MOTHERS, WIVES AND CHA

Mothers, Wives and Changing Lives

WOMEN IN MID TWENTIETH-CENTURY
RURAL WALES

B. J. Brown and Sally Baker

UNIVERSITY OF WALES PRESS
CARDIFF
2011

www.uwp.co.uk

British Library CIP
A catalogue record for this book is available from the British Library.

ISBN 978-0-7083-2334-2
e-ISBN 978-0-7083-2335-9

Typeset by Mark Heslington Ltd, Scarborough, North Yorkshire
Printed in Wales by Dinefwr Press, Llandybïe

This book is dedicated to R. Merfyn Jones,
Graham Day and Duncan Tanner

In memoriam Duncan Tanner (1958–2010)

Acknowledgements

We extend our thanks to the many people who agreed to be interviewed for this book and who subsequently gave so generously of their time, providing fascinating and moving narratives of their earlier lives. We also need to thank numerous friends and neighbours who for years have provided us with information and anecdotes regarding the recent past of rural Wales that stimulated our interest in the socio-politics of a region of Britain in many ways very different from the one in which we originated, long before we began formally researching it.

We are especially grateful to Derek Robbins of the University of East London, who provided critical feedback on an earlier draft of this manuscript, and it was at his urging that we explored the parallels between our respondents' lives and culture and Bourdieu's ethnographic work. We have benefited enormously from the enthusiasm and expertise of colleagues at Bangor University, especially Merfyn Jones, whose work on the subject initially interested us in researching this fascinating region, and Graham Day, whose willingness to share his vast knowledge and experience in the sociology of Wales is invaluable. Particular thanks are also due to Howard Davis (who has an uncanny ability to spot potential problems) and to Ian Rees Jones. We have not been able to use in this volume all of the material that we collected during the interviews. We have further publications planned. It was a privilege to have planned the future work with Duncan Tanner, Professor of Modern History at Bangor University, who was generous in his encouragement of scholars lesser than himself. His recent untimely death has stolen from us a guide and a friend. This volume builds therefore on the intellectual capital of different scholars and disciplines, and represents a trajectory which was at times arduous but was also enormously rewarding.

The fieldwork for this book was funded by British Academy Grant SG-45236 and we are most grateful for this support.

Contents

அ

1

Introduction: Womanhood, Wales and Culture

☙

Wales is a land steeped in history, yet the histories most readily brought to mind are often ones from which women are curiously absent. Whether they involve industry and labour struggles or more distantly glimpsed legends, it is increasingly recognized that many of the better known histories of the nation have focused their attention away from the spheres of domestic and community life, where women were most active, and have under-theorized the role of women in creating and supporting the social movements that have shaped the distinctive history of the country. Women have made a major contribution to Wales as it is today, but so far there have been few authors who have brought the story of their struggle to light. Inspired by extended interviews with forty older adults in Wales who were invited to describe their early lives, we have written this volume partly in an attempt to place the hitherto hidden history of women in rural twentieth-century Wales under scrutiny. We illustrate this with historical examples and first-person accounts from people reminiscing about their own and their families' histories.

In this respect, this book follows a different pathway from much work already published. A further important part of our project in the current volume is to show how insights from the social sciences can give us important new ways of interpreting the data of oral historians. We draw on many techniques – oral history, narrative theory, hermeneutics and even theories usually associated with literary criticism – but our major theoretical focus will be upon the work of the French sociologist Pierre Bourdieu (1930–2002). This interdisciplinary approach will allow us to understand people's biographies as both historical and sociological documents. Bourdieu's theory allows us to understand broad cultural and symbolic patterns in communities as well as to account for anomalous findings. The use of Bourdieusian notions shows that domestic life is important for the transmission of culture and illuminates women's crucial role in this. As we explored these themes, it became apparent that this kind of analysis offered a valuable supplement to much existing scholarship on Wales, which had not explored the relationship between public/political/professional life and the domestic sphere.

In this chapter we will lay out the ground and describe the context for the volume as a whole. By way of introduction, we will explore the historical antecedents to the situation in Wales in the mid-twentieth century and the role of nineteenth-century developments in the formulation of twentieth-century 'Welsh culture'.

Wales has often been thought of as a traditional place where gender is concerned, yet in this volume we will describe how women took leading roles in a number of important events, such as religious revivals. Additionally, in their tens of thousands, women promoted education, a love of learning and culture and a sense of ambition that has taken many of the current generation of Welsh men and women into the sciences, the arts and into public life. This desire for knowledge and aspiration towards 'better things' characterized community life in homes, schools, chapels and eisteddfodau, and in the last century women have played a vital, yet underappreciated, role in fostering it. This book unearths the hidden debt owed to Welsh women in laying the foundation for feminist advances and present-day cultural, professional and political achievement in Wales.

The role of women in the recent history of rural Wales is an area that has received scant attention from social scientists and historians. We draw upon family stories told about women's roles in education, the chapel and the family itself to address some of the important gaps in the knowledge base relating to women and Welsh culture. Although this book is primarily concerned with these spheres, we will also explore women at work, in the context of the work in which our participants found themselves – frequently teaching, but also, for example, farming. Whilst the issue of women at work in Wales has been covered in some depth previously by other authors, our intention here is to focus on the cultural work involved in accumulating, sustaining and reproducing modes of life, cultures of learning and in creating social capital, rather than to focus on the labour processes of material production found elsewhere.

A further source of inspiration for this book arose from earlier work that we conducted that set out to explore the personal narratives of people from rural Wales who had attended university. Time and again, women were mentioned – as mothers, grandmothers, schoolteachers and Sunday school-teachers – as providing the foundations for a love of learning and a sense that culture was important and something that everyone could enjoy. This we have characterized as an 'aspirational habitus', drawing on Pierre Bourdieu's work, to assist us in thinking theoretically about the relationship between knowledge, culture and community. We will explore this idea of an aspirational habitus further in chapter 6. The value of such conceptual tools lies in their ability to make sense of the relationship between highly particularized reminiscences, the broader historical context and social theory, linking the personal to the political, the individual to society and the private to the public, to build up a picture of mid twentieth-century rural Wales.

We unearthed a wealth of reminiscences, accounts, anecdotes and personal narratives attesting to the role of women in rural communities in twentieth-century Wales. Yet, as we have noted, much of the history and sociology of Wales has tended to stress themes relating to economic life, working relationships and practices and the role of religious nonconformity. In scholarship on all of these issues, the occupational experience, political role and theological hegemony of men has been paramount.

By contrast, prompted by the richness and the explanatory potential of the fieldwork data that we acquired, we became concerned to record and document the accounts of women who lived through the economic, cultural and political transformations of rural Wales in the middle years of the twentieth century. The bulk of our material will concern events and experiences from 1940 to 1970, but we will also trace forwards and backwards from this period to illustrate precursors and important sequelae, especially for feminism, in the latter half of the twentieth century. Although the reminiscences concern small communities in north, mid and west Wales, they convey an orientation to the world as well as a complex of knowledge and aspiration that were manifested through everyday practice. These included, as we have mentioned, the aspirational habitus, but also a sense of intellectual entitlement and the idea that literary interests and culture were 'good things' and matters from which everyone, even the poorest person, had much to gain. This also tells us how these women's lives involved the groundwork for the second wave of feminism in the 1960s and 70s. The manifestation of this in the rural communities in which our participants grew up and spent most or all of their adult lives, provides an important conceptual foundation to issues of politics and employment. This yields a fascinating insight into women's roles in supporting and affording the cultural and political activities of the region in the last sixty or seventy years. Indeed, this work on the part of women seems to go well beyond mere 'support' and there are intimations that women had considerably more creative control over many matters than has hitherto been supposed.

The very idea of a distinctive 'Welsh culture' is itself enigmatic. The passionate conviction that contemporary Wales is heir to a centuries-old tradition of spirituality and learning coexists with the somewhat uncomfortable contention that Welsh culture is a late nineteenth-century invention. Yet, however it originated, the important feature is that it was meaningful to the people themselves. An image of Welsh culture was entertained by many participants, which provided a sense that their aspirations were achievable and that the world beyond the village school would be appreciative of their contribution.

As we have suggested, these processes were part of a much more widely articulated, yet slow, process of social change. We will show how women's cultural labour in Wales not only sustained communities but prefigured and encouraged the changes in gender roles, which involved the current generation of adults, including our participants. We use the theoretical tools of sociological enquiry so that experiences related by participants can be incorporated into grander theoretical schemes, enabling us to explain notions of culture and politics at the community, or even national, level. Thus, we attempt to bridge the divide between the local, vernacular commemoration of the past and the patriotic formalism of official culture.

It is the everyday institutions – the school, the chapel, the family, the Sunday school – that played a formative role in shaping family and community relations. It is these 'small things' and their part in framing and constituting family life and communal relationships that we explore here. The micro-history of marriages, childhoods and communities plays a role in determining the experiences and accounts of relationships between men and women. The organization of sexual difference was important in structuring social institutions, social relations and material realities, and we will explore the connections between these through our participants' accounts. In this way, our volume will complement previous works that have explored the lives of women in Wales, such as Betts (1996), Beddoe (2000; 2003) and Rees (in Herbert and Jones, 1995) and, we hope, move the debate forward and enhance its theoretical footing.

Well-known community studies, including work by Davies and Rees (1960) and Emmett (1964) touched on women's lives, but there was not usually an in-depth exploration of women's position or identity – the community as a whole was the focus. However, Frankenberg (1957) did venture into the complexities of the politics of gender, discussing the position of women, both as individuals and as a group, in a manner unusual for scholarship of that time. John (1991) published a history of pre-war women in Wales and Aaron (1994) edited a contemporary account of women's position in Wales, overlaid with ideas derived from Anglo-American feminism. Recently, writers have turned their attention to the position of women in twentieth century Welsh politics (Chaney et al., 2007).

This book owes a great deal to our participants who agreed to be interviewed about their early life-experiences and reminiscences.

We will meet them more formally in chapter 2 and sketch out the contours of the processes through which the data was collected and analysed. However, at this stage a few further introductory remarks are in order to set out the manifesto for the book and to outline what we are hoping to contribute to the historiography and sociology of Wales.

Our work differs from much of the existing scholarship on Wales in that it uses a different range of analytical techniques, which have in the past been more closely aligned with social analysis. This enables us to make links between the micro-politics of everyday life and the domestic sphere and professional, public and political life. In this way we hope to show that what happens in Wales has an international academic relevance and is emblematic of more general social experiences and processes. Likewise, we will complement much of the work on education in Wales, such as that by Jones (1997) and Jones and Roderick (2003), by our use of Bourdieusian theory and our exploration of women's role in transmitting the rich seam of cultural capital that was present in so many otherwise materially disadvantaged Welsh communities.

Histories, memories and the imagination of tradition

The sense of identity found in Wales and the very fabric of its history is inherently controversial. To some it epitomizes the 'invention of tradition' described by Hobsbawm and Ranger (1983), where histories are exposed as recent creations. Whatever the literal truth of the history of Wales however, it is important to devote some consideration to this, as the *sense* of history is itself important.

At present the status of Wales is well known. Largely rural, it typically discloses high levels of disadvantage when measured against criteria related to income, employment or housing. In the face of this, however, our participants described something that they saw to be enduring and distinctive about 'Wales' and the 'Welsh'. Despite a single national designation, there is considerable differentiation within its borders. Life in industrial urban south Wales is considerably different from life in Snowdonia. However, as Jones (1992a: 330), observes: 'the Welsh have for centuries sustained an identity . . . despite . . . a recent history that has witnessed massive immigration and integrationist pressures'. This sense of national identity can be traced over the last century and a half. Jones (1992a: 332) argued that during this period a distinctive Welsh self-image was formulated: 'cliched and inadequate as were the observations of outsiders, there developed during the nineteenth and twentieth centuries a distinctive Welsh self image, an identity rooted in a specific combination of social and economic conditions'.

The spiritual climate in Wales was influenced by a distinctive religious history. Religious Nonconformity was explicitly permitted by the 1689 Toleration Act, which granted freedom to Dissenters, who had gained strength during Cromwell's rule as Lord Protector and in the subsequent Restoration period. The Act itself led to the open development of many differently inflected variants of Christianity. The first chapels in Wales were built soon after the Act was passed. At around this time, influential books such as Vicar Prichard's *Welshman's Candle* (*Canwyll y Cymru*) and the first Welsh translation of *The Pilgrim's Progress* were widely circulated and read. The key feature here is that the development of Nonconformity was accompanied by developments in literacy in the Welsh language, thus helping to cement the relationship between chapel life and learning. The major events shaping religious belief and observance in Wales came with the advent of Methodism in the eighteenth century. In Wales, this involved some notable women, such as Ann Griffiths (1776–1805). Jones (2004), states that in 1801 only 34 per cent of places of worship in Wales were Nonconformist. By 1850, this had risen to some 70 per cent. Of the total number of worshippers in Wales in 1851, 77 per cent claimed affiliation to the Nonconformist tradition. Jones (2004: 178) observed that by the middle of the nineteenth century, there was no part of religious or secular human life that Nonconformists had not penetrated, but, 'by 1850 the religious element had faded in intensity and we see it being secularized and nurturing a social ethos'. Jones, (1982: 43–4), when writing about north-west Wales, noted that 'chapels . . . dominated behaviour outside of the mere act of worship' and that 'their presence was central to the life and structure of slate-quarrying communities: a complex network of allegiances and a powerful organisational framework, nonconformity came to hold a position of quite particular importance'. He also described how villages grew around their chapels and the intense hold that the chapels held on the community (Jones, 1982). Jones (2004) maintains that Nonconformists, again and again, tried to give a united leadership to the nation.

The Nonconformist movement, punctuated by periodic 'revivals', held a firm grip on Wales until the mid twentieth century. Foreshadowing the key roles that our participants described for women, teenage girls were among the most charismatic preachers in the 1904–5 religious revival (Orr, 1975; Whittaker, 1984). Jones (1982: 63) considered that 'Nonconformity gave to Wales a self-confidence and security which also often engendered self-righteousness and a generally smug belief that Wales was the most faithfully religious corner in the whole world' and that 'During the 1904–5 revival echoes of a belief in the special mission of the Welsh people could at times be heard ... "the young men of Wales", it was prophesied at one revivalist meeting, "are to lead the way in the salvation of the world".' 'Many in 1904–5 thought that God had chosen the Welsh people to be his especial agents' (Jones, 1982: 64).

Although there was a rapid decline in Nonconformist congregations in the latter half of the twentieth century, many older people are still actively involved and a strong legacy remains. Davies (1994) noted the emphasis on 'self-culture' in Nonconformity, involving an interest in education and the alignment of this with religion itself. Although Welsh society changed greatly in the late twentieth century (Chaney et al., 2007; Jones, 2004), the idea of a Welsh culture has proved robust and forms a lived historical background to the experiences related later in this book.

The idea of this 'Welsh culture' stretching back through the centuries has been undermined by many historians, who have argued that much of it was invented in the nineteenth century (Jones, 1992a; Morgan, 1983). There have been challenges to the very notion of a Welsh culture. Jones (1982: 55) was explicit regarding the origins of Welsh culture and the identity of its 'propagandists':

for in a quite profound sense the Welsh radical tradition, and the cultural apparatus which sustained it, was a genuinely ideological construct . . . the programme of late-nineteenth-century Welsh liberalism was built around land reform and disestablishment. The cement which held the political alliance together was Welsh culture and its institutions, and this culture and these institutions came to be thought of as synonymous with nonconformity and radical liberalism. During the 1880s and 1890s the middle-class nonconformist elite, through the agencies of chapel and press, re-defined the idea of Wales in its own image, deftly excluding its opponents and sometimes also its supporters.

The idea of the *gwerin*, a kind of hard-working simple country folk, was popularized in the poetry of W. J. Gruffydd and helped to consolidate an idea of a classless or one-class Welsh democracy. The Wales of the *gwerin* (Morgan, 1986a), traditional, of the land and Welsh-speaking, became both symbolically and actually 'a storehouse of a specifically Welsh rural identity and as such was specifically politicised' (Gruffudd, 1999: 159).

The idea of rural Wales as being populated by the *gwerin*, including quarry workers, tenant farmers and purveyors of craft skills steeped in local culture, was also promoted in the educational philosophy of Sir Owen M. Edwards. Yet Edwards himself was influenced by John Ruskin's preoccupation with the value of craft skills and rural working life. Thus, the idea of the *gwerin*, says Jones (1982), was an 'ideological achievement' of middle-class Nonconformists. Yet there is a further serious point here. The patterns of social class perfected in industrial life in England have never mapped easily on to the situation in which Welsh people have found themselves. Consequently, the notion may have gained in popularity because of the comparative ease with which people felt it embraced their identity and their situation.

The collective sense of identity in Wales in the mid nineteenth century and discourse about its culture and politics was also dominated by the so-called 'treachery of the Blue Books'. This came about when, in 1846, William Williams, himself a Welshman and serving as MP for Coventry, pressed the government with his concern about the state of education in Wales. The government responded by appointing three commissioners, R. R.W. Lingen, Jellynger C. Symons and H. R. Vaughan Johnson. They toured Wales, but were handicapped by the fact that they spoke no Welsh and frequently relied on the testimony of English speakers – often Anglican clergymen – in Welsh-speaking areas. They completed their reports in April 1847, presenting them to Parliament in three blue-coloured volumes. Schools in Wales, they argued, were inadequate. Often, the teachers spoke only English and only English textbooks were available in areas where the children spoke only Welsh. Welsh-speakers, they reported, had to rely on the Nonconformist Sunday schools to learn to read and write. This much confirmed Williams's fears. But the commissioners did not confine themselves to the state of the schools. They concluded that the Welsh were ignorant, lazy and immoral, particularly the women, and that among the causes of this were the use of the Welsh language and Nonconformity. Commissioner Lingen especially condemned the people and their culture. It was this latter excursion into sniping at the culture and the morality of the Welsh that provoked a furious reaction in Wales.

Yet, only half a century later a very different image of Wales prevailed: 'National identity came to be associated with specific political and religious beliefs . . . a sense of identity fuelled by notions of religious purity, by the intimacy of chapel services and the strains of communally known and sung hymns' (Jones, 1992a: 338–9). It is apposite that the reconstruction of the image and re-engineering of the culture of Wales and the Welsh took place in the latter part of the nineteenth century, a time of industrious rebuilding and reconstruction. The Nonconformist intellectuals and middle classes were inculcating the notion that Wales had a heritage of scholars and poets to be proud of (Jones, 1992a).

This much must be understood to appreciate the cultural meaning of what follows later in this volume. These are debates and events familiar to scholars of Welsh history, but they are also part of the lived experience of Welsh culture, as we shall see.

To further specify, contextualize and periodize the experiences we will be focusing on later, it is worth briefly outlining the situation in nineteenth-century north-west Wales, a region in which many of our interviewees were raised. Jones (1982: 53), eloquently describing the situation in the late nineteenth century, stated that 'Gwynedd came to be effectively two societies, culturally and religiously defined, with their respective elites struggling for control of the local state', the two societies being the Liberal consensus and Tory Gwynedd. Jones (1982: 342) defines Liberal Wales as 'nonconformist, closely associated with the Welsh language, temperate, and based on the community of interest between small farmers, industrial workers, and small businessmen and professionals in the *gwerin*'. Surprisingly, perhaps, Jones (1992a: 338) notes that

> there were many Anglicans involved in Welsh liberalism . . . but the engine house was nonconformist, and increasingly, the two forces – one political, and the other denominational – embraced and sustained each other. All the demands of this political movement, articulated on public platforms and in a vibrant radical press by nonconformist ministers and their radical allies, derived, often explicitly, from the aspirations of nonconformity . . . all suited . . . the interests of the denominations.

Jones (1992a: 338–9) describes the situation as

> a religio-cultural rather than a national discourse . . . it created a series of definitions of Welshness that excluded much of the actual population of the country and constructed a history of nonconformist heroes with which many could not identify. Welshness thus became a cause to which one adhered, rather than a country to which one belonged . . . this powerful mix of politics, religion, culture and place, had, by the turn of the century, created what appeared to be a hegemonic Welsh identity. That this identity was based on an assumed and proclaimed homogeneity can hardly be overemphasized.

Jones (1982: 50) emphasizes that the interrelationship between language, class and politics wasn't static or automatic, offers major problems in interpretation and explains that the problems are 'compounded by the inexactitudes of the self images of the propagandists of Welsh culture and by the rhetoric which nourished these images' (p. 55).

Morgan (1981) states that, during the 1880s, 'dramatic transformations swept through the land which added up to a kind of national renaissance'. This

> expressed itself at the most popular grass roots level. The Welsh language in some ways proved more vigorous than ever in the years after 1880. It had new status and protection. In 1885 a group of cultured patriots ... founded a Society for the Utilization of the Welsh Language. (Morgan, 1981: 95)

Historians such as Jones (1982) and Manning (2002; 2004) have pointed to the way in which, especially in north Wales, Welsh culture involved an active reconstruction of the past and a carefully crafted sense of history, foregrounding the role of matters such as work, language, piety, the arts and scholarship, and that 'inadequate and uncomfortable realities became increasingly substituted by myths' (Jones, 1992b: 38). The revisions and counter-revisions of commentators on Welsh culture and history make it difficult to discern what the tenor of life might have been for people prior to the late nineteenth century. What is significant are the popular notions of Welsh history and culture that many people of our participants' generations espouse. Whilst they may not be consistent with historians' accounts, they serve to add value to the presumed tradition, incorporating images of the 'glorious past' used in the cultural construction of history, of bards, and of labourers with intellectual tastes. We will show how this culturally enhanced image of the past was adaptive and useful when people were aiming to transcend the circumstances in which they were brought up and attend university, and when they sought to manage their identity as people deserving of institutional recognition, the award of degrees and career success.

The structure of this volume: themes and variations

In the next chapter, we will begin by introducing our participants and outline the biographies of six key interviewees whose stories we shall return to regularly throughout the volume. In this chapter also we will describe in more detail our approach to the interviews and their analysis and consider the kinds of meanings that can be deduced from data of this kind. We will continue the process of providing context for our interviewees' lives and the relationship between what they told us and the collateral information about their places and periods from other studies and investigations of Wales at that time. We will also lay out our understanding of how culture may be conceptualized and studied in the Welsh context and, in the light of the importance of relationships and practical activities to the biographical narratives with which we shall be concerned, explore the possible contributions of Bourdieu's theories of culture to this debate.

In chapter 3 we consider the role of gender identity in the lives of our participants. This concern stemmed from our observation that many of our participants reminisced about women who had transcended gender-role expectations in their occupational, educational and domestic lives. Moreover, they had done so in a nation which had a reputation for social conservatism and a suspicion of emancipatory movements, from women's suffrage to second-wave feminism. We place this in the context of recent feminist scholarship on the role of women in Wales, but also consider its relationship to Bourdieusian theory. The insight that gender can be seen as a kind of generative schema, capable of creative reinterpretation to suit particular circumstances, is apposite here. Gender roles were usually not transcended completely, but aspects of traditionalism or motifs of respectability were retained, so that many women's lives were a mixture of conservatism and transgressive or radical involvement in activities not generally considered feminine.

Chapter 4 pursues the notion of gender in the domestic sphere. On the one hand, there were clear gender roles of the kind that would be recognized by most scholars of family life. Yet, women were clearly not powerless. Participants' reminiscences disclosed examples of women being able to activate social capital, in the form of networks of friends and relatives, so as to secure resources and solve problems. Household finances were managed and offspring were steered towards the kinds of jobs that offered security and an escape from the hardships of outdoor work on the farm or in the quarry. Mothers were remembered as instilling a sense that doing well in the education system was a passport to better things and in contributing to the cultural life of the community. In Bourdieusian terms women were crucial as members of the group who enabled the pooling of social and cultural capital so that certain members could succeed. Accounts of mothers here resonate with the idea of the 'Welsh mam' described in Deirdre Beddoe's work – a woman who was hard-working, pious and preoccupied with cleanliness. Moreover, as scholars of education have noted elsewhere, women were hard at work managing the risks attached to pursuing educational success, too.

This focus on education is continued in chapter 5, which explores further the relationship between women and educational culture. People in our study often had fond memories of women who had played significant roles in their early lives as teachers, Sunday-school teachers or who had invested themselves so that others in their family or social group could go on to university. Mothers and grandmothers were described as if they were a driving force that propelled our participants' generation through the education system. Poverty was described as limiting the educational opportunities of many families, but equally it was a spur to success in some cases, as education was seen as a means of escape. It opened the doors to prized non-manual, indoor jobs with additional benefits, such as pensions. Especially for young women, the teaching profession offered opportunities, not only for achieving symbolic recognition, but also for earning an independent living whilst retaining ties to their communities.

Chapter 6 considers women's role in the genesis of cultural capital, where, as mothers, grandmothers, aunts and family friends, they were described as being hard at work transmitting knowledge and enabling cultural participation. We show how these apparently mundane cultural activities, like participating in Bible-knowledge quizzes, helping to create plays and poetry, playing the piano and so on, were a part of, and helped to facilitate, the generation of cultural capital. Reminiscences about the role of women in cultural activity are intertwined with the sense that this also fostered the opportunity to gain more from other cultural resources, such as newspapers and radio plays. At the same time, as

culture developed and was passed on, there was a political awareness of how society worked and a desire to convert this capital,
where possible, to more symbolic credentials such as prizes in
eisteddfodau and educational qualifications.

Whilst we allude to the pervasive presence of chapel life in the
early lives of our participants throughout this book, in chapter 7
we consider the role of religion and spiritual life more explicitly.
Whilst the last half-century has seen a decline in participation in
formal worship in Wales as elsewhere, there is a palpable legacy of
chapel life in contemporary Wales. In the early lives of our participants, Sunday schools were remembered as being interesting and
fun. Chapel life provided a platform for the generation and reproduction of culture, in the form of literature, language, poetry and
music, as well as a sense of shared history. Particularly in sects
originating from Methodism, there was often a strong emphasis
on egalitarianism and, in some variants, an emphasis on gender
equality, too. Equally, gossip could be cruel and congregations
exclusive, but participants emphasized that chapels were not as
dour or forbidding as the popular image cultivated in Welsh literature. Indeed, the view that chapel was something which allowed
people to retain a sense of dignity was expounded by a number of
participants.

The theme of dignity returns also in chapter 8, where we
consider the idea of respectability and how people describe themselves and people of their parents' generation striving to lead
respectable lives. In this chapter we will explore how women were
cast in the role of moral guardians. There were instances recalled
of people being excluded from chapel congregations because of
perceived transgressions, such as becoming pregnant, although
these were often described as temporary withdrawals, akin to a
cooling-off period, rather than permanent arrangements. It was
other chapels or other periods in history, rather than one's own,
that were said to be forbidding and unforgiving.

Keeping quiet about matters relating to romantic attachments
and sexuality was about preserving discretion and maintaining
harmony as much as it was about formal prohibition. In some
cases, however, the parents of young women who became pregnant would bring up the baby as if it were their own, so mother

and child enjoyed a sibling relationship, so as to preserve the notion of respectability. Respectability was also vouchsafed by duties such as taking care of relatives or having clothes that were sufficiently fashionable and did not look like hand-me-downs. Respectability could also be maintained by sending one's children to a town several miles away for the very cheapest cuts of meat, rather than allowing one's hardship to be visible to neighbours and local tradespeople.

Finally, in chapter 9 we reflect upon the meaning of these findings, for both sociological theory and social policy. The life stories and reminiscences collected here offer opportunities for observing the accumulation and conversion of capital in the social cultural and symbolic spheres. Seeing the social lives and social process in this way, as progressive conversions of capital from chapel life to education to occupational advancement, enables us to explain the extraordinary resilience of the Welsh language and Welsh culture.

2

Narratives, Biography and Culture: Situating Participants' Life Stories

❧

The history of Wales and the role of orality, literacy and culture in its national trajectory and sense of itself means that it is particularly interesting and valuable to explore the life stories told by people who embody these values and whose lives represent, in miniature, the struggles toward national identity and self-determination in the mid and late twentieth century. In doing this, we shall concentrate upon the lives of a group of people who shared their life stories with us and also draw upon what has been called in the social sciences the 'narrative turn'. This has provided many methodological opportunities to identify 'life patterns' and develop understandings which are capable of being extended beyond personal accounts and also demonstrate community experience and meanings (Plummer, 2001). As MacAdams and Janis (2004) contend, personal narratives help to configure an individual's understanding of self, and the construction of identity has a degree of purpose and unity in making sense of oneself and one's circumstances.

The empirical work which provided the narratives upon which this book was based arose from a study of life in twentieth-century rural Wales, via the medium of older peoples' biographical narratives. The data for this volume were provided by separate groups of respondents, participating in two related but distinct research projects. All participants lived in rural north Wales and ranged in age from fifty-one to eighty-four years at the time of interview.

The interviews were carried out between 2004 and 2006. Whereas participants in the first group were made aware that the researcher was interested especially in their decision to enter higher education, the second group was told that the major focus of interest was their experiences of growing up in rural Wales. Despite the differences in the focus of these two projects, the respondents independently and spontaneously produced accounts of the significant place of religious Nonconformity in their lives and community. This prompted the focus in this book on recollections of the process of cultural transmission and reproduction in religious and community life, as a result of the centrality of chapel to participants' accounts. Forty participants were interviewed, all of whose first language was Welsh. A summary of participants and their details is presented in the Appendix.

During the middle years of the twentieth century, the region in which these participants grew up and lived was economically disadvantaged and dominated by religious Nonconformity, which was politically aligned historically to the Liberal party. A majority of the population spoke Welsh as their first language. The region covered Anglesey, Caernarvonshire, Meirioneth, Cardiganshire and much of Denbighshire, Carmarthenshire and Montgomeryshire. It was unique within the UK in terms of its religious and sociolinguistic characteristics. This area has been termed '*Y Fro Gymraeg*' ('The Welsh Language Area') and was mapped by Aitchison and Carter (2000). Detailed descriptions of the social life of the region during the middle years of the twentieth century are found in Madgwick et al. (1973), Emmett (1964), and Davies and Rees (1960). By the middle of the twentieth century, *Y Fro Gymraeg* was becoming secularized, yet the influence of Nonconformity was still pervasive. Public houses were closed on Sundays and many people were troubled by events such as whist drives being held and disapproved of activities such as going out to dances. 'Welshness' was such a well-recognized concept that there existed in the Welsh language a word to describe it, *Cymreictod*. Sundays in Wales were so distinctive that people interviewed by Madgwick et al. (1973) referred to the importance of retaining the 'Welsh Sunday'.

Participants in our study came from a variety of socio-economic backgrounds. A small number had endured extreme hardship when young, due to factors such as domestic violence or the death of a parent. A sample containing both women and men was aimed for, drawn from across *Y Fro Gymraeg*. The choice of individuals per se is not crucial in the biographical method; the data yield information regarding the individual in the social setting. The narratives reflect the cultural background prevailing, the experiences and processes involved and the use of symbolic capital around the axis of social mobility and education. Many participants had followed careers as teachers or academics. This bias was unintentional, but the composition of the participant group reflects many of the kinds of ideas that we discuss about the notions of habitus and aspiration. It is no coincidence, and in some ways an advantage in discussing the process of capital accumulation, to have fortuitously met so many people who embodied this process themselves. It is especially interesting in the light of the high value that Nonconformity placed on education; teaching and preaching were prestigious occupations in the region (Madgwick et al., 1973), so that people aspiring to 'success' often aimed for such careers. This has implications for our findings, in that many of our participants were highly educated and often had an excellent knowledge of Welsh history, politics and literature. Most had been involved with Nonconformist chapels and many had experienced childhood in Nonconformist families. Some had simply been exposed to Nonconformity through village life. One participant had been brought up as an Anglican but joined her husband's Nonconformist chapel upon marrying, and one participant, unusually among our sample, grew up in a devoutly Anglican family.

Interviews were conducted using an adaptation of the technique used by Chamberlayne et al. (2000), commencing with the interviewer asking a single generative question, prompting the participants to talk about their life, starting from childhood. The participants then led the interview by expanding their narrative in any way that they chose, the interviewer only interrupting to ask for clarification or to follow up particular points.

Whilst interviews are inevitably constructive activities and predispose a focus on the self and one's story which is perhaps different from that experienced in many other interactive settings, they remain the mainstay of much biographical and oral–historical inquiry. An interview is a form of interaction, and indeed is as 'natural' as any other, and is widespread in societies with social scientific or public opinion polling traditions (Atkinson and Silverman, 1997). An interview becomes a conversation, perhaps a 'conversation with a purpose' (Bingham and Moore, 1924). Shakespeare (1998) suggests that research interviews develop their own conventions, which are often familiar to participants. Interviews are culturally rooted communication situations in which narrative meanings are reinforced, but may also be challenged and negotiated between interlocutors (Westcott and Littleton, 2004). A research interview renders certain topics salient, and participants may agree to be interviewed because their life trajectories mean that the topic, such as the role of education or spirituality in one's life, constitutes a particular concern or special interest (Taylor, 2001). To Taylor and Littleton (2006: 28), interviews represent a kind of 'congenial performance context for first person narration which speakers find pleasurable' (Redman, 2005; Taylor, 2005).

Another way of understanding the place and meaning of interviews is connected with our earlier point regarding how different circumstances may elicit a different version of talk. If situated talk is a new version of what has been said before, perhaps different in detail from previous tellings, but not a wholly original, never-before-expressed innovation, then the talk elicited in research interviews can be analysed as part of the ongoing habitus, project or trajectory of the speaker. In other words, it is a kind of ongoing identity work on the part of the speaker (Taylor and Littleton, 2006). This could also imply that a biographical research interview might even provide a context for speakers to rehearse new versions, making it a particularly interesting context for the summative and reflective identity work among older people in whom we are interested (Taylor and Littleton, 2005).

The analysis of our participants' accounts proceeded in line with the recommendations of Chamberlayne et al. (2000), by discussion of the interviews on a case-by-case basis among a research team from the authors' host departments, identifying themes and pivotal moments in the narrative. Notes and records of these discussions formed a further layer of data for analysis. The analysis was informed by the issues raised in the background literature concerning the types of identities, interpretative repertoires and narrative forms that helped in the understanding of how culture, spirituality and education might be constructed, reproduced and imbued with meaning. Bourdieu attached a good deal of importance to practice and lived experience. The strength of this approach in discovering novel aspects of recounted experience is attested by the fact that the centrality of religion to our participants' lived experience had not been anticipated. It emerged from the data in a grounded fashion.

As a further check on the veracity of the interpretative structure devised, the analysis was fed back to selected participants for confirmation that the researchers had understood the material in the way in which the participants had expected. As they talked about their own or the wider community's involvement with Nonconformity, participants made a number of detailed and specific references to its role in cultural life and the preparation this gave for education and the acquisition of credentials in the wider world. This prompted a reflection on the applicability of notions of cultural capital. We were struck by the diligence with which it was described as being accumulated. As analysis progressed, the data were examined systematically for themes relating to cultural and symbolic capital, especially concerning Nonconformity.

A further check on the credibility of the data was provided by the fact that at the time many of our participants were young, many of the key community studies of Wales were being undertaken. A picture of relatively closed, static communities emerged from work by, for example, Rees (1950) and Davies and Rees (1960). Owen (1960), in his study of Glan-llyn, shows the social functions of familialism and kinship in sustaining the potency and strength of Nonconformity. In common with the accounts from our participants, face-to-face interaction tended to be based on local status-group distinctions and differentiations, and the class-based polarizations that preoccupied English and North American sociologists were much harder to detect.

Lives, narratives and trajectories

To understand the narratives more fully and to enable the reader to appreciate the particular identity projects and trajectories involved, we will refer to a smaller subset of the participants in detail throughout this volume. Whilst all forty participants will contribute to different points in the story that we tell about the lives involved, some participants seemed to embody aspects of the way of life in an especially conspicuous manner, such as the value of hard work, overcoming disadvantage, piety, a sense of responsibility towards others and so on. To facilitate this, in the section that follows we will provide brief portraits of six key participants to whom we will return regularly throughout the chapters that follow.

Geraint

Geraint was born in the mid 1940s and grew up in a small town in north-east Wales. Geraint's family background was very much more comfortable than that of most of our participants. His father owned a small business, which was inherited from his father before him, and his mother was a housewife. Geraint was aware that, as a boy, he was more fortunate than many of his peers. His parents were part of 'high society' in the town – his father was a councillor, a Freemason and a deacon in the Calvinist Methodist chapel that the family attended. Geraint attended the town grammar school, was academically very able and went to university at Oxford, to a college with Welsh connections. He was the first member of his family to benefit from a university education, although his father and uncles certainly would have wanted to go to university if they had been able to afford it. Geraint, being a member of the first generation in which maintenance grants for higher education were available, was expected to attend university by his family and family friends. After graduating, Geraint stayed in England for some years, spent a short time in academic research, then worked as a teacher and moved into educational administration and teacher training, eventually achieving a senior position in rural Wales. Although his early career had been spent in England, Geraint married a girl from a neighbouring village to his childhood home; they met whilst they were teenagers and his wife became a teacher. Geraint has retained a lifelong involvement with the chapel, as well as with various local charitable organizations. Geraint's children are now academics.

Alwena

Alwena was born in the early 1940s and grew up in north-west Wales, in an area in which most people were employed in agriculture or quarrying. Alwena described in some detail a childhood of considerable hardship. Her father was a manual worker and died from tuberculosis when Alwena and both her siblings were all less than six years old. Her mother subsequently raised the children single-handedly. It was difficult for everyone, particularly as Alwena's mother seemed to have very little support from the extended family. Alwena attributed much of this lack of support to the fear that was associated with deaths from tuberculosis, but was also frank in her condemnation of what she saw as callousness from relatives towards her mother's plight. Alwena's mother supported her children and herself by a combination of domestic cleaning jobs and meagre state benefits, where these were available. Very few people were affluent in Alwena's community, but fifty years later she vividly remembers the poverty that her immediate family endured and the way in which they were poorer and more stigmatized than most other people.

Alwena went to a newly created comprehensive school rather than to the grammar school that was nearby, because her mother could not afford the uniform required for the grammar school. She left school at fifteen to learn shorthand and typing, then gained employment locally as a clerk. Alwena met her future husband when she was sixteen and he was a student at a nearby university. She remembers a lot of hostility regarding their relationship from her extended family, on the grounds that her boyfriend was an Englishman. They married when she was nineteen and then moved to England to enable her husband to pursue his career.

They had two children. Alwena loved being a mother, but found middle-class English life rather boring. At the same time, she was unimpressed by her children's teachers in their primary school and therefore decided to undertake teacher training herself, on the grounds that she could do better than the lacklustre teachers whom she had encountered as a parent. The teacher-training course that she followed was a flexible one and thus she was able to combine teacher training with raising her family. She began her career in primary teaching and was quite quickly promoted to a headteacher's position, where she remained for the rest of her career. In her mid fifties, disillusioned with government policies that were affecting primary teaching, Alwena took early retirement.

She returned to live in north-west Wales with her husband and by then adult children. Although Alwena has now acquired the material and educational trappings of a middle-class professional, she still identifies with 'workers' and is very critical of 'bosses' who treat workers unfairly. The interview for this book was conducted in Alwena's house, and whilst one of the authors was joining Alwena for tea after the interview, her son telephoned. It transpired that her son had become involved in an industrial dispute at work that had turned particularly nasty, and that he had been arrested, charged and bailed to appear in court in connection with this. Alwena was wholly supportive of his actions, stating that the employers in question were exploitative, but she did express concern that her son's workmates, who had also been involved, would leave him to 'carry the can' alone. That was her worry; she was proud that her son had challenged abusive practices and defended less powerful people.

In the same way that, in comfortable retirement, Alwena retained her sympathies for employees rather than employers, her attitude towards organized religion had remained consistent. She spoke a lot about hypocritical members of churches during her interview, making references to the devoted members of the chapel of her childhood who had displayed such a lack of compassion towards her mother, as well as to an elderly neighbour of hers in England who died, in Alwena's eyes, alone and abandoned by his son, who was a vicar. Alwena's two sons are employed in manual work related to agriculture.

Erin

Erin was born in the 1950s to a tenant hill-farmer in Snowdonia; her mother was a housewife. Erin's father was involved with the Anglican Church; her mother was Nonconformist, but didn't attend chapel. Erin suspects that this was because her mother was not Welsh-speaking. Her mother died when Erin was fifteen. Erin hated school and found schoolwork difficult; she enjoyed helping her father on the farm and was much more interested in farming than her brother was. She left school at fifteen and went to the local technical college, completing a course in care, after which she worked in a residential hospital for learning-disabled people, although she still worked on the farm whilst doing this. She married, had a baby and then stayed at home, continuing to work on the farm. She ran the farm along with her father until the early 1990s and then by herself after her father retired (single-handedly, because her marriage had broken up), until the foot-and-mouth crisis of 2000, which she found overwhelming. After she gave up the tenancy of the farm, she returned to a job in the care sector.

Erin has spent her life working in either very traditional women's work, or in work that is perceived to be virtually entirely a male domain. Erin maintains that throughout all her years in farming she encountered absolutely no hostility from male farmers at all, although she does remember being the only woman farmer in the area. She felt completely accepted by her farming colleagues and, although she is very aware that farming is not considered a woman's career, she had no reservations about going into farming and cannot remember ever feeling 'pushed' into it by anyone. She loved it and simply did it because of that. Erin's daughter is a single parent, lives with her mother and works part-time as a carer.

Mabon

Mabon was born in the early 1950s and brought up on Anglesey. His parents came from opposing ends of the social scale. His father was from an affluent family locally; within the family possession were two farms and a number of shops in the village. Yet his mother's family had endured searing poverty – she was one of many siblings, her father had been disabled in the First World War and her mother had died when she was young. Although very able academically, she had not pursued education because of the family's dire economic circumstances. Although she married a man from a much wealthier family, her husband – Mabon's father – died when Mabon was five. She did not remarry, and raised Mabon as a single parent. However, unlike Alwena, she did enjoy the support of her extended family. Mabon's father's family provided her with an income which enabled her to raise Mabon without needing outside employment, and the family seems to have been harmonious; as a child, Mabon remembers visiting the shops within his paternal grandfather's family to fetch the bread and groceries.

Although Mabon was an only child, his cousin lived with him and his mother throughout his childhood. Her father suffered from severe shell-shock induced by the First World War and caring for him was a full-time occupation for her mother, so she lived with Mabon and his mother. Thus, Mabon's childhood family circumstances were a curious combination of severe disability, and hardship due to bereavement, with economic privilege. Mabon attended local schools and was enormously encouraged in his schoolwork by his mother. Unusually for our participants, he was involved in the Anglican Church and was an active and a successful participant in eisteddfodau. He remembers that, because of his success in eisteddfodau, it was assumed that he would go to university. He studied law at a Welsh university. After graduating he returned to north Wales and has worked as a lawyer in the region ever since. One of Mabon's children is now an academic, his other child is studying for A levels.

Lowri

Born in the 1920s, Lowri is the daughter of a Methodist minister and 'minister's wife'. She has a sister and spent her childhood and adolescence in rural north Wales, moving briefly to mid Wales at one point. Lowri's family matched the stereotype of Liberal Nonconformist Wales – her mother knew former British Prime

Minister Lloyd George sufficiently well to converse with him if they saw him in public. They were a highly educated family, part of Welsh literary society, but with very little economic capital. Lowri's family participated in radical activism; they and their friends were pacifists and were subjected to violent attacks during the war because of this. Her parents actively assisted workers during the General Strike. Lowri's life has followed a similar pattern. She studied at a Welsh university and subsequently followed a career as a teacher and then as a teacher trainer, eventually achieving a very senior position in this field.

Since retirement, Lowri has led an extremely busy life, continuing to do so even today in her eighties. She is involved with Welsh-language writing and publishing, prison reform, anti-drugs work and the Alumni Associations of the institutions in which she worked and studied. Nonconformity is still central to Lowri's life. She embodies a mix of considerable social conservatism, such as a strong belief in temperance, and traditional views on gender-appropriate behaviour, combined with a social radicalism that even today would outdo that of many younger activists. Lowri never married or had children.

Cadi

Cadi was born into a farming family in north-west Wales in the early 1930s. She has a large number of siblings due to her father marrying again in middle age, after having been widowed, and having had big families with both wives. Her father's family were comparatively wealthy farmers. Although they were 'working' farmers, there was a lot of land owned within the extended family and they were affluent enough to employ maids who lived in. When Cadi left school, she went to a 'farm college' to study farm business and administration. She married into a neighbouring farming family and had a number of children.

Cadi was widowed relatively young, whilst her children were still at school, and she then embarked on a sizeable legal struggle to gain the right to become the tenant of a farm that she wished to rent for her eldest son, who was seventeen and wanted to farm.

Cadi believed that she was the first woman in the country to have 'proved her case' under such circumstances. The interviewer was not privy to the full details of this litigation, but Cadi described it as a considerable battle and, from what we understood, the decisive factor involved Cadi demonstrating collateral owned by the extended family. After acquiring the tenancy of this farm, Cadi farmed it with her son, becoming a farmer, rather than a farmer's daughter or a farmer's wife. Although the members of Cadi's family obviously possessed considerable wealth between them, Cadi's mother-in-law seemed to be the sole member of the family with control over the family land and finances. The family enjoyed a good relationship with this matriarchal figure, yet they seemed to occupy roles as her tenants and employees. Cadi was keen for all her children to gain a university education. They were the first members of the extended family to go to university and are now all engaged in agriculture or various business activities.

Taken together, the life stories above, supplemented by the other thirty-four personal narratives upon which we shall draw, illustrate a representative set of positions and trajectories from the participant pool. Families containing small business-people, farmers and ministers rub shoulders with those whose early childhoods have been marked by family bereavement and poverty. The attempts to deal with hardship are often collective family struggles undertaken over generations. The ability of our participants, whose family backgrounds were modest, to, for example, attend university, was the culmination of familial and community identity work and accumulated cultural and economic labour over a prolonged period of time. In this we see strategies not only of reproduction, but also translation and transubstantiation, as the work of social mobility is accomplished.

Of particular interest to the present project, with its emphasis on accounts of relations between community members, is Somers's (1994) conceptualization of narrative as a way of focusing on identity in a relational context. The relational aspect of narrative is created and storied by individuals, yet narrative provides a means of linking the individual to their context. Somers (1994) positions narrative as 'ontological' rather than 'representational'; that is, it is to do with being, rather than merely serving as a description of something whose real existence goes on elsewhere. Originally, modes of narrative were seen as representational forms, with the narrative providing order to the 'chaos' of lived experience by the external voice of scholars. By contrast, in Somers' framework (1994), not only do stories guide action, but people construct multiple and changing identities and locate themselves or are located 'within a repertoire of emplotted stories'. Merton et al. (1979) introduced the idea of the 'sociological autobiography', and Stanley (1993: 45) notes that:

> there is no need to individualise, to desocialise, 'the individual', because from one person we can recover social processes and social structure, networks, social change and so forth, for people are located in a social and cultural environment which constructs and shapes not only *what* we see but also *how* we see it.

Stanley argues for the centrality of 'the social' in people's lives and that people act towards things on the basis of the meanings that the things have for them: meanings which are a product of differential social interaction in society (Blumer, 1969: 2–6). Hence, one can refer to the importance of the individual biography – as a 'social biography' – in understanding how meanings are shaped, reacted to and acted upon, through a diverse range of processes of social interaction.

Our participants grew up in Wales at a time when a 'Welsh culture' was still perceived by many to exist in Wales, infused with religious Nonconformity which owed much to the Methodist movement (Jones, 2004). From the nineteenth century to the present day, identity politics in Wales involves multiple socio-spatial identities and 'manifold borders or boundaries that give form to these identities' (Jones and Fowler, 2007: 91). Identities and their related boundaries, spaces and 'territories' may be meticulously constructed, narrated and maintained at local and community level and represent a way of sustaining knowledge. Being able to distinguish oneself and one's kin from the English, or from people in neighbouring villages, helped to define identity. Added to this were multiple distinctions of piety, respectability, occupational grouping, congregation membership and family history, any and all of which might be used in defining a sense of self.

The sense in which biographies are related to the broader social fields in which they were played out was of concern to Bourdieu, too. In his essay 'L'illusion biographique' (1986a), he was critical of approaches to biography that saw a unified self following a linear trajectory. Such an approach would be incomplete, akin to describing a trip on the Metro without acknowledging the 'structure of the network, that is, the matrix of objective relations between the different stations' (ibid.: 71). Instead, Bourdieu preferred a view of life trajectory as a 'series of positions successively occupied by the same agent (or same group) in a space itself in flux and undergoing incessant transformations' (ibid.). For Bourdieu, 'what exist in the social world are relations – not interactions between agents or intersubjective ties between individuals, but objective relations which exist "independently of individual consciousness and will"' (Bourdieu and Wacquant, 1992: 97). Rather, life trajectories and the biographies told are the outcome of the various social fields inhabited by the individual and their attendant value in the overall economy of symbolic exchanges.

At the outset of our project, we were intrigued by the facility with which participants were able to navigate the transition between the familial and communitarian culture of the home, the chapel and the workplace, on the one hand, and the apparently more contrived, centralized public culture of the education system beyond Wales, on the other. This parallels the dilemma identified by Bourdieu (1991a) and Robbins (2005) between the indigenous, somehow organic and natural-feeling cultures of childhood and the family, versus the more metropolitan, constructed culture that many of our participants would have encountered in higher education. That is, as Robbins (2005) puts it, between the life-world and the system-world.

This is not to suggest that the kinds of experiences undergone in early life in the family or community are somehow privileged or unproblematic. The spoken language is the sedimented world of shared meaning that individuals have at their disposal. For Merleau-Ponty (1945), speech is not the clothing of thought, rather it is its body. Thus, experience is constituted through the kinds of narratives that people are able to construct about themselves and their lives and by making sense of past and present events through 'storying the narrative', by assembling or integrating these events within a narrative, or perhaps a series of related narratives (Somers, 1994). These 'storied narratives' provide the basis for actions derived from memories, expectations or projections.

In this perspective, personhood is not absolute but embedded in a dynamic and often at times collective *ontological narrative*. In such narratives, says Somers (1994), 'cultural representations become more important than class attributes', thus directing us to investigate participant identities by looking at actors' places in their relational settings, or what Bourdieu would call their 'habitus'. Where participants tell their stories, interwoven with the stories of those around them, their biographies yield opportunities for researchers to 'grasp the life as a whole (or a major part) in all its inconsistencies and contradictions' (Roberts, 2002: 52).

The lives of many of our participants in the present volume invite comparison with the features of Welsh culture outlined in chapter 1. That is not to say that the notion of a nation with cultural, musical or scholarly traditions so assiduously accumulated by the 'Nonconformist elite' is literally true in any simple sense. The more interesting questions revolve around the way in which participants came to embody aspects of the culture and how their subsequent trajectories came to reflect this aspiration and striving, and how it was so deeply ingrained in the collective practice or habitus of the families, village and chapel communities involved.

Habitus involves 'the disposition to act which individuals acquire in the earliest stages of socialisation and which they consolidate by their subsequent choices in life' (Robbins, 1993: 159). The habitus of a person, family or community refers to more than just explicit norms and values, because it is embedded within everyday actions, much of which is subconscious, hence the use of the term 'disposition'.

The idea of habitus is not unique to Bourdieu. The origins of the concept in the social sciences go back much earlier. According to contemporary commentators such as Wendy James (James and Allen, 1998) and Elspeth Probyn (2004), Marcel Mauss was the first to deploy habitus as a sociological concept. James also notes that originally the term habitus was used medically to describe the outward appearance of the face and body as somehow revealing the individual's state of health or sickness (James and Allen, 1998: 20). For Mauss, striving to comprehend 'l'homme total', habitus is an important concept. It joins 'the local connectedness of form and content, . . . the tangible aspect of human life . . . in relation to the body and its material experience, the techniques of work, and the rhythmic enactment of ritual and symbolic performance' (James and Allen, 1998: 15). Habitus has been elaborated to include aspects relating to embodiment, agency and the interplay between past, present, individual and collective phenomena to make sense of cultural behaviour and experience (Reay, 2004a). Bourdieu defines habitus as the 'system of acquired dispositions functioning on the practical level as categories of perception and assessment or as classificatory principles as well as being the organising principles of action' (Bourdieu, 1990a: 13). One's habitus is an individually operationalized set of expectations and understandings based on the collection of experiences that one encounters that shape one's sense of the 'rules of the game'. Habitus is a 'generative schema', consisting of systems of durable, transposable dispositions (Bourdieu, 1977: 85) which are implicated in the reproduction of social order. According to Sulkunen (1982: 108), the 'habitus of a group or class defines a symbolic order within which it conducts its practices – in everyday life as well as in the feast'. One's habitus is the product of one's individual history but also of the whole collective history, of family and class (Bourdieu, 1990a: 91).

Bourdieu attempted to think about how material conditions of social class and economic inequality could be manifest in culture and in the individual's social–psychological organization:

> the social order is progressively inscribed in people's minds. Social divisions become principles of division, organizing the image of the social world. Objective limits become a sense of limits, a practical anticipation of objective limits acquired by experience of objective limits, a 'sense of one's place' which leads one to exclude oneself from the goods, persons, places and so forth from which one is excluded. (Bourdieu, 1984: 471)

As we have argued elsewhere (Baker and Brown, 2008), in the case of Wales, it is possible to extend Bourdieu's concept, and speak of an aspirational habitus. Participants, even though they were often from economically disadvantaged backgrounds in rural Wales, often described to us how the sense in their families that education was valuable culminated in their going to university. Educational values were embedded in culture and remembered as being held by people in the wider community, even among those who had little formal education. Habitus is not merely about restriction and exclusion. It may equally well serve as a generative construct, which explains how many of our participants from rural Welsh backgrounds, who experienced economic disadvantage on a regional and individual level, successfully entered and navigated their way through university and the professions. Their habitus developed in a particular historical context, spanning the generations who lived through the mid twentieth century. We take habitus in a flexible, non-deterministic sense, facilitating the growth of individuals into new circumstances, as well as trammelling them within familiar ones (Reay, 2004a).

The Welsh language may have prefigured Bourdieu, containing a concept similar to that of 'habitus', namely '*buchedd*' or 'way of life'. Jenkins's work (1960), originating in the same period as some of our participants, chronicled the concept of *buchedd* in some detail in a village in Cardiganshire. Jenkins describes one group as having a *buchedd* corresponding to the background of many participants in the present study – religious Nonconformists with a pervasive respect for knowledge, from whom the disadvantaged but aspirational first-generation university students allegedly came. The idea of *buchedd* itself may also be part of the mythical past, fabricated by middle-class Nonconformists (Jones, 1992a), yet like the notion of Welsh culture, its power lies in its image, which disadvantaged or marginalized people can carry with them as they aspire.

The *buchedd*, among our participants at least, involved aspiration and striving. Whilst sometimes the achievements were modest, the sense of striving and aspiration, as well as the sense of working for the well being of other family or community members, was a distinctive feature of many of the accounts of family life.

As the brief vignettes of participants' lives which we presented earlier have also illustrated, the idea of a classless *gwerin*, comprising working people from all walks of life, so beloved of W. J. Gruffydd (1881–1954), is difficult to sustain in the light of the manifest inequalities of status and material resources that left their mark on people's biographies and inform their reminiscences many decades later.

Some clues as to the intersection of inequality with community life in Wales are provided by Day and Fitton (1975). They contend that the chapel rarely overturned the economic or class order but tended instead to reproduce it, even within an ostensibly egalitarian organization. Those who had acquired status or esteem outside the chapel were more likely to hold office within the chapel congregation. Those who had gained this secular status and esteem were likely to be exponents of Jenkin's *buchedd* A and were positioned favourably, where matters of piety and respectability were concerned. Consistent with the arguments of Bourdieu and Boltanski (1978), class structure may not have been preserved in concrete, but a distinct hierarchy remained, and perhaps the perceived position of people and families in this structure conserves the ordinal ranking of different classes. There may be distinct differences in the extent to which people were able to claim embodiment of *buchedd* A, which may well have followed contours of status, esteem and gender. It might more easily be accrued if one were a farmer rather than labourer, a man rather than a woman, or a minister rather than an ordinary worshipper.

The existence of a concept such as *buchedd* underscores the reflexive quality of much human inquiry into the social world, in that individuals and social systems are capable of self-inquiry and self-conceptualization. As Archer (2007: 61) claims, this reflexivity involves a process of 'mediating deliberatively between the objective structural opportunities confronted by different groups and the nature of people's subjectively defined concerns'.

Indigenous cultural frameworks of thinking, means of making sense of the world and values often leave their mark on later generations, after the material conditions in which those values originated have changed. In Wales, this residue may derive from forms of social organization revolving around family and cliques based on occupational or religious identification. Several studies have noted that these groups and the *buchedd* they espoused served to enhance social embeddedness and integration and afforded a measure of social control, promoting standards of behaviour within the community (Day and Fitton, 1975; Jenkins 1960; Plowman et al., 1961).

Yet at the same time, *buchedd* could be remarkably elastic in practice. Indeed, Jenkins (1960) describes what he calls *buchedd* A and *buchedd* B. *Buchedd* A was the conventional, respectable Nonconformist existence, whereas *buchedd* B involved 'living a life in the world', which might involve a more carefree approach to pleasures such as drinking and gambling. As Williams (2002) further points out, there might be exponents of both *buchedd* A and *buchedd* B in the same household. *Buchedd*, then, is a supple construct, and, as we shall see, despite some participants' deviations from the notion of respectable Nonconformist existence, the communities and congregations were sufficiently robust to enable the support and recuperation of a person's or family's status, should a lapse occur.

Emmett (1964: 12), commenting on Jenkins's account of *buchedd*, appears to have noticed something similar:

> In Llan *buchedd* A and B are not separate. At a superficial glance, the division appears to be there . . . unlike Jenkins's *buchedd* A people, most of them value Wales more than they value wordly achievement: they would rather see their sons shovelling manure or working in the factory than see them go to London. They would like their children . . . to have good jobs and good opportunities, but they know that to get them they would have to leave the community . . . The fact that intelligent, well-informed people have stayed in the community in the past means that the community is worth staying in now . . . an 'almost *buchedd* A' group see their fellows: not in the main, as an opposing group, but as individuals . . . Their children are therefore not kept apart . . . their children intermarry with people who drink, mix with drinkers and probably drink themselves.

The close relationship between Welsh Methodism and education (White and Suggett, 2002) meant that the congregations formed as a result of evangelical and revival movements were primed with literacy, enhanced by the availability of the Bible in Welsh (White, 2007). Nonconformist religious movements in Wales were distinctively literate and, with the involvement of lay preachers and the encouragement of extemporized 'oral prayer' on the part of the congregation, an ethos was created of personal reading, understanding and interpretation. This was often accompanied by a sense of painstaking work to acquire the knowledge, skills and opportunities to exercise them – the accumulated labour of cultural capital. More than this, within the narrative accounts, connections are made between life events to demonstrate a sequence, process and order and to establish a sense of direction and meaning (Gergen and Gergen, 1984: 174; Brockmeier, 2000). They may also reflect individuals' and groups' attempts to shape a personal unity or coherence through 'stories' (Widdershoven, 1993: 7).

At the same time, stories are inevitably selective. In many 'stories that people tell about themselves, reference to a limited number of past (and possibly future) actions is made in telling their own life' (Van Langenhove and Harré, 1993: 97). This process of selection and limitation is itself a social one. As Emmett (1964: 10) says:

> Llan people see the people of their community in terms of places and see farms and cottages with families attached and both people and places are always seen embedded in and embroidered by the history of Llan's past fifty-odd years. The history is not one of important events: the two world wars left the lives of most Llan people unmarked. It is a history of scandal and jokes, a gossip history, whose power on people and beauty for people it is hard to express. Part of this power derives from the fact that everyone is familiar with that past; anyone can describe it.

In addition, the 'stories of the self ' (and the wider group) may shift, being reformulated and reproduced in relation to different and changing social audiences. From the historian's point of view, personal narratives may also contain 'historical accounts' of specific individuals and groups. A difficult issue has been how to chart and interpret the complex interlinking of time and narrative within individual and group accounts. Language, narrative and representations of past events are perhaps themselves part of the logic of practice – how we tell stories about ourselves is redolent of our particular habitus and the field in which events are retold. This structuring appears in the details of talk, for example, in brief references to past and future (Taylor, 2005), memories (Taylor, 2001) and the unfolding of a life story (Reynolds and Taylor, 2005).

As Linde (1997) describes, personal narratives may be shaped by broader collectively held narratives. In this volume, our interest is not necessarily in the narratives of a bounded collective or particular institution. However, the practice of telling and retelling stories is significant for Linde. 'The life story is . . . comprised . . . of the most significant narratives of a speaker's life, which are told and retold, reinterpreted and reshaped for different situations' (Linde, 1997: 283). In a sense, the stories themselves represent the practice of a particular kind of *buchedd* or habitus. For example, a life story may function for a speaker in a particular interaction to support a claim to an identity as a 'respectable' person. Understandings prevailing within the wider society enable or govern this kind of identity work, for example, because of the work being done by a speaker to reconcile it with other identity claims or positions into which they have been enlisted by their life circumstances.

Seeing the stories people tell as reflecting a particular habitus or *buchedd* and seeing the participants as actively embodying the capital that they have acquired, gives us a way of acknowledging the continuity of a storyteller's reflexive project to construct a biographical identity, examining links across the multiple occasioned and situated tellings of 'who I am'. This kind of approach addresses a common criticism of many discursive explorations of identity, in that they emphasise 'flux, variability and incoherence' at the expense of exploring continuities in the life narrative (Crossley, 2000: 528).

In important respects, the remainder of this book documents the kind of habitus or *buchedd* claimed by our participants and shows the dynamics of their accounts of their lifetimes' work towards it. This struggle was, as we shall see, by no means straightforward, for to gain prestige in one area might mean that it had to be foregone in another. Speaking Welsh with aplomb might be valuable in chapel, but in term of professional advancement, English might be the language of choice. In the next chapter, we will explore how this process of gaining and maintaining position in the social field could be undertaken in the occupational sphere.

3

Women and Society 1940–1970:
Culture, Gender and Politics

෬

This chapter will begin with a brief overview of the existing scholarship on the role of women in Wales, with particular reference to the mid twentieth century. This will provide a means of interrogating and interpreting our own data, some of which we will present in this chapter. We will discuss the extent to which some women among our participants were able to transcend the allegedly strict gender-role traditionalism noted by most earlier scholarship. Once again, the question of culture is paramount, and participants were often reflexively aware of the work done by women to accomplish and sustain music, learning, piety and community memory, underscoring the importance of Bourdieu's insights about practice, reflexivity and symbolic capital.

Most scholarship of Wales in the twentieth century describes a strongly patriarchal nation. Accounts have pivoted around male activity, such works frequently being concerned with economic or political life (Ginswick, 1983; Morgan, 1982). The traditional industries and forms of employment upon which the economy rested were very male dominated, through successive legislative manoeuvres and changes in custom and practice in the nineteenth century. Quarrying, mining and agriculture contained few formal roles for women and thus women did not usually constitute high-profile figures in these spheres (Egan, 1988; Howell, 2003; Jones, 1982; Williams, 1991). We will argue that in fact women's influence and activities were crucial to these and other spheres in the mid twentieth century, but that this was not always obvious or transparent. The occasional high-profile woman has been discussed in previous accounts. Lucy Thomas (1781–1847) was dubbed the mother of the coal industry after taking over her husband's business in 1833. Lady Charlotte Guest (1812–95) gained fame not only as a translator of Welsh folktales but also, on her husband's death, as an industrialist, continuing the running of his ironworks (Guest and John, 1989). Frances Hoggan (1843–1927) was born in Brecon but travelled to Paris, Düsseldorf and Zurich to pursue her studies in medicine, becoming not only the first woman doctor in Europe, but also a writer on topics such as education for girls in Wales and black women after slavery in the US. In the twentieth century, there are figures such as Margaret Haig Thomas (1883–1958), who promoted women's suffrage, and Megan Lloyd George (1902–66), who was active in both Liberal and Labour politics through our period of interest.

Until relatively recently there has been comparatively little written in depth about women's lives in Wales per se, or about interactions and relationships between men and women in Wales. Beddoe's *Out of the Shadows* (2000) is titled presumably to highlight the occluded and shadowy existence of women for many earlier chroniclers of Welsh history. Some historical accounts have described the marginalization and low status ascribed to women. For example, Jones (1982) describes the way in which there was no role at all for women in the slate quarry and the low status that the women in quarrying communities had in the eyes of other people in the locality. Women are sometimes ghettoized, in the sense that they are dealt with as a chapter within a book (Herbert and Jones, 1995). Rosser and Harris's study (1965) of familial relationships in Swansea reveals women beginning to break out of the domestic sphere after generations of being located in that position. Rosser and Harris's work, however, was solely about an urban population. The post-war community studies of rural Wales, such as Emmett (1964) or Davies and Rees (1960) – with the exception of Frankenberg (1957) – tell us little about women, other than their activities in the domestic sphere, en masse, such as in the Women's Institute, or in the occasional specific social role, such as the nurse or the schoolteacher. These community studies did not use gender as a central focus for analysis. They were also written before Bourdieu and other theorists that we use in this book were published in English, let alone Welsh. Indeed, writers on Wales have so far been rather reluctant to adopt the theoretical interests found in historiography and cultural studies elsewhere, as Croll (2003) notes.

It might seem that Wales provides a relatively stable picture of gender traditionalism, and that this perhaps reflected a traditionalism at the level of politics, economics and employment. Much previous work, whether or not undertaken from a feminist perspective, has usually emphasized the rigidity and pervasiveness of gender roles present in Welsh life until the late twentieth century. John (1991), exceptionally, describes women transcending these gender roles. She does this not simply in terms of describing the activities of individual, often extraordinary women, but also in the context of the activities of women as a group, concentrating on aspects of the lives of Victorian and early twentieth-century women in Wales. John gives a rich, complex account of the position of women, demonstrating how women could and did step out of the domestic sphere, how they were involved in protest and undermining authority as well as radical feminist activity, yet how at the same time women were charged with upholding morality. John explores Welsh and Welshness, as well as how England and English tradition affected the lives and identity of women in Wales. The influence of domestic ideology is also explored, raising questions of the social and cultural construction of masculinity. John's is primarily an historical work, rather than a sociological one, and thus social theory is not drawn upon to any great extent.

Jane Aaron et al. (1994) explored the lives of women in both Welsh- and English-speaking communities in Wales. Much of this work charts the change in women's lives during the latter half of the twentieth century, for example by looking at changes in family life, employment patterns and the division of domestic labour. Some stereotypes are challenged. The discussion on domestic violence questions the image of the Welsh 'mam' ruling over a domestic haven, and the chapter on the lives of farmer's wives undermines notions of a rural idyll. The effect of English colonization on Wales is explored, leading to a discussion of the persistence of the influence of English ideas of morality on Victorian Wales. Aaron et al. were primarily concerned with the lives of women in late twentieth-century Wales from a feminist perspective, consistent with the socio-political sensibilities of this time. Although social and cultural theorists are mentioned, there is, aside from feminism, little formal sociological analysis; rather, the emphasis is on the position of women in the late twentieth century and the events which led to this.

Deirdre Beddoe's work (see *inter alia* Beddoe, 1986; 2000) merits special consideration. In the 1980s her interest was in the imagery surrounding women in Wales. From her contention that 'Welsh women are culturally invisible' (Beddoe, 1986: 227), she goes on to argue that Welsh identity has traditionally been based on three male groups: 'coalminers, rugby players and male voice choirs' (1986: 227). By comparison, women are 'a bit of trimming on the male image of Wales' (ibid.). This invisibility, she contends, arises from three factors, namely 'patriarchy, capitalism and history' (ibid.: 228). She describes Wales as 'a patriarchal society, in which the activities and views of men are held in far higher esteem than those of women' (ibid.). Through the industries with which Wales has been associated from the industrial revolution, capitalism has dominated Welsh culture. In south Wales, the coalminer repre-sented both 'wealth' and 'rebellion' (ibid.). Beddoe believed, that in Wales, as in many capitalist societies, women's unwaged work often goes unnoticed. Beddoe is also attentive to the selective and constructive aspects of history which is 'not only divided along class lines but along gender lines too' (ibid.).

In her subsequent work, *Out of the Shadows*, Beddoe (2000) paints a picture of women's lives in twentieth century Wales that is highly consistent with the stereotypical gender roles of that time. The women's lives are depicted in and through the matrix of traditional gender roles, with only very slight indications that, at least for some women, these roles could be transgressed. This collection of short accounts by women of women's lives in Wales in the 1950s and 1960s can perhaps be seen as consistent with the spirit of those times and the climate of attention as to how women's lived experience is dominated by gender roles and gender inequality. Whilst this is in keeping with the feminisms of the late twentieth century, we do not end up with an intimate feel for the complexity of gender relations and roles and their inter-action with other facets of society, perhaps because many of the accounts are brief and the authors use broad brushstrokes to paint their pictures.

By contrast, our interviewees depicted a rather messier, more paradoxical picture than most of this previous work suggests. Women and men talked about their own memories and lives, as well as the lives of the previous generation and even the genera-tion before that. There was plenty of evidence that many women fulfilled traditional roles, either within the domestic sphere as wives and mothers (or carers), or in paid employment, as domestic servants, nurses, teachers or as farmers' wives and daughters. Many participants talked about the way in which churches and chapels were entirely male dominated and controlled. Yet the picture that emerged was a highly complex one; this was not simply a tale of patriarchal privilege. Women could and did traverse tradi-tional gender roles, and some respondents remembered women doing this as far back as the first decades of the twentieth century. The presence of powerful women under patriarchal systems is not unusual, although such women are usually powerful only within certain spheres defined by men. The reminiscences of our participants clearly suggest that in the rural Wales of *Y Fro Gymraeg*, women were able to gain strength and power in patri-archal systems, especially in spheres predefined for them by that patriarchal culture. Yet their power in turn informed, influenced, transformed and reproduced the cultures in which they were embedded. So let us explore here the situations in which our interviewees described women transgressing gender boundaries.

Stepping out of gender roles at work

Three of the women that we interviewed had spent their lives, or at least a large part of their lives, working as farmers. The centrality of their work in this area and their leadership role leads us to describe these women as farmers, as opposed to farmers' daugh-ters or farmers' wives. This distinction is important – the women themselves certainly considered it so. All three of the women were born farmers' daughters, but their role in later life was considered somewhat different to that of a farmer's daughter or wife. Two of these interviewees were very aware of their unusual status, one identifying farming as being 'male' and a woman farmer as 'odd', but one woman didn't mention this, seeming to take her life as a farmer very much for granted. Farming in Wales has been characterized as a patriarchal occupation (Price and Evans, 2009). At a time when developed economies were seeing many factors of production moving out of family hands and into corporate ones, agriculture (perhaps because there was a net decline in labour overall) tended to remain dominated by family concerns (Price and Evans, 2006), especially in Wales (Howell and Baber, 1993). Indeed, the decline in agricultural business in Wales in the nineteenth and early twentieth centuries appears to have been particularly acute compared with the rest of the British Isles. By the mid twentieth century, the average farmer's return in Wales was only a third of the average for the UK as a whole (Ashby, 1944; Howell and Baber, 1993: 294). It is against this background of emiseration of agriculture in Wales that the lives of our farmers unfolded.

The youngest woman farmer whom we interviewed was Erin, whose life story we outlined in chapter 2. She had been a sheep farmer in Snowdonia from the 1970s until 2001. In terms of gender roles, she maintained that she had never encountered any hostility at all as a woman farmer, even from much older male farmers, although she recalled that she didn't know of any other women farmers and would always be the only woman at sales. Erin was entirely positive in her description of her interactions with male farmers, although she was certainly aware of her gender:

> They just accepted it. They like having a girl to tease at the sales. I like farming and everyone accepted me. I don't think they're hostile to women, most of them aren't, I didn't come across them anyway, maybe I just know the nice farmers, I don't know anyone who's got a problem with it.

Interestingly, when this farmer left secondary school, she had initially entered a 'feminine' career, undertaking a course for entry into the caring professions at the local technical college and then finding employment at a residential hospital for learning-disabled people. During this time, she helped her father on his farm, the tenancy of which she subsequently took over after his death. Another twist to her narrative was that the event that finally motivated Erin to farm full time, initially with her father and then with her husband, was the birth of her daughter. An eventual divorce left Erin as a single parent running a hill farm alone. Although Erin undertook all the work on the farm, just as a man would be expected to do, the only time that she mentioned her status as a woman making farming an unsuitable occupation for her was at that point where she described why she finally gave up the tenancy of the farm: 'I farmed alone until the year of foot and mouth – that's enough girl – not a life for a girl any more, all the paperwork. The paperwork and the pressures, I don't think it's worth it. Since the foot and mouth it's got worse and worse.' Ironically, then, it was not any of the 'masculine' aspects of farming that caused Erin to give it up, but the enormous economic difficulties and stress that so many hill farmers in Wales have experienced in recent years. When Erin left farming, she received much support from her former male colleagues, a number of whom stated that they admired her courage in leaving a way of life that she had grown up with and to which she had given most of her adult years. Lest we believe that the transgressing of gender roles is a clean-cut simple affair, on leaving farming Erin returned to more traditionally feminized roles, such as working with learning-disabled people and helping care for her daughter's new baby. Erin spontaneously speculated on why she had become a woman farmer. She did not consider herself to have been particularly rebellious or radical when young and she had not felt coerced or even persuaded to take up farming. Yet she did mention always having felt closer to men than to women, and wondered whether losing her mother when young and her subsequent close friendship with her father may have been a factor. Erin also wondered whether perhaps the presence of the Women's Land Army in the region during the war might have made people more accepting of women farmers.

Cadi, whom we also described in one of the biographical sketches in chapter 2, was born in 1932 and farmed on the Llŷn

Peninsula during the 1970s and 1980s. Cadi was born a farmer's daughter, but she had 'never thought I'd be a farmer'. Yet in middle age she found herself widowed with children – her son was still in the sixth form, but had ambitions to be a farmer, so she wanted to rent a farm for him. But, in Cadi's words:

> they wouldn't let it to a woman – you had to prove yourself, that you had enough money. I understood that I was only the second woman [in Britain] to have proven my case. The will had to be proven for me to have the money. The struggle was enormous: the worst thing I ever went through.

However, like Erin, she did not remember opposition once she had acquired the farm; the other farmers 'treated me allright'.

Whereas Erin and Cadi had actively sought out careers as farmers, Angharad was in a different situation. There were indications that she had rather more mixed feelings about her life as a farmer than Erin and Cadi. Angharad was born in Denbighshire, a farmer's daughter. Her career plans as a teenager in the early 1950s did not involve farming: 'well I wanted to be a hairdresser but I didn't have the choice. They said I had to stay at home and work.' Her parents were both chronically ill and could not physically work hard. Although she 'loved the outdoor work', Angharad mentioned that she still cuts people's hair. She never thought that being a woman farmer was strange: 'but there were a lot of things I couldn't do, like when they were doing the threshing and that – you didn't want to mix with all the men did you?' Angharad went inside to prepare the food for the men at these times. Although she did not want to 'mix with the men' and was comfortable in traditional feminine spheres, Angharad mentioned that whilst farming, she had worked with horses and tractors.

This was in contrast to another woman farmer in Denbighshire that we were told about, the mother of Elsi, one of our participants. Elsi's mother was born a farmer's daughter in 1918. Her own mother died when she was ten and she left school at fourteen to work on the family farm with her father. It sounded as though this was partly through necessity – an older brother had already left home and was farming elsewhere in the area, while another

brother who would have run the farm had become mentally ill
and was a long-term hospital patient. These circumstances had
consequences; like Erin, Elsi's mother was very close to her father,
'they were friends'. Although we are talking about a woman who
began her career as a farmer in the 1930s, Elsi commented that:

> I think she was quite accepted, yes, because she left school at four-
> teen and then that was her job. She would milk, she would do all
> apart from the fieldwork, she never drove the tractor for instance. I
> think when I was very young it was actually the horse, not the horses
> I knew, she wouldn't have had the physical strength to hold, but we've
> got photographs of her holding the horse in the field, so she must
> have – although you can never tell whether it was just put up for the
> photograph.

Contrast the activities of these women farmers with the duties
usually considered appropriate for farmers' wives and daughters
– the care of the hens, the feeding of calves and piglets and work
in the dairy. Yet even for these female farmers who stepped out
of traditional gender roles, there were tasks that they considered
inappropriate for them as women. Erin considered high stress
levels, economic problems and excessive paperwork not suitable
for her; Angharad didn't wish to mix with men who worked on
the farm, although she would drive tractors; yet Elsi's mother did
everything, apart from tractor work.

Women farmers were breaching gender traditionalism in a very
obvious way, by doing a job that was considered to be effectively
exclusively in the male domain. Another respondent, Gwen, told
us of her two great-aunts who ran a cake shop together. Although
this is consistent with notions of what constituted suitable employment for women, these two women were described to us as quite
eccentric and autonomous:

> I'm thinking back to my great-aunts now – they were quite strong
> women as well and two of them came over to Anglesey and ran a busi-
> ness, a cake shop. They did it themselves – that would have been the
> 1960s. It was probably the women [in charge] in our family anyway. I
> never thought of it as being rather strange. My grandfather of course

[was] the head of the family as it were, but they [the great-aunts] went off and did their own thing on Anglesey. Actually I remember someone saying that they had books in the shop as well, like a library. My uncle, as far as I can remember, he didn't have any part in running it.

Whilst from these quotes we cannot make general statements about the female population of Wales as a whole, these examples show us that the androcentric world of work was not impenetrable to women. Farming perhaps, more than mining, offered this opportunity because there were fewer legal and bureaucratic restrictions on who could enter the occupation and do the work. Although, as we can see from the above accounts, sometimes acquiring the wherewithal to do so involved a considerable struggle on the part of the women concerned. A further factor which seems to have eased these women's transition into farming was the family connection with the industry. This meant that their assumption of the role was familial and gradual, so relatives, friends and neighbours would have time to get used to them in the occupation, even if, like Cadi, there had been a break to raise a family. Moreover, farming often involves long hours of work in isolation, so unlike the anomaly of a woman, say, in a factory or in the close quarters of a mine or quarry, it would not be immediately conspicuous or worthy of remark.

The women who ran the cake shop mentioned above were doing something consistent with female sex roles. Culinary skills and retail employment were long associated with women's work, as too in Wales were books and learning. Thus, in all these cases, we can see aspects of continuity with women's work and their assigned sphere, as well as transformational or emancipatory elements. The avoidance of work with tractors, avoiding the men involved in threshing or persisting with hairdressing, stand as curious motifs of femininity and modesty amidst the more socio-economically substantive incursions into male-dominated occupations. Here we see the symbolic qualities of the female sex role loyally sustained, in the face of deviations in other aspects. Thus, rather than a unitary feminine role to which all women in a socially conservative nation were consigned, the vicissitudes of rural life offered some opportunities for greater gender complexity.

Femininity and masculinity, as they are practised, seem to be dispositional schemes that might best be seen as *generative rather than determining,* and can be understood as an embodied 'generative grammar, but is not an inborn generative grammar . . . It is a principle of invention, a principle of improvisation. The habitus generates inventions and improvisations but within limits' (Bourdieu, 2005: 46).

At the same time, Bourdieu (2001) reminds us that the influence of masculine domination is pervasive and may survive attempts by individuals to shift it. In his view, masculine domination 'comes from the fact that it combines and condenses two operations: it legitimates a relationship of domination by embedding it in biological nature that is itself a naturalized social construction' (Bourdieu, 2001: 23). The symbolic violence of not being permitted to take on the tenancy of a farm, the retention of social and occupational gender separations, such as not working with male co-workers or not driving the tractor, suggest the resilience of traditional gender categories, even as they are absorbing challenges. The female working body can generate material embodied change in the structure of gendered relations. Yet this itself can also serve as a reconstruction of symbolic gender orthodoxy. Often, both possibilities are co-present in any given social setting. Nevertheless, material embodied changes rising from practice and then feeding practice in a generative sense can slowly, imperceptibly at times, challenge and transform the gendered habitus of social actors as they work.

Another way of thinking of this is as a process of 'somatization of social relations of domination' (Bourdieu, 2001: 23), as, through gendered practice, symbolic distinction becomes inscribed into and onto bodies as two opposing, yet complementary, forms of habitus or schemes of dispositions. Where participants feel comfortable being with their bodies, what they or their relatives felt able to do are subject to a form of subtle governance. In this respect, inspired by the phenomenology of Merleau-Ponty (1945) before him, Bourdieu used the phrase 'the feel for the game' in articulating how the social actor binds together his central constructs of habitus, capital and field.

This tension between a curious conservatism in some aspects of the practice of one's gender role, combined with a transgressive

or radical involvement in activities not generally considered feminine, was a pattern disclosed in other spheres, too, such as religious
organizations and politics.

Stepping out of gender roles in religious institutions

As we have noted, chapel communities played a central role in the
development of Wales as a nation and in the social and community lives of people to whom we spoke. Our participants talked
of other ways in which some women broke out of gender roles
within religious institutions. All of our interviewees spoke about
their memories of church and chapel life. Most people remembered these institutions as being dominated and led by men, at
least on the face of things. It was common to hear our respondents commenting thus: (Euros) 'women were Sunday-school
teachers but they weren't leaders in the chapel, but they were
allright for Sunday school and socials, preparing the tea'. Indeed,
most respondents remembered women Sunday-school teachers
or women playing the organ in churches or chapels, but not
women in leadership or influential positions. Lloyd, who grew up
in Denbighshire in the 1950s and 60s, whilst talking about the
possibility of women preachers in his Calvinist Methodist chapel,
commented: 'I'm not sure there'd be any rule, because it was a
democratic decision, it just didn't happen. No woman's name I
think would have been put forward.' Geraint, whose father had
been a deacon in the Calvinist Methodist chapel that the family
attended in the 1950s when he was a boy in Denbighshire,
observed that: 'certainly there were very capable women there,
but the structure within which they worked didn't allow that [a
woman preacher] to happen'. Yet Geraint continued: 'chapels did
not give women a clear leadership role did they? So what you
saw from the outside was male deacons. The outward impression
would be that it was a male-dominated thing, but that wasn't the
case in actuality.' Geraint then gave an explanation, from the point
of view of his family's involvement in chapel administration, of the
ways in which women did indeed exert considerable influence in
chapel, through influencing men (often their close male relatives)

and through their work in Sunday schools, as creators and transmitters of cultural capital.

Later, we will explore women's influence in religious institutions. For the moment, our interest is in the admittedly small number of women who were remembered as explicitly taking leading roles in male-dominated churches and chapels. Sometimes women were simply perceived as generally influential, such as a former teacher who was very active in a Calvinist Methodist chapel in north-west Wales in the 1950s: (Alwena) 'she'd be in the forefront. She put a lot of input into it she really did. So she was the one, the only one [woman] I think. She was more prominent than him [her husband].' Euros remembered a woman preacher visiting west Wales in the first half of the twentieth century, although this was highly unusual: 'I remember one lady coming to preach there occasionally and that was a great novelty.' Euros gave an insight into why this woman preacher may have been able to transcend such rigid gender boundaries: 'she was a M—— [family name] from Swansea, she was a very influential lady, her husband was very influential.' Yet, despite her husband's and family connections that were perceived to have assisted her, Euros also remembered her personal qualities: 'her ability as well to be fair, certainly. She'd have her way you see, she was one of the rare birds in the system, but I remember it quite well.' Other respondents, too, remembered women adopting leadership roles in churches and chapels, but on the basis of what was perceived to be merit, not through influential husbands and families. Gwenda was a member of a Baptist chapel in north-west Wales in the 1950s and 1960s and remembered that women deacons were not considered unusual in their chapel. Gwenda's mother was a deacon herself in the early 1950s:

there were more men yes, but there were I think three lady deacons at the time. I don't know whether we [our chapel] were special, the women did have influence. They had a full part to play in how things were run and certainly if they had something valid to give or to say, then that was received well. It wasn't 'Oh let the little woman talk' sort of thing. The lady deacons of the fifties and sixties were the salt of the earth, they really were sensible, practical people, with practical solutions to things. They weren't second-class citizens at all.

Interestingly, at least in Gwenda's eyes, these women deacons were not seen as participating in sexual politics; they were not battling for anything, they were just doing it. Gwenda told us that her chapel was perceived as liberal. We need to mention here that although her chapel was in a Welsh-speaking town and was attended by many people who spoke Welsh as their first language, it was considered an 'English' chapel. As well as perceiving her chapel per se as 'liberal', Gwenda did speculate that perhaps 'Welsh' chapels were 'stricter' and would never have tolerated women in leadership roles; in particular, those that she designated as 'the Methodists' were seen to be more 'old fashioned'. Other interviewees, too, often mentioned the Calvinist Methodist chapels as being 'strict' and 'old fashioned' and highly patriarchal. Yet first-hand accounts told a different story. Elsi attended a Calvinist Methodist chapel in the 1950s and remarked that:

> we did have a lady deacon. She was actually chosen. Quite exceptional, because there was a lot of jealousy from some of the men who thought they should have been deacons. She was so lovely, she was a very, very good person you know, deserved it. It wasn't 'oh yes we should have a woman'. I think this woman was really good.

There are several points to note here. First, given the tendency of much other scholarship to identify chapel life with piety and social conservatism, it might seem surprising that so many participants reported women in influential roles. Second, the spiritual life of the community was not homogeneous, as it might appear to the outside observer, but subtle lines of distinction were drawn. Participants distinguished between their own chapel, which was thought of as progressive, and others which were more 'strict' or conservative. Intriguingly, whilst the Calvinist Methodists were regarded as strict by some participants, those who had been members of such congregations were quick to point out, for example, that they had had a 'lady deacon'. Thus, the conservatism was always seen as coming from somewhere else. Equally, it showed the participants were keen to assert the progressive nature of their particular chapel congregation. Third, there is a sense in which gaining social capital in chapel communities is, in the

Bourdieusian sense, a matter of accumulated labour. The 'lady deacon', for example, was believed to have earned this recognition through her work for the chapel.

Equally, we can see how the distinctive capital accumulated through communal acts of worship and related cultural activities helped to sustain distinctions and draw boundaries. Participants' identification of their own community of worship as being more progressive than the others suggests that the work done for women to achieve advancement was valued and positioned as a point of distinction between one's own and other congregations.

Yet at the same time, the leadership roles of women were somewhat limited. The women who were remembered taking on these roles were seen as somehow exceptional in their work for the chapel or their talents, rather than this being the common experience of women in chapel congregations. Moreover, it is only in very recent times that women have served as pastors or ministers, yet as we have argued elsewhere (Baker and Brown, 2009), the groundwork for this appears to have been laid much earlier, before a distinctive second-wave feminism was widely detectable in the UK.

The progress of women in this sphere reflects a long-standing alignment between women and piety that, as we have suggested, was formulated in the nineteenth century. Beddoe (1986) describes how the idea of pious Welsh women is a common theme and notes the many stories of Welsh women who committed spiritual acts of self-sacrifice for religious reasons. Beddoe refers to the painting 'Salem' (1908), depicting a chapel scene, by Sidney Curnow Vosper (1866–1942). Here, a woman in 'traditional' Welsh costume (itself a nineteenth-century invention) is shown between the pews of a small chapel near Harlech, as if about to take her seat amongst the other congregation members. In a sense, then, the women succeeding in gaining position in chapel life are gaining capital in a field with which they had been powerfully associated. This may have assisted both the women themselves and the chapel communities in formally recognizing their role, suggestive of the relatively slow change in the patterns of division and domination that we detected in the world of work above.

Women and political activism

The worlds of work and chapel were not the only domains in which we heard of women stepping outside of gender roles. Women were active in the 1926 General Strike, the 1934 hunger march from Tonypandy to London and in the 1984 miners' strike. The high profile of women in Welsh-language activism from the late 1960s onwards is well documented (Piette, 1997). Indeed, some language activists are also known as writers, such as Meg Elis, Menna Elfyn and Angharad Tomos. Some of our interviewees told us about their involvement in the Welsh-language movement: (Eunice) 'that's what I remember really about university. They had women protesting and women being taken to prison as much as the men really, they were as influential as the men.' Indeed, women were so active in Cymdeithas yr Iaith Gymraeg (the Welsh Language Society) that, as Angharad Tomos memorably wrote:

> When someone actually asks me specifically about the role of women in Cymdeithas yr Iaith, I've got to sit back and think 'Which are the women?' because they don't stand out as separate or a peripheral group in Cymdeithas. They are the group. Take the women from Cymdeithas, and it wouldn't be the same movement at all. That's why, come to think of it, we've never had a 'women's section' in Cymdeithas. Because if we did form such a group, what would you call the rest? (Tomos, 1994: 259)

Women have also been prominent in Plaid Cymru, although there is conflicting opinion as to their degree of influence (Charles and Hughes-Freeland, 1995; Watson, 1990).

We interviewed Ceinwen, whose mother (and father) had been involved in a high level of political activism before that surge of activism of the late 1960s and 1970s in which so many women played a substantial part. Ceinwen's mother had achieved fame in Wales through her actions in the 1950s when she and her husband refused to pay their local rates when living in west Wales, unless they received the rates demand in Welsh. Their refusal to pay resulted in them being summonsed more than a dozen times to appear before the Magistrates Court. They insisted that the court proceedings should be in Welsh. These court proceedings resulted in this couple's furniture being seized on three occasions. In 1960, they finally received a demand for the rates in Welsh. This family group was seen as particularly radical, involved in industrial action and Welsh politics. It would seem that interest in politics and the fact that 'we were fighting for the language' subsumed gender issues. Although Ceinwen's mother was politically active and for a time was the main wage-earner whilst her husband, in 1964, gave up his work as a miner and took care of the family, Ceinwen does not ever remember her talking about feminism. When Ceinwen was asked if, as a child, she remembered men and women being of equal status, she replied, 'Of course. I'm surprised the question would even be asked.'

This family was far from patriarchal, but it was an interesting combination of factors which led to the decision that Ceinwen's mother should become the wage earner. The family became concerned for her father's welfare (although he was in good health) when a close friend was killed underground, and Ceinwen's mother, as a teacher, could earn a higher salary than her father could as a miner. Ceinwen described her father as 'an excellent cook and far better around the house', her mother being a 'very indifferent housewife'.

Ceinwen never for a minute doubted that women were of equal status. But she made it clear that her family were political radicals and members of a Congregationalist chapel, with an emphasis on equity. In some ways, Ceinwen's family lived feminism before the second wave of feminism was widely discussed. Her mother worked full time, when women with children usually did not, and she had also been a town councillor, campaigning on issues that feminists later became concerned with, such as childbirth conditions, help for single women with children and housing. Ceinwen did remember gender restrictions in wider society, though, mentioning that one Welsh county in which they had lived was 'incredibly sexist' because it would not employ married women as secondary teachers. But then Ceinwen's family 'did what we wanted', were proud of their radicalism, associated with other radicals and clearly had confidence in their own ideals and values.

Another one of our interviewees, Geraint, whom we described in chapter 2 and whose family were involved in the chapel, remembered Ceinwen's mother. She 'was a chapel-goer but phenomenally radical. She's a phenomenal person and in a sense [she] showed that it was OK for women to do things like that. She became famous simply by being the first person not to pay their income tax or local tax.' He noted that her husband was radical, too, but fitted into a particular tradition: 'being a communist as it were and a miner, was more in a certain tradition of radicalism', while 'she was quite something'. We were interested to learn that, like her mother, Ceinwen had reversed gender roles in her own marriage in the 1970s and 1980s. She worked full time while her husband brought up their children.

The role of women in Welsh politics and Welsh-language activism has been viewed with some ambivalence by feminist commentators. Aaron (1994: 183) detected that 'feminism is still frequently viewed with suspicion by Welsh identified communities as an alien and divisive Anglo-American phenomenon'. Aull Davies (1994) notes that in some nationalist writings it is supposed that gender inequality will cease to be an issue when national autonomy is achieved. Despite the activity of women in Welsh-language movements, it was much more recently that they achieved senior leadership roles in the movement as a whole.

Nevertheless, the vignettes presented here show a curiously high degree of flexibility concerning gender roles, especially among self-identified radicals. Once again we must be cautious about claiming any generality for the experience. Rather, we present the stories here to show what was *possible*, despite the apparently conservative spirit abroad in Wales at the time. It is intriguing, also, that those involved described no ostracism, bullying or other friction with neighbours, acquaintances or schoolmates as a result of these apparent transgressions. Hence, a degree of tolerance and acceptance is implied, as the people concerned certainly did not live reclusively. By assiduous cultivation and capitalization of the self in activities which were valued in the community, such as farming, chapel life or activism in support of working people or the language itself, credit could be gained that would facilitate exceptions being made. For our participants, these deviations might have been viewed by others indulgently as eccentricities at the time, yet their cumulative effect could be seen as the precursor of more far-reaching changes in gender relations that would occur later (Baker and Brown, 2009).

Transgressing gender roles in personal life

Some women transgressed their traditional role and its associated morality and piety as a consequence of unhappy personal circumstances. Arsula has lived her entire life in a town in Gwynedd. She married in 1950 when she was twenty-one and soon after gave birth to a boy. Sadly, by then her husband had become violent. Parts of Arsula's story are depressingly familiar from accounts of domestic violence at that time (Hague and Wilson, 2000). She went to the police about her husband once but 'they didn't want to know'. It was clear to her that the police would act only if she was killed, because then 'that would be murder'.

Arsula left her husband and went to live with her mother in the same town. She was effectively without any means of support. She described her husband as being 'supposed to pay twelve shillings a week', but he did not. She took no further action, as she wanted no contact with him. With the help of her mother, who cared for the baby whilst Arsula worked as a ward maid at a local hospital, Arsula then brought her child up alone. She remembers no ostracism for being a single parent. She suspects that was because, coming from a small community, 'they knew what he was like'; but, 'if they did talk I wouldn't have cared. I wasn't going to put up with that.' Arsula didn't know of any other woman who had left a violent man and was aware that, in the eyes of some, a woman leaving her husband was a 'scarlet woman'. She knew women who stayed in violent marriages who 'had a hell of a time'. Arsula believed that they were 'afraid of talk, wanted to be respectable', keeping it 'all behind closed doors'. Arsula is confident, with regard to her status and the decisions that she took many years ago: 'men – the dominant race [laughs]. We were independent. My mum did it, so did my grandmother [her mother and grandmother also brought up children on their own as a consequence of being widowed young].' Yet Arsula does remember the enormous practical problems for any woman wishing to escape a violent marriage: 'I don't know what I would have done without my mum. There was no help. I suppose I'd have still left but I don't know how.'

Dewi, born in 1946, described a chaotic childhood with his mother, who had a number of male partners, one of them violent, none of them his biological father. Dewi and his mother moved house frequently because of difficult economic circumstances and his mother changing partners. At one point Dewi lived with his aunt, his mother being effectively destitute and unable to care for him. Although Dewi remembered clearly the difficult circumstances that he experienced as a child, like Arsula he did not remember any ostracism from any part of the community. He believed that the quarrying village in Gwynedd in which he grew up 'wasn't that kind of village' and that 'there were only low wages, so times were hard for quite a few of us'. At one point, Dewi's mother cleaned the local chapel in exchange for accommodation. Far from institutions like the chapels excluding people like his mother, Dewi was of the opinion that they 'could not have afforded' to exclude them, as people in such circumstances made up such a high proportion of the village's population.

One male interviewee, although remembering women who did step out of gender roles (he considered his own mother to have been one of them) perceived that for many girls in the 1950s, a brief period of rebellion or independence was followed by life-long domesticity:

> (Harri) I had a feeling that they had this little brief, they were almost like mayflies in a sense. In their teens, they'd go dancing and this sort of thing, then all of a sudden they'd either get married and then get pregnant or they'd get pregnant first then get married, which was very common, and then they just slumped into a housewife's role and that was it, their lives as individuals were virtually over.

Once again, we can see that the models of womanhood that were apparently preferred in community life in Wales were not, in these accounts, all-powerful, nor were they pursued through the entire life course. Instead, these accounts suggest that there might be circumstances where a good deal of flexibility was allowed. Taken at face value, these accounts suggest that there was a good deal of what Gwenda called 'sensible, practical' problem-solving so as to preserve people's dignity and well-being, whilst enabling the broader processes of work, marriage and chapel life to continue. In Bourdieusian terms we could see this as reflecting the generative creativity of a particular kind of habitus, such that new solutions were implemented regarding life events that were potentially threatening to the way of life. Perhaps, rather than an inviolable set of prescriptive rules, gender roles can be seen as a kind of working project, where participants themselves and other community members collectively worked to maintain their symbolic integrity, but tolerated deviation where this was deemed practically necessary. This aligns with Emmett's descriptions (1964: 104) of the practicality with which young women who became pregnant were accommodated, despite the apparent severity of the 'chapel code'. This flexibility is an issue to which we shall return in subsequent chapters.

This possibility of practical solutions being foregrounded in the local habitus may help us explain other features of life for women in Wales in the mid twentieth century. The apparent lack of involvement in the women's movement on the part of women in Wales in the 1960s and 1970s may not have been entirely the result of conservatism or the subsumption of political activism to Welsh-language activities. The reminiscences presented here open up another possibility. Perhaps some of the freedoms for which women campaigned in England or America were not necessarily unknown to women in Wales. They may not have had formally or legally sanctioned equality, but, as we have seen, there were locally negotiated and interpersonally mediated means for women to enter male-dominated occupations, participate in chapel communities, engage in political activism and escape violent marriages.

Women, after all, did not transition fully to men, or men to women. Rather, they were able to take on aspects of the role of the other, whilst many facets of their role remained intact and conventional. In explaining social practice, Bourdieu emphasized the relational and generative aspects of social life (for example, 1998: 3), as well as the agents' dispositions and the structured situations in which they act. The resourcefulness and practical flexibility of the participants and their family members in response to the opportunities available suggests that Bourdieu's analogies with generative grammars are apt. The flexibility of moral systems was also noted by Emmett (1964) in her study of a north Wales village. The manifest position concerning the proper conduct of girls and women is often negotiated flexibly and pragmatically in practice. It is perhaps significant that the gender role nonconformity was, in the case of the farmers and the political activists especially, actualized through family relationships. Supportive parents or partners, commitments to bring the wishes of one's offspring to fruition and so on seem to have been key elements in facilitating the process.

This potential for flexible and, in some cases, creative and generative reinterpretation of gender, normative expectations and moral values deserves further investigation. Indeed, for Bourdieu (2001), the stability of gender relations itself over time is surprising, something he addresses through the 'paradox of doxa'. This refers to the way in which there are so many unquestioned practical actions (doxa) performed every day, which might cumulatively suggest an almost inevitable tendency towards change in gender relations. Yet these actions often seem to have the paradoxical effect of sustaining and stabilizing gender relations. Here, masculine domination represents 'the prime example of the submission to the social orthodoxy' (Bourdieu, 2001: vii). The subversion of the ordered gender system is at the same time serving to render it sufficiently flexible to be durable.

The practical responses to events in working, spiritual, political and family life allow the grander structures of the social field to be preserved as a result of these local, practical accommodations. It is perhaps this generative practicality that allowed women in Wales to enjoy a degree of freedom and recognition that had at the time yet to be gained by their counterparts in England. As Emmett (1964: 118) notes, 'consistent logic is not the aim of most conversation'. Instead, social exchange is the raw material from which social relationships are created. The solutions to local and temporally bounded dilemmas are both informed by – and themselves transform – the grander structures and processes in the social field.

4

Havens in a Heartless World: Accounts of Gender, Femininity and Domestic Life

☙

The original inspiration for the fieldwork reported in this book came from our puzzlement regarding the educational success of so many people from apparently deprived backgrounds in rural north Wales who subsequently graduated from university. Early in the process of collecting life stories, it became clear that a number of people from backgrounds with even a good deal of poverty had attended university. At the time that the fieldwork was conducted, the UK government was keen to increase the proportion of people participating in higher education. Educational researchers were equally keen to assert that there was something about higher education institutions that was intrinsically hostile to young people from less well-off backgrounds (Archer and Hutchings, 2000; Bamber and Tett, 2001; Bowl, 2003; Hutchings and Archer, 2001; Tett, 2000).

In this context, universities themselves and those who worked in them were urged to change, so as to accommodate a new breed of student who was supposedly less acclimatized to the university experience (Baker et al., 2006; Srivastava, 2002). The experiences recounted by participants from north Wales forty or fifty years ago thus had an intriguing resonance with the debates in educational policy in the present. The means by which people who had experienced poverty in childhood could aspire to university and succeed, even at elite institutions, when they got there, was worthy of further investigation. If their strategies could be elucidated, then widening access policies could readily be enhanced.

Unfortunately, as might be expected, the answer was not so easily yielded. The accounts from participants of their early experiences of learning were a world away from the present. The specificities of culture, class and community, as well as the education system itself, had changed out of all recognition. However, in this chapter we will begin a speculative reconstruction of the kind of culture that prevailed in the childhood of our participants and try to show how, despite many accounts of hardship, some people sought to hoist themselves up by their bootstraps and gain educational qualifications. This depended on the orchestration of many cultural resources: the family, the chapel and the Sunday school, as well as schools themselves and the teachers in them. In this chapter we will begin by considering the role of the family in this process and, in particular, the role of mothers. We consider how mothers were often ambitious for their children and how this was both animated by and itself fed into collectively held notions of Welsh culture and history. From Bourdieu's work on the idea of habitus, we will consider how this set of aspirations was reproduced and carried between generations, forming what we have termed elsewhere (Baker and Brown, 2008) an aspirational habitus. We shall show how the seeds of many participants' careers were sown at women's knees in mid twentieth-century domesticity.

In the previous chapter, we considered some examples of gender roles being subverted and even reversed in some circumstances. However, as we have also seen, despite these exceptions, our interviewees all remembered distinctly traditional gender roles prevailing in the mid twentieth-century *Fro Gymraeg*, regardless of factors such as the locality from which people came, their socio-economic status, religious denomination or even personal circumstances.

Geraint, one of our key informants, born in 1945 in Denbighshire, described an adolescence more fortunate than that of some of our other interviewees. His father was a stereotypical pillar of the community – a Freemason, a councillor and a man with a well-established small business that had been passed down to him from Geraint's grandfather. Geraint described a family situation that reflected the 'ideal' of that era:

> there was a clear separation between my mother's role and my father's role ... it would have been my mother who was more influential on my own direct upbringing ... it was a time when women didn't go to work if they had young children ... I think she had the capacity to do something other than that but really never had the opportunity ... I don't think she had any misgivings about what she was doing. I think that was the role that she accepted ... I think she saw her role as being one of supporting her husband, as supporting us as children as we were growing up ... Going back to my mother's influence at home, she would have had the most influence on me, in helping me read for example and spending time with me on things like reading at an early age. My father would not do anything like that ... when I was small I suffered from quite a severe stutter and my mother decided that she'd find somebody to help me out and she actually found a teacher ... I went to this chap and learnt a few poems – he certainly wasn't an expert on stutters – but he was effective.

Here, we can see the inherence of social capital in relationships or, as Bourdieu (1986b: 248) would have it, 'the aggregate of the actual or potential resources which are linked to possession of a durable network of more or less institutionalized relationships of mutual acquaintance or recognition'. Being an 'established' family in the neighbourhood would no doubt enable the mobilization of relationships to secure help for family members. On the other hand, sometimes the family's social capital was manifested by not using resources which were available, perhaps in the form of credit or charitable facilities.

Eirlys grew up in a more impoverished home in a slate-quarrying village in north-west Wales. Her father worked as a quarryman and, although her family did not have the sort of financial stability or social status that Geraint's parents enjoyed, her mother didn't work either, 'because all women stayed home'. However, her mother was 'boss in the house'. Eirlys talked at length about the admirable effort that her mother made managing the family finances on such a limited income. She described how managing on a quarryman's wages was so difficult that many of the quarrymen's wives would buy groceries from the Co-op on credit and subsequently have to pay for them on the day that their husbands received their *taliad mawr*, or bonus, from the quarry. But her mother, 'always made sure she had half a crown in her purse on *taliad mawr* day so that she wouldn't have to go and meet my father to get his pay packet to go to the Co-op to pay the bill'. Eirlys perceived that the sexual division of labour that she witnessed as a child had also existed in the previous generation – her mother's father had allegedly told her mother that 'a girl's place is in the home'. Eirlys remembered this with some resentment on behalf of her mother – the family narrative was that Eirlys's mother had wanted to become a vet, but this was out of the question because she was a girl. Of course, we do not know whether there would have been other barriers – such as financial or academic ones – preventing her mother from qualifying as a vet, but the factor remembered was her gender. The sense that earlier generations had missed opportunities was a powerful component of the aspirational habitus and was seen as an important reason to succeed oneself, as we shall discuss later.

Eirlys also remembered her mother-in-law's aspiration for her own son:

> [my husband] wanted to be a farmhand like his father, but his mother said 'no, you are not going to work on a farm'. She couldn't send him to university, she couldn't afford it, so she sent him into an office to work . . . if you were in the civil service you had security, you had a pension . . .'

The social capital – in terms of the strength and direction of encouragement exerted – could be exercised within the family. The allure of office work as a destination for young adults from more aspirant homes was noted also by Emmett (1964: 41), whose informants were attracted to what was called a 'clean job'.

Eirlys herself could only remember one occasion on which she was told that a career option was simply not open to her because of her gender:

[my father said] 'you're not going in the army' – because I was a girl
– my dad didn't want me to go into the army. I was his favourite little
girl you see and the fathers are more for the girl than the boy, aren't
they. Girls can do no wrong.

Erin, to whose life story we have returned several times in the
course of our narrative, was one of the woman farmers who
had transgressed gender roles in her employment. She described
the approval of her family and the surrounding community, yet
remembered that 'farmers' wives weren't supposed to work' – her
own mother did not.

Another of the women farmers, Cadi, referred extensively to
rigid gender roles during her interview, but remembered her
husband's mother, who lived on the neighbouring farm: 'she
had influence – she was Queen Bee . . . she never lost control
of anything . . . she didn't even give them [the adult children working on the farm] wages'. But then this was a woman
with her own financial means – she had money, 'more than her
husband'. However, she was described as being very well-loved
within her family – she was not viewed as tyrannical, although we
were told that her refusal to relinquish control of the family land
and finances until her children were in late middle age did cause
serious problems.

The mothers of some of our interviewees, although conforming
to traditional gender roles in many ways, were not able to choose
to adopt the role of the 'ideal' full-time mother of the mid twentieth century. These were the women without husbands to
support them. Interviewees whose mothers were in this position
gave moving accounts of the enormous amount of work and sheer
poverty that their mothers had endured – yet they also remembered that their mothers were still determined to fulfil the role of
a 'good mother'.

Alwena, whose story we outlined in the biographical sketches in
chapter 2, lost her father to tuberculosis when she was four, leaving
her mother alone to bring up three children under six years old.
The nature of her father's illness had unpleasant social repercus-
sions for the family, as well as condemning them to poverty:

very few people came near us really. I think they were frightened of catching TB because it was a killer . . . so my mother had a very, very tough life. She supported us when we were tiny – I think she just had a small pension and we were relying on school dinners for our main meal. Mother was very poor, had to work at cleaning jobs – although people did understand. Like most people in those days you had a coal fire which you had to cook on, so when you got up in the morning the fire wasn't really hot enough to heat anything substantial. So we used to have bread and milk in the morning and in the winter my mother would heat the milk, it heated quicker than water and we'd have that with a bit of butter in it . . . my mother was always there in school holidays and on a Tuesday and a Thursday she was at home because when we came home there was always a nice fire in the grate and a meal on the table you know, you used to skip home feeling happy that your mother was going to be there. But on the days that she wasn't there . . . She was a fantastic mother . . . her children were the forefront of her life. She never left us one evening on our own, never.

Many interviewees talked to us about family financial hardship and hard work, yet described how their mothers took full responsibility for family life in the domestic sphere, although they may have had other substantial responsibilities relating to work and contributing to the household income as well. Many of these women obviously transgressed traditional female gender roles out of necessity. We were therefore particularly interested to contrast such reminiscences with the memories of our more affluent or middle-class participants. Geraint and Gwerfyl both remembered their mothers helping run the family small businesses, but being primarily concerned with the welfare of the family. Lowri and Euros both had fathers who were Calvinist Methodist ministers and described tensions in their mothers' role as the 'minister's wife', a role which led to tremendous expectations in terms of their time, energy and conduct, but also resulted in serious financial hardship. We will explore the position of the 'minister's wife' further in a later chapter.

Perhaps the interviewee who most obviously described a mother being bound by gendered expectations and roles was Nona, whose family enjoyed a greater degree of affluence and social standing than most other people. Nona's father was a well-known doctor in north Wales, deeply involved with the chapel and temperance movement. She remembered him being quite remote and formidable, spending much time in his study, which was out of bounds to Nona and her sister. Although she was much closer to her mother, Nona and her sister spent nearly all of their time with their live-in nanny. Nona's account suggested that her mother did little of the day-to-day care of the children or domestic work. Nona's reminiscences describe her mother as being acutely aware of the gendered role of a middle-class woman of that time. She was able and well educated, but work of any sort would have been out of the question. She was a keen member of the local golf club but, characteristic of such organizations until quite recently, there was a sort of gendered apartheid prevailing there in terms of when women could and couldn't use the greens. Nona was adamant that even if there had been a possibility of her mother being able to breach such rules, she would not have felt able to do so, simply on the grounds of the social shame of a woman behaving thus. As Nona and her sister grew older, Nona's mother studied for qualifications in law – yet even after completing her studies, she did not ever practise.

Nona's mother's social position and her expectations of middle-class women were described as lasting influences on Nona and her sister. They were both expected to (and did) go to university; yet upon marrying and having children, they gave up all paid employment and took the view that as far as work was concerned, their husbands' careers were more important. As her children grew older and more independent, Nona became involved with community and public life, assuming responsibilities in the chapel and sitting as a magistrate.

A consistent theme among our participants was the way in which they remembered aspiration for both boys and girls. This nearly always involved educational aspiration, because it was assumed that this would lead to career success and social mobility. (We will look at educational aspiration and success in further detail in chapter 5.) In seeking to understand how our participants formulated the origins of these accounts of aspiration and in attempting to unpack the role of women, one common theme introduced by our informants was that of socially ambitious mothers.

Fathers were usually described positively: (Arwel) 'my father had very little understanding of what higher education was, other than it was clearly a good thing and he was always immensely supportive, emotionally and financially'. However, overall, they did not appear to be the real driving force. Again and again, this was attributed to mothers. (Geraint) 'she was the one who pushed me to think of college of the two of them . . . she was quite persuasive'.

This theme, detectable in both men's and women's narratives, often involved participants describing mothers who had missed out on affluence and social status themselves and who therefore wanted their children to have these privileges:

> (Alwena) my mother used to say work hard in school and get your-self a decent job. And a decent job in my mother's mind would either be working in a bank or for the government. No way could we go to college, there was no question of that. We didn't have any money did we . . . because of the hardship she didn't want us to go scrubbing floors um you know when she was little, she went out at fourteen then and there were maids in ordinary farm houses, sleeping in the attics, freezing cold, having to get up at six to make the fires for the family and they were only ordinary farmers, because labour was so cheap. So my mother really used to say you're not going to be slaves for other people. So she encouraged us, but the only drawback was that she wouldn't let us join the library because in those days people used to say that you'd catch TB from books . . . we'd had no books at home . . . so we were in the 'A' stream at grammar school, but very disadvan-taged because we had no books . . . she didn't want us to go to a shop, just behind a counter, she wanted something better for us.

Many interviewees remembered their mothers living out educa-tional ambitions, in particular, through their children, but we shall return to that in a later chapter. What we are concerned with here is aspiration per se. Arwel summed up such aspiration eloquently as he talked about his mother's 'tremendous aspiration' that he should 'do well' and the 'great pressure . . . psychological pressure . . .' that he felt from his mother:

the goal was as I say always the next hurdle. I think that's the way my mother in particular kind of drilled all this into me ... I don't think I grew up taking in with my mother's milk some idea that I should go to university. What I did take in virtually with my mother's milk was this tremendous aspiration she had that one should do well at exams ... there was great pressure on me from my mother to do well once I think she realised that I was quite good at it, that I was quite good at schoolwork. It wasn't just – my mother had gone to secondary school in the 1930s so she had some experience of academic education. My father had none, my father left school at the elementary stage ... she also knew quite a lot of people who did have university backgrounds, mainly visitors to the area, people that came and stayed for a short time, mainly people from English backgrounds, mainly people with Oxbridge experience, so she was aware of all that, and I think of the social privileges that was associated with it. However, there was only a certain amount she could do really, there was more a psychological pressure because she didn't understand much about higher education, she'd never experienced it herself and none of her family had.

Another participant also described a mother who had enjoyed little education herself, but nonetheless aspired socially:

(Harri) there was quite an interesting dynamic going on between them [parents] ... my mother used to claim that he had no ambition, that it was her who had driven them from being domestic servants and shop workers to actually being in business ... but he [father] was able. He was an able intelligent man but she reckoned he lacked ambition which she had to make up for. He had ambition for his children but not for himself ... mam was quite a social climber in her little way. She had social ambitions not only for herself but for her children ... But then there was that you know, especially in the quarrying districts. This is where it didn't affect girls, but for the boys it was a bloody awful job, you got diseases and they'd say 'my boy's not going to do that'. There wasn't that imperative for the girls. But again ... in some of the more religious families, they were very ambitious for their girls as well. They didn't seem to distinguish between them.

The quote from Harri, alluding to the integration of academic ambition with a particular religious orientation and way of life is redolent of the issue of *buchedd*, especially *buchedd* A (Jenkins, 1960). Like Day and Fitton (1975), we can see how possession of the more prestigious *buchedd* is interanimated by esteem in the workplace, the chapel or the community. As we have suggested earlier, this concept of 'ethos' or 'way of life' (Conran, 1997: 1) has a good deal in common with Bourdieu's 'habitus'. Ceinwen also made a similar reference, remembering that it was the children of people who went to chapel who were usually the ones encouraged to achieve academically. Habitus, says Bourdieu (1985a: 13), is an experience but also itself a form of capital.

Some participants were acutely aware of what some of the (even modest) aspirations that their parents had for them were about: (Dewi) 'all I do remember is that like most parents they didn't want us to go to the quarry to work because of the conditions, because of the silicosis, it was known even then'. Having a particular aspirational habitus (or indeed *buchedd* A) was thus not merely about the gains in respectability or lifestyle, but could be about survival itself. There were a number of poignant memories relating to the eleven-plus exam and the awareness of the social consequences of failing this. Many of our participants remembered the delight (and relief) of them and their mothers when they or their siblings passed, but one man had clear recollections of the huge disappointment when he did not:

> (Dewi) tried the eleven plus, failed . . . I remember the very, very day I went to school . . . and my father gave me a Parker fountain pen for good luck . . . and I remember having the results and I'd failed and I'd let mum down and I thought ooohhh, but – I got through life.

This participant was not from an 'aspiring' home – his mother was frequently a single parent, he had a series of stepfathers, one of whom was violent towards his mother, and the family experienced severe poverty. Yet he was clearly well aware as a boy of the shame and failure associated with failing the eleven plus. Unlike the families of some of our other participants, Dewi's family would not have been in a position to compensate for him having failed the eleven plus by sending him to a private school or employing the various other strategies to mitigate the effects of educational setbacks that were sometimes used by parents at that time.

The acquisition of educational credentials, such as success in public examinations, can be seen as a kind of 'conversion' of capital. The diligent accumulation of labour involving building up social capital and cultural capital can, if one is successful, yield symbolic capital through the educational assessments that confer legitimacy.

> When one knows that symbolic capital is credit, but in the broadest sense, a kind of advantage, a credence, that only the group's belief can grant to those who give it the best symbolic and material guarantees, it can be seen that the exhibition of symbolic capital (which is always expensive in material terms) makes capital to go to capital. (Bourdieu, 1993: 120)

Whilst some participants and their parents had a rather fuzzy concept of where the symbolic capital would lead, there was a sense that it could facilitate further opportunities for educational and occupational advancement, thus giving the chance, such as mentioned by Harri and Dewi, for one's sons not to have to work in a quarry. The acquisition of a little capital can enable a larger haul of capital later.

Some interviewees had a sense that previous generations had been similarly encouraged towards educational aspirations, especially by women in the family: (Gwen) 'it was very strong in my grandmother, she'd felt that my mother and her brother, my uncle, should do very well . . . to get on, to work hard and to make a better life for yourself really. They [the women] were quite strong.' One of our oldest participants, Euros, who was born in 1926 and grew up in west Wales, came from a family that were unusually academic – his mother had been one of the first women in Wales to go to university. He described his mother as being ambitious for all eight of her children, but because she was married to a minister and had such a large family, they had very little money. Her academic background was believed by Euros to have influenced her aspirations for her children. All of them but one went to university, but when Euros's brother stated his ambition to become a minister:'my mother said "no I'm not having two in the family, it's a difficult vocation" . . . we went into teaching for the simple reason that you got grants then, that was the main reason I suppose'. Although we heard many accounts of women missing out on opportunities due to poverty, men's ambitions were often thwarted for the same reason, particularly during the first half of the twentieth century: (Dafydd) 'my father was very good in school and wanted to be a banker . . . but my father was one of seven or eight children and his father died when he was fifteen . . . so he had to leave school and work on the farm to raise the family'. Significantly for our interest in women's lives during the period in question, this culture of aspiration was remembered as including girls as well as boys:

> (Elsi) whatever we'd chosen they would have supported us you know, there was never any thought of 'oh you're a girl it's a waste of time, go in for nursing or domestic science', nothing ever like that . . . doing well, yes that was very important . . . she [mother] was very aware of doing well . . . I think girls were expected, where we lived, girls were expected to, if they had the brains, to do it . . . they never thought we'd ever be farmers [like themselves] . . .

Although Elsi explicitly linked aspiration for girls to those girls with 'brains', there were indications from other participants that mothers still had ambitions for daughters who were less academically able. Geraint described his sister as having 'academic difficulties' and remembered that his mother 'had aspirations for my sister, she kept looking for ways of improving her lot'. This included sending Geraint's sister to a local fee-paying school when she failed her eleven-plus exam, although his parents felt that they had 'sold out' on one of their firmly held principles by using the private education sector. Geraint's sister eventually went nursing – 'they wanted a career for her, yes'.

Another interviewee whose family ran a small business but who did not have the same position in the local community as Geraint's parents, also remembered her parents having ambitions for a sibling who found academic work difficult: (Gwerfyl) 'my sister wasn't as bright as us . . . so she was encouraged to get an apprenticeship so she went as a hairdresser . . . they wanted her to have some training or some career'. One interviewee came from a family which she felt did not aspire, and now, nearing retirement after a lifetime of poorly paid cleaning jobs, is quite critical of this: (Eirlys) 'this was a failing in my family really, we were never pushed . . . they weren't ambitious for us which they should have been really'. She remembered how, at sixteen, she began working as a nursing cadet in the local hospital, but left after realising that her friends working in other jobs were earning much more than her:

> so I left. And to this day I regret it, to this day. I should have stuck it out but my mother never said 'you can't leave, you've got to do it' . . . I always used to say to my mother 'why didn't you make me?'

Eirlys was also aware of how the culture of aspiration, or *buchedd* A, if you will, played a part in animating social life and transmitting cultural capital. She talked a good deal about the role a friend's mother played in working to create culture and help convey it to the local children.

> My friend's mother . . . was with the amateur dramatic society in D—— where they lived. She even produced a play herself for all the children in [the village] when I was ten . . . she wrote a play . . . everybody got involved . . . she should have been a teacher but she never had a chance . . .'

Looking back, Eirlys believes that, 'I think being friends with her, it helped me as well'. This particular family may have been unusual, in that they had lived for a short time in England before returning to the village where Eirlys lived. Later, this friend went on to have a career that Eirlys admired but envied. She did outstandingly well at university, and Eirlys remembers going to watch this friend in a leading role in a play performed entirely in French and feeling honoured to have been invited, although unable to understand any of it. Eirlys's friend eventually became the headmistress of a highly academic girls' school in England and, whilst giving the account of her friend's achievements, Eirlys constantly attributed her success to her friend's mother's cultural and educational influence.

This account is emblematic of a notable tendency in our data. The sense of ambition, aspiration, the value attributed to education and culture and the pressure to 'do well' often came from other female members of the immediate and extended family. Of course, women schoolteachers and Sunday-school teachers were frequently mentioned as being inspirational. We will explore this later, but for the purposes of this chapter we are particularly interested in the influence of women in the family. One interviewee, Eunice, whose mother had been widowed when Eunice was five, remembered the influence of a number of female relatives:

> when we were studying she'd [mother] make a fire in the front room so we'd have peace and quiet and everything, she was very supportive, very very keen . . . I'd lost my father, my father had a sister . . . so she was very influential in the family as well, a role model . . . and my mother only had two sisters as well, so its very woman, not many men.

Yet, unusually for our study, she noted that:

> my aunt was . . . quite good at school and they weren't encouraged, there wasn't many who went on at that time. It wasn't expected for girls to do well . . . they had also lost their mother and she was the only girl with three boys, so she had to leave school to look after the boys. It was the girl who had to leave and . . . not go to college . . . the boys from the family went to college.

This kind of situation is envisaged also by Bourdieu and Boltanski (1978: 208), where they talk of the members of a group pooling their respective capital so that the benefits can be greater. This may, in the case of the participants described above, result in selected family members going to university, but also in benefits filtering back to those – parents or sisters – who stayed at home.

This pooling of capital sometimes involved household members who were not necessarily blood relatives. A few participants remembered other women in their households who were held in great affection. However, where specifically academic encouragement was mentioned, this was invariably in relation to mothers. The other female household members – often informal nannies or household helps – were never described as being influential in the formation of the interviewees' career ambitions:

> (Dafydd) we used to have a kind of nanny, she was a widow from N——, she was called Mrs P—— and we used to call her Pa and she used to help my mother because there was a lot of washing and that, she used to help with the looking after the children, so she was with us for years, so she stayed with us sometimes if the weather wasn't too good ... we used to love Pa, she was very kind to us ... she was like one of the family really, but I wouldn't say she influenced us – very partially compared to parents really.

Dafydd's account of Pa not influencing them was in the context of their social and educational aspirations. It was clear, from his memories of a harsh, Spartan upbringing on a remote hill farm, that Pa played a key role in the emotional climate of the home, but the sense of educational ambition was matrifocal. This particular reminiscence illustrates how households could be flexibly organized, too. Whilst husband and wife usually formed the core of a family group, it was possible for this to expand to include other relatives and family friends. People like Pa were not formal employees, but rather were people who stayed around and helped out. Families were clearly not structurally isolated from broader kinship systems.

In one case, Nona, who experienced a middle-class upbringing with far less hardship than Dafydd, described being cared for by a formally employed full-time live-in nanny throughout her childhood. Even so, in small households with limited resources, this could yield a considerable degree of intimacy. Nona remembered her nanny sharing living space with her and her sister and is sufficiently close to the nanny to pay her regular visits in sheltered accommodation some miles away, although Nona herself is now over sixty. Nona's family continued to provide for her nanny even after Nona and her sister had grown up. Yet, although Nona spoke warmly and fondly of her nanny and in many ways her nanny clearly was 'part of the family', once again

Nona was clear that, in terms of social and educational ambition, she took her cue from her parents, particularly her mother, not her nanny.

We did wonder that if perhaps girls were being encouraged by their ambitious mothers with a view to 'marrying well'. Educational credentials might increase a daughter's value in the marriage market, and this might afford a route for converting the cultural capital so acquired into economic or symbolic capital. However, our participants did not remember such an attitude prevailing:

> (Mabon) I don't think there was that attitude . . . but maybe if you were living in Bangor or a bigger town than P . . . [small Anglesey village] which was just a small village, that might be different . . . but certainly I think in the countryside I don't think that was ever the case.

A further possibility is that participating in post-compulsory education served like a social club or dating agency to meet young men with good prospects. Yet this was explicitly discounted by some participants, for example Gwen: 'I never picked that one up at all – it was just to have a career, to do the best you could.' But marrying well was certainly an added bonus:

> (Elsi) we were never encouraged to talk about boyfriends or anything like that . . . but it was in the background I think . . . they were very pleased when I met and married Geraint and my sister then married his best friend who'd also been to Oxford, so they were very pleased about that, that they'd both been to Oxford, I suppose it reflected glory in a way . . . but marriage was never talked about like that [marrying well].

Among our participants there was one person who remembered a very clear exception to these attitudes. He was a man from a quarrying village in Gwynedd who could recall many women who were ambitious for themselves and their children of both genders, but said his own ex-wife had quite a different attitude towards their daughter as late as the 1960s: (Harri) '[she thought university was] 'a waste of time if you're going to get married . . . marrying a middle class man that was her ambition . . . [she was]

very much into gender roles'. He 'quarrelled extensively' with his wife about their daughter – he wanted their daughter to have a career. His wife wanted their daughter to go into bank until marriage, because 'it was middle class'. He observed that 'the ones that went to university and college didn't assume these roles in quite the same way'.

Lowri, now in her eighties, whose father was a Calvinist Methodist minister in Denbighshire, described her mother's life as being completely within the domestic sphere, as the carer of the family and a support to her husband in his role as a minister. Lowri still regards this as the only appropriate position for a woman to occupy if she has children. Yet she sees no conflict between women occupying the domestic sphere and exerting influence. She maintained that women did not need a 'public role' to be 'counted'. She was clear about the value of women supporting husbands in positions which involved trust:

> I do believe this very very strongly, in a job like that . . . you're a very lonely person . . . however fond you are of people, there's a certain decorum and etiquette in a job – you don't get too close because people want to feel that you're being distant about their affairs and then you've got to have a partner otherwise you burst almost. You've got to have a sounding-board and it's got to be someone completely trustworthy and I think the women carried these subtle burdens all the time . . .

The ideas expressed here correspond closely to the historical trends identified by commentators on the family. Women's roles from the nineteenth century involved nurturing the husband and acting as an 'angel of consolation' (Lasch, 1975: 5). Indeed, the very idea of the family as being a 'haven in a heartless world' presupposes a degree of warmth and emotional connection, compared with a world outside which is rational, commercial and not infrequently brutal.

The inculcation of the love of learning within the family represents a strategy for the accumulation of cultural capital and also a means of gaining improved life chances for children, which may involve the whole family in inculcating ambition and providing social and material spaces into which the children's academic careers can unfold. We heard again and again how, within rural Welsh communities, boys were encouraged to become teachers and ministers and girls were encouraged to go into teaching or nursing or to work in a bank. A number of participants stressed that this reflected the paucity of choice of local employment at the time, especially for women – usually their only other alternative, in the middle of the twentieth century, was to work as a shop assistant. Some of these kinds of employment, such as shops or banks, as Emmett (1964: 41) reminds us, also represented a source of Anglicization, especially where young people were concerned. This is a dilemma in aspiration and social advancement to which we shall return later.

Some of our participants discussed feminism and their memories of hearing about feminist activity in England or America. However, in line with many other accounts, feminism was not seen as a movement central to social development in Wales. For example, Cook and Evans (1991) describe how women's suffrage movements got off to a slow start in Wales and women's activities tended to be subsumed into nationalist (Masson, 2003) and language activism (Piette, 1997). Many interviewees considered that feminism had been largely irrelevant in Wales. Two female interviewees and one male participant all maintained that political activity in Wales in the 1960s and 1970s prioritized language campaigning – these two female participants had both been Welsh-language activists and considered this to be more important than feminist struggles.

Older women participants talked about feminism in terms of well-worn stereotypes and jokes – 'women's libbers' and 'burning bras'. They did not remember any feminist activity in Wales, but knew about it because they had seen it on television. Again and again we encountered the paradox of women who had themselves challenged gender roles in many ways maintaining that they had very little interest in feminism, or, in the case of older women, laughing at memories of their initial encounters with the second wave of feminism.

One further irony experienced whilst conducting these interviews was that the only person who ever declared an involvement in the feminist movement was in fact a man, Arwel. Arwel had attended some of the first meetings initiating the UK women's liberation movement in the early 1970s and was well versed in the debates of that time regarding gender traditionalism and the division of labour. He considered himself very much a product of 1960s radicalism and had also been active in nuclear disarmament and anti-Vietnam campaigns. One reason that Arwel gave for enjoying university so much was that it gave him the opportunity to become politically active, having previously had few outlets for this interest, as a result of growing up in a remote village in north-west Wales.

Two women interviewees, now in their eighties, both from Nonconformist households, described very clearly how they were sheltered from knowledge of the extremes of female oppression – for example, domestic violence. They both stressed that until they were young adults, they simply weren't aware that such things happened. Lowri believed that her parents actively shielded her from such knowledge whilst she was young to prevent her from becoming cynical or negative regarding human nature. As an adult, Lowri became involved with social justice issues, pacifism and penal reform, along with her parents. It would seem that despite sheltering her whilst she was growing up, her parents did not wish her to always remain naive about such problems. Meinwen articulated a slightly different experience. Although she grew up in a disadvantaged quarrying village in Snowdonia where domestic violence will have undoubtedly existed, she was unaware of it because she simply 'didn't know anyone like that'. There are indications that, even when she was in middle age, Meinwen believed that violence against women was unusual. She recalled that when she first heard about writers like Germaine Greer, her reaction was 'where are all these oppressed women?' This ability to profess ignorance of aspects of life which were deemed unsavoury was also noted by Emmett (1964: 114) and reflects the sometimes meticulously managed barriers of discretion that communities could deploy.

Interesting also was the way that some participants used literary material to make sense of their situation. Lowri and Meinwen both referred to the rural hardship experienced by women described in the novels of Kate Roberts. They both expressed the opinion that, although such hardship undoubtedly existed, Kate Roberts had somehow overblown it or dwelt upon it to the exclusion of other more positive aspects of the community. Lowri believed that Kate Roberts had developed a very negative view of people because she heard many discussions regarding the seamier side of life when she had been too young to put this in perspective. In other words, there had been a failure of the process of discretion that we mentioned above. Meinwen proffered the opinion that 'Kate was unhappy' and that this coloured her writing. Meinwen also considered that perhaps she had an insight into this, as a number of her older relatives had attended school and grown up with Kate Roberts. This highlights a further aspect of the habitus in question – the value attached to the management of impressions. As Emmett (1964: 114) understands: 'If people are to live harmoniously with each other and, indeed, with themselves, they must pretend not to know half of what they do know about each other.' It is particularly remarkable that the reminiscences and perceptions of influential women that we have mentioned so far came from people who grew up in what has often been chronicled as a very patriarchal society. We should not be entirely surprised by this, however – under patriarchal systems women are allowed influence in certain spheres, which have often been defined by men (Collis, 1999), such as the domestic sphere, and are frequently responsible for decisions relating to the upbringing of children (Di Stefano and Pinelli, 2004).

An important point of contact between what we have reported here and earlier literature comes from Beddoe's characterization (1986) of the 'Welsh mam', who was 'hardworking, pious and clean', a mother to her sons and responsible for the home; she appears in Richard Llewellyn's *How Green Was My Valley* (1939). Beddoe notes that before the rise of industry in the eighteenth and early nineteenth centuries, women worked on the land alongside men, yet later they became 'economically *dependent* upon [their] husband's and son's wages' (1986: 230). In this account, the 'mam' or mother figure, however, was depicted as holding sway in the domestic sphere only.

The ingenuity of women in manipulating the domestic arrangements and meagre resources so as to facilitate the well-being and success of their children has been noted elsewhere (Lovell, 2004). Moreover, mothers are sometimes to be found hard at work managing the risks of educational marginaliza- tion and failure in their children (McLeod, 2005). Reay (2004c) points to the gendered nature of emotional work in family life and educational aspiration. Our point here is that the influence of these women, even those whose activities were confined to the domestic sphere, was far greater than most accounts of history in Wales have allowed for. The other feature of our interviews that is inconsistent with so much of what has been chronicled regarding the lives of girls and women in Wales, is that many people did remember encouragement and aspiration for girls. Although we did encounter heartbreaking reminiscences regarding women who were completely oppressed by callous authoritarian men and girls whose families actively prevented them from gaining an education, this was not the pervading dominant picture.

Women telling stories about the hardships that other women suffered nearly always framed the narrative in terms of extreme poverty. Again and again, this was the factor that was perceived to make women really unhappy and life barely worth living.

Alwena remembered the humiliation that her mother suffered as a widow with small children, being subjected to the scrutiny of an early equivalent of a social security official. She remembered that this man would scour the house looking for signs of anything that might indicate a source of income, and that if as children they spotted him in the village they had to get to their mother first to warn her.

Eirlys, too, remembered her mother going without because of poverty, although she described her father as a gentle kind person who did give what money he earned as a quarryman to his wife – he just didn't earn enough for the family to live comfortably.

Gwerfyl, however, had vivid memories of her father-in-law, a callous man who caused his wife to suffer – not by physical violence, but by extreme miserliness. In this case, the level of hard- ship that this man's wife (and children) experienced was deemed to be completely unnecessary, as, despite having a very big family, he was a comparatively wealthy farmer when measured against his neighbours. Gwerfyl described him as being like something 'from another century' and remembered his wife not even being given sufficient money to buy good clothes for chapel. This seemed particularly poignant as the man in question was a deacon and lay preacher, and we were told that his wife was pitied for being forced to endure such poverty. His conduct was all the more notorious in the light of his willingness to invest in his farm quite substantially, in a way which other farmers in the area could not afford. Gwerfyl was horrified when she first encountered the conditions in which her future mother-in-law lived. She felt that her father-in-law's attitude was epitomized when a travelling rug salesman called and her mother-in-law wanted to buy a mat. Her father-in-law stated that he wasn't going to waste money on something 'that you put your feet on'.

Clearly, Gwerfyl's mother-in-law was vulnerable to hardship as a result of her gender, insofar as she did not have independent means and as a married woman was at the mercy of her husband's extreme miserliness. Yet Gwerfyl maintained that this man didn't reserve this sort of treatment just for his wife, or indeed women generally. It was, she said, the sort of man he was, and he had caused problems throughout the extended family. None of his many sons remained at home to work on the family farm, although he was desperate that they should – they all left because he refused to pay them any wages. These sons are now well into late middle age or retirement, and all followed professional careers – not one became a farmer or had any desire to take over the farm on their father's death.

These observations show how the transmission of culture, knowledge, motivation and material assets was by no means simple. Whereas people with few material means were successful in retaining a sense of dignity in the face of hardship, sometimes, under other circumstances, clear advantages such as a family farm held no appeal for the rising generation.

In this chapter we have shown that in our participants' recollections, the desire for them to succeed was a salient feature of their childhoods in almost all cases. Moreover, women played a central role in this process. In the light of demonstrable occupational and educational inequalities in developed nations through the twentieth century and the relatively small proportion of women at university during much of that time (Martin and Goodman, 2004; Soloman,

1985), the sense of girls as well as boys being encouraged to achieve might appear unusual. Whilst conventionally gendered expectations were disclosed in a few cases, listening to these memories one might be surprised at how egalitarian these aspirations were. Of the encouraging adults that participants described, we might be led to speculate regarding the degree of influence that these women had in the wider community. Participants remembered highly influential mothers, grandmothers and aunts, but also, as we shall see later, spoke of other women who influenced them educationally – school-teachers and Sunday-school teachers especially.

The comments from our participants are consistent with Miles's observation (1999) that mothers were 'moral guides and inculcators of ambition', desiring upward mobility for their sons, but usually for daughters as well. The question remains as to how we might best conceptualize the process of inculcating the ambition and organizing the children's educational experiences that are reported to have occurred in so many participants' backgrounds.

Authors such as Diane Reay (for example, 2004c) have described this in contemporary parents as a kind of 'emotional capital'. It is emotional in her account because it involves a good deal of stress and worry, at least for those who implement it assiduously. In contemporary life, the efforts to ensure that children are placed in schools with good league-table positions, the concern about their doing homework or being adequately prepared for entrance examinations, the everyday experience of ensuring that they are up and dressed in time to make sometimes arduous journeys to distant 'good' schools – these are the tasks for which emotional capital is required. This represents a kind of investment in children. As Reay describes it:

> The gendered practices which make up involvement in schooling are exemplified in the complex contradictions of 'a capital' which is all about investment in others rather than self – the one capital that is used up in interaction with others and is for the benefit of those others. (2004c: 71)

Emotional capital as a concept tends to focus on the accumulated emotional labour of ensuring success in the education system.

On the other hand, perhaps because the practical experiences of getting through the education system were long gone for our participants, the focus of many of their accounts was instead on ambition and aspiration and its role in the family. This returns us to the question with which we began this chapter, that of how people from backgrounds that were not privileged managed to project themselves into a post-compulsory education system which was at that time highly selective and exclusive. It is here that the idea of aspirational habitus comes into its own as a way of enfolding both the ambition and practical strategies that our participants and their families displayed.

Ambition fostered by lack of opportunity in mid twentieth-century Wales was chronicled by Jones (1960), showing how education provided escape and status for young people. While Jones (1960) could be accused of being over-credulous about the idea of Welsh culture, what is significant here was the sense that education would elevate those who undertook it. Bourdieu and Boltanski (1978: 214) talk about a similar process of demoralization and speculation. Demoralization might include awareness of the hardship and occupational diseases that were associated with quarrying and the conviction that this would not be a fitting life for one's children: in other words, a loss of faith in the occupation's ability to perpetuate, reproduce or advance itself. Speculation involves long-term investment being made in the children, such that they are prepared and equipped to take their chances with another kind of career – a 'clean' job or one 'with a pencil'.

Lest it be thought that the Welsh have a monopoly on aspirational habitus, Warmington's research (2003) in England also showed that some disadvantaged people aspiring to university perceived it as a means of escaping welfare dependency and marginalization, and some Scottish research has shown that disadvantaged students see higher education as a gateway to desirable employment (Tett, 2000). The progressive demand for education is, for Bourdieu and Boltanski (1978), indicative of the desire of social groups to maintain or change their position and hence the structure of relations between classes. What is specific, however, about these reminiscences is that they describe a process which was considerably more than wishful thinking. Unlike Reay's mothers (2004c), there was often only a very hazy appreciation of how the education system worked, yet the culture of the family itself seemed to promote this interest in knowledge and thus a tendency to grasp educational advancement as the most ready-to-hand reconversion strategy.

There are distinctive parallels between Jenkins's study (1960) of a village in Cardiganshire where he discerns the different and distinct varieties of the *buchedd* of differing groups. The most obvious parallels are between the educational aspirations described here and religious Nonconformists with a pervasive respect for knowledge, from whom the disadvantaged but aspirational first-generation university students came, although, of course, *buchedd A* may also be part of the carefully constructed, mythical past, fabricated by nineteenth-century middle-class Nonconformists (Jones, 1992a).

The idea of families as 'havens in a heartless world', rather like the book of the same title by Christopher Lasch (1975), is somewhat ironic. Much as Lasch shows how, far from being havens, families are interpenetrated by cultural currents and economic forces, we have shown here how the aspirations fostered in the home served important functions for the people and communities concerned. The period that our participants described was one that saw a loss of job opportunities in the staple industries of farming and quarrying and a consequent loss of vision as to the collective future of these occupations and industries. The generation of cultural capital is intimately connected with the development and sustenance of the aspirational habitus and associated reconversion strategy through the education system. This builds upon and sustains the traditions of an imagined past and might, if one's speculation was fortunate, facilitate escape from the grinding poverty and occupational risks of manual labour in the present.

5

Education and Attainment: Women's Roles in Informal and Formal Schooling

⋈

Introduction: women and Welsh culture

In the previous chapter, we discussed the role of educational aspirations for boys and girls in our participants' reminiscences and focused on the role of women as mothers in promoting and reproducing this aspirational habitus. Our attention in the previous chapter was taken up with people's narratives about that which happened in the home, from mothers encouraging children, to their providing the wherewithal for them to study and enabling them to see learning and school achievement as something that was valuable.

In this chapter we shall explore the relationship between women and educational attainment further. As well as in the home, there were other roles that women took to sustain, elaborate and transmit the cultural capital associated with education. We will discuss women as educators and the experiences of women receiving education, including the degree of influence that they described themselves as having, both within their places of employment and over their young charges. The pivotal position of women in informal and formal education in England has been well documented. Elsewhere, we have commenced the examination of this process in Wales (Baker and Brown, 2008; 2009), but, to our knowledge, this has been far less well explored in Wales than England. There is surprisingly little scholarship regarding girls' and women's relationship to education or opportunity in Wales or Welsh-speaking communities, although Wales traditionally had many women schoolteachers and Sunday-school teachers.

Therefore, it is valuable to commence the unpacking of this enigma of women and their relationship to education and hence opportunity in Wales in the mid twentieth century. As we have noted, the period under discussion by our participants saw substantial declines in the farming industry and in quarrying (Lindsay, 1974; Richards, 1995). This was reflected in changes in the demand for labour and the supply of economic capital to *Y Fro Gymraeg*. It became difficult, as we have also noted, for those involved in these industries to envisage a future, and such a process of demoralization would yield a particular acuity to the search for alternatives. It is this context which perhaps shaped the desire for change and facilitated it being encoded in the *buchedd* or habitus. For Bourdieu,

> The habitus entertains with the social world that produced it a real ontological complicity, the source of cognition without consciousness, of an intentionality without intention, and a practical mastery of the world's regularities which allows one to anticipate the future without even needing to posit it as such. (1987a: 12)

Participants were not formally forecasting the socio-economic changes that have taken place latterly, such as the reconfiguration of European economies in terms of 'service industries', but were nevertheless aspiring to undertake a shift in the occupational topography which would be personally and collectively congenial.

The centrality of the relationship between women and education in Wales upon which we shall concentrate in this chapter is evidenced by other data, too. For example, when Bangor University was first established (as the University College of North Wales) in 1884, a third of its students were female (Williams, 1985), a high proportion for that era. Moreover, there is a tradition of Welsh women literati, such as Kate Roberts (1891–1985), who sought to depict the hardships of life for women in the quarrying neighbourhoods of north Wales in fiction such as *Traed Mewn Cyffion* (Roberts, 1936; Morgan, 1991). Even so, the dominant images of educated or cultured people in Wales have been male. It is only rarely that women such as Mererid Hopwood have achieved high honours at eisteddfodau (Equal Opportunities Commission Wales, 2005). However, it appears that a proportion of women in Wales have enjoyed a relatively high level of education and have been teaching for quite some time.

There is a sizeable body of scholarship on gender influencing education from countries other than Wales. There has been much work done regarding the influence of mothers on the educational aspirations and achievements of both boys and girls (DeGarmo et al., 1999; Schoon and Parsons, 2002). Dyhouse (2002) has documented the role of mothers in the transmission of cultural capital, and others, such as Schaller et al. (2007), underscore the value attached by migrant mothers to their children's education, especially when they have had little themselves. Miles (1999: 335) noted that if education could be likened to an infectious disease, 'women have acted as important carriers'. Previously, Jackson and Marsden (1962) wrote about maternal influence in education, highlighting the importance of mothers' support for working-class entrants to grammar schools. Kelsall et al. (1972) stressed the importance of maternal support of higher education for educational success.

Our participants' accounts suggest that the influence of women on the educational ambitions of both men and women who grew up in mid twentieth-century Welsh-speaking communities was considerable. As we have seen, participants disclosed the presence of independent, influential women in their families and communities who were a substantial driving-force and were in a sense the harbingers of the social and cultural differences that were apparent in the 1970s, as the 'second wave' of feminism yielded cultural and legislative changes. Middleton (1987) documented a similar process in women who grew up in post-war New Zealand.

Our original interest in the educational success of people from north Wales prompted our initial focus on the role of mothers in facilitating the preparedness of their offspring for education and on how mothers could be apparently such powerful vectors for this form of capital, in circumstances which on the face of it might appear far from promising. Wales furnishes examples of this process that pre-date the cultures of aspiration noted for children by Schaller et al. (2007) and might add to the insight that mothers invest so-called 'emotional capital' in their children's education (Reay, 2000).

Educational ambitions and personal sacrifices

In seeking the origins of accounts of education being valued and in attempting to unpack the role of women, an important starting-point is a theme that we alluded to in the previous chapter, that of mothers who had missed out on the education that they had desired and who therefore wanted their children to have that experience. Both men and women had felt this, such as Eryl:

> my mother had to go working to support – she was one of six and she was the eldest – I reckon she could have gone for further education given the opportunity. So that was a major factor in that my mother wanted us to go to further education if at all possible to make up for what she had to do without.

Some of the interviewees were acutely aware that they were among the first generation, or often were the first member, of their family to attend university:

> (Geraint) in some sense, going to college on behalf of the generation previously, who hadn't been able to go to college – you're almost going to college as a proxy for other people . . . they had felt a certain frustration at not being able to take advantage of university . . . I expressed it in what was a very poor poem . . . but the fact that I wrote it clearly meant something . . . the thought of for example failure at university would have been horrendous . . . you would not be letting yourself down, you'd be letting down a whole generation of people for whom you were there as this proxy.

As we have indicated previously, Geraint's family had a business and some position in the community, so could be seen as being poised to undertake the conversion process whereby capital in community life could be converted to other, more widely recognized cultural emoluments. A number of participants, as if signalling the readiness of their families to undertake this process of conversion, stressed that previous generations/other members of their family had possessed the ability to gain entry to university, but circumstances such as poverty had prevented this:

> (Ceinwen) my father always said he [his brother] was a brilliant mathematician and it was a crying shame that he'd never had that university education and the girls of the family as well, they were very, very good mathematically . . . they were all aware that they'd missed out on that university education . . . they were keenly aware they'd missed out . . . I had an uncle . . . a carpenter by trade and he never had the opportunity to go to university, in fact he sacrificed that so that his younger sister could go to university . . . my father always said . . . they all should have had a university education . . . after my grandfather led that strike and subsequently became unemployed, university education or even secondary school education was out of the question for them . . .

Here there is a sense that, as a result of financial circumstances, if one family member went to university it meant that others could not, as if educational opportunity was a distinctly finite resource. Therefore, family members who did go to university were in a sense going on behalf of the others left behind. The fact that this was a collective speculation resulted in the obligation to succeed being especially keenly felt by the individual who had been in receipt of the university place.

The sense of a powerful mixture of emotions being passed down through generations is evident, with some family members feeling enormous pressure to succeed, having achieved the privilege denied to their forebears, and other family members feeling cheated. Interviewees talked of how many members of their extended families had been denied an education and identified their mothers as being particularly important drivers behind them entering university. Many participants spoke of the same phenomenon:

(Eryl) definitely my mother was a driving force . . . We never discussed it, going to university, but there was positive pressure to do well at school.

(Gwen) my mother was a primary school teacher, so the idea of education and a strong work ethic I think was instilled into us from a very early age, from my father as well, but I'm sure with her it was because she was in teaching as well, she wanted the best for us and wanted us to do well, that's always been her theme . . . I'm the eldest so I suppose that's another factor too but she herself was trained at [the teacher training institution] here and I was asking her the other day how her mother influenced her and she said oh yes it was very strong in my grandmother, she'd felt that my mother and her brother, my uncle, should do very well.

As in the previous chapter, our female informants all remembered that their mothers were ambitious for them. Encouragement to succeed educationally was offered to both boys and girls, again widely remembered to have come particularly from mothers. In chapter 4, Arwel described taking this in with his 'mother's milk', and this was echoed by other participants: (Gwen) 'we were encouraged to do our best and to aim high, that came through my mother particularly . . . she would have been the driving force behind that'. The sense of ambition for children of both genders to acquire an education is in contrast to much prior research, but was clearly evident in the interviews that we conducted.

(Interviewer) Would your mum have been as ambitious for you if you'd been a girl?

(Mabon) I think so yes. I think the same would have applied because she wanted me to have the opportunities that she didn't . . .

(Lloyd) encouragement and aspirations [for boys and girls] were pretty much the same – some of the cleverest pupils in my year were the girls.

Ceinwen was one of the first members of her family to go to university and, interestingly, remembered gender as 'not being an issue'. Hers was a radical family, involved in industrial action and

Welsh politics – it would seem that their interest in politics and the fact that 'we were fighting for the language' subsumed gender issues. Although this family placed great importance on education, it was Ceinwen who went to university, not her brother. Her perception was that girls 'are naturally more academic'.

However, much of this may have been a facet of widespread post-war aspiration. Euros, from a highly educated family – all but one of his seven siblings went on to university – whilst talking about life in the first half of the twentieth century, commented that: 'Very few girls went on to college, I think my sister was an exception really.'

We should note that although Euros used the expression 'college' here, he was using this as a generic term that referred to 'university' as well. Indeed, the University College of North Wales was affectionately known by some locals as 'college'.

Euros believed that although his sister was clever, the overriding reason that she went to university was because of the family from which she came – the family contained many scholars, teachers and ministers. As we have mentioned, Euros's own mother had been to university, one of the first women in Wales to do so. However, Euros remembered many girls going to teacher training institutions: 'but I can't think of many who went to university, certainly at that time . . . I think many of them weren't ambitious enough . . . they were quite happy with a nice job . . . get married I suppose'.

Yet the picture of ambition and the sometimes restricted opportunities was often a little more complex than this. Cadi was born in 1932 and was brought up on a farm on the Llŷn Peninsula. Her parents were ambitious for their large family of five boys and five girls: 'they both wanted us to have an education'. Her parents were keen for the children to gain entrance to grammar school, as it was felt that this opened the door to better opportunities. However, Cadi's older sister failed the scholarship examination, so their father sent the younger children to different primary schools in the hope that they would have a better chance. Cadi describes her mother as 'a very, very clever woman' but one who had left school at the age of fourteen. After their education, one of Cadi's sisters went to work in a bank and one became a nurse.

Cadi herself wanted to stay and work on the farm, so she went to a 'farm school' to learn bookkeeping. Later, Cadi's own daughter went to university to study accountancy. Cadi said she had 'never thought of anything else [but university] for the children'. Cadi described herself as 'quite keen on education' and said, 'if they're clever enough they go'. She described how, in her experience, post-compulsory education was seen as being for both boys and girls: 'by that time it was for all'. Cadi remembers popular careers for girls included working in a bank, being a teacher or a nurse. Despite the encouragement from home and community, there was a limited range of careers available: 'it was lack of choice wasn't it?'; 'it was a shop assistant or – that was the choice'. Nevertheless, banking, teaching or nursing were seen as eminently 'respectable' careers and were sought after by young people – 'it was something with a pencil that they wanted to do', Cadi told us.

By the time he was a teacher in the 1950s, Euros remembered more ambitions and opportunities for girls: 'quite a number from B——— [village in north-west Wales] of course who had an eye on Bangor University'. Some of the women that Euros did meet at university in the 1940s were very impressive:

> I remember in college some very high-powered women ... I remember you know some very fine careers too ... I don't know whether there was any pressure on them ... when I was at college I wasn't aware of the difference between men and women ... it wasn't palpable, it didn't affect you in any way ... I'm male, I'm probably biased ... but there certainly wasn't any envy at all looking back in college.

Sometimes, despite the ambition, the opportunity to gain qualifications was somewhat truncated.

> (Alwena) My mother used to say work hard in school and get yourself a decent job. And a decent job in my mother's mind would either be working in a bank or for the government. No way could we go to college, there was no question of that. We didn't have any money did we ... because of the hardship she didn't want us to go scrubbing floors um you know.

93

So, despite the encouragement, there were sometimes economic constraints on how far this educational ambition could be taken.

As far as some people were concerned, the examples and encouragements toward educational achievement came from the community culture around them as well as from parents. The chapel is an obvious source of these aspirations, but sometimes the means of becoming aware of educational opportunities was more informal.

> (Ceinwen) I remember quite early on hearing about Ph.D.s. I have a very vivid memory of our milkman's son collecting milk money on a Friday evening and he was doing his Ph.D. . . . and my mother would keep him talking for hours. He'd have this little bag for collecting the milk money and he'd be running the money through his fingers and talking about this Ph.D. and I remember thinking then, that's what I want to do . . . I can't have been more than ten . . .'

But this encouragement of education and careers for girls did not mean that gendered expectations were absent in schools or in terms of pupils' careers. Erin remembered gender stereotyping in the school curriculum in the late 1960s: 'I hated needlework . . . you had to make your apron and cap for cookery in the needle-work class – only the girls. I still think boys should be doing some sort of cookery . . .'

Erin was one of the few interviewees who talked of hated 'girls' subjects' at school. We suspect that this may be because many of the other women interviewed were academically able, and had experienced grammar schools or the top streams of comprehensive schools. Erin attended the same school, at the same time, as another male participant who remembered much educational encouragement for female pupils. Yet he also remarked that in this school the 'A' stream 'had everything' at 'the expense of the C and D streams'. Erin was in the lower streams, 'hated' school and left as soon as possible. We were told that in this school, pupils of different ability were even taught on different sites geographically. Although the male interviewee from this school remembered girls going to university, Erin remembered that there 'wasn't much to do for girls' – shop work or typing, unless they went nursing. Success in the education system could be a way into a different cultural milieu where a novel opportunity structure was laid out, even at secondary school.

Interviewees remembered gendered career patterns for more academic girls, too: (Mabon) 'as far as girls were concerned, most [of them] really were being geared towards becoming teachers . . . girls were always thinking of becoming teachers. I don't think they had anything else in their minds'. This observation was supported by Gwen, who became a teacher herself:

> I didn't consider any other career. I was quite happy. It was what I wanted to do. I think it was always something I wanted to do . . . it was wanting to do a combination of having the music, of wanting an opportunity to do something that you could have a career at and that would bring you work and bring you a steady wage . . . it was seen as an acceptable career.

And again by Elsi: 'I chose [a career as a teacher] myself . . . my sister went to teacher training college as well'.

However, it was remembered that both boys and girls were encouraged to become teachers: (Mabon) 'I don't think any other careers were being advanced basically in the school'. We will return to the subject of careers in teaching later in this chapter. The allure of this particular career was partly because the teacher training course was one of the first kinds of post-compulsory courses to attract financial support, before this was available for degree-level courses. Moreover, the progressive professionalization of teaching over the course of the twentieth century entrained a particular relationship between qualifications and a subsequent career in teaching. It was manifestly vocational and had clear links to a job whose previous generation of occupants were often fondly remembered and admired, and who had enjoyed security and status in the community.

However, some interviewees gave accounts of mediocre schools and of how determined their mothers were to avoid their children being disadvantaged by such schools:

> (Dafydd) my mother wanted us to pass the eleven plus, so we went to N—— [village in north-west Wales] school, most of us went for about a year . . . it was very important to pass the eleven plus.

(Elsi) my mother didn't – they couldn't really [move us to another school] with no car or anything . . . so my mother actually did get exam papers, old eleven plus . . . possibly because she felt that she'd like to have gone on, but circumstances made her leave school at fourteen . . . doing well idea, passing the eleven plus because you went to the grammar school . . .

There was a sense that the sacrifices that had been made and the opportunities foregone were making themselves felt across the generations. Dyhouse (2002), whilst focusing on the middle years of the twentieth century, noted that maternal support and sacrifice was commonly undertaken to assist boys, especially among those from modest backgrounds. The capital entrained and embodied in the households of our participants, through chapel participation and Bible study, was put to work as assiduously as any contemporary UK parent might seek to place their child in a school with an advantageous position in the 'league tables'. As Bourdieu (1984) notes, the 'liberal professions', of which teaching is arguably a member, are prime sites for the reconversion of capital. The sense of sacrifice in pursuit of the accumulation of capital is borne out in comments from our participants. Some mothers had missed out themselves and wanted their children to have the opportunities that they had not had, and were ambitious for both boys and girls. This is also reflected in scholarship focusing on the situation in England.

The discourses of 'missing out', 'sacrifice' and 'poverty' appear to serve important functions, in terms of securing the sense that the family has a measure of cultural capital. The absence of formally certified educational qualifications (Bourdieu, 1986b), in this formulation, is not because of personal failings, stupidity or lack of awareness. It is, rather, because of other circumstances constituting a *force majeure*, such as poverty. In a sense, then, it is a way of securing the notion that people had abilities, knowledge and cultural capital that was manifest in family and community life, but was merely not apparent in terms of official certifying institutions. This sacrifice is a kind of capital in the form of accumulated labour. In Bourdieusian terms we can read this as embodied capital, of value added to the individual or family through labour and through deferred gratification – 'sacrifice'.

Narratives of poverty

The role of poverty in restricting or truncating educational ambitions for both boys and girls was apparent in the stories participants told about their families. These family tales often contained an implicit contrast of the hardship of days gone by with the relative affluence of the present. Those of our participants who were in their late fifties and early sixties were of the generation who went to university in the 1960s at a time of educational expansion and when maintenance grants became available. Yet some of our participants talked of their parents and grandparents, indicating how for some families the idea of girls and boys gaining an education had long been an attractive one and how the educational accomplishments of both men and women were valued.

Mabon gave a moving, detailed account of the hardship that his mother's family had undergone. His mother had been one of five children and her mother had died when she was young. Her father had lost an arm in the Battle of the Somme:

> (Mabon) he was a postman, he used to look after them with one arm, he used to dig the garden, plant the veg, so they were a family of very limited means and there were difficulties in pensions . . . very, very little income . . . about two bedrooms and they used to share beds . . . she came out of [secondary school] with about nine equivalent of O levels . . . nobody could finance her to go on.

When asked if he thought that his mother's educational chances would have been different if she had been a boy, he said 'I don't think it would have made much difference at that particular time . . . in that family it was just the lack of money more than anything else'.

Teaching

One strategy to enhance their stock and standing, as described by participants from some families, where circumstances permitted, was to enter the teaching profession. It has been suggested that there is a feminist subtext to the very history of teacher training in the UK, inasmuch as it was one of the earliest careers legitimated for women (Cohee et al., 1998; Hirsch and Hilton, 2000). Thus, early in the twentieth century, young women were positioned as playing a key role in the stewardship of educational capital.

We have already seen how teaching was actively promoted as a career for women and men. Gwen, a teacher, was aware that in her family teaching had been considered a desirable vocation by the generations before her. Gwen was told by her mother that her grandparents 'had been very, very happy' for her mother to become a teacher. They were 'delighted when she got in'.

Dyhouse (1995) identifies women as being ambitious in their roles as teachers and as influencing boys and girls. Not only did our participants remember much explicit encouragement to become teachers, but both men and women remembered charismatic female teachers influencing them:

> (Gwen) I think, you know, what will have had a great influence when you're at school is your teachers ... absolutely ... as a class we greatly admired our music teacher and that would have been a tremendous spur for us ...

> (Arwel) later ... in my sixth form ... particularly and outstandingly my English teacher who really did encourage ... the emphasis she put on real intellectual work ... she showed enormous confidence in myself ...

> (Harri) when I first went to grammar school, the French teacher was a woman, the Welsh teacher was a woman, the English teacher was a woman. Apart from French where they recruited a man later, throughout my school career I was taught in literature, in English and Welsh, by women ... it didn't alienate us at all. It didn't make us think that literature was effeminate either.

Yet two interviewees were less than complimentary about remembered specific male teachers and there was some investment made by parents to avoid them: (Elsi) 'in the village school ... the male teacher taught us then to eleven and he wasn't considered a very good teacher ... so consequently no-one ever passed the eleven plus . . . so quite a few of them then moved their children'. Cadi, remembering schools in the 1940s, referred to a lot of the teachers at the time as being 'old men' who were 'no good' – they were replacing the younger male teachers who had been called away because of the war.

Education and teaching didn't just take place in schools and colleges. Nonconformity gripped Wales until relatively recently, and the emphasis that Nonconformists placed on education and 'self-culture' has been well documented (Davies, 1994). All participants remembered this Nonconformist influence, particularly on the Sunday schools and the Sunday-school teachers, who in many people's memories were female:

> (Ceinwen) I could read and write before going to primary school. We were taught to read and write in the Sunday school. I remember the old lady with the blackboard and the chalk and we were taught the alphabet. I vividly remember the first lesson doing the letter A . . .

> (Gwen) my impression is that it [the influence] would have been women. My own days I think it was women. [The sol-fa system] . . .is a strong influence in lots of Welsh communities, you can sing great works by Mozart or Handel because they've been transcribed into the sol-fa notation . . . it's embedded in some communities still . . . so there was an influence and education going on there . . .

Gwen remembered her mother talking of her love of Sunday school in a previous generation: 'my mother was saying that about when she was a child . . . Sunday school was an important part of their life . . . the place where you could hear stories . . . she really looked forward to that, having something fresh and new to read'. Nona, whose own mother was a Sunday-school teacher, remembered that the Sunday-school teachers prepared children for their exams and other educational and cultural events such as eisteddfodau. She was touched when, many years later, one of her close friends from childhood who had followed a highly successful academic career, revealed that as a child her friend had 'always wanted to be like your mum from Sunday school'. The role of women in the Sunday schools attached to chapels was clearly very prominent in the minds of many participants, and there is much more that could be said about this experience. We will explore this further in chapter 7.

We have shown that participants remembered a substantive role accorded to women in teaching, both informally in Sunday schools and formally in schools. Once again, we see here that there were women in positions of influence, at least where children were concerned, inspiring and educating the next generation of people living in communities which were often seriously disadvantaged.

School teaching was, in a sense, a means by which value was put back into the community by a largely female, educated labour force:

> (Mabon) they would go to college and lots of them would go to Bangor . . . so they would go there and they would try and find a job locally . . . perhaps because they were very Welsh-speaking . . . I don't think many would have thought of going away to work, always with the intention of coming back to your area.

This was also supported by the benefits that would accrue to the individual teacher, assisting with the support of the family: (Mabon) '[teaching] was a job for life, it was paid very well at that time'. Euros, from a big intellectual family but with little money, summarized the career goal of his siblings and himself: 'almost inevitably teaching. . .we went into teaching for the simple reason that you got grants then, that was the main reason I suppose'. Ceinwen's mother was able to earn more as a teacher than her father could as a miner. This contributed to the family's decision that Ceinwen's mother would become the wage-earner, although it should be noted that this was a somewhat unconventional family.

Teaching provides a key to understanding how inroads into gender inequality were made at a time when these were not necessarily readily accomplished in other walks of life. The movement has been termed 'the feminization of education' (Francis, 2000; Arnot et al., 1999) and seems to have begun much earlier in our participants' communities than in the UK as a whole, inasmuch as it opened up possibilities for personal and familial advancement.

Moreover, at least judging from the accounts presented here, it was an occupation that permitted links to be retained with the local area; people who pursued this career were perceived to be likely to remain in the area to pursue their chosen career. The speculation involved in enabling a member of the family or community to attend college was underwritten by the probability that this was indeed an investment for the community, because of the likelihood that the skill acquired would be used in the community. Thus, an entry to the teaching profession represented both a reconversion and an acquisition of capital strategy.

The opportunity to attend university and/or the possibility of entering the teaching profession involves a step from embodied or objectified cultural capital to the fully institutionalized, educationally credentialled version. Here, we see the full significance of educational qualifications that 'matter' in the wider world, which are sanctioned by legal guarantee, formally independent of the person of the bearer and have symbolic value. 'One sees clearly the performative magic of the power of instituting, the power to show forth and secure belief, or, in a word, to impose recognition' (Bourdieu, 1997: 51).

Power, patriarchy and forms of exclusion in education

Mabon believed that among schools as employers, a change in attitude towards women only occurred in the 1960s and 1970s. Before that:

> (Mabon) you only had the primary schools . . . you had the headmaster who was male, all the other teachers were female . . . as far as schools were concerned, they were starting to change in the sixties and seventies and I think they did change during that period.

Similar changes were occurring in other educational institutions:

> (Euros) I spent most of my life [working] in the [teacher training college] and the women there were important people, but it was assumed even there you see that women would take certain jobs. For a long time it was assumed that the man would be the vice-principal but then that changed. Early in my days there we had a woman

vice-principal. But then certain things changed in my time but apart from a few phobias there wasn't any jealousy or envy.

The picture is therefore complex. Participants remembered encouragement for both girls and boys, and women of influence were remembered clearly, yet gendered restrictions were also spoken of, such as in chapter 3, when we reported Ceinwen remembering that one Welsh county in which her family had lived during the 1950s was 'incredibly sexist' because it would not employ married women as secondary teachers.

Euros had similar recollections. He started teaching in the early 1950s and, although he had lots of women colleagues: 'there was a rule of course, if you got married one partner had to go . . . [the rule was] just about finishing then . . . I remember one couple in B——— [village in north west Wales], she had to go but she was eminently qualified'. It is interesting that Ceinwen remembers specifically that married women were not employed as teachers, yet Euros perceived it as being a matter of neither party of a married couple being employed. These comments represent snapshots of an historically inconsistent relationship that existed between government, local authorities and women working in teaching. Teaching was a profession that women were entering in significant numbers from the late nineteenth and early twentieth centuries and prior to the First World War only about a third of local authorities operated a so-called 'marriage bar'. However, as Oram (1989) documents, between 1921 and 1923 a majority of local education authorities introduced marriage bars as a response to teacher unemployment and funding shortages. Some women teachers were sacked and others were required to resign upon marriage. Consequently, the number of married women who had succeeded in remaining in the teaching profession had dropped to about ten per cent by the 1930s, although married women were sometimes retained to provide temporary cover in so-called 'supply' work. It was only later, after the Second World War, that the 'wise married woman' (Oram, 1989: 24) was encouraged to remain in the profession in many areas. It was not until the late 1960s that married women were encouraged to enter teacher training. However, the process of implementing marriage bars was different in different local areas and clearly, even in the 1930s, was never entirely complete.

Despite the difficulties that our participants and people they knew faced, the teaching profession remained a popular choice for academically minded girls in Wales through the twentieth century. However, they did not necessarily achieve powerful positions. In counterpoint to the theme of women undertaking influential teaching roles, two male participants remembered overtly powerful male head teachers:

> (Geraint) the head teacher would really decide for you . . . in a sense he would have denied access [to a career] if he thought that someone wasn't suitable. The headmaster told you what you would do . . . 'maths is your poison'. And that was my careers advice.

> (Arwel) the headmaster . . . moved me up a year [at primary school] . . . it may well have been really quite important . . . I probably found that very challenging and I probably reacted very well to that . . . so a teacher, at a very young age, I think was quite important as well.

Despite the many memories and anecdotes pertaining to numerous inspiring women teachers, only one participant referred to quite such an explicitly powerful female teacher. This was our interviewee Eunice, speaking of her own mother's retired headmistress, who, when Eunice was a teenager, still lived in her village in Snowdonia. According to Eunice's account, this retired teacher remained as fierce towards the whole community as she had been towards her pupils decades earlier.

Why education?

In contrast to the ideas expressed by so many of our participants, namely that the Welsh were a literary, cultured people, one respondent had an alternative explanation for the whole idea of educationally aspiring Welsh people: (Ifor) 'even the so-called "culture" . . . which is alleged to be high-minded and intellectual was a rather sad way of trying to escape from the dreadful conditions'. But he did note that: 'there was a sense of aspiration to get out of manual labour and the same tendency applies throughout Wales'. Some of the other participants' observations echoed this:

> (Lloyd) they [his parents] always set a high store by education . . . as a means to a better life more than anything.

> (Dafydd) it was primarily to get a good job I think, something away from farming and hard labour jobs . . . if you had a good education it opened doors didn't it, you could go to any job.

> (Harri) [for working-class girls] university was a way out for them just as it was for boys . . . [encouragement for girls] altogether it depended on the parents . . . it was the men as much as the women . . . there was no distinction between them [boys and girls], they all went to college.

Conclusion

Our participants' view of educational encouragement and gender in Wales in the mid twentieth century, its relationship to the economic and labour-force changes of the period and how it was inflected by questions of power and influence, was a complex one. The participants gave some idea of the complexity of their perceptions when they offered their spontaneous views as to why some children were encouraged educationally and others were not.

Mabon suggested that his mother may have been particularly ambitious for him because he was an only child. Gwen wondered whether her educational ambitions had been affected by her position as the eldest child. Mabon was not at all sure that his success at school was because he was a boy: 'it's very difficult to say . . . I was being pushed but maybe I had more ability than some people . . . my cousin who was the same age, she had the ability as well and she was progressing through school at the same rate as me'. Mabon proffered some insights into the situation:

> I know of other people who had the ability to go forward but who were certainly not being encouraged by their family to do so and that

was maybe because of their family background than anything else. In rural Wales, especially Anglesey or wherever I think it's more complex. It all depends upon the parents' backgrounds and upbringing as well . . .

Mabon is alluding to a notion reminiscent of Bourdieu's habitus, especially the involvement of a 'disposition to act which individuals acquire in the earliest stages of socialisation and which they consolidate by their subsequent choices in life' (Robbins, 1993: 159). As we have argued, the habitus of a person, family or community refers to more than just explicit norms and values, because it is embedded within everyday actions, many of which are subconscious, hence the use of the term 'disposition'. Mabon talked quite extensively about this in his interview, remembering children who 'had ability' but who did not 'go on' and leave the area, because they came from families where 'they didn't do that'. They found paid work immediately after leaving school because that was 'what they'd always done', in a manner strikingly reminiscent of the account of Bourdieu and Passeron (1977) of how some students appeared to be at odds with the ethos of the higher education system.

Lest it be thought that Wales in the middle years of the twentieth century was filled with people assisting each other up the cultural capital ladder, it was clear that some people remembered distinctions being drawn between those who were legitimate recipients of assistance and those who were not. Arwel remembered a certain social prejudice shown by the teachers to many of the children in his school that would not have encouraged educational aspiration or achievement: 'there was a culture . . . which did tend to write off a large number of kids . . . they were seen as a problem . . .'. Taking this reminiscence at face value, there appears to be a mismatch between what Bourdieu would describe as the habitus of the social group to which the children belonged and what has latterly been called the 'institutional habitus' of the education system. Drawing from the work of Thomas (2002), McDonough (1996), Reay (1998) and Reay et al. (2001), institutional habitus describes 'the impact of a cultural group or social class on an individual's behaviour as it is mediated through an organisation' (Reay et al., 2001, para. 1.3). Bourdieu viewed the education system as the primary means through which class order is maintained. Possibly Arwel was referring here to some kind of disjuncture between the children's habitus and that of the school – the teachers had identified such a habitus as being problematic. But this disjuncture was not a gendered one – instead, it was seen as having more to do with the cultural discrepancies between some families and children and the education system.

The message from our participants was uncompromising – there was real encouragement for girls as well as boys to gain an education. Of course, there are other factors within families that result in educational encouragement for particular children, such as their position relative to other siblings. Yet our participants' narratives were littered with references to educational encouragement and achievement for girls and women, both in various generations of their own families and in the communities around them.

The accreditation or certification for their efforts that some women achieved, especially through school teaching, was itself informed by the prevailing political–economic system. Poverty was a constraint but sometimes it was a spur, in the sense that the 'good' wages in teaching, relatively independent of the then declining fortunes of quarries and farms, could be a valuable bulwark against starvation.

Like Scotland, Wales could be said to be an 'understated nation' (McCrone, 2005) and, within it, women may be seen as an 'understated' social group. It is this cultural context that helped to sustain those patterns of inequality, but at the same time helped lay the groundwork for social change in the latter part of the twentieth century. Experience, as Pasteur is alleged to have said, favours the mind prepared.

Walkerdine and Lucey (1989) explored at length the way in which mothers of young children nurtured 'educational' development at home and the notions of 'sensitive' mothering linked to this, and were interested in how such notions resulted in criticism of some working-class mothers. Although Walkerdine and Lucey were writing about a later generation of mothers and children than that of our participants, the parallels of mothers located within the domestic sphere being responsible for and influencing children's educational development are clear.

Whilst the claims for generality from forty life-stories are of course limited, we can point to some interesting differences between the features of participants' accounts here and the situation identified by historians of nineteenth-century Wales, such as Jones (1982). Then, at a time of buoyant employment in quarrying, the male working class itself was intellectualizing and sacerdotalizing itself. Tales abound of the break-times in the '*caban*' in the quarry being occupied with reading, music or theological or political discussion. In the mid twentieth century, in a context of declining employment in the industry, the intellectual efforts of the community were more closely focused on reconversion, in the form of pursuing more widely recognized educational qualifications and different occupations. In this context, the involvement of women as teachers and their increased entry into the labour market represents the mobilization of a 'reserve' (Bourdieu, 1984: 134) on the part of the communities concerned.

Our participants' comments thus show a number of tendencies that have important historical and theoretical implications. Some features of the culture – and the very fabric of family life itself – seem to have been actively promoting the continuation of education for young women. This occurred through both encouragement and example.

There were demonstrable occupational and educational inequalities in developed nations through the twentieth century and only a relatively small proportion of women at university during much of that time (Soloman, 1985; Martin and Goodman, 2004). There was an exception to this, of course, and that was during the years of the Second World War. Older female participants, who had been at university during this time, mentioned that the influence of male students was virtually negligible, because 'there weren't really any there'. Thus, girls being encouraged to achieve might appear unusual. Yet, in the light of the role played by education and teaching in the acquisition of institutionalized cultural capital and career opportunities of women, it is perhaps less surprising that girls' educational achievement was so encouraged.

As we suggested in chapter 4, the role of education was seen to be crucial as a way of escaping the hardships of manual work, as the remuneration declined in relation to the physical risks. Equally, through example and by means of actual practice in families, the idea of education for girls, especially where this would lead to teaching qualifications, was generally seen as desirable. From its outset in 1884, the University College of North Wales admitted many women, and the reminiscences of our participants suggest how this spirit of education being good for girls and good for the community was experienced at an everyday level.

6

Cultures of Aspiration: Women and the Genesis of Cultural Capital

०३

In this chapter we will consider a little further the notion of cultural capital and how it can illuminate the role of education and the role of women within our participants' accounts of their early lives. As we have seen through our earlier chapters concerned with the family and with women's role in education, there is a sense in which women were important vectors of cultural capital, whether as mothers or schoolteachers, or in a variety of roles more peripheral to family life, such as the movers and shakers in chapel congregations and even as amateur dramatists. Overall then, we have sought to underscore how, through their labour in such activities, women were accumulators and custodians of cultural capital. In these quotidian roles, such as teachers, Sunday-school teachers, mothers, grandmothers, aunts and family friends, they were encouraging social and educational aspiration in children. These kinds of relationships seemed to have been central in creating and passing on this 'aspirational habitus' among participants, which, importantly, was often seen as offering opportunities to girls as well as boys.

The place of cultural capital itself in encouraging cultural participation has been noted by many authors (Ganzeboom, 1982; Sullivan, 2007), who note that in many societies there is an association between cultural knowledge and cultural participation. This relationship may well be a circular one, as Sullivan observes. High levels of knowledge and skill allow people to understand

and enjoy cultural stimuli, therefore making cultural participation more likely; equally, cultural participation may also promote and deepen people's cultural knowledge, which in turn will allow greater cultural appreciation, making subsequent proficient cultural participation more likely.

Sullivan (2007) goes on to elaborate the relationship between cultural capital and academic ability:

> It is clear that parents with high levels of academic ability, broadly defined, transmit this to their children in various ways. Academic ability can be defined as any form of intellectual skill or knowledge which is rewarded in academic assessments within schools and other educational institutions. Of course, considerations other than a student's intellectual performance can affect the grades or other rewards given by the school. Academic ability is seen as distinct from these other characteristics and behaviours which may be rewarded in the school, such as 'appropriate' behaviour in class. (Sullivan, 2007: 3.3)

Bourdieu himself placed a good deal of stress on the importance of linguistic sophistication as a key to success in the realm of cultural capital: 'Obvious in the literary disciplines but more subtle in the sciences, the ability to manipulate academic language remains the principal factor in success in examinations' (Bourdieu et al., 1994: 21). Bourdieu asserts the importance of proficiency in academic language, in both the arts and sciences, and that students who have a grasp of formal language, rather than being restricted to informal language, are at considerable advantage and are more aligned with the institutional habitus to be found in the education system. Other authors have addressed similar points. For example, this account recollects Bernstein's distinction (1973) between 'restricted' and 'elaborated' codes in language. The restricted codes, he argued, were found largely in working-class communities and families. They were characterized by a low level of vocabulary and limited syntactic variety and, whilst intelligible to the middle class, the latter were apt to use the 'elaborated code' which belonged to the educated classes and which had a flexibility that enabled the expression of analytical and abstract ideas and arguments.

Bernstein has been accused of promulgating crude stereotypes of what it is to be working or middle class (Rosen, 1972). Others have pointed out that complex arguments can be formulated in non-standard, vernacular dialects (Labov, 1972), yet there is widespread agreement that proficiency in the culturally valued forms of language and educational demeanour are associated with being able to gain from the education system. 'Cultural habits and . . . dispositions inherited from the family are fundamentally important to school success' (Bourdieu and Passeron, 1977: 14).

The roles, activities and commitments described by participants as characterizing domestic life in the mid twentieth century suggest that female members of families and chapel congregations were investing considerable importance in their role as cultural custodians. We have already seen many of the ways in which women influenced and educated, both formally and informally, younger members of the community. Further examples will be encountered when we explore the role of women in Nonconformity.

The idea of incorporating gender into analyses of cultural capital is not necessarily new. Dumais (2002) introduced the idea that gender is crucial in determining the role of cultural capital in increasing educational achievement and shows how gender and social class interact to produce different benefits from cultural capital.

Bourdieu argues that 'the scholastic yield from educational action depends on the cultural capital previously invested by the family' (1986b: 244), and that 'the initial accumulation of cultural capital, the precondition for the fast, easy accumulation of every kind of useful cultural capital, starts at the outset, without delay, without wasted time, only for the offspring of families endowed with strong cultural capital' (ibid.: 246). We encountered numerous examples of women inculcating their stock of cultural capital in the rising generation in the context of family life, priming them for success in the education system. Gwen's reminiscences illustrate the pivotal role of the women in two generations of her extended family regarding the transmission of cultural capital. We shall quote this at length to give a sense of the connectedness of the narrative and the connections made by the participant herself between the different facets of the experience:

my mother was a primary-school teacher, so the idea of education . . . I think was instilled into us from a very early age, from my father as well, but I'm sure with her it was because she was in teaching as well, she wanted the best for us and wanted us to do well, that's always been her theme . . . I'm the eldest so I suppose that's another factor too but she herself was trained at [a teacher training institution] here and I was asking her the other day how her mother influenced her and she said oh yes it was very strong in my grandmother, she'd felt that my mother and her brother, my uncle, should do very well. My grandma trained as a nurse and would have grown up in the [a village in north Wales] area and I think she went to London and then came back to north Wales and then eventually got married and settled in [the same village that she grew up in] and ran a post office and then my mother grew up in that environment, so did my uncle and my uncle was given the option to take over the post office, but that was of course quite a hard life and he was given well not an ultimatum, but this is an opportunity for you, do you want that or not and I don't think he wanted that, so he went on and he did some work in finance. And then so she was telling me that with my grandmother who got him the papers and stuff and sent away for the papers to apply for the job . . . I'm thinking back to my great aunts now – they were quite strong women as well and two of them came over to [north-west Wales] here and ran a business, a cake shop – they did it themselves, I don't know the actual background. That would have been the fifties wouldn't it? They ran a business and my great uncle he also had another business in the town, a different kind of business. And the family probably, this had been instilled into them as well, to get on, to work hard and make a better life for yourself really. The women were quite strong . . . I think they [the great aunts] were quite highly regarded, my impression . . . to me you see I never thought of it as being rather strange . . . it would have been my grandfather of course who would have been head of the family as it were with the post office, but then these went off and did their own thing in Anglesey . . . they made a comfortable living at it . . . I remember someone saying they had books in the shop as well, like a library . . . a funny combination. I'm wondering where that came from. When you're in the middle you don't think to ask do you . . . one of the two was quite strong, the other was quiet by nature . . . but my uncle as far as I can remember, he didn't have any part in running it. It was my aunt who was the main one, who stood in the shop and sold all the cakes, the other one did all the cooking and baking because I remember going in there, this lovely aroma of cooking. I don't remember the books.

This particular account merits being quoted in full because it shows how a sense of there being a family tradition of doing these kinds of jobs comes to animate a person's sense of who they are and where they come from. For several generations, the extended family is being depicted as being enterprising, keen on education and taking on roles as skilled professionals or entrepreneurs. There is also here another common theme in our participants' accounts, that of coming back to the area. This echoes Emmett's contention (1964) that in the neighbourhood she studied, people forewent opportunities to further their careers in England in order to stay in the area or return to it: 'The fact that intelligent, well-informed people have stayed in the community in the past means that the community is worth staying in now' (Emmett, 1964: 12). In the 1950s, whilst these neighbourhoods might have seemed remote to someone accustomed to metropolitan life, there was nevertheless a sense of attachment to place which encouraged people to return after periods of work or study elsewhere.

This account from Gwen, with its emphasis on family traditions and the atmosphere encouraged in the family, illustrates also how the acquisition of cultural capital outside the formal education system was intimately bound up with success within the education system. We can see this particularly in the form of the routes most clearly available for women into nursing and teaching. Several other interviewees referred to this connection, too, and these career options are mentioned by Emmett (1964). One participant remembered his parents playing a leading part in what he called 'village life', in particular the eisteddfodau and the chapel. He felt that his parents' involvement in such activities led to a collectively shared expectation on the part of others in his rural community that he would go to university. Another respondent revealed a connection between participation in the eisteddfodau and expected academic achievement: (Mabon) 'within the community yes I think they expected me to go somewhere because I always used to take part in eisteddfodau'. Mabon's descriptions of his mother suggest that she had acquired considerable locally recognised cultural capital by the time that she was raising him, despite the severe hardship that she had experienced herself when growing up. He remembers her winning prizes at eisteddfodau too, being 'first in Wales' in a Bible-knowledge quiz and writing plays for the church that were always performed. She was clearly able to transmit this cultural capital to her son, enabling him to succeed academically: (Mabon) 'she would always play an active part in the work which I did and really she was very good with Welsh and English poetry . . . and enjoyed looking at what I was doing'.

From accounts like these we can see, even in the absence of formal educational verification of a person's cultural worth, there were means of acquiring markers of prestige through the indigenous structures, processes and institutions that had been set up informally, via competitions, eisteddfodau and activities within church or chapel, which could confer the 'certification' or legitimation for talents which was lacking from other sources.

Thus, the cultural capital present here is perhaps more fully of the objectified kind, in that it is marked with artefacts and objects, the competitions won, the poetry, the plays enacted and so on. What is also clear is that this stage or moment in the cultural process subsumes the earlier phase of embodied capital. That is, the labour involved at mastering poetry, drama or Bible study accumulates a kind of 'embodied' capital, in Bourdieu's sense, which can be exchanged through the process of cultural participation for more widely recognized forms of prestige.

As we have seen, women played a substantial role in the workforce as schoolteachers and sometimes even teacher trainers. Many of our participants also remembered women teaching outside these institutions, frequently in a private capacity, and the pupils were also often remembered as being female:

(Harri) there was a piano school in Ll—— (a quarrying village in north-west Wales), a private one – none of the pupils there were boys, they were all girls, every last single one of them. Not one of my male friends could play the piano, virtually all of my female contemporaries could.

Another interviewee told us of a ballet school – with an exotic-sounding French name – that she and her friends attended as children, in a small town near this quarrying village. This seemed to be an institution exclusively for girls, run by one woman.

Such cultural pursuits might be expected in affluent middle-class communities, but it is significant that these reminiscences pertain to severely economically disadvantaged areas, with many of those in employment eking out a subsistence lifestyle with meagre wages from quarry or farm work. From the information that we have been given, the pupils of such establishments were by no means always from the more privileged families.

When we consider this, along with the activities of the many women in Sunday schools and their involvement in teaching music, singing and preparation for eisteddfodau, we begin to realize the scale of women's contribution to the generation and transmission of cultural capital in rural Wales. One participant summed up the influence of women in chapel thus: (Harri) 'theirs was a more general cultural influence I think rather than a religious one'. In cases like Gwen's (above), we can see how people's biographies demonstrate that their sense of culture, family history and identity were bound up with their success at university or social mobility.

The effects of 'Welsh culture' and the sense of history represent a relatively unexplored aspect of habitus, but the importance of a sense of history or cultural identity was noted by Bourdieu: 'the subject is not the instantaneous ego of a sort of singular cogito, but the individual trace of an entire collective history' (1990a: 91). For many, there is a distinctive sense of identity, history and associated habitus (McCall, 2001), which structured family life and persisted through geographic movement and intermarriage.

A pervasive image of Wales is that of a nation that valued education, producing 'preachers and teachers', despite debate as to whether this notion is a romantic invention (Morgan, 1986b). The 'stereotypical' image of the Welsh orientation to education is reflected in the founding of the University College of North Wales, where in the late nineteenth century scholarships were funded by subscriptions raised from the local quarrymen and working-class farmers to educate their own children (Williams, 1985).

Despite the intimations of an aspirational habitus in participants' accounts, it was widely remembered that only a small proportion of people would attend university. In a sense, the targets of these aspiring people 'thus glitter in the eye of history as signs of the labourer's conception of the nature of society' (Reddy, 1977: 84). Therefore, the images of history and culture are particularly important in constructing participants' orientations to education.

Cutting across the themes in this chapter is a concern with 'Welsh culture'. Some participants explicitly subscribed to its existence and its influence, but in others it was present in an occluded form, participants mentioning aspects of life and influences that would be unusual elsewhere in urbanized areas of the UK. It can be seen from the participants' comments that images of culture and images used in the cultural construction of Welsh history may make additions to constructions of habitus.

The influence of religious Nonconformity

The cultural and educational role of chapel communities in Welsh life and in the generation and sustenance of cultural capital can usefully be illuminated by means of Bourdieu's extensions (1986b) of the notion of capital to explain cultural and symbolic affairs. Cultural capital is concerned with knowledge, skill, education and related advantages that can lead to higher status in society, closely approximating the accretions of knowledge, aspirations and spirituality which have been claimed to be central to Wales's identity (Philips and Harper-Jones, 2002). The influence of the chapel was mentioned by nearly all participants. Participants recollected the 'educational' and 'self-improvement' ethos of the chapel providing an encouraging culture:

> (Eryl) the chapel was a major influence on my life and on certain members of the [school] class. The chapel encouraged reading, literary culture . . . it especially helped me when I had to perform and go in

front of an audience, so that was part of the Welsh culture . . . before you got to college you had done it before and chapel was really important in that.

Other participants revealed a very direct assistance from the chapel in their memories of receiving a formal education in Sunday school. Another participant felt less directly affected, but certainly sensed its presence in society:

> (Arwel) a great deal has been made and probably rightly, of the influence of Nonconformity and RE and Sunday schools . . . in creating a literate, disputatious culture in Wales which lent itself in a sense to university education . . . I did go through some of that . . . felt that education was a good thing . . . it wasn't a crucial influence . . . but one was certainly aware that Wales did have a lot of teachers and preachers who had had an education whereas the other people in my community had not . . .

The early religious experiences of the participants played an important part in acquiring a love of learning and an intention to go to university; a 'cognitive habitus' in Nash's sense (2005) of the term. The chapel exposed them to people in roles for which an education was needed, such as ministers and teachers, who played a significant role in these communities. Such experiences are implicated in the kind of habitus the participants describe themselves acquiring as children.

A number of interviewees attributed their aspirations to attend university to a lack of other opportunities, as a result of local socio-economic problems:

> (Eryl) it was automatically assumed that I was going to university because . . . in B—— [a village mainly dependent on a dying slate industry], at that time, what else do you do?

> (Geraint) there was that feeling that you should get an education to avoid the pit, avoid the quarry.

> (Arwel) I knew . . . plenty of slate quarry workers . . . I didn't want to do physical labour . . . I knew what it was . . . I'd seen people physically

digging ditches, I'd seen people coming home from work covered in slate dust and . . . I very consciously didn't want to do that . . . as a kid I'd suffered from ill-health . . . the only way I was going to be able to do anything was if I used my brains . . .

Ambition fostered by lack of opportunity in mid twentieth-century Wales was chronicled by Jones (1960), education providing escape and status for young people. Whilst Jones (ibid.) could be accused of being overly credulous about the idea of Welsh culture, what is significant here was the sense that education would elevate those who undertake it.

The previously quoted interviewee clearly described his own strategies for acquiring cultural capital and how this may have led to his success at gaining access to university:

(Arwel) [an interest in politics is] . . . a very educative process . . . means you become a voracious reader of newspapers . . . a massive capital plus, a cultural plus . . . I listened a lot to Radio 4 . . . plays by Arnold Wesker . . . so it was politics and also what in a sense flowed from that in terms of the mass media . . . finally there was reading . . . often ill at school . . . perhaps I learnt more sitting at home with a bad chest looking out at the rain and reading . . . and then talking to local people . . . who came into the house . . . I often feel that I learnt more in that informal way than I did formally at school and that does lead you to the kind of cultural capital argument . . . I think I would venture a speculation that actually what got me to university was the cultural capital which I had acquired largely by default . . .

In describing life as an adolescent in rural Wales during the early 1960s, this participant follows Jones (1960: 102), who observed, rather quaintly, that 'during this period of adolescence children are even more open to the influence of newspapers, the cinema and the wireless'. New capital, then, can be acquired from wider culture as a result of the initial work done in the early years of family life.

Other participants alluded to the acquisition of cultural capital and cognitive habitus through politics and educational involvement:

(Ceinwen) that political awareness was there and culture was tied in with that, so there was always discussions of politics, of philosophy ... books were everywhere in our house ... it was taken for granted that education was one of the central parts of life ... in general terms education was very highly regarded in the community ... literature was very important for my parents ...

Ceinwen's father had attended Workers' Educational Association classes, instead of the university education that he had been unable to afford, and through this became active in politics, which led him to philosophical and literary interests. Ceinwen's parents were certainly keen autodidacts – she remembers their enthusiasm when a Welsh-language bookshop opened in Aberystwyth and the frequent trips subsequently made to the shop when her parents purchased volumes on a vast array of subjects. This kind of cultural capital was relatively autonomous from economic capital: (Eifion) 'although I came from what would be economically a very deprived background, I think culturally and academically it was a very privileged background'. Although these people were not from affluent households, they were acquiring 'embodied cultural capital', investing in self-improvement through learning, preparing them for the acquisition of more institutionalized forms of cultural capital and prestige. Cultural capital, following Bourdieu (1986b), has an incremental quality – the earlier, informal varieties and the establishment of an appropriate 'cognitive habitus' (Nash, 2005) later lead to the acquisition of concrete forms.

Two other influences were mentioned by many participants, in the form of influential schoolteachers and peer support. Schoolteachers were mentioned as a factor enabling access to higher education by nearly all the interviewees. Often particular teachers were perceived as helpful, or as we have seen, explicitly powerful. One participant remembered some overt discrimination against certain pupils in schools, but based on the pupils' perceived ability, not social class.

Some participants remembered being encouraged by schools and teachers to 'do well' at school, even though they thought that their teachers may not have expected them to eventually go to university, because 'we were not that sort of family'. It was widely remembered that there was educational encouragement for pupils, but it seemed to be related more to whether the pupil was perceived to be 'able', than to their socio-economic background. The social environment within which education takes place is important in the inculcation of an aspirational habitus. A significant element in the social realm of the school involves the individual's peer group, and many participants mentioned this.

Some interviewees remembered a subculture developing amongst their peers that motivated them academically:

> (Arwel) one [influence] was my fellow students as it were at school . . . major influence within that was my closest friend . . . we certainly sparked each other off . . . there was a number of people who went to university who, at that time, sort of encouraged each other . . .

> (Gwen) I'm sure there was a degree of competition . . . you were spurred on because everybody else was going to do this, that and the other.

The quotes here suggest that an academically orientated peer culture can propel people towards higher education. In Bourdieusian terms, these peer-group experiences help to provide what Reay (2004b: 79) calls 'a feel for the game' which is usually characteristic of a middle-class educational habitus. These reminiscences stress the acceptance of the educational game found in the peer groups of the participants. Our participants were almost always involved in a social life that enhanced their readiness to acquire cultural capital.

Many of the participants unequivocally attributed their success at university to aspects of their 'Welsh culture'. This included the influence of religious Nonconformity, but some people clearly identified a Welsh culture encouraging education and self-improvement. The eisteddfod was frequently mentioned. One described how success in the eisteddfod for her uncle had compensated for him not going to university: (Ceinwen) 'he sat the eisteddfod exams to become a member of the *Gorsedd* . . . for a man who had sacrificed a university education for somebody else, that was very, very important'. Another interviewee, growing up in a town decimated by a shrinking slate industry, recollected that: (Eryl) 'the quarrymen were keen to get on . . . that was part of the Welsh culture . . . maybe the Welsh did want to learn and go further'. Such beliefs are consistent with what Jones (1982: 57) described as 'a certain mythologising about the cultural attainments of the quarrymen'. This sense that the quarry workers in rural villages had intellectual tastes is present in Smiles's accounts of labourers reading the works of nineteenth-century intellectuals. The theme of these accounts is that the interests of the quarrymen were unexpectedly highbrow.

Other participants explicitly identified the value that the Welsh (and 'Welsh culture') put on education and the results of this: (Geraint) 'people who didn't go to university but were manifestly qualified to do so were not in Welsh culture'. This, in context, was not directed at those who had not been able to attend as a result of poverty or caring responsibilities; rather, Geraint had in mind people who were merely disinclined to go to university. (Eryl) 'so the culture you grew up with . . . it was automatically assumed you were going . . . it was the way of the world, expected'. What is important here is that the habitus of the participants is freighted with evocative images of a centuries-old literary and musical tradition, a sense of how their forefathers kept their mercurial intellects alive despite their toil in the quarry or on the farm. As Douglas (1986) reminds us, sometimes history has little to do with the past but 'everything to do with the present'.

One participant here stressed repeatedly that there were 'no barriers' to him and his disadvantaged peers going to university: 'we could get out of this trough – we did'. However, one interviewee did remember that, 'there was a great deal of it's not for people like us', echoing Bourdieu's notion (1990a: 64–5) that habitus defines the boundary between what is thinkable and unthinkable. Of course, statistics relating to university entrance during this era will confirm that for many people, it was not for the likes of them. The impression is that of a community whose members had an embedded aspirational habitus toward education per se, yet due to past economic circumstances they were denied a university education. When it became a possibility, many members of the community enthusiastically embraced the idea of university education. It is as if the adults were trying to enlist the children into the kind of aspirational habitus that prevailed in educational settings.

There were more distant members of the social group forming an historical backdrop to the participants' stories. Interviewees remembered hearing about individuals in the community who had gone to university previously – the boy from the same terrace who had achieved a First some years ago, an actor from the same grammar school who had gone to Oxford, the milkman's son who was doing a Ph.D. – indicating that such things were possible. Such academic successes seemed to have been highly regarded in these rural communities and encouraged the respondents.

In many of the narratives there was a sense of politicization – despite past oppression, participants had every right to a university education. This seems to have motivated and enabled many to cope with the social difference encountered at university.

One participant observed that there was not a class system in Wales when he was growing up, but a 'caste system'. He classed himself as a 'very poor Brahmin' – his family were 'subsistence' farmers, but he considered them 'very rich' culturally and educationally. As we have seen, some scholars have disputed this notion of Wales being a 'classless' society. Jones (1982: 55) described the promulgation of a classless idea as the 'main ideological achievement' of the late nineteenth-century middle-class Nonconformist elite. In addition, as our participants noted, the continuing involvement of educated, qualified people in the community, as teachers, ministers or other professionals, enabled the sense that such experiences were part of the community rather than separate from it.

The aspirational habitus narrative emphasizes how 'our family' or 'our people' always had the 'embodied cultural capital', but somehow were unable to translate this into the institutionalized form. This also reconciles hardship with the sense of having a rich cultural heritage – the latter was always there, but merely occluded by the lack of opportunity.

The image has been long-lasting and powerful. Many of our participants felt that they had a distinctively 'Welsh experience', which seemed to have contributed to their habitus, informing educational aspirations:

The habitus acquired in the family is at the basis of the structuring of school experiences; the habitus transformed by the action of the school, itself diversified, is in turn at the basis of all subsequent experiences . . . and so on, from restructuring to restructuring. (Bourdieu (1972), in Bourdieu and Wacquant, 1992: 134)

Images and ideas of Welsh culture, as well as national identity and the cultural construction of Welsh history, infuse the aspirational habitus described. The everyday practice of ordinary people is habitus, which becomes culture, inasmuch as it is imbued with value. As we have discussed, some historians (for example, Jones, 1982; Manning, 2002; 2004) have pointed to the way that Welsh culture has involved actively reconstructing the past. The insight from Bourdieu is that by recreating and reconfirming this sense of history, people are adding value and creating the kind of culture which can compete with the more prestigious varieties flourishing in universities and which can enable the holder's transition smoothly from child to student and ultimately to academic or professional.

Many of the people that we have interviewed were of a generation where people from disadvantaged backgrounds were for the first time able to afford to enter university. At this time, universities were dominated by privileged social groups, so it is interesting to explore how these disadvantaged participants from rural Wales experienced university and the associated social mobility. The 'Welsh factor' is relevant because so much of the imagined history and imagery associated with Wales is linked with learning and erudition. The construction of history and imagery that has contributed to national identity in Wales also found its way into participants' sense of identity, and, in line with Bourdieu's formulation, this contributed to their stock of cultural capital. This appeared to affect the ease with which they were able to assimilate capital in the form of educational experiences beyond their home community.

As we have seen, participants identified the aspects of Welsh culture that in their backgrounds had been involved in the acquisition of cultural capital, which then facilitated their acquisition of more institutionalized forms through university education

(Bourdieu, 1986b). Two participants maintained that although the acquisition of cultural capital had played a part in their attending university, they did not believe it had originated in Welsh culture – indeed, they problematized the very notion of Welsh culture.

Poverty and oppression were remembered, but participants felt strongly their right to be at university. Their habitus enabled them to feel comfortable in the university environment, despite being aware that their social backgrounds were very different from those of their peers at university. Participants' habituses seemed to have a transformative aspect, reminiscent of Richards's sense (2005) of 'advancement' and 'investing' in the self associated with education. This facilitated their move into the middle classes after university as they adopted new professions and lifestyles.

Our participants' experiences were made possible by the rural isolation of the communities – social activities and opportunities for collective experiences of identity were organized through chapel, Sunday school, family and education. This lent a particular tenor to the experiences. It was relatively easy for the aspirational aspects of culture to prevail over hedonistic ones, as the value of piety, education and culture was adumbrated by the adults in the community. The relative isolation of the communities in question and the corresponding significance of their social occasions afforded the consolidation of this value system, rather than its dilution.

These communities en masse were unable to readily convert their capital into economic capital, to perform what Bourdieu called the process of 'transubstantiation' (1986b: 242). Although escape from family and community traditions of manual labour and an improved economic position were sometimes achieved, the currency in which participants dealt was still primarily symbolic and educational. Nonconformists often acquired sufficient capital to enter the bourgeois salariat, but never as a group, or rarely individually, achieved the economic capital needed to join the most economically dominant group in Wales. People who grew up in the same villages and sat in the same schoolrooms as Nonconformists, but who were not in possession of the same sort of symbolic and cultural capital, were acknowledged by participants as not always capable of achieving even this mobility.

Consistent with the arguments of Bourdieu and Boltanski (1978), the previous class-structure may not have been preserved in every detail, but there are residual hierarchies which mirror the pattering of wealth, status and prestige seen in earlier epochs. Perhaps the last half-century has seen a deepening and diversification of the process of reconversion, which has nevertheless preserved the ordinal ranking of different classes. This would fit the argument of Day and Fitton (1975) that the chapel rarely overturned the economic or class order but tended instead to reproduce it. We speculate that the distribution of types of capital between different groups was, in line with Bourdieu and Boltanski (1978), modified, without any substantial change in the dominant or dominated position vis-à-vis other groups.

In this region there was an emphasis, through the activities of the chapel and encouragements to marry within the community, on keeping cultural capital alive within that community. Where conversion to symbolic capital did occur, such as in the form of qualifications gained, the person did not necessarily leave entirely, as with Ceinwen's memory of the milkman's son, who became an academic in a university within the region, or those who returned to their communities as teachers. This yielded similar interest in capital acquisition and conversion in the rising generation.

On the other hand, perhaps our data confirms Bourdieu and Boltanski's notion (1978) that under the guise of the 'disappearance' of populations lies the hidden work of reconversion. The life trajectories of our participants show that many Nonconformists effected a reconversion, raising their position whilst abandoning their condition. The rural, chapel-going communities reminisced about by participants may not exist in the same form in the present, but through a process of reconversion, the families and groups who were most successfully engaged in their cultural activities were best enabled to facilitate their rising generation to enter the higher education system and hence the professions.

Among the congregations in which the participants grew up, a localized symbolic capital was created and owned by those able to recognise it. Their knowledge of prior struggles between the polarized groups, between the English and the Welsh, was crucial to the creation of this symbolic capital. In this context, piety and biblical study is meaningful because it differentiates one group from another. The creation of this kind of symbolic capital helps normalize the economic disadvantage suffered, and self-legitimates theological radicalism, allowing the bearers of the capital to consider themselves distinctive and more gifted compared to other, more dominant, groups in the hierarchy, such as the English. The power of symbolic capital is evident, as many of our interviewees subscribed explicitly to the 'myths' of Nonconformity. The valorization of Welsh culture occurred in the context of several centuries of relative cultural and economic disadvantage, and to those who subscribed to them, Nonconformity and Welsh culture gave a sense that their lives were part of a venerable tradition upheld by their learning. Imbued with value, the everyday practice of ordinary people becomes culture, in Bourdieu's sense. Moreover, the ability of members of these groups to exchange the cultural capital laboured for in the chapel, the eisteddfod and the village schoolroom for more broadly recognized symbolic capital, such as degrees, professional qualifications and middle-class job opportunities, helps to underscore and vindicate their efforts.

In Bourdieu's original formulation, ideas about different types of capital were developed in order to explain how social-stratification systems were preserved and the dominant class-reproduction strategy was legitimized (Adam and Rončević, 2003: 159). We have shown how some of our participants' recollections suggest that by assiduous cultivation of cultural capital, by intergenerational nurturance of aspirations and through social networks (although in many ways limited) that confronted children with experiences of cultural accomplishment, the seeds were sown for a shift in occupational structure and a mid twentieth-century perturbation in gender roles. These domestic, social and occupational changes themselves prefigured the larger and more culturally conspicuous social changes of the 1970s. In an important sense, then, the women that our participants remembered made this wave of feminism possible. Whilst these women might not have described themselves as feminist, many of them could be described as harbingers of the movement that led to gender equality being placed on the national policy agenda.

Throughout this discussion of the 'aspirational habitus', it is clear that the influence of women pervades all aspects. Their influence in the home and the ambitions that they had for their children, their work as teachers in schools and Sunday schools and other contexts which involved transmitting cultural capital and inspiring young people, along with them assuring the next generation that a good education was their birthright, laid the foundations for numerous people who grew up with severe disadvantage to later follow careers as academics and professionals.

7

Religion and Spiritual Life

ॐ

Introduction

As we have seen, religion and spiritual life have been described by many authors as central to Welsh culture, society and politics. Despite the contention that the popular image of Welsh culture was constructed in the nineteenth century, the role of religious Nonconformity, particularly variants of Methodism, has been substantial, as we have discussed. So far, the conventional story has it that in religion and spiritual life, men were ministers, elders and deacons in chapel communities. Whilst this may be largely true, here we will further explore, from the evidence provided by our participants, the role of women in these communities and congregations. As we mentioned earlier, there were some accounts of women becoming deacons, but such exceptions reflect a much larger tradition of service by women contributing to chapel life. With this work, perhaps, came a degree of influence or 'subtle governance' which infused the organizational life of the chapel and the cultural and spiritual work it undertook.

Nonconformity was a term originally applied to religious dissenters after the 1662 Act of Uniformity mandated the use of the Book of Common Prayer as the basis for Church of England liturgies. Through the nineteenth and first half of the twentieth centuries, the centrality of chapel life to many Welsh communities amounted to what Chambers and Thompson (2005) call 'Nonconformist hegemony' in Wales. Bruce (1995: 521) mentions how the Nonconformist churches in nineteenth-century Wales acted as 'the repository of Welsh cultural identity and anti-English political sentiments' and how, in Wales, religious affiliation was 'politically charged'.

The aforementioned hegemony underwent a decline in the post-Second World War era. Yet the residual influence of this form of symbolic life has generated a great deal of interest in contemporary accounts of Welsh identity (Jones and Fowler, 2007).

As we examined the transcripts of interviews with our informants, it is clear that, taken at face value, they disclose not only the role of religious practice in transmitting cultural capital, as we have seen in the previous chapter, but the importance of women in formulating and sustaining this culture. Moreover, whilst Nonconformity has often been seen as a relatively homogeneous movement, what was striking is the way in which participants noted a whole range of finely grained distinctions between themselves and their chapel and others. Whilst broadly defined as 'Nonconformity' by many authors, the perceived distinctions between, say, Congregationalism and Calvinistic Methodism, were important in sustaining a sense of social identity. Once again, Bourdieu helps us in understanding how a congregation's religious practice was invested with value over and above that of others, and we shall be drawing on notions of cultural capital and distinction in the exposition that follows.

All participants mentioned their involvement with religious institutions, and most participants talked about it extensively. Some mentioned the Anglican Church, but overwhelmingly our interviewees talked about 'chapel', meaning either Calvinist Methodist chapels, Congregationalist chapels or, in the case of one participant, the Baptist chapel. Participants were convinced of the importance of chapel life in the making of modern Wales: (Lowri) 'we're living on the legacy [of Nonconformity] – it'll be very interesting to see if the legacy will go on to the next generation now'. Participants nearly all remembered their involvement with religious institutions as a very positive aspect of their youth. Sunday schools were generally remembered as being interesting and fun. Again and again, it was women members of the chapel that our participants remembered, although chapels have nearly always been previously documented as highly patriarchal institutions.

129

It was unsurprising that our interviewees remembered the women and their activities, given that women were so often the people running Sunday schools and the activities with young people. No one, for example, mentioned the content of the sermons given by men – yet they presumably would have heard many of these. Those interviewees whose fathers were deacons, lay preachers or ministers remembered them attending meetings from which women were excluded, regarding the running of the chapel. Yet no one expressed any real interest in what took place at such meetings. The interest was in the Sunday school, the competitions, the Band of Hope, the music and singing – usually organized and led by women.

One interviewee, Mabon, had a mother who was very involved in the Anglican church. Nearly everyone else from 'religious' families was a Nonconformist, yet Mabon described childhood activities very similar to those of our Nonconformist participants, that is, Bible study, competitions and eisteddfodau. We have described earlier the way in which Mabon's mother transmitted cultural capital to Mabon and how this was frequently linked to her activities in the church. Yet as we explored the issue of religious life in the interviews, it became apparent that women were central to the task of creating and maintaining culture in the context of chapel life.

For most of our participants there were clear boundaries between Anglicanism and Nonconformity – people were either one or the other, and this was important to their identity, sense of self and sense of the value of their religious life. Some of our participants also talked about the divisions within Nonconformity, distinguishing themselves as Calvinists or Congregationalists, for example. In this respect, our interest in Bourdieu's work reminds us of *Distinction* (1984), in which he explores the 'specific logic' at work in the 'economy of cultural goods' (p. 431). Making distinctions, in this view, is important in how social groups define themselves and imbue their cultural life with value.

Yet the barriers between different communities of faith and chapel congregations were not rigid or impermeable. We encountered examples of cross-fertilization between religious denominations. Two interviewees who were from less conspicuously devout families described attending a service three times on a Sunday when they were children. This frequency of attendance was not uncommon, but these participants attended a combination of Anglican church and Nonconformist services. The denomination of the place of worship that they attended clearly was not a crucial limiting factor for their parents, or presumably for the ministers and other congregation members.

According to the accounts offered by participants, religious life can be understood substantially in terms of the acquisition, development, maintenance and transmission of the cultural resources that it offered. In contrast to Bourdieu's original formulation, where the key elements of religion are trickled down through a church hierarchy, the Welsh interviewees emphasized the democracy of chapel congregations, demonstrating another manifestation of the symbolic capital of Nonconformity. Prior to 1832, only a small proportion of the population was entitled to vote, and at the time of the establishment of Methodism, the notion of a vote for every person was radical. In Welsh Nonconformity, the laity contributed to the structuring of the culture of religion and the collectively held fund of capital.

This chapter will, for the most part, be concerned with Nonconformity. This invites ideas about religious life and spiritual capital as they were articulated by Bourdieu and his followers, but this focus will not exclusively define the material we cover. In line with the focus of this book as a whole, we will be particularly interested in the role that women played in spiritual life.

Nonconformity and symbolic capital

We can develop and extend Bourdieu's notion of symbolic capital, reflecting the biographical dimension of our participants' narratives. Many participants identified Nonconformity as central to their childhoods, commenting on the democratic and egalitarian ethos of their chapel communities, leading to a generalized respect and support for people in the community as a whole. It enabled participants to imbue their practice with symbolic value and contrast that with what was seen to be the hierarchical and authoritarian structure of Anglican Christianity. Chapel life, supported at a national level by eisteddfodau, provided a forum for the generation and reproduction of culture, language, literature, poetry and music, as well as a sense of shared history which was itself valorized. The notions of symbolic, religious and spiritual capital illuminate how community and chapel activities were infused with importance and imbued with value in a way which could be compared with others in the social field.

Bourdieu defines symbolic capital as 'the acquisition of a reputation for competence and an image of respectability and honourability that are easily converted into political positions as a local or national noble' (1988: 291). The profit of symbolic capital is distinction. A group is thus able to set itself apart and make itself more prestigious in relation to other groups by developing distinct actions, behaviours, norms, dress and rituals (Bourdieu, 1999).

Participants regularly mentioned aspects of Nonconformity that were described as giving their faith 'more than other faiths', particularly the egalitarian, democratic nature of Nonconformity, its Welshness and the education of chapel members via the chapel, facilitating the accumulation and transmission of cultural capital. This spirit of egalitarianism has a long pedigree, and was noted in 1847 by the Commissioners of Inquiry into the State of Education in Wales (1847: 4): 'It is all among neighbours and equals . . . every one who has got anything to say is under no restraint from saying it'. Some of the groups which emerged from Methodism in the early nineteenth century, particularly the self-termed Primitive Methodists, were led by men with manual occupations, such as Hugh Bourne (a wheelwright) and William Clowes (a potter), who voiced forceful opinions favouring gender equality. Our participants' accounts suggested that the symbolic capital accessed was universal within these communities, but expressed differently by men and women.

Symbolic capital can be thought of as the amount of 'honour' or 'prestige' or the 'right to be listened to' possessed by a person with regards to acting structures; it is a crucial source of power. Bourdieu (1984) argues that symbolic capital is a self-construction by actors in the face of difference to their social group. Through an understanding of their social history, a group is able to produce a perpetuated self-identity that can be facilitated through use of symbolic capital. A group is able to legitimize itself, its rituals and its language. Language is particularly important here. The communities that we discuss were Welsh-language communities. English was spoken as well, but Welsh was the preferred language. This was integral to the identity of these communities and could be used to exclude non-Welsh speakers.

To some participants, some aspects of the symbolic capital of chapel were seen to be particularly superficial:

> (Alwena) a lot of them are hypocrites. I saw that when I was a child. They used to go to chapel with their new clothes to show off their new hats and things and to see what other people have had. There was a lot of that going on. And backchatting, talking about you . . . I think it was the time – if you didn't go [to chapel] it would be frowned on . . . but when my father died, my grandmother lived in the village, my grandfather, and they were very big churchgoers, they never missed a Sunday and we used to go and sit in the pew behind them.

To Alwena, then, there was a sense in which the displays of chapel or church attendance, certain people's displays of piety and even their clothes were somehow ostentatious and lacking in what she believed to be deeper religious feeling.

As well as representing a means of support and of tying communities together, the chapel congregations were perceived by some to be judgemental and exclusionary: (Erin) 'chapels seem to be worse . . . more narrow minded . . . that's the impression. You hear these horrendous things about girls having babies and being kicked out forever. I haven't heard that about churches but it wouldn't surprise me'. There were other reports of a somewhat censorious and exclusionary attitude being taken by church or chapel congregations. Five of our participants commented explicitly on this. One participant referred to a group of people who did not aspire educationally or socially and mentioned that these people were not involved in chapel and usually lived in 'council' accommodation. Two other participants referred to certain quarrying villages in north-west Wales as having a high proportion of 'unfortunate' people in them. Further conversation suggested that these interviewees were deploying a kind of discourse reminiscent of the way that some contemporary commentators talk about the so-called 'underclass'. The means of making distinctions, then, was ready to hand in the social and conceptual habitus of these communities, and was recalled as being important in congregations' sense of identity and difference from non-members.

One interviewee, Alwena, remembered very clearly having been part of this excluded group, although her grandparents were members of the chapel. Her father had died of tuberculosis when she was very young and her mother had been left to bring up the family single-handedly. 'No one came near the family'; the children felt stigmatized and endured extreme hardship. This participant was frank in her condemnation of what she perceived to be the hypocrisy of her neighbours, both Nonconformist and Anglican: 'you'd find more Christians in a pub'.

Yet this censoriousness and cliquishness, in the view of some participants, was somewhat overstated, and owed as much to fiction as it did to actual practice:

> (Lowri) Anglo-Welsh literature gave a completely foreign and wrong idea. People like Caradog Evans, the picture they gave and you've got it a bit in *How Green was my Valley* and things like that, you have the business of the single woman who'd had a baby being denounced. I think it's a picture that's been given by people who've given up going [to chapel] and want to give a good reason.

For Lowri, the harshness of the presumed judgements was more imagined than real and owed as much to fiction as it did to actual practice. Indeed, in accounts such as Lowri's, there was a complex intersection of fiction, memory and history: (Lowri) 'in the Anglo-Welsh stories in a way you've got types and they don't reflect the real characters of society'. She made reference to the work of Caradog Prichard (1904–80), a writer from Bethesda whose *Un Nos Ola Leuad* was a somewhat melancholy novel about mental health, written from a child's perspective. It was one of the most enduring and widely translated Welsh-language stories of the twentieth century and was informed by Prichard's experience of his mother's mental illness and the hardship of his early life, which, Lowri asserted, had 'none of the cosiness of other families'. Lowri also drew upon other writing to make sense of the situation in which she grew up in Wales in the mid twentieth century. Making reference to the Welsh poet Waldo Williams (1904–71), she said:

> Williams the poet referred to 'the Holy network of God – keeping thee and him and her and me' – and that was the right thing for the stage for what we're discussing now [women supporting and caring] – because there was always someone there to look after – and we're back to your nonconformist community and church . . .

For those involved in chapel communities, there was a complex and tight-knit social network which involved 'keeping' one another. This might involve care and support but also keeping alive the language, the presumed traditions and culture and the system of values and moralities which suffused and sustained community life. Dafydd also stressed that the popular image of Welsh chapels as dour and cold was wrong – 'it wasn't like that'.

Nevertheless, what is interesting here is how chapel congregations were readily perceived as being tight-knit and potentially cliquish – that they were communities of practice with a common outlook, set of morals and aesthetics. This enabled both members and non-members to demarcate the social world of the village and identify the place of different groups within, in connection with their self-ascribed symbolic capital.

Alongside symbolic capital, Bourdieu also defined the capital present and utilized through religious organizations, religious capital. Bourdieu's perspective on the field of religion emphasized the agency of religious officials in shaping its dynamics. However, other commentators, such as Dillon (1999: 411), argue that there are multiple 'micro' producers upon the religious terrain. Dillon asserts that as everyday religious actors consume religious goods, they also exercise religious authority and produce new meanings.

In addition to religious capital, Verter (2003) additionally defined spiritual capital as a derivative of cultural capital, in terms of the traits, knowledge and habits passed down through the generations. The construct of spiritual capital can be understood in terms of an embodied, objectified and institutionalized state. The embodied state sees spiritual capital as 'the knowledge, abilities, tastes, and credentials an individual has amassed in the field of religion' (ibid.: 159). This is capital embodied in the habitus of a religious community and was clearly described by our participants. Spiritual capital flows through 'the power that . . . religious organizations exercise to legitimate an arbitrary array of religious goods, promote the demand for these goods, and feed the supply by bestowing qualifications on a select group of authorized producers' (ibid.: 160). In this view, spiritual capital in the embodied state is 'the knowledge, abilities, tastes, and credentials an individual has amassed in the field of religion' (ibid.: 159).

Iannaccone (1990) promotes a notion of religious capital which includes religious knowledge, familiarity with ritual and doctrine, and social relationships with fellow worshippers. Religious capital can be accumulated by individual congregation members as well as by the religious movement, sect or church as a whole. Iannaccone's model suggests religious capital acts as a conservative and cohesive social force. At the same time, 'religious participation is the single most important means of augmenting one's stock of religious human capital'. Hence, 'religious capital is both a prerequisite for and a consequence of most religious activity' (Iannaccone, 1990: 299). In this view, religious capital is both produced by and enhances satisfaction with religious practice.

These views are more aligned with the democratic and communitarian spirit of chapel congregations where, as we shall see, there was a great deal of emphasis on the congregation voting on issues of importance to the chapel and of the contribution of the laity to spiritual life. However, that which we wish to retain from Bourdieu's insight is the idea that capital was being created and sustained through religious observance and the related social activity.

What is distinctive in the Welsh case is the relationship between religious life and a whole variety of forms of civic, cultural and educational activity – as Chambers and Thompson (2005) call it, 'public religion'. In Wales, the gains of Nonconformity were particularly noticeable in the nineteenth century. The most numerous Nonconformist chapels to be found in Wales were Calvinistic Methodist and Congregationalist (also known as Independent (*Annibynwyr*). Jones (2004: 178) observed that by the middle of the nineteenth century there was no part of religious or secular social life that Nonconformists had not penetrated, but 'by 1850 the religious element had faded in intensity and we see it being secularized and nurturing a social ethos'. Jones (1982), when writing about north-west Wales, noted that 'chapels . . . dominated behaviour outside of the mere act of worship' and that 'their presence was central to the life and structure of slate-quarrying communities . . . a powerful organizational framework, nonconformity came to hold a position of quite particular importance' (Jones, 1982: 43–4). Jones (2004) says that the Nonconformists were determined to provide a united leadership to the nation. By the end of the nineteenth century Nonconformity was becoming associated with political radicalism (Chambers and Thompson, 2005).

Nonconformity plays a unique part in the remembered history of Wales. Nonconformity is characterized by theologically centred activism, Biblism and conversionism, creating a personal ethic. The set of doctrines and beliefs of Nonconformity led to a culture prevailing in *Y Fro Gymraeg* resulting in, famously, Sunday closing: a suspicion of mass culture, such as disapproval of whist drives and dances (Emmett, 1964: 92). This was still evident in the 1960s. Madgwick et al. (1973) illustrate the erosion of this Nonconformist culture through secularization. The residual influence of this form of cultural life and the symbolic value attributed to it generates great interest in contemporary accounts of Welsh identity (Jones and Fowler, 2007). Such identities may be constructed, narrated and maintained at community level, representing a way of sustaining knowledge, culture and symbolic capital (Carter, 2006).

The spiritual and religious capital generated through participation in religious life might not be equivalent or universally recognized, however. The spiritual capital of the 'posher ladies' at the Anglican church would not necessarily translate easily to a Calvinist Methodist congregation.

Many older people in Wales are still actively involved with Nonconformity. They retain a sense of the differences between the different faith-groups and the collective identities fostered. Whilst historical commentators have identified common themes in the various denominations and communities, our concern here is more with the distinctions understood by participants themselves within this broader movement.

The rapid evolution of culture and spiritual life that took place in rural Wales in the late nineteenth century and the beginning of the twentieth century is consistent with Bourdieu's notion of symbolic capital. There was a frenetic accumulation of value and the development of formal and informal techniques to ensure its sustenance, growth and transmission. Paradoxically, as this happened, there was a decline in the faith itself, although this was punctuated by religious revivals, such as the one of 1904–5. It is noticeable that our interviewees rarely talked of spirituality – they talked of practical theology, the social values of Nonconformity.

The idea of symbolic capital is particularly incisive here because the key feature of this image of Welsh culture was that it was carefully crafted, although by the time our participants became aware of it, the secularization of Wales was under way and the religious element was fading.

The sense which emerges from many sociological accounts of chapel life in rural communities is of austerity and severity, where to transgress against the strict moral codes 'was to be placed outside respectable society' (Chambers and Thompson, 2005: 33; Welsby, 1995). This preoccupation with the punitive and exclusionary role of chapel morality obscures the ways in which change could be accommodated and anomalies in gender roles and conjugal life could be assimilated. The chapel as an active social matrix that could sustain community cohesion in the face of changes in people's circumstances, accidents and transgressions has been relatively underexplored.

Women and chapel life

Given our focus on women's role in rural communities in Wales in the mid nineteenth century and given Bourdieu's intimation (1991b) that religion is a patriarchal institution, let us look at what participants had to say about gender roles as they were manifested in chapel or church communities.

The role of men as the prime movers and figureheads in chapel congregations was identified by many participants. (Nona) 'I think it [the chapel] was very much the men's domain. My father used to go to something called the *seiat* where they'd discuss the service the week before – it was just the men. The deacons were men'. Despite the pre-eminent role of men in the formally recognized positions in the chapel, we were given some insight into the role of women, such as minister's wives, by Lowri, whose father had been a chapel minister: 'yes I think privately he [father and minister] consulted her [mother] a great deal'. The role of the minister's wife, however, was one which could represent a burden for the woman concerned, as well as a pathway of influence:

> (Lowri) as the century merged . . . a minister's wife didn't think that she ought to turn up at everything, she had a life of her own and I remember someone here talking about a minister's wife and saying, one of the deacon's wives, she said 'she doesn't come does she' and I remember saying 'oh I didn't know the church had made an arrange-ment for her, they're paying her a wage as well?' They expected that gratis . . . the minister's life, it was a very difficult life economically with a wife not working, but until the war had finished, even if they wanted to work they couldn't. It was only a widow who would go in for teaching for example . . . in most cases it was after the war. So many of them would have been teachers anyway . . . they almost sanctified it [being a minister's wife] – put it this way – there was a role and they would have been considering.

Here, Lowri characterizes the expectations upon a minister's wife – that she should attend the place of worship where her husband preached and should not take up full-time employment, so as to leave her time and energy free for chapel or church activities. Yet, as Lowri points out, there was no remuneration and the expecta-tion was that all the work would be undertaken voluntarily. As well as ministers' wives themselves, this also applied to other women in the chapel community: (Lowri) 'many of them were members of churches with a faith, with a belief that you sacrificed yourself, that you don't go after your own ends and I think that makes the whole difference to your life doesn't it?' Alwena had a similar sense of women's roles in churches and chapels:

> I did think that [the church was male-dominated] [the women were] only for doing the flowers. It was very stereotyped in this area then. I

would have said that they [chapel] were just as bad, no, in fact I don't know if they were worse . . . behind the scenes, like a lot of places today, they relied on them [women].

This ambivalence over women's roles – being relied upon, yet not being in positions of formal leadership – was remarked upon by other participants, too. According to Lowri, women counted, yet men had to be seen to take the lead in chapel or church business:

> if you think that women counting of necessity means being public . . . their role wasn't a public one except in women's meetings, that's perfectly true, but when there were men present the men took the lead at those times, but that didn't mean the women didn't count.

The gendered division of labour was recalled as being prevalent in Anglican as well as chapel congregations. Women did a great deal of informal work but were seen to be excluded from positions of influence:

> (Erin) [church was] very woman-orientated I think . . . [women] probably doing the dirty work and they weren't working [outside the home] anyway, most of the women, most wives, mothers, weren't actually working women . . . they [church] think themselves a bit posher [than chapel] . . . why should it be middle class though, all classes should go there . . . but the council estate didn't, it was the nicer ladies, the posher ladies that were doing all the things . . . things were set in stone . . . its always been done like this . . . [the church] women – doing the flowers, doing the cleaning, what's wrong with them being a vicar . . . they just did the work I think.

In Erin's account, the women are described as hard at work, yet, as she notes, they were not in the top position. A further distinction worthy of note in these quotations from Erin is the idea that church, as distinct from chapel, was sustained by the work of 'nicer', 'posher' ladies. This recollects Iannoccone's contention (1990; 1994) that the more austere, demanding theologies, such as might be found in chapel rather than Anglicanism, are the preserve of poorer people.

The forms of shared symbolic capital: democracy and education

Our attention was drawn to notions of symbolic capital because participants regularly mentioned aspects of Nonconformity that were described as giving their faith 'more than other faiths'. Two issues were discussed by the majority of participants, women and men. First, the idea that 'every member of the chapel had a vote', leading to a strong sense of chapels being equitable, democratic institutions, rather than the hierarchical structure which the Anglican Church was said to have. Second, a distinctive feature was the education of the chapel members via the chapel – the transmission of cultural capital, in which women were centrally involved. We will explore each of these themes in turn.

Many interviewees stressed that the Nonconformist chapels of which they had been members were democratic, equitable bodies and that all adults had a vote on important issues. Participants made the distinction that this was unlike the Anglican church, where decisions were believed to be taken by the priest and church elders: (Geraint) 'it'd [the chapel] be very egalitarian in that way'. Geraint remembered that Congregationalist chapels, in particular, were very egalitarian and voted on many things. One interviewee was more cynical, implying that it was possible to manipulate the democratic vote:

> (Euros) everybody has a vote in Congregationalist in theory. [laughs] Well you can have your way can't you? Um you can get somebody to propose, somebody to second, then you ask for a show of hands and most people you know will put up their hands. It takes a brave man or lady to oppose . . . all members would vote.

One woman interviewed had attended an Anglican church when young and upon marrying had attended her husband's Calvinistic Methodist chapel. She commented on the difference:

> (Angharad) in the church you know it's the vicar's word that goes, but in the chapel it's the deacons . . . In the church, if the vicar said we're doing something, that's the last word. With the chapel it's not quite the same . . . the congregation get it [a say in running things] in the chapel

as well. The congregation have more of a say in the Methodists than in the church.

Although this participant had not been brought up in the Nonconformist tradition, she did notice the greater degree of democracy when she joined the chapel.

The idea of a vote for every member of the chapel had practical and symbolic consequences. One interviewee, Ceinwen, interpreted it as a way in which women were treated equally, in an era when they were often discriminated against. She spoke at length about gender equality in the chapel. She attended a Congregationalist chapel and speculated that this might have a different tradition to Calvinistic Methodism. She considered that the principle of equity was central to her chapel and took it for granted that women 'were fully equal'. Ceinwen was one of a few interviewees who remembered women deacons. Interestingly, although she maintained that gender was 'not an issue', Ceinwen remembered that it was only men who sat in the *set fawr* (literally, the 'big seat', the place in front of the pulpit in the chapel in which elders would be seated). But the important thing to this participant was that everyone had a vote and decisions were taken by vote. Ceinwen came from a family of radical political activists and she linked this to their participation in Nonconformist worship.

This sense of the egalitarian ethos of Nonconformity was echoed in a number of accounts. Another interviewee, the daughter of a Calvinist Methodist minister, whose family had clearly possessed much symbolic and cultural capital, linked the democratic tradition of the chapel with radical social action. She recalled her mother working in a soup kitchen and her father supporting the General Strike of 1926. She linked the democracy of Nonconformity with the support of people in 'dreadful' socio-economic conditions: (Lowri) 'that sort of maintenance [of Nonconformist principles] by the whole society helped people keep their dignity'. Jones (2004: 212) made a similar observation when writing about Nonconformity in south Wales in the nineteenth century: 'It is fair to say that the faith proclaimed by these chapels gave comfort and strength to thousands and the host of societies that met within their walls gave a human warmth to harsh lives'. In this context it is noticeable that most of our inter-viewees actually talked of social values, rather than 'faith'.

This passionate support of egalitarian causes harmonizes with a long tradition of Nonconformists supporting radical social action. Jones (1982: 63), in his account of the north Wales quar-rymen, details the substantial role that Nonconformity played in the quarrymen's struggles: 'the chapel was much more than a place of worship; it was also an organiser and an identity, the focus and the expression of the community's values'. Lowri linked this ethos with that of respecting all people, no matter what their social station or their personal idiosyncracies: 'I think within Nonconformity in particular that's part of the business isn't it...in our house we never had any inclination as to who was worthy of respect and who wasn't. Everybody was worthy of respect'. In a similar vein, within chapel communities, several participants observed that, for example, becoming a deacon did not depend on one's socio-economic status:

> (Geraint) the way in which the chapel for example dealt with people, there was no class division at all, people could become deacons from any walk of life, there was nothing there to – my father was deacon, the local primary headteacher was a deacon, another deacon was a joiner. They were all male of course . . .

Many of our Nonconformists subscribed explicitly to this notion of classlessness, although the same participants indicated that they were aware of locally meaningful hierarchies among the people involved. This sense that all were worthy of respect, could hold office, vote on decisions affecting the congregation, learn and teach and come to their own understanding of the biblical message, aided collective participation in culture and the genera-tion of shared cultural capital. Whilst, as others such as Day and Fitton (1975) have argued, the distribution of respectable *buchedd* A tended to follow other contours of status and prestige, here the assertion was often that one's status in the occupational world, for example, did not matter in terms of holding office in the chapel.

In some cases participants recalled this democratic spirit over-coming gender boundaries. Women deacons were recollected in particular chapels as early as the 1950s and 1960s, as we described in chapter 3. Women deacons were certainly unusual – most people did not remember them at all – but those who did remember them stressed that it was part of the 'beauty' of Nonconformity. Participants contrasted this with the Anglican Church, in that it was stressed how in chapel there was no hierarchy or governing structure preventing women from becoming elders; if an individual chapel voted for a woman to be made a deacon, then that would happen.

It was repeatedly stressed that 'anyone' could become a deacon and that 'everyone' was respected within the chapel, irrespective of their socio-economic position. Yet, at the same time, some participants indicated that there were people who were not part of this respected and respectable non-hierarchical society.

Equally, another participant, Dewi, as we described in chapter 3, had experienced a very difficult upbringing. His mother had a series of partners, one of whom was violent, and she was often short of money. They moved house frequently and at one point he lived with his aunt as a consequence of his mother being homeless. He remembered his childhood being very difficult practically, but he did not remember any sense of exclusion. Dewi believed that his mother and he were accepted within the community because there were quite a number of people in similar circumstances living in their village.

Similarly, in the previous century Jones (1982: 45–6) described some people in Nonconformist communities whose conduct did not always equate to Nonconformist ideals: 'there were plenty of pubs, drunkenness and unruly behaviour . . . the nonconformist monolith had its underbelly, defined in drink, which it needed, as much to embrace as to keep at a distance' (p. 47). Although Dewi was describing a somewhat chaotic family life some fifty years later, there exists the same sense of tolerance among the perpetuation of a myth of respectable classlessness.

Lowri talked at length about another tenet of Nonconformity – that everyone can aspire, no matter what their social station. Lowri had followed a career as a teacher and lecturer, and throughout her career, as well as in her work as a reformer and activist, she considered it 'an essential need' that she 'expected the best from people – because you often get it . . . although you're wily enough to know that the best might not happen'. Lowri mentioned the thirteenth chapter of Corinthians, 'eager to believe the best': 'the old Nonconformist network often brought out the best in people because if they know [that] in the name of God it's expected – but of course .we don't, we're sinners aren't we – but high expectation is an important part of life'. Lowri was unusual among our participants in that her conversation was peppered with Biblical quotes, rather than simply revolving around the social values of Nonconformity. Nevertheless, this shows how radicalism and the support for working-class causes were tied into Biblical precedents. This is reminiscent of Dorothy Smith's observation (1990: 197) that 'all texts are indexical' because their 'meaning is not fully contained in them but completed in the setting of their reading'.

This sense of expectation and aspiration for oneself and one's fellow congregation members, no matter how abject their circumstances, was intimately connected with the next theme that we distinguish, that of how cultural and symbolic capital was transmitted to subsequent generations.

A number of people interviewed emphasized the importance of Nonconformist institutions in educating the community, especially young people. Women were the major players in this process. The role of Nonconformist chapels in educating children, most commonly through *Ysgol Sul* (Sunday school) is well documented (Snell, 1999), women being the major players in this process (Baker and Brown, 2008; 2009). This education involved religious education and teaching children literacy. Also important was music, often introduced using the sol-fa technique, a simplified system of teaching music. The way in which many people felt that their involvement in Nonconformity when young had encouraged them to aspire academically and assisted them in moving into academia or the professions has been previously described (Baker and Brown, 2008). As we explored in earlier chapters, the role of women in wider society in educational aspiration and the transmission of cultural capital is well documented (Dyhouse, 1995; 2002).

Yet our participants were not merely describing the acquisition of cultural capital; they also gave clues as to how it was invested with value and meaning, as symbolic capital. They were not simply being educated, or even being educated in a Sunday school, as many young people were. They were learning within a Welsh Nonconformist chapel. Many interviewees had very positive memories of Sunday school and remembered other people being enthusiastic about Sunday school too.

(Geraint) Sunday school was very important, you'd learn the alphabet for example. That would be women teaching you, women until you were in your late teens and then there's more chance of a man.

(Dafydd) I used to enjoy Sunday school, it was a social thing, you'd meet other children the same age as you, did interesting things, did acting for the Christmas play and you had to study for written exams and you won prizes if you did things. In those days you only had radio, you didn't have telly or anything and it was something to do, although we weren't conscious of it, it was something to do, I found it interesting.

Other interviewees also remembered the songs and music of chapel: (Nona) 'women were involved in the music and the choirs but that's definitely influential actually because you deal with the younger people don't you?' Dafydd remembered that 'lots of people were very musical'. His own father used to sing and win at the eisteddfodau and 'could sol-fa a hymn at first sight because he was so familiar with it'. Women were explicitly remembered as being culturally influential in the chapel: (Harri) 'the women helped organise the Band of Hope [a Nonconformist youth organisation], they helped organize the eisteddfod . . . theirs was a more general cultural influence I think, rather than a religious one if you see'. In this case, it was clear from the rest of Harri's interview that by 'cultural influence' he meant 'culture' in terms of musical and educational accomplishments, rather than in the broader anthropological sense. The Sunday schools, musical activity and involvement in eisteddfodau help explain the complex social networks through which a sense of 'Welsh culture' could be nurtured, reproduced and translated into other contexts.

Nona also had very clear memories of the cultural influence of women in the chapel. She recalled that they 'had a lot of influence on the children', preparing them for exams, running Band of Hope, organizing Christmas events and eisteddfodau. Nona's mother had been a Sunday-school teacher and she was flattered to have been told by one of her mother's former pupils, a woman who had subsequently undertaken a distinguished academic career, that 'I always wanted to be like your mum from Sunday school'.

Participation in local and national activities like the eisteddfodau help to explain the complex social networks through which symbolic capital could be nurtured and reproduced and give 'credence', as Bourdieu (1993: 120) has argued.

The capital nurtured in the Sunday school could be 'exchanged' or 'converted' into something akin to Bourdieu's symbolic capital at both local and national level in eisteddfodau, which were not only festivals of culture, but also inasmuch as they offered the possibility of winning prizes, functioned as a forum in which value could be traded. The role of women in this process of investing chapel activities with meaning and value was clearly identified by most participants.

Thus, the symbolic life of the chapel communities was set in such a way that women, as Dyhouse (2002) has observed, were creating, reproducing and maintaining the symbolic capital involved, the love of music, poetry and learning that the Welsh had claimed as their own in the late nineteenth century (Jones, 1992a). The memories and comments from our interviewees are consistent with Jones's observations (2004) about how music, poetry, literature and hymns are important in Nonconformity.

Once this kind of capital had been acquired, the minds and bodies of the congregation were the bearers of symbolic value, the repositories of knowledge, piety and cultural skill. Prayer itself was a kind of cultural capital: (Dafydd) 'most of the men prayed from the heart, no reading or anything, no paper, they were very gifted in oral prayer you know because they'd probably done it for years'. Prayer from the heart was the culmination of many years' discipline and investment in piety, rather like the sportsmen described by Wacquant (2004). Many of our participants made comments regarding the perceived ability of the numerous people who were leading lights in Nonconformist chapels, but who had not experienced a formal education and had thus been 'held back' in society.

The accounts presented here illuminate the processes involved in investing the life and work of chapel communities with value and how the knowledge and cultural proficiencies achieved were exchanged on a national level in eisteddfodau. The capital involved infused much of Welsh-speaking rural Wales, *Y Fro Gymraeg*.

Educational researchers have often used Bourdieu to explain how education involves the acquisition of particular kinds of cultural capital which favour the middle classes (Reay et al., 2005). Yet the Welsh case described here provides some counterpoints to this picture. The capital that participants described was not concerned with improving the person's 'employability' in any simple sense, nor was it readily connected with or converted into economic power or wealth. Some of the participants, perhaps as a result of hard work and a suite of aspirations based upon this model of equity and learning, had gone on to have distinguished careers. But the kind of culture they described was not primarily orientated in this direction.

The striking feature is the creation and acquisition of symbolic capital by people who did not belong to the most economically powerful cohort in Wales. The kind of culture from which our participants originated was Liberal or radical in politics, pious and apt to regard the Anglican church as Conservative, hierarchical and somehow decadent. The 'Liberal Wales' that Jones (1982) described was the movement that, in the nineteenth century, laid the foundations for the kinds of experiences that we describe in this book.

The success of Nonconformists and the chapel movement in colonizing the intellectual and moral high ground in the late nineteenth and early twentieth centuries is illuminated by the narratives presented here. The chapel activities are invested with value in their own right and have an exchange value in comparison to other groups in the nation. One of our interviewees was aware that 'there was a lot of self-made men who got their sense of importance from the chapel' in Nonconformist congregations. The awareness of symbolic capital was well developed.

It should be noted that Nonconformity yielded a cultural dominance rather than an economic one. Jones (1982) points out that the Liberals never replaced the Tory elite as wielders of economic power in Gwynedd, and when the landed fortunes were eroded in the twentieth century, the local economy disintegrated. The term 'symbolic capital' as a means of characterizing what is gained through the cultural activities pursued and promoted by our participants in their early lives is apposite. It enjoys a relative autonomy and was not necessarily linked with material advantage.

Bourdieu (1997) proposed that forms of capital are interchangeable – they are interconvertible one into another. Interconvertibility occurs when a single, specific form of capital is exchanged to create a different type of capital. Interconversion is strongly metaphysical in that it involves exchanges between material and non-material forms. This is a process which Bourdieu describes as akin to transubstantiation. Acquiring cultural capital through education might lead to a person subsequently acquiring greater economic capital in employment, for example. Those who are richer in economic capital can more readily acquire cultural capital, and their offspring are more likely to succeed in the education system.

The situation that we are describing, however, is one in which the free exchange of forms of capital was limited. In many cases, the local economy in which participants grew up was one with limited opportunities for acquiring economic capital. Symbolic and cultural capital were not readily converted into economic capital in any direct manner, since this was simply not present in their communities. This recollects the words of the participant we met in chapter 6 who considered himself a 'very poor Brahmin' and whose family were 'subsistence' farmers, but whom he considered 'very rich' culturally and educationally.

The creation of symbolic capital and the role of women within this process in chapel communities deserves further comment. Among the Nonconformist congregations of rural Wales in which participants grew up, as we have suggested in chapter 6, a localized symbolic capital was created and owned by congregation members and the wider community of enthusiasts for Welsh culture. Demonstrating a proficiency in extemporized prayer, participating in Bible study competitions and eisteddfodau, all represented ways in which one could gain credibility, status and legitimacy within these close-knit communities. Being able to perceive, appropriate and elaborate upon the symbolic capital opportunities in chapel life suggests that the community carried with it some kind of historical knowledge of the divisions present within the social order. In Bourdieusian terms, it may be that those who sensed that there was an unequal distribution of economic capital would be able to generate more symbolic capital than those unaware of the inequality.

Conventionally, in Bourdieusian scholarship, symbolic capital represents a way in which the 'legitimate vision of the social world' (Bourdieu, 1987b: 13) is created and sustained. Relationships, practices and conventions which were once matters of convenience for wealthy or powerful groups come to look natural, legitimate or as if they are the only possible way of doing things. In this context, however, the cultural and symbolic capital of the chapel communities was not entirely about naturalizing and legitimating an unequal state of affairs. The spiritual practice and piety was not without knowledge of prior struggles between the polarized groups of rich and poor, employer and worker, gentry and commoner, which was crucial to the creation of symbolic capital in this context. Religious observance and Bible study were meaningful partly because they were a means through which people were able to differentiate one group from another.

A close analogy with the situation that we are describing can be found in Bourdieu's *Distinction* (1984). Based on studies of the occupational, cultural and social structure of French society in the 1960s, Bourdieu observed a number of partly overlapping social groups – there appeared to be certain occupations with distinctive associated lifestyle clusters. On the one hand, there were artistic producers and teachers who had relatively high cultural capital, yet who, despite their position in the middle classes, had relatively low economic capital. On the other hand, there were industrial and commercial employers whose position at the high economic capital pole in social space bore little overlap with the artistic producers at the opposite pole of high cultural capital.

We could see the chapel communities as affording a similar process. The members might not be wealthy by the standards of the time, but were nevertheless hard at work labouring to create the cultural and symbolic capital of which they were proud.

Knowledge of Biblical details, participating in spiritual life and putting oneself and one's fellow congregation members forward for competitions and festivals were transformed from the ordinary to the extraordinary through a process of cultural consecration: 'Cultural consecration does indeed confer on the objects, persons and situations that it touches a sort of ontological promotion akin to a transubstantiation' (Bourdieu, 1984: 6).

In connection with this, as we have already noted, a number of writers have talked about an intensive period of 'self mythologization' that was undertaken in Wales from the late nineteenth century onward (for example, Manning, 2002; 2004). This was extended to the occupational sphere, too. For example, the special and impenetrable skills of the quarryman existed, it was said, 'because the rock did not speak English'. The symbolic capital of Nonconformity involves a fusion of occupations, from minister, teacher and doctor to farm labourer and quarryman, into the notion of a common people.

Our interviewees' comments resonate with Jones's observations (1982) that Nonconformists were instrumental in promoting the notion of a *gwerin* in Wales. The Wales of the *gwerin*, traditional, organic and Welsh speaking, became both symbolically and actually 'a storehouse of a specifically Welsh rural identity and as such was specifically politicised' (Gruffudd, 1999: 159). Many of our Nonconformists explicitly subscribed to this notion, although the same participants sometimes indicated that they were aware of locally meaningful hierarchies among the people involved. The power of symbolic capital to enlist the consciousness of a community's members was evident, as many of our interviewees explicitly subscribed to the 'myths' of Nonconformity – democracy, equity, respect, the *gwerin* with superior knowledge and of course, Welsh culture itself.

According to many sources, this ascendancy of Welsh culture and its investiture with symbolic capital is of relatively recent date:

> Ever since the sixteenth century when Wales was incorporated into the English state and the status of its language downgraded, a deep strain of inferiority had infected the Welsh national consciousness. The legal and objective inferiority conferred on Welsh nationhood,

especially on its most obvious point of differentiation, namely its language, produced in successive generations of Welsh people a subjective sense of ambivalence and often shame concerning the essence of their own national identity. (Morgan, 1999: 36)

The valorization of Welsh culture occurred in the context of cultural and economic disadvantage stretching back over previous several centuries. It is a determined attempt to climb out of the disadvantaged position by recuperating value attached to the language and religious practice. Culture and piety are the pursuit of politics by other means.

When confronted with accounts of the role of chapel communities in their early lives, it is difficult to be precise as to whether participants are talking about cultural, social or symbolic capital. The sometimes indissoluble relationship between these forms was recognized by Bourdieu. Bourdieu and Wacquant (1992: 119) state that the other types of capital take the form of symbolic capital when they are 'grasped through categories of perception that *recognize* its specific logic or, if you prefer, misrecognise the arbitrariness of its possession and accumulation' (original emphasis). Although symbolic capital has its roots in the other types of capital, it is a form of 'denied' capital, since it conceals the underlying interested relations. Symbolic capital is subjective and is perceived as making legitimate demands for recognition.

In Bourdieu's original formulation (1990b), symbolic capital legitimates power relations. In the case of our participants, this notion is somewhat more complex. Rather than merely legitimating power relations in any simple sense, the constructions of Welsh culture are part of a reassertion of identity and value in the face of the historically marginalized position of Welsh people. Ideas of democracy and a sense of equity at a local level in chapels may have masked localized power relations, but at the same time the idea of Welsh culture was part of a broader struggle against nineteenth-century English attempts to brand Welsh-language activities as backward and an impediment to education, a struggle in which women played key parts. As Jones (1992b: 337) says: 'the ascendant Wales of this period was fashioned from the hopes and fears of nonconformism; indeed, the identity associated with piety and chapel lay at the heart of this construct'.

The very notion of Wales is itself a felicitous construction, specifically formulated as a piece of this complex array of symbolic capital (Wood, 1997). Although the idea of a *gwerin* with a common culture is believed to be a recently constructed historical image (Morgan, 1986a), it is intimately aligned with the egalitarian notions of mutual respect, support and democracy that formed a central part of our participants' lived experience.

Experiences recounted by our interviewees concerning their early lives, added to the panoply of historical motifs found in popular accounts of Welsh culture, suggest that in this case the local symbolic capitals had been developed with their own history. This history is effective in the present, serving to reaffirm the value of literature, music and piety, imbuing it with a sense of tradition. This underscores and validates the everyday politics of the recent past, in which women assumed many key roles, in our interviewees' childhoods.

8

Moral Guardianship and Respectability: Lives Beyond Suspicion

೦ః

Introduction: situating respectable Welsh womanhood

Since the nineteenth century, when the Blue Books declared that eight out of ten Welsh women were 'unchaste and insensible to female virtue', there has been a special relationship between femininity, morality and piety in Wales. Well into the twentieth century it was as if the nation were still smarting at this criticism and seeking to negate it. In 1850, three years after the publication of the Blue Books, the Nonconformist minister Evan Jones (Ieuan Gwynedd, 1820–52), founded a magazine to promote a different version of Welsh womanhood, *Y Gymraes* (The Welshwoman). In this publication, Jones aimed to raise the educational standards of women in Wales and disprove the allegations of immorality levelled by the authors of the Blue Books.

Jones's intention was to present an ideal image of the Welshwoman, who was respectable, moral and religious – what he called '*gwir Gymraes*', or a 'true' Welshwoman. The journal contained articles with advice on subjects such as housekeeping and cooking, as well as on religion, marriage, temperance and morality, with the aim of encouraging the female readership to follow these stipulations in their everyday lives. In addition, Jones produced statistics to show that the number of illegitimate children in Wales was no higher than in England, contrary to the implication of the authors of the Blue Books.

The publication was supported by Augusta Hall, Lady Llanover (1802–96) (who was also noted as the originator of the 'traditional' Welsh costume for women), but it was published for only two years, due to Jones's failing health. After his untimely death, *Y Gymraes* ceased publication in November 1852 and was taken over as a joint publication by *Y Tywysydd a'r Gymraes*. Over twenty years later, in 1879, *Y Frythones* (The Female Briton) appeared, under the editorship of Sarah Jane Rees (Cranogwen, 1839–1916). Rees herself was greatly affected by the religious revival of 1859 and, as well as being a Band of Hope leader and Sunday-school teacher, was a campaigner for temperance. *Y Frythones* ceased publication in 1891 and it was decided to revive *Y Gymraes*. The first issue of the new *Gymraes* appeared in 1896, edited by Alice Gray Jones (Ceridwen Peris, 1852–1943), and the magazine continued until December 1934.

We have described the development of this publication not so much because of its intrinsic interest, but because many of those involved were also key players in the reconstruction of Wales, through costume, temperance and religious revival. The relationship between morality and skills of household management in publications like this echoed the areas of concern to the authors of the Blue Books. As well as the presumed sexual impropriety of women in Wales, their household skills were believed to be lacking. The Reverend Richard Morgan gave this evidence to the Commissioners:

> They learn anything but delicacy of thought and feeling and when they grow to womanhood and marry, they know next to nothing of the management of a house . . . The loss of chastity before marriage (the scandal of the Principality) is the rule rather than the exception. I do not think the duties of wives and mothers are well understood, still less fulfilled. (Commissioners of Inquiry into the State of Education in Wales, 1847: 488)

This background means that questions of morality and respectability were closely allied with the religious piety that we saw in the previous chapter. It also means that distinctions regarding who was respectable and who was not infused community life in villages in *Y Fro Gymraeg* in the mid twentieth century.

Like the opinions offered by the witnesses to the Commissioners in the mid nineteenth century, twentieth-century respectability could be exercised in terms of many factors. It might involve household management, child care, money management and the avoidance of debt, cleanliness, the kind of clothes worn, as well as the management of actual or implied sexuality. Previously we have described situations such as Eirlys's mother saving enough so as not to have to meet her husband urgently on *taliad mawr* day in order to pay debts. Yet respectability, moral guardianship and the active practice of lives beyond suspicion required far more than this.

In this chapter we will seek to examine the notion of moral guardianship and the idea of women seeking to lead respectable lives in more detail. At the outset it appeared to us that, like the idea of habitus itself, far from being a static morality, the exercise of respectability, originating from a generative principle, required a vigilant social acuity and constant, complex negotiation.

In the decade since Beverley Skeggs (see, for example, 1997) famously placed the issue of respectability on the sociological agenda, there have been many fruitful attempts to apply the notion to social phenomena. The practice of femininity in school (Allan, 2009), cleanliness and the transformation of the labouring classes in the nineteenth century (Crook, 2006) and the construction and maintenance of social distinction in rural Ireland (Muldowney, 2008) have all been illuminated by this concept. Skeggs's insight (1997) that respectability was used by her informants as a means to accrue some symbolic value to their devalued and vulnerable class position prompts reflection on how the notion may be extended further to show how that it is imbricated with the past.

Bourdieu sees moral convictions, customs and judgements as being established through convention and, in a move reminiscent of Foucault (1975), as matters of discipline and normalization. Thus, Bourdieu saw matters of morality as being very closely bound up with symbolic capital, or with the power of conse-cration. Symbolic capital may serve as a kind of credit that social actors or groups have as a result of having gained a social posi-tion which is regarded as legitimate and which may be grounded in cultural or economic capital. Thus, morality, in this view, is grounded in social practice and habitus rather than in any pure moral philosophy (Bourdieu, 1986c).

Respectability is bound up with social capital, which is 'a capital of social connections, honourability and respectability' (Bourdieu, 1984: 122). Bourdieu's notion helps us to explain how moral convictions, habits and judgements guide people in pursuing meaningful lives and in distinguishing between right and wrong, good and evil. Also, as we have seen in the previous chapter, moralities and striven-for respectabilities on a social level may serve as means of discrimination, stigmatization and exclusion. In the course of social life in village and chapel communities, people orientated and positioned themselves and one another not only in a moral, but also in a social space. Both of these, although distinct, are thoroughly intertwined with one another.

In connection with this, Bourdieu sees strong moralities as hallmarks of less powerful, more working-class and downwardly mobile social groups. As he saw it, the working class 'refers often explicitly to norms of morality or agreeableness in all their judgements' (Bourdieu, 1984: 41). In this view, those who are at the bottom of social hierarchies are apt to subscribe to moral conservatism in religious and sexual matters. The middle classes, by contrast, are instead inclined toward a moral system which is more psychologically minded and focuses on personal needs.

Further insights on the issue of respectability have been provided by Skeggs (1997), who notes how it is often the working classes who have been identified as dangerous, polluting, threatening and pathological – curiously like the picture of the Welsh painted in the Blue Books. To Skeggs,

> Respectability is one of the most ubiquitous signifiers of class. It informs how we speak, who we speak to, how we classify others, how we study and how we know who we are (or not). Respectability is usually the concern of those who are not seen to have it. (1997: 1)

Respectability means belonging, inclusion and being accepted, being treated with respect, acknowledged and recognized as an individual. Our participants reported a diligent adherence to perceived rules. Nona's mother played golf, but would never have broken golf-club rules regarding the hours during which women players were permitted to use the greens.

Yet achieving respectability in the sense of becoming middle class sometimes meant surrendering something.

> (Harri) when I was a kid, anyone who had middle-class pretensions, doctors, lawyers, spoke English. Even though they could speak Welsh perfectly well, they spoke English, they spoke English to their wives and this sort of thing and that was a badge of having made it . . . that was being broken down in my teens, in the fifties . . . we would insist as kids on speaking Welsh . . . it was really strange but there was something respectable about English-type jobs, like being a secretary, being a bank teller.

English, then, was still the language of upward mobility, as noted also by Emmett (1964: 33): 'Speaking good English and being accredited with social superiority are closely connected.'

Gaining status through professionalization and entry to the middle class was one way of securing respectability. There were, however, other means of being respectable and ensuring that one's social circle was free from any moral taint. This was particularly important, since upwardly mobile middle-class careers were not available to everyone in small communities.

Regulating respectability

Where popular culture and literary representations of Wales were concerned, the notion of women being excluded from chapel congregations and socially ostracized if they became pregnant outside marriage was a common one. Yet participants' recollections of this were equivocal and suggested a more subtle and sometimes contested picture. Exclusion was not necessarily imposed in an authoritarian manner, nor was it necessarily permanent, once the *casus belli* had been resolved.

Our participants gave some examples of this kind of thing. Lowri, a minister's daughter, remembered her father's 'church discipline' being such that a couple were asked not to come to the chapel, because of their ongoing extramarital relationship, in the 1930s. However, subsequently they married and were accepted back in, so that the process of exclusion had more in common with a kind of cooling-off period for the benefit of the injured parties who might be offended, rather than permanent banishment. As Lowri remarked, it was also the case that people excluded themselves if there was any likelihood that their actual or imagined conduct might attract disapproval. Thus, a picture emerges of a kind of consensual disengagement during periods of people's lives which could have been morally contentious or which had upset other congregation members. Indeed, this disengagement might be seen a means of managing potential conflict. In a small community, the parties involved in problematic situations would very likely have been someone's husband, someone's daughter, wife or best friend, and if they had gathered together in one place, tempers might easily have frayed.

In the lifetimes of our participants, however, things were changing:

(Geraint) the period of people being thrown out of chapel because they were pregnant is before my time ... I'm talking about the fifties ... I suspect that there would have been people who wouldn't have gone to chapel, eliminated themselves, whereas in the previous generation they'd have been thrown out. I can see that if someone had done something like that it would have been quite tricky. They'd have censored themselves.

A further account of shifts in attitudes and practices was provided by Eirlys: 'well, when I was young, sixteen or seventeen, my [future] sister-in-law got pregnant and they wrote her out of the chapel, the Methodists, they took her name out of the book. But my chapel [*Annibynwyr*] wouldn't do that.' Eirlys went on to relate how when this young woman was thrown out of the Methodist chapel, she attended the Anglican church instead – 'she was accepted in church'. Perhaps in this case the exclusion reflected family sensitivities as much as those of the broader congregation: 'it was her own father who did it because he was the deacon and he was so old-fashioned he just wrote her out ... I think they would have done it [anyway] ... very tight.' 'They said to her "you're not a member any more", so she says "tough", well what did we care. We was young. I think they were a bit too narrow-minded.' There were also distinctions drawn between different denominations. Chapels were seen to be more austere in their approach. Erin, whose father was involved in the Anglican church and whose mother did not attend chapel, grew up with a particular impression of chapels: 'chapels seem to be worse . . . more narrow-minded . . . that's the impression . . . you hear these horrendous things about girls having babies and being kicked out forever. I haven't heard that about churches but it wouldn't surprise me.' This process of distinction between different groups of people sometimes involved geographic and spatial boundaries as well. Arsula recalled hearing that the rural areas were even more apt to be socially conservative than towns and that rural chapel communities were 'bad' to single women with children. The people were 'narrow-minded in C——— [a town in north Wales] but more in the country'.

Thus, the core of social and sexual conservatism was often represented as being somewhere else – in another community, a different chapel, out in the countryside or 'before my time'. Nevertheless, the kinds of standards of conduct that chapel communities were believed to sanction cast a long shadow over the childhood and young adulthood of participants. Even where social change was in the offing and youngsters were reacting against this milieu, they necessarily had to define themselves in opposition to the pervasive notions of respectability which informed how people saw one another and how they saw themselves.

This is reminiscent of an idea attributed to the anthropologist Ernest Crawley and further elaborated by Freud (1930), namely the 'narcissism of small differences'. In this view, negative feelings are directed at people who resemble ourselves but who differ in some small or subtle respect. The ability to make these distinctions is important in enabling social distinctions between otherwise similar communities or congregations to be maintained and to sustain a sense of identity.

As Skeggs (1997) proposed, the ideas about respectability held by a community mediate positionings and responses to sexuality. Respectability, in this view, is a discourse of normativity. That is, it represents a way in which actual or implied sexuality, poverty or deviance is evaluated. It enables distinctions to be drawn, legit-imated and maintained between groups or families. Among our informants, respectability and the taboos surrounding sex did more than this. Sometimes they enabled certain topics to remain unspoken.

Most interesting in this regard are accounts of how accidental pregnancies were managed, where, despite rumours of a severe response by some congregations, very often participants recalled the matter being resolved so as to preserve both notions of morality and the dignity of those involved. Eirlys again provided a story:

> and I remember my other sister-in-law, she got married in white, but she was pregnant, but her father didn't know, she never told him. And he found out, but because the baby was nearly due when she got married and he was so thick that he didn't know and he even went to the minister to tell him, 'well look you've married my daughter and she's pregnant' and he made a big thing. And the minister turned around and said 'it doesn't matter whether she was pregnant or not, I'd have still married her. If I'd have known, I'd have still married her.' He was more modern you see. Times had changed. It was a Methodist chapel, the same chapel, but later [in 1964, about eight years after the incident of 'writing out' described above]. But that was just my father-in-law's ways. He was, well he thought he was, a religious man. And he was a deacon you see. And that's how they used to do it in his time. But people didn't care whether she was pregnant or not did they? What did it matter? But to him it mattered. No, of course they didn't care, it was just his way, very old-fashioned. Lived in the Dark Ages as far as I was concerned . . . her father had written her off and I think for a while she didn't like her father. Now my father would never have done anything like that, kicked anyone out of chapel . . . I mean he [her father-in-law] used to smoke and he used to drink. Then he saw the light . . . then he turned religious.

Eirlys's and Geraint's accounts suggest that the period of harshness, when people who had violated the perceived respectability of the community were physically and socially excluded, had somehow occurred before their time. In Eirlys's case there is more evidence of conflict, such that the younger generation in the 1950s and 1960s, as well as the minister in the story above, were of a more liberal cast of mind and that 'they didn't care'. Severity, in these accounts, was apt to happen in another time and place, rather than in the present. It occurred among a different generation, or in another chapel community which was more dour and severe than one's own. Perhaps also we are seeing an elision between Jenkins's *buchedd* A and *buchedd* B (1960), where other chapels, periods in time or religious congregations are seen as exemplifying *buchedd* A and one's own, whilst still conferring respectability, are more pragmatic and compassionate towards excursions into *buchedd* B.

Indeed, the older generation and their perceived distance from the concerns of the young could be a source of entertainment. The man in Eirlys's story who did not realise that his daughter was pregnant was the father of Eirlys's boyfriend (who subsequently became her husband). He was also a lay preacher in the Methodist chapel and, whilst Eirlys and her boyfriend sat on the sofa together in the living room, they were entertained by hearing him practising his preaching upstairs and rehearsing sermons. The moral guardianship of women then did not necessarily mean enforcing rules, but ensuring that people were able to operate within them, through a strategic process of information management and discretion.

Despite these intimations of social change, where the purportedly rigid mores of the past were subject to renegotiation, there were a number of accounts of more severe responses to pregnancies. Cadi recounted how a girl and boy at school with her in the 1940s became romantically involved, culminating in the girl's pregnancy. The boy stayed at school, whereas the 'girl disappeared to have the baby'. Eventually she returned alone. 'I think it was given away or something. She still lives around here.' Indeed, such was the residual stigma and the perceived need for discretion attached to this event, that Cadi said that she would not tell the researcher the name of the women concerned in case the researcher knew her or came across her in the course of the research.

The discussion of sexual morality was sometimes recollected as a kind of humorous diversion:

(Euros) looking back to my boyhood days, when there was talk about women being rather lax in their morals, it was regarded as a joke – I don't know how our parents felt about it, but we regarded it as a bit of a laugh. I can't say we were peeping toms but we kept an eye open occasionally. It's a complicated subject when you look back.

This complexity reveals itself at several levels. On the one hand, sexuality and its regulation, especially where young men considered young women, was a matter for humorous camaraderie, yet at the same time, where young women themselves were concerned, matters were of considerable personal importance.

Lapses, in the form of accidental pregnancies, did not necessarily represent an irretrievable loss of position within the community. The period of time spent 'away' was sometimes the signature of such an event and sometimes meant the achievement of a means to its resolution:

(Dewi) I think just before I left school, there was one girl, she was a beauty, an English girl, she got pregnant, its bad enough now, but in the fifties, oh no, poor girl, she had to go away to have the baby – I think she kept it . . . I remember her name clearly, that's the only one I remember having to leave the village . . . everybody knew what was going on, I suppose they did gossip, but they didn't throw stones at her or anything, there was nothing like that at all when we were growing up.

Dewi's account thus also stresses the process of separation as a means of managing the morally problematic situation. Whilst in this case the pregnancy is described as common knowledge, the way in which it was managed enabled the perceived problem to be negotiated with little overt conflict.

There are some intriguing implications here. The code of silence surrounding manifest or suspected violations of the mores of respectability may have been facilitative as well as repressive. Cadi's making a point of not telling the name of the person concerned preserves their dignity, but also conveys the message that this is a matter which demands discretion and enlists the listener's co-operation. Keeping quiet about matters such as pregnancy, even where one's own father was concerned, enabled a degree of harmony to be maintained in family and community life and lay at the heart of this moral guardianship that deflected confrontation, allayed suspicion and preserved the appearance of the highly valued *buchedd* A.

The value of this discretion was underscored by Cadi's description of what happened in the case of other women where knowledge of their circumstances leaked out and confrontations ensued. In the case of another pregnant girl: 'I remember chapel being nasty . . . it was just one or two of them wasn't it . . . I remember one woman – it was about a man – "she should be thrown out of chapel".' Such censorious views, even if expressed by only a few congregation members, could lead to exclusion by the rest of the congregation and its leaders, anxious to avoid further confrontation and conflict. Cadi believes this woman was indeed 'chucked out' – 'I heard about it happening.'

This is reminiscent of Skeggs's point (2004) that the pursuit of respectability and normality enables normalcy to be both a kind of capital within the field of the family and a form of symbolic capital that represents accumulated privilege in other fields. Being respectable could even be thought of as a kind of capital in itself, which authorizes and sustains one's own and one's family's position in social space. This could lead to some particularly convoluted arrangements in certain families.

For example, Angharad, born in 1939, described her situation as follows:

> it's a little bit complicated actually – I was brought up by my grandmother but I didn't know until I was, oh about ten years ago. I thought I had two sisters but one was my mother you see. They never told me anything until my sister, I thought it was, died. So you know I've been brought up by my grandparents. She [her biological mother] married afterwards and had another child.

Thus, Angharad's family had kept this secret successfully for over fifty years, suggesting that Emmett's notion (1964: 14) of 'not knowing' was being brought into play, whereby people chose 'not to know' about behaviour that would be 'frowned on'. Angharad spontaneously mentioned this, but out of respect for what was clearly still a sensitive issue, the interviewer did not probe further. Perhaps the circumstances of her birth were still shrouded in mystery, since she did not mention a biological father. At the time of her birth, presumably, there would have been a number of people in the family and elsewhere who were aware of who her mother and probably her father really were, but this had been kept from her, presumably in the interests of minimizing gossip and any stigma attaching to her or the rest of the family.

This practice may not have been unusual, as it was noted by Emmett (1964: 104):

> It often happens that the child is reared entirely by his maternal grand-mother as his mother and his mother as his sister … this happens more often when the father is unknown or when it seems certain that the father will not marry the mother … The mothers then have a better chance of finding a husband.

The morality and respectability to which people and communities subscribed represent a particular 'grid of visibility' (Rose, 1996: 55) of conduct, where certain kinds of conduct such as sexuality and reproduction were brought under special scrutiny. This did not mean that they were eliminated, but rather that they were managed through processes of discretion, spatial separation and through complex reconstructions of family life such that the potential taint could be minimized. The effort, or accumulated labour, involved in maintaining this separation and the complex, multiply layered social realities to which it gave rise can be thought of as a kind of social capital. The social networks in Bourdieusian notions of social capital are also networks through which it was possible to maintain boundaries between purity and danger in the sense proposed by Douglas (1966). Moral guardianship involved not so much enforcement, but rather a kind of management of social reality so that morality appeared to be maintained.

In Skegg's work (2004: 25), she suggests that a process of self-authorization takes place at a local level by taking a new perspective on oneself and one's situation and by revaluing the positions that we are expected to inhabit. In a culture where the predominant economic experience is one of poverty and economic advancement is unlikely, then the maintenance of a social capital that emphasizes and accumulates piety and respectability is ever more important.

People who inhabited positions which were of little value in terms of the broader socio-economic system of the UK, could give themselves value and 'authorize their existence as valuable people through the practice of respectability'. This was often not a form of respectability borrowed wholesale from the English middle class. As we have seen, the sense that something special defined chapel communities that was missing from the Anglican Church was pervasive. This, then, was a kind of respectability defined partly in opposition to the middle class. Whilst this was informed by the legacy of the Welsh response to the Blue Books, it did not represent a simple taking-on of the views of the economically dominant group, but represented a reworking of perspective and value.

More recent studies which have explored respect and dignity in other communities have emphasized the lengths that people will go to in order to maintain this sense of dignity and self-respect and to ensure that they will be recognized as worthy of respect by others (Hoffman and Coffey, 2008). Indeed, people are often willing to undergo considerable material hardship in order to retain the sense that they are treated with respect.

As we have intimated, participants' descriptions of the nature of life in villages in rural Wales during the time in which our participants were growing up suggest that moral boundaries and the codes governing respectability could be applied flexibly in specific cases. Some participants, like Dewi, described a childhood with frequent disruptions and a good deal of poverty and hardship, due in his case to his mother's difficulties in maintaining employment or stable relationships. Yet Dewi did not report any experiences of stigma. Indeed, a particularly accommodating view seems to have been taken, and Dewi and his mother seem to have been shown considerable kindness by the people in the villages in which they lived.

Exceptions could be made in other ways. Whilst the expectation was that married couples would stay together, Arsula described how the community condoned her escape from a violent marriage.Yet she also noted how women who left their husbands were usually seen as 'scarlet women' and that others endured many years of domestic violence, for fear of 'talk' if they attempted to leave.

There were, however, other issues and conditions which were deemed to merit a degree of separation. Alwena's father had died of tuberculosis and, as a precautionary measure, she and her siblings had to be X-rayed once a year to check for disease in their own lungs.Whilst during most of the year they mixed freely with other children in the village and at school, for the period of time surrounding the chest X-ray they were kept separate from the other children.The separation here seems to be largely symbolic in nature, since even if they had had tuberculosis themselves, they were unlikely to be more infectious when the X-ray was due. When they did mix with other children they did not get bullied or experience any other social stigma – 'the children were ordinary children'.Thus, despite some rather peculiar and inconsistent precautionary measures, the stigma and separation were temporary rather than pervasive.

As Skeggs (1997) found in her work, the idea of respectability was not entirely coterminous with material well-being or being middle class. It was possible to be 'respectably poor'. It is as if one's efforts to maintain respectability and keep up appearances in the face of economic hardship were appreciated. Alwena, whose widowed mother was very poor, was highly conscious of the family's marginal status, although they tried hard to remain among the respectable poor.

Sometimes, when people had no other sources of livelihood, work could be found for them. Dewi's mother, whose position was sometimes very vulnerable, as we saw in chapter 3, was given work cleaning the chapel that they attended in exchange for accommodation:

> yeah I went to chapel . . . mum used to watch after the chapel, clean it and I used to give her a hand every two weeks. Mum used to go to chapel in the morning, I used to go in the afternoon and mum used to go in the evening . . . mum was never a member of anything but she used to look after the chapel . . .

What was clear from Dewi's account was not so much ostracism and censoriousness, but instead a sense in which the rest of the community and chapel congregation aided them in maintaining a façade of respectability and a sense that his mother was contributing to the community.

This offers further insights into how the notion of respectability was maintained. Taking Dewi's account at face value, it seems as if this represents a further socially mediated means of maintaining a sense of respectability for the family in difficulty. Rather than 'charity', which people might be reluctant to accept, this involved work which was more palatable so that a sense of fair exchange could be maintained. Respectability, then, could be a collective effort. Moreover, as more recent studies of respect among the poor have shown, this may facilitate a more positive account of oneself among those whose circumstances have taken a turn for the worse (Hoffman and Coffey, 2008). Importantly, too, this account from Dewi involves alignment with the chapel. A sense of closeness to religious institutions has also been noted as representing a valuable source of self-worth in people who are subject to poverty and stigma. For example, Collins et al. (2008) write of 'church ladies' and 'good girls' as desired identities among people struggling for self respect amid misfortune.

Embodying the family honour

Achieving a pristine and unselfconscious state of respectability was clearly not an easy feat for women in patriarchal societies beset by problems such as poverty, bereavement, domestic violence or unwanted pregnancy. As has been noted by scholars of self-presentation, much care is taken to regulate the way in which women present themselves in their everyday lives (Goffman, 1959; Sawin, 2002). In the personal accounts presented here it appears that, as they performed their respectable selves, women in Wales in the mid twentieth century sought to achieve a state in which their respectability became naturalized beyond any possible doubt – beyond suspicion – thus supporting their right to be involved in village or chapel life.

Part of this naturalizing process involved caring for others. As well as one's immediate household and children, caring for relatives represented a duty through which a kind of symbolic capital could be gained and disdain could be expressed toward those who were seen to be less diligent in their caring duties.

Eirlys's mother cared for a number of elderly relatives; Eirlys recalled her saying 'I would carry my mother on my back' and expressing disgust at families who put the elderly in homes. Eirlys felt the same way: 'I think I would have done the same.' These displays of care and nurturance are similar to the displays of piety we have discussed elsewhere. Whilst they perform an important practical social role in providing care for the elderly and infirm, there is a symbolic quality to them, too, especially inasmuch as they augment the social image of the carer and her family.

Women's self-performances as respectable ladies pivoted on a certain kind of representation of nature. That is, it is as if women combined nurturing instincts with an allegedly innate propensity for proper etiquette, good taste and culture. Their task of embodying and displaying a habitus of respectability was not limited to managing their family members' good reputation, but was inscribed on their own selves through a painstaking work of 'social magic' (Moi, 1991).

Respectability, like the displays of gender described by Guano (2007) in Genoa, is a practice that 'blends a degree of volition with a fiction of naturalness', that fixes and essentializes respectability and its related gender identities, as if they were somehow natural and not a matter of personal agency.

Men's involvement in community life, whether in the chapel as a minister, elder or lay preacher, or in working life, was often a form of creativity. The skill in oral prayer or Biblical knowledge was often remarked upon as an especially admirable feat – although, as we have heard, these apparently spontaneous performances were sometimes carefully rehearsed in the privacy of one's own home.

To Roger Abrahams (1983), men's interventions like this are creative, whilst respectability, often the domain of women, lacks such performative ingenuity, and is, in fact, just a mere repetition of static norms. In conjunction with this, we can see vestiges in our participants' accounts of what anthropologists have termed the 'honor/shame complex' (Peristiany, 1974; Schneider, 1971) and, as part of this, the notion that, as the embodiment of their family's honour, women's virginity and sexuality were actively policed by their male kin. The lay preacher who did not realize that his daughter was pregnant and subsequently remonstrated with the minister who married her could be seen as an example of this.

Yet the maintenance of respectability and the process of creating the associated symbolic capital was a much more complex, strategic and resourceful practice. This could especially be seen where matters of money and possessions were concerned. As Eirlys said, when speaking of her mother: 'she was very disciplined with money . . . she never owed anything . . . she wanted a three-piece suite once and her friend bought one on credit . . . my mother didn't.' Eirlys's mother 'feared' debt, so decided that she would save up for her three-piece suite:

> oh and about twelve months had gone and her friend said did you get your three-piece and my mother said no. Well there you are she said, I've got mine and I've paid for it. Have you saved the money to buy one? And she hadn't had she, so she didn't get her three-piece [laughs] can you imagine, it was horrific. The things we had to do without, absolutely do without.

The 'doing without' however, had to be kept private, lest it affect the family's reputation in the broader community. As regular attenders at chapel and Sunday school, they were conscious of the need to have clothes that would enable them to command the respect of the rest of the congregation: 'some days we couldn't go because we didn't have nice shoes'. The role of new clothes in chapel attendance was also underscored by Alwena's comments in chapter 7 – there was a lot of mutual evaluation, and, perhaps just as importantly, self-evaluation going on. From participants' reminiscences, there were many distinctions made on the basis of clothes. The wearing of second-hand clothes in poor families such as Alwena's seems to have been accompanied by particular feelings of shame:

> (Alwena) a parcel would come of clothes and they were horrible clothes. You know for us girls there would be jumpers with collars

on like the boys wore. And I remember having boots passed on to me from this parcel, they were too big but I had to wear them. They were winter boots and I remember going to collect a girl that lived next door . . . and she remarked on my boots to draw attention to them . . . I've never forgotten that . . . it was very hurtful . . . I didn't mind that I had to wear them, things like that, that you were different . . . we had hand-me-downs from my cousins . . .

Hand-me-downs and charitable packages of clothes were, by the fact that they were not freely chosen and in the fashion of several years before, apt to make the wearers feel especially devalued in the economy of respect. They might attract unkind remarks from other children and detract from one's ability to maintain the performance of a socially valued individual. Yet at the same time, despite appearances of poverty, Alwena was keen to stress the widely recognized underlying respectability and virtue of her mother: 'if you spoke to anyone in this district who knew my mother – honest, hardworking woman who put her children before her'. There were, nevertheless, opportunities for managing the impression other villagers and local tradespeople had of the family.

(Alwena) my mother used to send me to B—— [a town in north Wales] . . . she didn't want to go to the butchers in B—— and ask for a scrag end or something, because everybody else would have baskets and be asking for a leg, she'd have to be asking for the cheapest cuts of meat.

If the child of the family went to buy the cheap meat and did so at a shop far from home, it would not be as shameful as if the adult did so. In Alwena's account there was no mention of any actual disapprobation from others; it was the imagined stigma of not being able to buy as much or of such good quality as others. Thus, the maintenance of a respectable image for the family could involve the deployment of considerable ingenuity to ensure that the limitations of their resources would not be disclosed to everyone all at once.

Whilst participants and social historians agree that wealth was in short supply in the communities with which we are concerned in the mid twentieth century, there were still perceived differences in wealth between different families. We have already described the acutely felt divide between those who occasionally had new clothes to attend chapel and those who had hand-me-downs, or those who had the cheapest, left-over cuts of meat and those who could buy a prime joint.

Even people considered well-to-do were commanding re-sources far less than those equivalent to the standard of living which might have been enjoyed by a middle manager, doctor or lawyer in the home counties of England. Yet the social divisions based on money and respect were nevertheless profound.

Eirlys remembered a man in her village who was appointed as a magistrate, and seeing him driving past in his Austin 7. This was, of course, a cheap, entry-level car – 'the motor for the million' – and elsewhere in the UK was not one likely to command respect. Yet Eirlys recalls people 'literally doffing their caps' as he drove by. 'I think they did respect him.' Eirlys's family themselves, despite the frugal attitude to furniture that we described above, were not without their own sources of capital. They owned their own house, which was 'quite something' in those days, since 'a lot of my friends lived in council houses'. The status of home owner-ship can be gauged from the fact that at the time small houses in north Wales were changing hands for considerably less than the average annual wage for manual workers. We do not mini-mize the achievement involved in owning a house or running a small car, but such reminiscences indicate that the economic status involved in the communities under discussion must be judged by a different standard from that which might apply to the UK as a whole. Resources which might have been considered small else-where were of considerable value.

This process of recognition was often practised only in one direction. Those deemed to be lower in the social hierarchy recog-nized those above them, but those who had been elevated affected not to notice those below. Arsula worked as a hospital ward-maid and said 'we were nothing, they [the doctors] ignored us'. As we have outlined in previous chapters, the cultural and symbolic capital embedded in roles in education and chapel elicited respect and some admiration. Eunice recalled the head teacher of her primary school: 'our headmaster, we were in awe of him, he was a deacon . . . so he was very influential as well, so we were keen to please'. Despite the relative paucity of economic capital available, some profoundly felt distinctions were drawn between people who were believed to have resources and those who did not. Cadi described how this had affected her own family background. Her mother had left school and gone to work as a housekeeper for a farmer. Even though he was considerably older than her, Cadi's mother married him when she was 'around eighteen or nineteen'. People in the neighbourhood felt that he had 'married beneath him'. 'We knew who was rich and poor we did . . . it was according to how you were born.'

The sense of having resources at one's disposal or being middle class was perceived to add to one's respectability and was believed to open doors and grant further opportunities. Eirlys described how she had been born 'in a private nursing home' and the prestige that this temporarily added to the family. She described how she had been born in 1943 in north Wales and her grandfather, who was reputed to have some savings, had paid for her mother to give birth in the nursing home, which evidently carried some cachet in the local area. Her grandfather had previously worked in the gold mines in the Transvaal before returning to Snowdonia to work in the quarries. Eirlys's older brother had been born in the local maternity hospital three years earlier and her grandfather had visited his daughter and her new baby. He was appalled to find mother and baby in a freezing ward, with the baby covered in a discarded army greatcoat because there was insufficient heating and no bedding. Consequently, he ensured that the next baby, Eirlys, was born in a private nursing home. Eirlys described how 'magistrates and things used to go into that home'. Her father, who was serving in the Second World War in the Welsh Guards at the time, was phoned by the nursing home to alert him to Eirlys's arrival. The call was believed to have caused something of a stir in his regiment. He got leave straight away 'because they thought he was somebody . . . he was only a private but they thought the family – "well she was born in a private nursing home"'.

These motifs of status, privilege and luxury were looked back upon all the more fondly perhaps because they were relatively rare.

Nevertheless, among communities where material luxury was rare, and often less than that enjoyed by similar working families in England, it retained a symbolic power which is perhaps nowadays difficult to appreciate.

Circumnavigating controversy

A further feature of the respectability that our participants describe their relatives and acquaintances affecting is its flexibility and its ability to keep different aspects of people's lives in different social compartments. We have seen this in the case of the information management where pregnancy was concerned, but there were several further examples related to us by participants.

One of these concerned a reminiscence relating to Lewis Valentine (1893–1986). Valentine was one of the founders of Plaid Genedlaethol Cymru (later Plaid Cymru) which was first proposed at a meeting between Valentine and fellow enthusiasts for Welsh language and culture, notably Saunders Lewis and H. R. Jones at the 1925 eisteddfod at Pwllheli. During the inter-war years, the party promoted education as well as the language and culture of Wales, and Valentine and his colleagues came to fame only as a result of an incident in 1936. With deepening international tension in Europe, the Westminster government was intent on building a bombing school on the Llŷn Peninsula. Building went ahead despite local protests. Valentine said that the government was intent upon turning this home of generations of patrons of poets, one of the 'essential homes of Welsh culture, idiom, and literature into a place for promoting a barbaric method of warfare' (Davies, 1994: 592).

On 8 September 1936, the bombing school building was damaged in an arson attack. Saunders Lewis, Lewis Valentine and D. J. Williams claimed responsibility. The trial at Caernarfon failed to yield a verdict and the case was referred to the Old Bailey in London. The 'Three' were sentenced to nine months' imprisonment in Wormwood Scrubs, and on their release they were greeted as heroes by fifteen thousand well-wishers at the Pavilion, Caernarfon (Davies, 1994: 592). (By this time,

Saunders Lewis, despite being the son and grandson of prominent Calvinist Methodist ministers, had converted to Roman
Catholicism.)

Geraint had the following anecdote to relate about Lewis
Valentine's relationship with his family: 'my grandmother . . . was
widowed very young . . . and my grandmother had two children
and was expecting a third . . . she had three children and nowhere
to go'. She had lived with her husband in police accommodation,
and when he died she and the children were asked to leave the
police house 'within a fortnight'. Geraint continued:

> she was a remarkable character, a very strong character . . . she wore
> black for the rest of her life which was another fifty years . . . she was
> incredible . . . she was very prominent in her local chapel, she was a
> Baptist . . . she was quite friendly with Lewis Valentine, the minister in
> Llandudno . . . When Lewis Valentine came over to our place to preach,
> he'd always go to my grandmother's to dinner. Lewis Valentine was
> one of the three . . . who in 1936 put the bomb and fire in Pen Llŷn.
> She knew Lewis Valentine before then, she knew him after then and
> although she knew him very well, she never understood this thing. 'Oh
> no, not my Mr Valentine.' So not everybody was steeped in this radi-
> calism, although she was steeped in Nonconformity. To her, there were
> two Mr Valentines, there was Mr Valentine doing some silly things at
> Pen Llŷn and Mr Valentine who preached to us every so often and she
> could not reconcile. And I think that's true of a lot of people actually,
> 'what on earth are you doing' and it would be men doing that sort of
> thing I suppose in the 1930s when the fire was lit . . .

This highlights something important about how a sense of
respectability and propriety could be maintained. Lewis Valentine
as a friend of the family was somehow a different person to the
Lewis Valentine involved in direct action and who had served a
prison term.

This ability to bracket out the more contentious elements of
a person's behavioural repertoire and treat them as if this were
somehow separate from more mundane engagement with them
was present in other accounts, too. Once again, Welsh-language
activism and politics provide examples. Some participants

described their own involvement in protests, yet as Eunice describes below, her mother showed considerable reticence where these issues were concerned. Eunice had been involved in actions such as breaking into and occupying BBC studios, and had been arrested:

> my mother, deep down I knew she was supporting us, but she didn't like us being involved in these things . . . there were quite a lot of older women there . . . I think that they were from middle-class families really, who knew what they were protesting about and the effect it was having on the language.

Again, we see this process of bracketing off certain potentially problematic aspects of experience which might involve personal danger or, perhaps more significantly, the danger of some lapse from respectability. In this regard it is as if the most important thing about social knowledge is what is excluded as well as what is included. It is, paradoxically, a good deal easier to be discreet, or as Emmett (1964) would have it, to 'not know', if one knows what one has to be discreet about. As contemporary idiom has it, these were the elephants in the room.

The ability to navigate around potential disruptions to the prevailing moralities and mores was evident in other areas of life, too. As we have described, Ceinwen's family was unusual, in that her mother was the main breadwinner and her father undertook most of the child-care. Whilst this was deemed to be unusual, there was some mitigation, in the sense that Ceinwen's mother's strength of character meant that any disagreement would be futile. As Geraint said:

> you wouldn't argue with [Ceinwen's mother] . . . I think they were unusual, certainly by Nonconformist Wales they would have been regarded as very unusual . . . [Ceinwen's father] being a communist as it were and a miner, was more in a certain tradition of radicalism, but [Ceinwen's mother], she was quite something.

The ability to transgress norms then had something to do with the ineffable personal qualities that an individual was perceived to have, and this somehow gave them credit in order to pursue less conventional paths.

Respectability and social change

The notions of respectability that we have described and the way that this was used to classify people and activities helps us to make sense of the responses to social change in the later part of the twentieth century. This was manifest in several ways. One of these concerned attitudes to feminism.

Despite the many roles that we have seen women taking on in this volume, which displayed a degree of flexibility and apparent liberalization where gender was concerned, news of second-wave feminism was greeted with some ambivalence:

(Geraint) they'd have been pretty traditional I think, this feminism stuff is American. In a sense, looking back, women had, take my father-in-law and mother-in-law, she ruled, there was no sense of a need as it were, because the actual sense of the situation was that there was this equality ... although the situation *de jure* was different and I guess they'd link feminism to ban the bomb and hippies etc.

For the women interviewed, too, feminism (or, as it was often termed at the time, 'women's lib') was understood through caricatures and not seen as having immediate relevance to their situation.

(Cadi) well you were shocked at first, throwing brassieres about, I was married by then, I missed all that ... maybe they weren't as interested as the English perhaps ... well they were loose women weren't they ... that's how you saw them wasn't it, we all had television by then.

(Arsula) We laughed ... burn your bras – they didn't do that in C——
[a town in north Wales] – I don't suppose they [the English] really did either.

The image of bra-burning, itself a fanciful addition by a *New York Times* journalist to a feminist protest at the 1968 Miss World contest in Atlantic City, seems to have captured the imaginations of participants. Moreover, it allows the concerns of second-wave feminism to be dismissed as something trivial, something seen on television, predominantly American or English, and of little immediate relevance or practical value to their lives. Perhaps, as Piette (1997) has suggested, the interest in changing the world was deflected into the struggle for greater recognition of the Welsh language. It may be, of course, given the events described in this volume, that there was already a measure of flexibility. Small communities with strong religious preoccupations may be constraining, but at the same time they often involve a relatively legible system of social capital that the astute participant can work to their advantage. The performance of respectability, the display of piety, the love of learning – these could all be means whereby women could exert influence over their own lives and perhaps, arguably, over community affairs, too. Without wishing to suggest that any of their activities were undertaken cynically for personal advantage, once one is able to read the symbolic social system, it is far easier to secure a comfortable place within it.

Conclusion: respectability and symbolic capital

Having examined how morality, respectability and moral guardianship were exercised through participants' accounts, it is possible to raise some new critical insight into the concepts and begin to explore how they may be interpreted within a broader theoretical framework.

On the one hand, respectability was a means of enforcement and, as we have seen, women were centrally involved in its genesis and maintenance. It can be thought of as a form of capital – through diligent performance of a particular kind of identity, one could accumulate a particular kind of social capital for oneself and one's family which might achieve symbolic status as it was recognized by other influential members of the community.

In a good deal of scholarship, respectability is seen as strongly contoured by class, with the wealthier and more hegemonic sections securing respectability for themselves most easily

(Proudman, 2005). Indeed, for Veblen [1899] (2001), respectability overlapped with 'pecuniary repute'. Respectable behaviour is 'emulated and disported' by the powerful and those who aspire to power and influence. Certainly, respectability brought potential female sexuality to the fore, yet this was very rarely in the form of sex itself. It was to do with one's clothes, one's shopping list, the occasional small signifiers of status or luxury, care for children and elderly relatives and, more rarely, it might involve a premarital pregnancy. Yet with each of these criteria, as we have seen, there were ways in which the matter could be resolved in some cases so that the potential for conflict or confrontation was minimized.

Perhaps, once again, our best chance of understanding the exercise of respectability is to see it as a facet of social capital which, if one played the game appropriately, led to the favourable regard of others and thus could be said to have achieved symbolic status. To some extent, respectability in this study showed emulations of elite conventions, particularly where this concerned clothes worn to chapel or to school, or the kinds of shopping one was willing to undertake in view of neighbours and local tradespeople.

The practice of respectability served to create and shore up social capital through the creation and maintenance of networks of social relationships. When one is judging one's neighbours one is drawn into some sort of social relationship with them. When one anticipates one's neighbours' judgement, one is imagining them and constructing their evaluation as if it were true. Respectability thus involves powerful relational intersubjective bonds which can exclude people from congregations, send people miles out of their way for cheap meat and have them grasping for their hats when a magistrate drives by. The creation of respectability and the exercise of moral guardianship in these circumstances is a profoundly social process. The capital attributable to an individual is a quality produced by the totality of the relationships between actors, rather than merely a common 'quality' of the group (Bourdieu, 1980: 2). In Bourdieu's formulation, symbolic capital exists, grows and is recognized through intersubjective reflection. Like social capital, it is based on mutual cognition and recognition (Bourdieu, 1980; 1986b; 1998a). This is how it acquires a symbolic character, and becomes symbolic capital. Indeed, for social capital to become effective at all, actual (or, as Bourdieu would have it, 'objective') differences between groups or classes, between the respectable and those who were not, between one chapel community and another, have to be transformed by the social group into symbolic differences and classifications that make possible symbolic recognition and distinction.

The creation of respectability and the exercise of moral guardianship in these circumstances is a profoundly social process. As Bourdieu maintained, 'the volume of social capital possessed by a given agent . . . depends on the size of the network of connections that he can effectively mobilize' (1986b: 249). Membership in groups and involvement in the social networks that developed within and between these and in the social relations this afforded could be utilized in efforts to improve the social position of the actors in a variety of different fields.

Chapel and church communities, voluntary associations, political parties and the like could be seen as examples of the embodiment of social capital. Differences in the control of social capital may explain why apparently the same kinds of events could yield different kinds of resolution or outcome. A pregnancy was managed discreetly or was scandalous, or the degree of virtue attributed to acts of caring was informed by the different powers of influence ascribed to different actors. Group memberships creating social capital are said by Bourdieu (1986b) to have a 'multiplication effect' on the influence of other forms of capital.

As Bourdieu describes it: 'symbolic capital . . . is nothing other than capital, in whatever form, when perceived by an agent endowed with categories of perception arising from the internalization (embodiment) of the structure of its distribution, i.e. when it is known and recognized as self-evident' (1985b: 204). As symbolic capital, distinctions are 'the product of the internalization of the structures to which they are applied' (ibid.). Respectability was so much more than simple rule-following. It involved being able to participate in, make legible and beguiling and even manipulate social realities in a way that increased one's own and one's group's status, as well as manage social problems and avoid conflict.

9

Culture, Capital, Learning and
Conversion in the Next Generation

CB

In this chapter, we will reflect upon the present-day relevance
of the findings of this volume. In the course of researching and
writing this book, we have discovered a great deal that was unfa-
miliar – and in some cases counter-intuitive – given the potent
stereotypes of village life in Wales.

We have been able to flesh out some of the detail concerning
how the Welsh of *Y Fro Gymraeg* were able to harness education
for their own purposes and achieve a modest measure of social
mobility. Armed with the seductive Victorian reconstructions of
bardic and scholarly tradition and with the cultural capital assiduously cultivated in the chapel and village school, some of them were
able to embark on university education and subsequent white-
collar careers. We have noted, like Emmett (1964), that these kinds
of jobs often involved, especially prior to the 1960s, an ambiva-
lent relationship to the Welsh language. Professionals – or those in
'clean jobs', as Harri noted – tended to speak English. Yet, by the
1960s, political lobbying and activism was placing the issue of the
Welsh language on the agenda of broadcasters, policy-makers and
officials in a variety of public and private organizations. The social
changes in Wales in the latter part of the twentieth century did not
lead to the Welsh language being abandoned, but instead led to it
being more fully embedded in public life. The question of cultural
and ethnolinguistic change in rural communities is an interesting
one which deserves further inquiry.

In describing people's accounts of their lives and those of others in the communities where they grew up, we have presented a highly particular milieu with, as we mentioned in chapter 1, a specific *buchedd*, or way of life. We have attempted to lay out some of this habitus, as people sought to make sense of their early life and background. Whilst everyone was different, many of them were religious Nonconformists with a pervasive respect for knowledge. Although a number of our participants had succeeded in attending university, and hence elevating themselves into what we might call the 'middle classes', the experience of poverty and self-consciously 'doing without' had shaped their early lives in many cases. The idea of *buchedd* itself, along with the idea of the people of Wales representing a common folk or *gwerin*, could indeed be part of a constructed past, formulated by middle-class Nonconformists (Jones, 1992). Yet what is important is the sense of identity that it conferred, the sense of being part of a particular culture or community and the value that this gave to cultural and religious pursuits which lent themselves to educational aspiration and university entrance.

The role of mothers is specifically addressed by Bourdieu:

> It is because the cultural capital that is effectively transmitted within the family depends not only on the quantity of cultural capital, itself accumulated by spending time, that the domestic group possess, but also on the usable time (particularly in the form of the mother's free time) available to it. (1986b: 253)

The social capital described here is often about investment in others rather than the self. It is 'used up in interaction with others and is for the benefit of others' (Reay, 2004c: 71). Yet, whilst this depletion may occur on an individual level, the trajectories described by our participants suggest that in terms of the family, the group or the faith community, there may nevertheless be a collective gain. The sense of going to university on behalf of other family members who had foregone the opportunity highlights the centrality of the family to cultural accumulation and reproduction of this kind. It is as if the changes that many of our participants were able to make in their lives were achievable because they were standing on the shoulders of other family members, who had cultivated the *buchedd* in themselves and their loved ones in the past.

The present study revealed noteworthy unexpected findings where gender and sex roles are concerned. Whilst people's accounts, recalled several decades later, are not definitive representations of reality, they are nevertheless important, because they represent how people see their past and, by implication, see themselves in relation to the present. In participants' accounts, dating from an age before second-wave feminism was believed to have reached the UK, women were gaining access to means of accumulating certain kinds of cultural and even economic capital. Set around these forms of cultural capital, and providing a context for it, was their social capital.

Whereas we have documented some unexpected anomalies in gender-role enactment – such as women running businesses and farms – the picture painted by our participants is also one in which women had a stake or a voice in family and community strategies of capital accumulation and conversion. The contributions ranged from school teaching and Sunday-school teaching to writing and organizing plays and other entertainments and even providing the time and space for children to succeed at their homework. Although a good deal of this work was in gender-conventional domestic spheres, there was an active and strategic quality to much of this work, and it suggests that women were adroitly reading the rules of the broader social field.

The role of women in homes, chapels and schools in the mid twentieth century in rural Wales has – at least judging from the accounts presented here – had considerable influence over the formations of culture, capital, piety and learning in the subsequent generations. In a sense, this is 'the legacy' of Nonconformity mentioned by our participant Lowri.

Despite hitherto limited applicability to explorations of gender, Bourdieu's insights are increasingly appreciated in examining gender and teacher education (Acker and Dillabough, 2007), women as intellectual workers (Eagleton, 2005) and the role of examination proficiency as a kind of cultural capital for Victorian schoolgirls (Jacobs, 2007). There was disagreement among our participants as to whether Wales during the middle years of the twentieth century was controlled by men or women, and over the relative powers that the two genders commanded. If we were to take Bourdieu's 'masculine domination' (1990c) in a strong form, men's universalizing, instrumental functions in chapel, church or working life would be seen as involving power over women's particularizing, expressive roles in the household or as followers, rather than leaders, in religious congregations. For Bourdieu, as we have seen, the construction of social order takes place in social practice. It is not merely to do with the agents' thinking or the beliefs to which they subscribe. The regularity of society and of social action originates in physical action and practical sense – the capacity bestowed by the habitus to produce ways of acting that align themselves with the social order so as to appear natural – a 'social necessity turned into nature, converted into motor schemes and body automatisms' (Bourdieu, 1990b: 69).

One way of seeing the gender roles as they were played out in participants' reminiscences is as a model of masculine domination in the Bourdieusian sense. Some interviewees, such as Mabon, were adamant that this was the case: that, for example, men controlled family finances and that, although the church 'would not have survived without them', women had no influence in church matters. Unusually, Mabon's own family were Anglican, rather than belonging to a Nonconformist chapel, yet his perceptions would presumably have applied to chapels too, where 'lady deacons' were a rarity.

By contrast, participants such as Gwen and Ceinwen would disagree. Gwen believed that in the chapel, as in other areas of life, men 'fronted', but behind the scenes women had plenty of influence. Geraint also spoke of 'powerful' women, who very often were instructing or advising the men who 'ran' the chapel. Geraint perceived the whole interaction between women and men as a rather complicated game that the whole community willingly played. He remembered, as a mathematically gifted boy of ten, constructing mathematical puzzles for the adults to solve. He was aware that the wife of a local accountant was far more competent than her husband and invariably knew the solution to the puzzles, but concealed this until her husband had finally worked out the solution. Even at ten, he understood the game and the rules and was aware that everyone was participating knowingly. Interestingly, Geraint perceived that women did not feel uncomfortable or humiliated by participating in this game. One could of course argue that being male and very young, Geraint would not have detected the more subtle feelings of women in these situations. Yet other participants, male and female, made similar comments about 'men fronting but women often in charge' or simply were clear about a complex interplay and evident paradoxes which sometimes allowed the genders remarkable flexibility in gender roles and how they sought to interpret them.

A further example of this concerns our discussion of respectability in chapter 8. The codes of silence and discretion which governed the exercise of sexuality and the possibility of pregnancy might look quaint or sometimes even brutal, by comparison with the emphasis on communication in contemporary relationships. Yet at the same time this allowed a certain amount of room for manoeuvre. One could accumulate respectability through other displays of piety or frugality and have sufficient credit in the economy of respect to enable other eccentricities to be overlooked, if appropriate appearances were sustained.

Once again the metaphors of capital are apposite, but this is capital as a process rather than an entity:

> social capital, a . . . metaphorical construction, does not consist of resources that are held by individuals or by groups but of processes of social interaction leading to constructive outcomes. Therefore, we argue that social capital is not located at any one level of analysis and that it emerges across different levels of analysis. The confusion over the meaning of this term, then, is a consequence of a metaphorical confusion of a substantive quantity (capital) and a process that takes place through stages (embedded, goal-directed relations). Locating and defining social capital is further complicated by the variability, contextuality, and conditionality of the process. Stages of social relations that lead to constructive outcomes for one group of people or in one situation may not lead to constructive outcomes for another group or in another situation. (Bankston and Zhou, 2002: 286)

The reminiscences of our participants suggest that in the highly particular circumstances of *Y Fro Gymraeg*, women were able to gain strength and power in patriarchal systems, especially in spheres pre-defined for them by that culture. Yet women's powers in turn inform, influence and reproduce the cultures in which they are embedded. Even in the arenas of religious institutions and communities that have nearly always been documented as patri-archal or even misogynist, some of the scholarship outlined by Anderson (2004) has underscored the more agentic role of women that is coming to light as researchers revisit women's histories. This much is in line with our findings. Yet so much depends on how one looks at these institutions, groups and social entities and how much of their workings one takes for granted.

Central to the relational approach is the grasp of ethnographic sites as essentially porous, and we must necessarily understand the boundaries as ambiguous and subject to external influence and migration. Thus, the value that was attached to being able to get a 'clean job' or a 'good job with a pencil' might often involve the transition to an English-speaking workplace. Equally, obtaining higher education might involve a movement to a different part of the UK. Nevertheless, among our participants, there remained close ties to the neighbourhood and community and its way of life.

Throughout this volume we have emphasized the parallels between the notion of habitus and the indigenous concept of *buchedd*, particularly the kind of habitus described by participants and what Jenkins (1960) called '*buchedd* A'. The idea of a habitus which was peculiar to the people concerned is an appealing one, for it might help us make sense of the stories they told, the clothes they wore, the kinds of songs and poetry which came most readily to mind, the alacrity with which they invested time and energy in Sunday schools and cultural events. As well as their readiness to engage in all these things, another persistent feature is the readi-ness with which they grasped the sense that it was all worthwhile.

In this way, *buchedd* has something in common also with Bourdieu's *illusio*, the continued belief in the aims and rewards in a particular field. For example, declarations of loyalty and love for Wales and Welsh culture, despite its historically marginal status, are examples of *illusio*. Certain ideals, even idealism and intangible dividends of the social field prevent total disaffection and disconnection, and thus ensure continued participation; as Dreyfus and Rabinow (1993: 41) call it, 'the self-deception necessary to keep players involved in the game'. The illusion then, a faith and investment in the worth of the stakes of the field (Bourdieu, 1990b: 66), is what holds together and brings energy to the field where cultural and spiritual activities, self and family improvement were practised. *Illusio* is the animating force that makes things meaningful, worthwhile – it is what turns *options* into *generative oppositions*.

In Bourdieu's view, this generative conviction – the *illusio* – is to do with the relationship between habitus and field (1996: 172). This explanation merits some unpacking. The field is a set of objective relations – a 'social universe' whose logic enjoys a degree of autonomy from that of larger-scale politics or the economy. It is made up of institutions and agents and their struggles over the stakes of the field (Bourdieu, 1993: 162–4). Thus we might see chapels, schools, eisteddfod organizing committees, families and individuals themselves seeking to gain legitimacy, for themselves and their 'products'. These were often aesthetic or cultural products – such as knowledge, music, poetry – and thus we recollect Bourdieu's remarks about the artistic or literary fields (1993: 164; 1996: 224), where the stakes have to do with the kinds of cultural forms that are granted legitimacy.

The habitus represents an internalization of one's position in and understanding of the field, both currently and in terms of one's personal and family history, which grounds generative practice. Whether individual or collective, the *illusio* is a felt or sensed connection between self, social context and purpose. It is a conscious but unquestioned faith. It is the conviction that this is the right way, given the field as it currently presents itself and one's historical and ongoing internalized position – the conviction that it is valuable to avoid debt, to treat everyone as worthy of respect or to feel a sense of obligation to others who have facilitated the opportunity to pursue higher education. This social cement, allied to broader sentiments of nationalism, provided a means of holding families and communities together and facilitating their transition.

This *illusio* helps explain why it was that, with the decline of local industry and occupational opportunities in the mid twentieth century, the people did not become deculturalized, but rather directed their efforts toward exchanging their cultural capital for credentials outside the immediate community – for qualifications and jobs 'with a pencil'. Bourdieu himself, in *The Forms of Capital* (1986), was most concerned with the conversion of economic capital into other forms. Yet the process has the potential to run in both directions. He also notes that the conversions that take place are likely to be those least costly in terms of the 'conversion rate' and which occasion the least losses in the conversion process. Consequently, whilst the capital accumulated through the social and cultural labour could not readily or effectively be converted into economic capital, it could most easily be turned into the symbolic capital of educational qualifications, awards and prizes.

As a general rule, social changes may produce struggles against 'down-classing' and lead to people generating strategies to maintain or enhance their social position by converting devalued resources – or capitals – into valued forms (Bourdieu and Boltanski, 1981; Bourdieu, 1984). Thus, the relationship between habitus and class position is not frozen in time but reflects a historical trajectory, either an individual one, through different social spaces – the chapel, the school, the university and a career in education, for example – or a collective one, through transformations of the social structure.

It is differences in the habitus and *illusio* which may explain some of the contrasts apparent between the story told by our own participants and the situation of ethnolinguistic minorities elsewhere. To pursue our Bourdieusian argument further, it is instructive to compare the situation described by our participants with Bourdieu's account of life in the Béarn region in France. This was a rural area and there are some apparent similarities with our own informants growing up in *Y Fro Gymraeg*. Both areas were characterized by a distinctive language or dialect and were economically disadvantaged, compared to the broader national configurations of which they were a part. Both areas relied to significant degree on farming, especially on small farms which afforded a subsistence existence for their proprietors and a few workers.

In *The Bachelor's Ball*, Bourdieu (2008) describes the decline of this culture and way of life, as farming declined in importance and the economic and cultural centres of life were increasingly found in the towns. The title of the book was prompted by his noticing that a large number of unmarried men could be seen at village social events. It appeared they had little chance of marrying and that the way of life they pursued showed every prospect of disappearing. In tandem with the decline in farming, ambitious young people became increasingly attracted to town life and young women especially, encouraged by their families, sought romantic engagements with young men in towns pursuing urban occupations. Women's preference for 'townsmen' rather than 'peasants' revealed broader changes in attitudes to the peasant condition. It reflected the progressive realignment of attitudes in line with the dominant groups in France at the time. Judged on this basis, the peasant farmers, their education, skills and the meagre capital that they can muster, have little value. The peasant had to reckon with a devalued image that the townsmen gave him.

In our case there were a number of differences from the scenario prevailing in the Béarn presented by Bourdieu and it is instructive to try to discern what they were, to explain the relative resilience of the particular *buchedd* or habitus. The devalued image suffered by Wales and its people in the nineteenth century is well documented and we have already mentioned the image portrayed in the Blue Books of 1847. Equally, the second half of the nineteenth century saw a great resurgence of interest in Welsh language and culture and the rewriting of the country's history in terms which stressed cultural and scholarly tradition. Despite historians' scepticism about some of this history, it formed the basis for the *illusio*, the sense that the cultural game was worth playing. Combined with the developing interest in Welsh nationalism over the same period and the continuing influence of Nonconformity, it served to consolidate the sense among participants' families that they had something special to preserve and pass on to the next generation. Moreover, by the mid twentieth century the infrastructure to practise and authorize this culture – the networks of chapels, the eisteddfodau and so on – were sufficiently well established to give a sense of authority, legitimacy and symbolic value to the recognition and prizes they conferred.

Rather than an exogamous marriage strategy for young women, as described by Bourdieu in the Béarn area, the participants here described a much more endogamous approach. Certainly, there was evidence of encouragement to marry people the rest of one's family found desirable with desirable occupations, but, as we have noted, there was some encouragement not to marry people who were English or anti-Welsh.

In Bourdieu's account, the education system was also seen as a factor in the process of devaluing rural life and rural occupations. The influence of schools was strong enough to undermine the family's strategies of reinforcing children to invest themselves in the land. Equally, the extended period of time spent in school was enjoyable to children and cut off farmers' children from the experiences, lifestyle and temporal rhythms of peasant society. Schooling, says Bourdieu, tends to destroy the values transmitted by the family and redirects children's affective and economic investments away from the reproduction of the family line. Yet, as many of our participants disclosed, studying was embraced by the Welsh and was not seen as being inconsistent with the Welsh rural condition. Bourdieu's Béarn peasant children were given, through their education, a sense that they could move on to wage-earning status rather than being subsistence farmers and looked forward to a young adulthood with a personal income and the rights linked to this. Among our informants, children of farmers and slate-quarrymen might be encouraged to gain an education and a more comfortable life, yet this did not involve estrangement from family or culture. The idea among parents that an education would prevent one's child having to endure a working life of manual labour was apparently widespread and chimed in with the status given to education as part of the *illusio* that we have described earlier. Education might lead to one getting out of certain occupational trajectories but it did not involve getting out of the culture – indeed, if anything, it facilitated one moving more deeply into it.

In the Béarn region, many farmers, with their slim marriage prospects, were unlikely to continue their family lineage. Such children as there were were unlikely to pursue farming after school, as the education system had enlightened them as to apparently more attractive prospects elsewhere, thus contributing to the demise of the peasant class. In our data, by contrast, it is as if the education system was seen as being a part of the common culture rather than situated in opposition to it. Schools and colleges were a reason to stay in the area for many who had succeeded in the education system, because they provided job opportunities as teachers or lecturers. This deepened the sense that the education system was part of the community and belonged to it, in a way that seems to have been absent in the Béarn.

Nevertheless, Bourdieu's analysis and our own work come into alignment when he says that the flight into education prevented revolt on the part of those who had been uprooted, by transmuting objective bankruptcy into reconversion, proletarianization into social promotion and by providing adolescents excluded from traditional activities, not with jobs, but with a kind of provisional occupation by staying on at school. As we noted earlier in this volume, when the slate industry was buoyant, much of the cultural activity was directed inwards, for the community's own entertainment and edification – the cultural life of the *caban* (quarry rest-room), or the *Ysgol Sul* (Sunday school).

We noted earlier the 'demoralization' of industries such as quarrying and farming in the middle years of the twentieth century, in terms of the loss of employment possibilities and the decline in the industries themselves. In response to this decline, as people sought to maximize their capital accumulation strategies this cultural activity was directed outward, towards enabling the rising generation in a process of conversion to obtain the educational credentials which would grant them recognition in the wider world of employment – the 'jobs with pencils' that were accessible once the indigenous culture had been converted into the symbolic capital of qualifications. Therefore, it could be said that the Welsh of *Y Fro Gymraeg* harnessed education for their own purposes. The social mobility, as the century wore on, was accompanied by language activism, underwritten by the bards' and scholars' *illusio*.

Whilst this was going on, groups of intellectuals and activists in Wales and beyond were formulating a new kind of nationalism, within which the notion of an unbroken history and a national language were paramount. In response to the threatened loss of

Welsh identity and the apparent indifference of existing political parties to that loss, Plaid Cymru was formed in 1925. The Liberal hegemony, established in Wales at the 1868 election, espoused 'Welshness' but had little thirst for home rule (Gruffudd, 1995: 221). The nationalism espoused by Saunders Lewis, president of Plaid Cymru from 1926 to 1939, eulogized Welsh-speaking districts such as the Llŷn Peninsula in north Wales, which was an area 'where Welsh speech has moulded a countryside rich in intelligence, noble in the purity of its idiom, and with its native culture harmoniously developed through fifteen centuries of unbroken tradition' (Lewis, 1936: 915).

As Gruffudd (1995) says, this serves to locate the Welsh not merely as the possessors of a peripheral piece of land, but also as a central part of western civilization. According to Saunders Lewis, Wales 'stands today on the very territory it occupied – the *only* territory it occupied – when [it] was part of the Roman Empire' (1936: 915).

Iorwerth Peate stated that Wales was: 'an immortal nucleus containing . . . the finest heart of the Western world's traditions. There has grown in Wales a society which possessed an inheritance of incomparable tradition, and . . . a culture almost as old as the world itself' (Peate, 1926: 4). A corollary of this view was that because this was such a perfect society, the Welsh therefore had a duty to civilization to ensure the perpetuation of their nation. This meant resisting English cultural encroachments. Saunders Lewis contextualized this territorial politics within a broader European dimension, defining Wales, not as a region of Britain, but as one of the historical nations of Europe (Jones, 1973; Gruffudd, 1995).

Nonconformity and Welshness were intimately linked. Jones (1982: 63) noted that 'Welsh Nonconformity was acutely conscious of its Welshness. Calvinistic Methodism was a Welsh denomination which, by the late nineteenth century, was clearly aware of its national identity. Other denominations, especially the Congregationalists, were also conscious of their standing as Welsh institutions.' In this book, we consider the Nonconformist denominations together, because, as Jones (2004: 198) observes: 'By the middle of the nineteenth century, it was clear that the Nonconformist denominations had much in common. Differences could barely be discerned . . . in their chapels, their ecclesiastical organization, their services or the various societies which were established for their members.' R. M. Jones's work describes how the Nonconformist institutions and communities created a pervasive, long-lasting form of symbolic capital in the form of notions of Welsh culture. The successful venture that this was is not only illustrated by ideas of Welsh culture persisting to the present day, but is clear by contrast with earlier, rather more negative, images of Wales and the Welsh. Jones (1992b) notes that in medieval Britain, the Welsh had usually been portrayed as thieves and barbarians. Giraldus Cambrensis, even though he admired the Welsh, condemned their alleged incest and homosexuality when writing in the twelfth century. Jones maintains that some of this prejudice survived into the nineteenth century – *Blackwood's Magazine* refers to the 'gloomy passion' and 'dull mysticism' of the Welsh (Jones, 1992b: 37). He suggests that the rebellions of workers and Chartists in the 1830s in Wales fuelled such prejudice: 'Wales became associated with both good and evil as the noble savage was supplemented by the threatening industrial savage' (ibid.: 38).

Consistent with this, was, as Jones (1982: 57) described, 'a certain mythologising about the cultural attainments of the quarrymen'. This sense that the quarry workers in rural villages pursued 'the life of the mind' is present in Samuel Smiles's accounts of labourers reading the works of nineteenth-century intellectuals. The theme of these accounts is that the interests of the quarrymen were unexpectedly highbrow and they strove to keep abreast of developments in the sciences and arts. The quarry has been described as 'an important cultural centre where much music was made and innumerable verses were composed' (Jones, 1982: 57). Jones (ibid.) also describes the *caban* (a sort of canteen) in the quarry, as being 'organised for educational, cultural and, at times, agitational activity'.

It was as if the austere world of farm, quarry and chapel could outdo in piety and culture anything mustered by the English. The Anglican Church was an 'alien church' whose strength came from wealthy English patrons (Jones, 1982: 64). It was 'linked with status, power and privilege; its bishops would sit in the House of Lords' (Morgan, 1999: 36). As Jones (1982) notes: 'The [Anglican] church was scorned, its parsons characterised at best as lazy, ignorant and drunken, at worst as tyrants forcing their church and their dogmas on a hard-pressed people'. Contrast this with the frenetic activity and Bible study of the chapel, its Sunday school and huge quantities of transmissible cultural capital in the form of education, song, music and oral prayer. These factors, along with the social activities of the chapel, not only fostered a sense of Welsh culture, but also a sense of something very special, far superior to that on offer in England or from the Anglican Church.

It was against this kind of backdrop on the part of the intellectual elite of Wales that the early lives of our participants unfolded. This is not to say that the work of Saunders Lewis and his associates were everyday reading in the majority of households, but rather that a notion existed of a distinctive Welshness and special quality to the neighbourhoods and countryside. As Isobel Emmett (1964), in her account of a village in north-west Wales, based on fieldwork conducted from 1958–62, says:

> Much of the life was like country life anywhere. But the chapel was woven through it all in a way that gave it distinction . . . that which makes country life meaningful is the talk; and the talk was in Welsh and so the life was peculiarly Welsh . . . They learnt the unique culture in which they lived . . . people learnt to think of their community past and present, in the light of their system of values . . . emphatically 'Welsh' values. (1964: 11)

The late nineteenth century had seen a flourishing of women's involvement in Liberal organizations with nationalist ambitions (Masson, 2003), yet during the period in which we are interested, much of this nationalist sentiment had been redirected into the politics of Welsh nationalism per se, into Plaid Cymru. Much of our period, however, pre-dates the resurgence of the more assertive nationalism and language activism that existed through the 1960s and 1970s, which followed the founding of Cymdeithas yr Iaith Gymraeg (the Welsh Language Society) in 1962.

It is in nationalism that we can also detect some clues as to the lack of overt class antagonism evident both in the documented history of Wales and, despite accounts of hardship, in most of the accounts from our participants. As Adamson (1991) contends, nationalism provides ideological cement to bind classes together in historical blocs, providing common ground for the synthesis and transcendence of particularistic class interests. Consequently, Adamson argues that nationalism had a class-neutral quality, which gave it an appeal to any class, class fraction or combination of classes. It was therefore not necessarily either a bourgeois or proletarian ideology. Whereas in the nineteenth century, the nationalism of Wales was the political practice of rural tenants and the indigenous urban bourgeoisie, by the twentieth century, nationalism had also united parts of the rural middle class and a fraction of the industrial working class.

During the period in which our participants grew up, Wales was undergoing further change, which was in turn being documented by a new generation of social scientists and ethnographers. Continuities with the late nineteenth century were identifiable. Madgwick et al. (1973) reported that three-quarters of their respondents in Cardiganshire engaged in regular religious worship. As Madgwick et al. remark, through the first six or seven decades of the twentieth century religion was a pervasive force. Whilst the Anglican Church in Wales had a large number of nominal adherents, Nonconformists tended to be active, with ministers predominantly Welsh in origin, culture and outlook, most speaking Welsh as their first language. Many had followed non-professional careers prior to taking up the ministry. In the view of Madgwick et al., it was ministers, rather more than schoolteachers, who were the link bringing the culture and politics of urbanized south Wales into rural mid Wales. The use of the Welsh language was one of the most distinctive elements in the culture of countryside and chapel. During the mid twentieth century, religious observance and its associated values were fundamental to this concept of Welsh culture. Anglicization was believed to be associated with what were seen as more disruptive aspects, such as drinking and going to dances. In contrast to the politically engaged and often radical variants of Methodism apparent at the turn of the twentieth century, by that century's middle years, ministers were not usually politically active (Madgwick et al., 1973).

At a local level this unity or solidarity could be perceived, too: 'There is little division between living and working in the lives of most Llan people. Quarrymen, factory workers, road cleaners, farmers, farm-workers, all live and work in a community and their lives form a satisfactory whole' (Emmett, 1964: 53). Indeed, the sense of unity based in geography, language, culture and common work-experiences formed particularly important strands in the self-image and everyday experience of people in our study and those whose experiences contributed to the earlier generation of community studies. Until relatively recently, with the formation of the Welsh Assembly Government and with the activation of policies directed towards more local decision-making, Wales had no independent institutional and political basis for national identity and had created an identity 'evoked overwhelmingly by literary and musical culture, and having as its mainspring the language question' (Nairn, 1977: 208).

This, then, was the situation at the time when many of our participants were growing up. The centrality of chapel and village life was still present – perhaps so much so as to seem mundane and unremarkable to our participants. At the same time, social change, in the form of a reduction in the domains in which Welsh could be used as the language of choice, was going on apace. Yet the erosion of the language was not going unremarked. Intellectuals and activists were reframing the landscape, language and what they saw to be traditions of the nation, infusing them with value, assiduously capitalizing them and talking up their symbolic power. This revalorization of language and history, whilst not specifically marked as a male or female issue in the original manifestos and position papers of the nationalist movement, was, as we shall see, intimately connected with women's concerns. In the family, the schoolroom or the religious congregation and in the spheres of work or village life, women were described by our participants as providing this very cement that held both nationalism and social life itself together.

The image of Wales which was refurbished in the nineteenth century and elaborated upon by Saunders Lewis, Iorwerth Peate and their collaborators in the 1920s and 1930s was not important because it was literally 'true'. The idea of traditions of culture and scholarship, or a common people living as a classless *gwerin*, are powerful because of their role as ideas. Notions of place, history and folk culture came to embody ever-more romantic ideas of nationalism. Urban corruption was opposed by rural purity, and the concept of 'homeland' shifts the understanding of territory from a material to a symbolic role: 'History has nationalized a strip of land, and endowed its most ordinary features with mythical content and hallowed sentiments' (Williams and Smith, 1983: 509).

Towards the end of the twentieth century, scholars were increasingly coming to explore the idea of the nation as being an imaginative discourse just as much as a material reality (for example, Bhabha, 1990; Parker et al., 1992; Samuel, 1989). Benedict Anderson (1991) writes of the nation as an 'imagined community' whose members are bonded by cultural, as much as explicitly political, networks. There is an appreciation of the symbolic attributes of land and landscape and their role in the construction and mobilization of national identity (Gruffudd, 1995: 220).

Particular languages have emblematic roles in the articulation of national identity, and debates about their preservation can thus assume wider symbolic significance. In this way, processes like education and worship become highly charged and politically contentious. It is this process of the reproduction and negotiation of a particular version of Welsh identity through the associated sense of history, culture and what it meant to be a man or woman that has occupied us through much of the present volume. This identity was often fundamentally cultural, in that it located Welshness within the representation of a particular geographical and historical context. Moreover, in many cases it was an identity that was, in an important sense, one which was relational – experienced in relation to space/place, family and community – and one which was practised – through family life, work, worship and community involvement.

The literal truth of the sense of culture may be questioned, but its power lies in the fact that it is a piece of the cultural puzzle – an image of culture and history which aspiring youngsters could carry with them, for example into the world of the university. Perhaps this reflects the 'Thomas Maxim': 'If men [*sic*] define situations as real they are real in their consequences' (Thomas and Thomas, 1928: 572). What is important for understanding culture is that which people think is real, and this should be remembered if the social reality of the Welsh experience is to be grasped.

At the same time, during the period about which our participants were reminiscing, the Welsh language itself was in decline. In Wales as a whole, report Madgwick et al. (1973), Welsh-speakers amounted to 87 per cent of the population in 1931, yet only 26 per cent in 1961. These figures hide the question of fluency, the steeper decline of monoglot Welsh and corresponding rise of monoglot English. The middle years of the twentieth century saw what came to be called 'language erosion' and the emergence of renewed concerns about a corresponding erosion of national identity. Some of these influences were characterized by Williams (1934: 325), who concluded that: 'Modern expansion, new cultural influences made possible by rapid transport, the cinema, the wireless, and the powerful influence of the teachers in the elementary schools since 1870 all enter into the linguistic changes that are taking place in Wales to-day.' As Aitchison and Carter (2000) formulate the issue, the key point was not that the Welsh language was being geographically displaced, but the progressive limitation of the domains in which it was used, and thus a restriction of its status, compared to the high point of its late nineteenth-century renaissance. Welsh flourished in domains such as the home, chapel, literature and in eisteddfodau and agriculture, whereas English was the preferred tongue of polite society. Science, law, administration and government were largely conducted through the medium of English.

In addition to the implications for theories of social, cultural and symbolic capital, it is perhaps valuable to revisit the issue of how this historical study can shed light on contemporary practical policy questions. As we have described elsewhere (Baker and Brown, 2008), the distinctive culture experienced by people growing up in *Y Fro Gymraeg* at this time might well have assisted them in gaining entry to higher education. Equally, the links that people maintained to their original communities and families also meant that access to higher education did not – in its early days at least – necessarily represent a 'brain drain', or cultural depletion of village life. Thus, a measure of continuity was maintained in their citizenship, and as schoolteachers, ministers or other professionals they were locally involved to enrich the lives of subsequent generations.

The question of learning and how it may best be fostered in Wales is of concern to policymakers. In *The Learning Country*, the Welsh National Assembly stated:

> The plain fact is that training and education are equally and intimately related to successful community development, social inclusion, wealth creation and personal fulfillment. There is a close synergy between the measures necessary to sustain learning and creativity, and achieving the benefits of economic growth, community enrichment and a wonderful quality of life for individuals. Innovation in the arts, sciences and technology stimulates, and is promoted by, a vigorous learning country. (National Assembly for Wales, 2001: 7)

To policymakers, then, a well-trained nation is a well-educated nation and one filled with fulfilled and well-renumerated employees. The document goes on to point to the way in which Wales lags behind the rest of the UK, in terms of the proportion of its population gaining qualifications, the rate of economic activity and in terms of wage levels. Whilst detailing a number of actual and proposed educational projects and policies, it is as if *The Learning Country* document, like the Blue Books over a century and a half earlier, is haunted by a notion of Wales as a nation in deficit which has a good deal of catching up to do in order to match its better-qualified and better-paid cohorts in England. Moreover, there is portentous talk of the dangers of a 'culture of low skills, low qualifications, low creativity, low expectation, and low enterprise' (National Assembly for Wales, 2001: 7), which is lacking in competitiveness and which, if allowed to proceed unchecked, will fail against the more flexible, enterprising economies of Europe.

Yet, as we have suggested, within living memory, there was a good deal going on in rural Wales which seemed to be eminently well suited to the Welsh Assembly Government's purposes. The desire for education, the social and cultural activities and the strong networks of social bonds appear very much in line with what *The Learning Country* seeks to generate, yet which appear far less in evidence in the policies of the devolved government, now that this has been adopted as a matter to be managed through the implementation of learning policy.

Within living memory then, life in *Y Fro Gymraeg* was strongly, yet locally and organically, 'capitalized'. We have suggested that the activities, practices, customs, knowledge and social fabric of villages in *Y Fro Gymraeg* could be seen in terms of Bourdieu's notions of social capital, cultural capital and symbolic capital. If capital involves 'what people find valuable and adjudge as valuable', then it is apparent that this includes a great deal of the piety, knowledge, prayer, frugality and respectability that participants remember.

The symbolic capital attained was also, to a large extent, derived from cultural capital, especially as it involved knowledge and the much vaunted 'love of learning'. This was also derived from social capital, as it was intimately bound up with social networks that enabled the organization of competitions and eisteddfodau, chapels and their congregations, informal help and support for relatives and neighbours, and much more. The communities that people described growing up in were ones which in general had a relatively legible structure of status, prestige and respectability, as well as small but significant differences in wealth. The predictability of this social structure perhaps lends itself also to a somewhat different concept of social capital, from Robert Putnam (2000), where trust is a key element. People's conduct was in an important sense predictable. This, then, represents an organic, practice-based, bottom-up kind of social capital, rather than one which is imposed from the Welsh Assembly Government downwards.

Our participants' accounts therefore speak to some fundamental debates about the relation between policy and community. There are difficult questions here as to how far learning and social networks can be rekindled through Welsh Assembly Government policy or legislation. Perhaps the best route for policy and the encouragement of education lies in further study of the culture itself. If policy is developed from the aspirations of local people and in so doing builds upon the commitments and social networks of communities, it is likely to be perceived as meaningful and valuable rather than distant and didactic. Oral histories have a role to play in informing contemporary policies. Even if parts of those histories are self-mythologized, they are valuable because they reflect how groups of people see themselves and enact their shared identities in the present.

The reminiscences of our participants chiefly cover the years from the 1940s to the early 1970s, yet their reminiscences and the people about whom they spoke represent a much longer tradition. When they were young, the older generation, such as people of their parents' and grandparents' cohort, would very likely have been born in the nineteenth century. Whilst contemporary historians point to the relatively recent nineteenth-century cultural revolution in Wales, to people in the present study village life and the values found there would appear to have a timeless, commonsensical quality which is difficult nowadays to appreciate. The love of learning and the sense that educational activities represented a sociospatial niche for them appears to have been important in undergirding the subsequent achievement of educational qualifications in many cases.

This intimation about the relationship between the *buchedd* or habitus of participants and that of educational institutions was strengthened as the study progressed. Our participants' stories were striking in that they revealed none of the sense of alienation often reported by present-day students from disadvantaged backgrounds who attempt university courses. Poverty and oppression were remembered, but those participants who had attended university felt strongly it was their right to gain an education and that they owed this to other family members who had forgone opportunities in the past.

There is evidence within the narratives that the idea of going to university was not just a whim, or even an aspiration, for these respondents. These participants had a very embedded educational aspiration, many remembering having been encouraged toward educational achievement from a very young age, hence our use of the term 'aspirational habitus', rather than simply 'aspiration'. Their habitus seemed to have enabled them to feel that they had a right to a university education and to feel comfortable in the university environment, despite being aware that their social backgrounds were very different from those of their peers at university.

Participants' habitus also seemed to have a transformative aspect, reminiscent of Richards's sense (2005) of 'advancement' and 'investment' in the self by gaining an education. This facilitated their movement into the middle classes after university, as they adopted new professions and lifestyles, yet enabled them to retain continuity with their 'core'. These narratives detailing embedded attitudes towards education revealed much regarding the ability of many of our participants to climb out of disadvantage. It is such a disposition that may need to be cultivated within present-day disadvantaged groups if social change is to result, rather than simplistic 'add-on' initiatives which do nothing to challenge deeply held beliefs, let alone assist in the reconstruction of habitus.

The process of the conversion that Bourdieu proposed between the forms of capital has been given a new and interesting cast by that which we found in this investigation. As we have noted, no matter how diligently people accumulated cultural capital, it was difficult for this to be converted into economic capital because the economy was dominated by subsistence-level employment. Even people who had their own farms or smallholdings, and who might be thought of as having some degree of material capital, were not readily able to live more affluent lives. The need to continually reinvest in the business could leave them and their families worse off than many of their fellows. To some, of course, with the addition of a university degree, the value of cultural capital could be understood in relation to advancement in the labour market. The value of cultural capital may also have been more diffuse, in that it contributed to an accumulated sense of prestige and cultural value. For Bourdieu, educational qualifications represent the 'certificate of cultural competence which confers on its holder a conventional, constant, legally guaranteed value with respect to power' (1986b: 248).

Because of the difficulty of turning the social and symbolic capitals into material assets, a rather different symbolic economy seems to have evolved in *Y Fro Gymraeg*, where material hardship existed hand in hand with cultural enrichment. It is this damming-up of the social, cultural and symbolic capitals which is crucial in creating this sense of yearning for educational achievement, for some sort of outlet for the desire for education. The puzzle for educators, policy-makers and those seeking to sustain 'Welsh culture' is how this can be encouraged to sustain a genuinely learning country, rather than one which is doomed to be the poor relation, forever trying to catch up with the land east of Offa's Dyke.

> If you want to build a ship, don't drum up the men to gather wood, divide the work and give orders. Instead, teach them to yearn for the vast and endless sea. (Antoine de Saint-Exupéry (1900–44), *The Wisdom of the Sands*)

Appendix:
Table Outlining Participants' Details

CB

Participant's name	Gender	Age (at time of interview)	Occupation	Area of residence whilst growing up	Parent's occupation
Gwen	Female	52	University lecturer	Mid Wales	Shopkeeper; teacher
Euros	Male	82	Retired university lecturer	West Wales	Nonconformist minister; Housewife
Lowri	Female	84	Retired university lecturer	North-east Wales	Nonconformist minister; housewife
Geraint	Male	63	Retired senior academic	North-east Wales	Butcher; housewife
Cadi	Female	80	Retired farmer	North-west Wales	Farmer; housewife
Arsula	Female	79	Retired factory worker	North-west Wales	(Father died when Arsula was young); mother's work unknown
Dewi	Male	60	Factory worker	North-west Wales	(No permanent father); cook
Dafydd	Male	62	Retired teacher	North-west Wales	Farmer; housewife
Lloyd	Male	54	University lecturer	North-east Wales	Farmer; housewife
Eryl	Male	51	Pharmacist	North-west Wales	Plasterer; housewife
Meinwen	Female	80	Retired teacher	North-west Wales	Quarryman; teacher
Angharad	Female	61	Housewife	North-east Wales	Farmer; housewife

Participant's name	Gender	Age (at time of interview)	Occupation	Area of residence whilst growing up	Parent's occupation
Ceinwen	Female	53	University researcher	West Wales	Miner; teacher
Eirlys	Female	60	Cleaner	North-west Wales	Quarryman; housewife
Alwena	Female	59	Retired primary headteacher	North-west Wales	(Father died when Alwena was young); Domestic servant
Nona	Female	62	Magistrate/ housewife	North-west Wales	Doctor; housewife
Elsi	Female	63	Retired teacher	North-east Wales	Farmer; housewife
Gwerfyl	Female	59	Teacher	North-west Wales	Market gardener; housewife
Eunice	Female	54	Teacher	North-west Wales	(Father was Nonconformist minister who died when Eunice was young); housewife
Eifion	Male	61	Retired university lecturer	North-west Wales	Farmer; teacher
Arwel	Male	56	University senior manager	North-west Wales	Publicans (tenants)
Gwenda	Female	61	Retired university administrator	North-west Wales	Manager; housewife
Harri	Male	64	Retired university lecturer	North-west Wales	Publicans (tenants)
Mabon	Male	53	Solicitor	North-west Wales	Mother widowed when Mabon was young – financially supported by family
Erin	Female	53	Farmer; carer	North-west Wales	Farmer; housewife

Note: These are not the only participants that the authors interviewed, but the above interviewees provided the narratives from which we quote directly in this book. Other participants' narratives were also utilized, in that consistent themes and images emerged, enabling us to gain a picture of participants' notions of life in rural Wales in the mid twentieth century.

Bibliography

CR

Aaron, J. A., Betts, S., Rees, T. and Vincentelli, M. (eds) (1994). *Our Sister's Land: The Changing Identities of Women in Wales* (Cardiff, University of Wales Press).

Abrahams, R. (1983). *Men-of-Words in the West Indies: Performance and the Emergence of Creole Culture* (Baltimore, Johns Hopkins University Press).

Acker, S. and Dillabough, J. (2007). 'Women "learning to labour" in the "male emporium": exploring gendered work in teacher education', *Gender and Education*, 19, 3, 297–316.

Adam, F. and Rončević, B. (2003). 'Social capital: recent debates and research trends', *Social Science Information*, 42, 2, 155–83.

Adamson, D. L. (1991). *Class, Ideology and the Nation; A Theory of Welsh Nationalism* (Cardiff, University of Wales Press).

Aitchison, J. and Carter, H. (2000). *Language, Economy and Society* (Cardiff, University of Wales Press).

Allan, A. J. (2009). 'The importance of being a "lady": hyper-femininity and heterosexuality in the private, single-sex primary school', *Gender and Education*, 21, 2, 145–58.

Anderson, B. (1991). *Imagined Communities: Reflections on the Origin and Spread of Nationalism* (London, Verso).

Anderson, M. C. (2004). 'Negotiating patriarchy and power: women in Christian churches', *Journal of Women's History*, 16, 3, 187–96.

Archer, L. and Hutchings, M. (2000). 'Bettering yourself? Discourses of risk, cost and benefit in ethnically diverse, young, working-class non-participants' constructions of higher education', *British Journal of Sociology of Education*, 21, 4, 555–74.

Archer, M. S. (2007). *Making Our Way Through the World: Human Reflexivity and Social Mobility* (New York, Cambridge University Press).

Arnot, M., David, M. and Weiner, G. (1999). *Closing the Gender Gap: Postwar Education and Social Change* (Cambridge, Polity Press).

Ashby, A. W. (1944). 'The peasant agriculture of Wales', *Welsh Review*, 3, 3, 206–11.

Atkinson, P. and Silverman, D. (1997). 'Kundera's immortality: the interview society and the invention of the self', *Qualitative Inquiry*, 3, 304–25.

Baker, S. and Brown, B. J. (2008). 'Habitus and homeland: educational aspirations, family life and culture in autobiographical narratives of educational experience in rural Wales', *Sociologia Ruralis*, 28, 1, 57–72.

Baker, S. and Brown, B. J. (2009). 'Harbingers of feminism?: gender, cultural capital and education in mid-twentieth century rural Wales', *Gender and Education*, 21, 1, 63–79.

Baker, S., Brown, B. J. and Fazey, J. A. (2006). 'Individualisation in the widening participation debate', *London Review of Education*, 4, 2, 169–82.

Bamber, J. and Tett, L. (2001). 'Ensuring integrative learning experiences for non-traditional students in higher education', *Widening Participation and Lifelong Learning*, 3, 1, 8–16.

Bankston, C. L., III and Zhou, M. (2002). 'Social capital as process: the meaning and problems of a theoretical metaphor', *Sociological Inquiry*, 72, 2, 285–317.

Barth, F. (ed.) (1969). *Ethnic Groups and Boundaries: The Social Organization of Cultural Difference* (London, Allen and Unwin).

BBC (2008). *Wales: History – the Blue Books, http://www.bbc.co.uk/wales/history/sites/women/pages/blue_books.shtml* (accessed 28/06/2008).

Beddoe, D. (1986). 'Images of Welsh women', in T. Curtis (ed.), *Wales: The Imagined Nation, Studies in Cultural and National Identity* (Bridgend, Poetry Wales Press).

Beddoe, D. (2000). *Out of the Shadows: A History of Women in Twentieth-Century Wales* (Cardiff, University of Wales Press).

Beddoe, D. (2003). *Changing Times: Welsh Women Writing on the 1950s and 1960s* (Aberystwyth, Honno).

Bernstein, B. (1975). *Class Codes and Control* (London, Routledge and Kegan Paul).

Betts, S. (1996). *Our Daughters' Land: Past and Present* (Cardiff, University of Wales Press).

Bhabha, H. K. (1990). *Nation and Narration* (London, Routledge).

Bingham, W. V. D. and Moore, B. V. (1924). *How to Interview* (New York, Harper and Row).

Blumer, H. (1969). 'The methodological position of symbolic interactionism', in *Symbolic Interactionism. Perspective and Method* (Englewood Cliffs, N. J., Prentice-Hall).

Borofsky, R. (1987). *Making History. Pukapukan and Anthropological Construction of Knowledge* (Cambridge, Cambridge University Press).

Bourdieu, P. (1977). *Outline of a Theory of Practice* (Cambridge, Cambridge University Press).

Bourdieu, P. (1980). 'Le capital social', *Actes de la Recherche en Sciences Sociales*, 31, 2–3.

Bourdieu, P. (1984). *Distinction: A Social Critique of the Judgement of Taste* (Cambridge, MA, Harvard University Press).

Bourdieu, P. (1985a). 'The genesis of the concepts of habitus and of field', *Sociocriticism*, 2, 11–14.

Bourdieu, P. (1985b). 'The social space and the genesis of groups', *Social Science Information*, 24, 2, 195–220.

Bourdieu, P. (1986a). 'L'illusion biographique', *Actes de la Recherché en Sciences Sociales*, 62–63, 69–72.

Bourdieu, P. (1986b). 'The forms of capital', in J. G. Richardson (ed.), *Handbook of Theory and Research for the Sociology of Education* (New York, Greenwood Press).

Bourdieu, P. (1986c). 'Social space and symbolic power', in *In Other Words: Essays Toward a Reflexive Sociology* (Stanford, CA, Stanford University Press).

Bourdieu, P. (1987a). *In Other Words: Essays Towards a Reflexive Sociology* (Stanford, CA, Stanford University Press).

Bourdieu, P. (1987b). 'What makes a social class? On the theoretical and practical existence of groups', *Berkeley Journal of Sociology*, 32, 1–18.

Bourdieu, P. (1988). *Homo Academicus* (Cambridge, Polity Press).

Bourdieu, P. (1990a). *In Other Words: Essays Towards a Reflexive Sociology* (Cambridge, Polity Press).

Bourdieu, P. (1990b). *The Logic of Practice* (Stanford, CA, Stanford University Press).

Bourdieu, P. (1990c). 'La domination masculine', *Actes de la Recherché en Sciences Sociales*, 84, 2–31.

Bourdieu, P. (1991a). *Language and Symbolic Power* (Oxford, Polity Press).

Bourdieu, P. (1991b). 'Genesis and structure of the religious field', *Comparative Social Research*, 13, 1–44.

Bourdieu, P. (1993). *Social Sense* (Frankfurt, Suhrkamp).

Bourdieu, P. (1996). *The Rules of Art: Genesis and Structure of the Literary Field* (Stanford, CA, Stanford University Press).

Bourdieu, P. (1997). 'The forms of capital', in A. H. Halsey (ed.), *Education: Culture, Economy, Society* (Oxford, Oxford University Press).

Bourdieu, P. (1998). *Practical Reason* (Berkeley, CA., Stanford University Press).

Bourdieu, P. (1999). 'Scattered remarks', *European Journal of Social Theory*, 2, 334–40.

Bourdieu, P. (2001). *Masculine Domination* (Stanford, CA, Stanford University Press).

Bourdieu, P. (2005). 'Habitus', in J. Hillier and E. Rooksby (eds), *Habitus: A Sense of Place* (Aldershot, Ashgate).

Bourdieu, P. (2008). *The Bachelors' Ball: The Crisis of Peasant Society in Béarne* (Chicago, University of Chicago Press).

Bourdieu, P. and Boltanski, L. (1978). 'Changes in social structure and changes in the demand for education', in S. Giner and M. Archer (eds), *Contemporary Europe: Social Structure and Cultural Patterns* (London, Routledge and Kegan Paul).

Bourdieu, P. and Boltanski, L. (1981). 'The educational system and the economy: titles and jobs', in C. Lemert (ed.), *French Sociology: Rupture and Renewal Since 1968* (New York, Columbia University Press).

Bourdieu, P. and Johnson, R. (1993). *The Field of Cultural Production: Essays on Art and Literature* (New York, Columbia University Press).

Bourdieu, P. and Passeron, J.-C. (1977). *Reproduction in Education, Society and Culture* (London and Beverley Hills, Sage Production).

Bourdieu, P. and Wacquant, L. J. D. (1992). *An Invitation to Reflexive Sociology* (Cambridge, UK, Polity Press).

Bourdieu, P., Passeron, J.-C. and Saint-Martin, M. (1994). *Academic Discourse* (Polity Press, Cambridge).

Bowl, M. (2003). *Non-traditional Entrants to Higher Education: 'They Talk About People Like Me'* (Stoke-on-Trent, Trentham Books).

Brockmeier, J. (2000). 'Autobiographical time', *Narrative Inquiry*, 10, 1, 51–73.

Bruce, S. (1995). 'A Novel Reading on Nineteenth-Century Wales: A Reply to Stark, Finke and Iannaccone', *Journal for Scientific Study of Religion*, 34, 520–2.

Carter, P. L. (2006). 'Straddling boundaries: identity, culture, and school', *Sociology of Education*, 79, 304–28.

Chamberlayne, P., Bornat, J. and Wengraf, T. (eds) (2000). *The Turn to Biographical Methods in Social Science: Comparative Issues and Examples* (London, Routledge).

Chambers, P. and Thompson, A. (2005). 'Public religion and political change in Wales', *Sociology*, 39, 1, 29–46.

Chambers, P. (2004). 'The effects of evangelical renewal on mainstream congregational identities: a Welsh case study', in M. Guest, K. Tusting and L. Woodhead (eds), *Congregational Studies in the UK: Christianity in a Post-Christian Context* (Aldershot, Ashgate).

Chaney, P., Mackay, F. and McAllister, L. (2007). *Women, Politics and Constitutional Change* (Cardiff, University of Wales Press).

Charles, N. and Hughes-Freeland, F. (1995). *Practicing Feminism* (London, Routledge).

Cohee, G. E., Daumer, E., Kemp, T. D., Krebs, P. M., Lafky, S. A. and Runzo, S. (1998). *The Feminist Teacher Anthology: Pedagogies and Classroom Strategies* (New York, Teachers College Press).

Collins, P. Y., von Unger, H. and Armbrister, A. (2008). 'Church ladies, good girls, and locas: stigma and the intersection of gender, ethnicity, mental illness, and sexuality in relation to HIV risk', *Social Science & Medicine*, 67, 389–97.

Collis, M. (1999). 'Marital conflict and men's leisure: how women negotiate male power in a small mining community', *Journal of Sociology*, 35, 60–76.

Commissioners of Inquiry into the State of Education in Wales (1847). *Reports of the Commissioners of Inquiry into the State of Education in Wales: Part 1, Carmarthen, Glamorgan and Pembroke* (London, Her Majesty's Stationery Office).

Conran, T. (1997). *Frontiers in Anglo Welsh Poetry* (Cardiff, University of Wales Press).

Cook, K. and Evans, N. (1991). 'The petty bell ringing of the boisterous band: the women's suffrage movement in Wales', in A. V. John (ed.), *Our Mothers' Land: Chapters in Welsh Women's History 1830–1939* (Cardiff, University of Wales Press).

Croll, A. (2003). 'Holding onto history: modern Welsh historians and the challenge of postmodernism', *Journal of Contemporary History*, 38, 2, 323–32.

Crook, T. (2006). 'Schools for the moral training of the people': public baths, liberalism and the promotion of cleanliness in Victorian Britain', *European Review of History*, 13, 1, 21–47.

Crossley, M. L. (2000). 'Narrative psychology, trauma and the study of self/identity', *Theory and Psychology*, 10, 527–46.

Davies, C. Aull (1994). 'Women, nationalism and feminism', in J. A. Aaron, S. Betts, T. Rees and M. Vincentelli (eds), *Our Sister's Land: The Changing Identities of Women in Wales* (Cardiff, University of Wales Press).

Davies, E. R. and Rees, A. D. (eds) (1960). *Welsh Rural Communities* (Cardiff, University of Wales Press).

Davies, J. (1994). *A History of Wales* (Harmondsworth, Penguin).

Day, G. and Fitton, M. (1975). 'Religion and social status in rural Wales: "buchedd" and its lessons for concepts of stratification in community studies', *Sociological Review*, 23, 867–91.

DeGarmo, D. S., Forgatch, M. S. and Martinez, C. R. (1999). 'Parenting of divorced mothers as a link between social status and boys' academic outcomes: unpacking the effects of socioeconomic status', *Child Development*, 70, 5, 1231–45.

Di Stefano, G. and Pinelli, A. (2004). 'Demographic characteristics and family life', *Current Sociology*, 52, 3, 339–69.

Dillon, M. (1999). 'The authority of the Holy revisited: Habermas, religion, and emancipatory possibilities', *Sociological Theory*, 17, 3, 290–306.

Dillon, M. (2001). 'Pierre Bourdieu, religion, and cultural production', *Cultural Studies, Critical Methodologies*, 1, 4, 411–29.

Douglas, M. (1966). *Purity and Danger: An Analysis of Concepts of Pollution and Taboo* (London, Routledge and Kegan Paul).

Douglas, M. (1986). *How Institutions Think* (Syracuse, NY, Syracuse University Press).

Dreyfus, H. and Rabinow, P. (1993). 'Can there be a science of existential structure and social meaning?', in C. Calhoun, E. LiPuma and M. Postone (eds) *Bourdieu: Critical Perspectives* (Cambridge, Polity Press).

Dumais, S. (2002). 'Cultural capital, gender, and school success: the role of habitus', *Sociology of Education*, 75, 1, 44–68.

Dyhouse, C. (1995). *No Distinction of Sex? Women in British Universities, 1870–1939* (London, UCL Press).

Dyhouse, C. (2002). 'Graduates, mothers and graduate mothers: family investment in higher education in twentieth-century England', *Gender and Education*, 14, 4, 325–36.

Eagleton, M. (2005). 'Nice work? Representations of the intellectual woman worker', *Women's History Review*, 14, 2, 203–22.

Egan, D. (1988). *Coal Society: History of the South Wales Mining Valleys, 1840–1980* (Llandysul, Ceredigion, Gomer).

Emmett, I. (1964). *A North Wales Village: A Social Anthropological Study* (London, Routledge and Kegan Paul).

Equal Opportunities Commission Wales (2005). *Changing Wales* (Cardiff, Equal Opportunities Commission Wales).

Foucault, M. (1975). *Discipline and Punish: The Birth of the Prison* (New York, Random House).

Francis, B. (2000). *Boys, Girls, and Achievement: Addressing the Classroom Issues* (London, Routledge Falmer).

Frankenberg, R. (1957). *Village on the Border: A Social Study of Religion, Politics and Football in a North Wales Community* (London, Cohen and West).

Freud, S. (1930). *Civilization and its Discontents* (London, Hogarth Press).

Friedman, J. (1992). 'The past in the future: history and the politics of identity', *American Anthropologist*, 94, 4, 837–59.

Ganzeboom, H. (1982). 'Explaining differential participation in high-cultural activities – a confrontation of information-processing and status-seeking theories', in W. Raub (ed.), *Theoretical Models and Empirical Analyses: Contributions to the Explanation of Individual Actions and Collective Phenomena* (Utrecht, E.S. Publications).

Gergen, Mary M. and Gergen, Kenneth J. (1984). 'The social construction of narrative accounts', in K. J. Gergen and M. M. Gergen (eds), *Historical Social Psychology* (Lawrence Erlbaum Associates, London).

Ginswick, J. (1983). *Labour and the Poor in England and Wales, Volume 3: South Wales – North Wales* (London, Frank Cass Publishers).

Goffman, E. (1959). *The Presentation of Self in Everyday Life* (New York, Doubleday).

Gruffudd, P. (1995). 'Remaking Wales: nation-building and the geographical imagination, 1925–50', *Political Geography*, 14, 3, 219–39.

Gruffudd, P. (1999). 'Prospects of Wales: contested geographical imaginations', in R. Fevre, and A. Thompson (eds), *Nation, Identity and Social Theory: Perspectives from Wales* (Cardiff, University of Wales Press).

Guano E. (2007). 'Respectable ladies and uncouth men: the performative politics of class and gender in the public realm of an Italian city', *Journal of American Folklore*, 120, 475, 48–72.

Guest, R. and John, A. V. (1989). *Lady Charlotte: A Biography of the 19th Century* (London, George Weidenfeld and Nicholson).

Hague, G. and Wilson, C. (2000). 'The silenced pain, domestic violence 1945–1970', *Journal of Gender Studies*, 9, 2, 157–69.

Herbert, T. and Jones, G. E. (1995). *Post-War Wales* (Cardiff, University of Wales Press).

Hirsch, P. and Hilton, M. (2000). *Practical Visionaries: Women, Education and Social Progress 1790–1930* (London, Longman).

Hobsbawm, E. and Ranger, T. (eds) (1983). *The Invention of Tradition* (Cambridge, Cambridge University Press).

Hoffman, L. and Coffey, B. (2008). 'Dignity and indignation: how people experiencing homelessness view services and providers', *The Social Science Journal*, 45, 207–22.

Howell, D.W. (2003). *Taking Stock: The Centenary History of the Royal Welsh Agricultural Society* (Cardiff, University of Wales Press).

Howell, D.W. and Baber, C. (1993). 'Wales', in F. M. L. Thomson (ed.), *The Cambridge Social History of Britain* (Cambridge, Cambridge University Press).

Hughes, D. O. and Trautmann, T. R. (eds) (1995). *Time. Histories and Ethnologies* (Ann Arbor, University of Michigan Press).

Hutchings, M. and Archer, L. (2001). '"Higher than Einstein": constructions of going to university among working-class non-participants', *Research Papers in Education*, 16, 1, 69–91.

Iannaccone, L. (1990). 'Religious participation: a human capital approach', *Journal for the Social Scientific Study of Religion*, 29, 3, 297–314.

Iannaccone, L. (1994). 'Why strict churches are strong', *American Journal of Sociology*, 99, 5, 1180–211.

Jackson, B. and Marsden, D. (1962). *Education and the Working Class* (London, Routledge and Kegan Paul).

Jacobs, A. (2007). 'Examinations as cultural capital for the Victorian schoolgirl: "thinking" with Bourdieu', *Women's History Review*, 16, 2, 245–61.

James, W. and Allen, N. J. (1998). *Marcel Mauss: A Centenary Tribute* (New York, Berghahn Books).

Jenkins, D. (1960). 'Aber-Porth. A study of a coastal village in south Cardiganshire', in E. Davies and A. D. Rees (eds), *Welsh Rural Communities* (Cardiff, University of Wales Press).

John, A. V. (ed.) (1991). *Our Mothers' Land: Chapters in Welsh Women's History, 1830–1939* (Cardiff, University of Wales Press).

Jones, D. C. (2004). *A Glorious Work in the World. Welsh Methodism and the International Evangelical Revival, 1735–1750* (Cardiff, University of Wales Press).

Jones, D. G. (1973). 'His politics', in A. R. Jones and G. Thomas (eds), *Presenting Saunders Lewis* (Cardiff, University of Wales Press).

Jones, E. (1960). 'Tregaron. The sociology of a small market town in central Cardiganshire', in E. Davies and A. D. Rees (eds), *Welsh Rural Communities* (Cardiff, University of Wales Press).

Jones, G. E. (1997). *The Education of a Nation* (Cardiff, University of Wales Press).

Jones, G. E. and Roderick, G. W. (2003). *A History of Education in Wales* (Cardiff, University of Wales Press).

Jones, R. and Fowler, C. (2007). 'Where is Wales? Narrating the territories and borders of the Welsh linguistic nation', *Regional Studies*, 41, 1, 89–101.

Jones, R. M. (1982). *The North Wales Quarrymen 1874–1922* (Cardiff, University of Wales Press).

Jones, R. M. (1992a). 'Beyond identity? The reconstruction of the Welsh', *Journal of British Studies*, 31, 4, 330–57.

Jones, R. M. (1992b). 'Wales and the English imagination from the 18th to the 20th centuries', in *Gulliver 31: Britische Regionen Oder: Wie Einheitlich ist das Königreich? German English Yearbook, Band*, 31, 34–41.

Jones, R. T. (2004). *Congregationalism in Wales* (Cardiff, University of Wales Press).

Kelsall, R. K., Poole, A., and Kuhn, A. (eds) (1972). *Graduates: The Sociology of an Elite* (London, Methuen).

Labov, W. (1973). *Language in the Inner City: Studies in the Black English Vernacular* (Philadelphia, University of Pennsylvania Press).

Lasch, C. (1975). *Haven in a Heartless World: The Family Besieged* (New York, Basic Books).

Lewis, S. (1936). 'The case for Welsh nationalism', *The Listener*, 13 May 1936, 915–16.

Linde, C. (1997). 'Narrative: experience, memory, folklore', *Journal of Narrative and Life History*, 7, 1–4, 281–89.

Lindsay, J. (1974). *A History of the North Wales Slate Industry* (Newton Abbott, David and Charles).

Llewellyn, R. (1939). *How Green Was My Valley* (London, Michael Joseph).

Lovell, T. (2004). 'Bourdieu, class and gender: "the return of the living dead"', *Sociological Review*, 52, S2, 35–56.

MacAdams, D. P. and Janis, L. (2004). 'Narrative identity and narrative therapy', in L. E. Angus and J. McLeod (eds), *The Handbook of Narrative and Psychotherapy* (London, Sage).

McCall, M. M. (2001). 'Three stories of loss and return', *Cultural Studies–Critical Methodologies,* 1, 1, 50–61.

McCrone, D. (2005). 'Cultural capital in an understated nation: the case of Scotland', *British Journal of Sociology*, 56, 1, 65–82.

McDonough, P. (1996). *Choosing Colleges: How Social Class and Schools Structure Opportunity* (New York, State University of New York Press).

McLeod, J. (2005). 'Feminists re-reading Bourdieu: old debates and new questions about gender, habitus and gender change', *Theory and Research in Education*, 3, 1, 11–30.

Madgwick, P. J., Griffiths, N. and Walker, V. (1973). *The Politics of Rural Wales* (London, Hutchinson).

Manning, H. P. (2002). 'English money and Welsh rocks: divisions of language and divisions of labor in nineteenth-century, Welsh slate quarries', *Comparative Studies in Society and History*, 44, 3, 481–510.

Manning, H. P. (2004). 'The streets of Bethesda: the slate quarrier and the Welsh language in the Welsh Liberal imagination', *Language in Society*, 33, 4, 517–48.

Martin, J. and Goodman, J. (2004). *Women and Education, 1800–1980* (Basingstoke, Palgrave Macmillan).

Masson, U. (2003). 'Hand in hand with the women, forward we will go: Welsh nationalism and feminism in the 1890s', *Women's History Review*, 12, 3, 357–86.

Merleau-Ponty, M. (1945). *Phénoménologie de la Perception* (Paris, Gallimard).

Merton, R. K., Coleman, J. S and Rossi, P. H. (eds) (1979). *Qualitative and Quantitative Social Research* (London, Collier Macmillan).

Middleton, S. (1987). 'Schooling and radicalisation: life histories of New Zealand feminist teachers', *British Journal of Sociology of Education*, 8, 2, 169–89.

Miles, A. (1999). *Social Mobility in Nineteenth and Early Twentieth Century England* (Basingstoke, Macmillan).

Moi, T. (1991).'Appropriating Bourdieu: feminist theory and Pierre Bourdieu's sociology of culture', *New Literary History*, 22, 1017–49.

Morgan, D. (1999). *The Span of the Cross* (Cardiff, University of Wales Press).

Morgan, D. L. (1991). *Kate Roberts* (Cardiff, University of Wales Press).

Morgan, K. O. (1981). *Rebirth of a Nation. Wales 1880–1980* (Oxford, Clarendon Press/University of Wales Press).

Morgan, K. O. (1982). *Rebirth of a Nation: A History of Modern Wales* (Oxford Paperbacks Ltd.).

Morgan, P. (1983). 'From a death to a view: the hunt for the Welsh past in the romantic period', in E. Hobsbawm and T. Ranger (eds), *The Invention of Tradition* (Cambridge, Cambridge University Press).

Morgan, P. (1986a). 'The gwerin of Wales: myth and reality', in I. Hume and W. T. R. Pryce (eds), *The Welsh and Their Country: Select Readings in the Social Sciences* (Llandysul, Gwasg Gomer).

Morgan, P. (1986b). 'Keeping the legends alive', in T. Curtis (ed.), *Wales the Imagined Nation: Studies in Cultural and National Identity* (Bridgend, Poetry Wales Press).

Muldowney, M. (2008). 'We were conscious of the sort of people we mixed with': the state, social attitudes and the family in mid-twentieth-century Ireland', *The History of the Family*, 13, 4, 402–15.

Nairn T. (1977). The *Break Up of Britain* (London, New Left Books).

Nash, R. (2005). 'The cognitive *habitus*: its place in a realist account of inequality/difference', *British Journal of Sociology of Education*, 26, 5, 599–612.

National Assembly for Wales (2001). *The Learning Country: A Paving Document* (Cardiff, National Assembly for Wales).

Oram, A. (1989).'A master should not serve under a mistress: women and men teachers 1900–1970', in S. Acker (ed.), *Teachers, Gender and Careers* (London, Routledge).

Orr, J. E. (1975). *The Flaming Tongue: 1900* (Chicago, Moody).

Owen, T. M. (1960). 'Chapel and community in Glan-llyn, Merioneth', in E. Davies and A. D. Rees (eds), *Welsh Rural Communities* (Cardiff, University of Wales Press).

Parker, A., Russo, M., Sommer, D. and Yaeger, P. (1992). *Nationalisms and Sexualities* (London, Routledge).

Peate, I. C. (1926).'Y genedl ac awdurdod', *Y Ddraig Goch*, 1, 2, 4.

Peel, J. D.Y. (1984). 'Making history: the past in the Ijesha present', *Man*, 19, 111–32.

Peristiany, J. G. (1974). *Honour and Shame: The Values of Mediterranean Society* (Chicago, University of Chicago Press).

Philips, R. and Harper-Jones, G. (2002). 'From Ruskin to the learning country: education policy, the state and educational politics in England and/or Wales, 1976–2001', *Educational Review*, 54, 3, 297–305.

Piette, B. (1997). 'Identity and language: the example of Welsh women', *Feminism and Psychology*, 7, 129–37.

Plowman, D. E. G., Minchinton, W. E. and Stacey, M. (1961). 'Local social status in England and Wales', *Sociological Review*, 10, 161–202.

Plummer, K. (2001). *Documents of Life: An Invitation to Critical Humanism* (London, Sage).

Pope, R. (1998). *Building Jerusalem. Nonconformity, Labour and the Social Question in Wales, 1906–1939* (Cardiff, University of Wales Press).

Popular Memory Group (1982). 'Popular memory: theory, politics, method', in R. Johnson, G. McLennan, B. Schwarz, and D. Sutton (eds), *Making Histories. Studies in History-writing and Politics* (London, Hutchinson).

Price, L. and Evans, N. (2006). 'From "as good as gold" to "gold diggers"': farming women and the survival of British family farming', *Sociologia Ruralis*, 46, 4, 280–98.

Price, L. and Evans, N. (2009). 'From stress to distress: conceptualizing the British family farming patriarchal way of life', *Journal of Rural Studies*, 25, 1–11.

Probyn, E. (2004). 'Shame in the habitus', *The Sociological Review*, 52, S2, 224–48.

Proudman, M. F. (2005). '"The stupid party": intellectual repute as a category of ideological analysis', *Journal of Political Ideologies*, 10, 199–217.

Putnam, R. (2000). *Bowling Alone: The Collapse and Revival of American Community* (New York, Simon and Schuster).

Reay, D. (1998). '"Always knowing" and "never being sure": institutional and familial habituses and higher education choice', *Journal of Education Policy*, 13, 4, 519–29.

Reay, D. (2000). 'A useful extension of Bourdieu's conceptual framework: emotional capital as a way of understanding mothers' involvement in their children's education?', *Sociological Review*, 48, 4, 568–85.

Reay, D. (2004a). '"It's all becoming a habitus": beyond the habitual use of habitus in educational research', *British Journal of Sociology of Education*, 25, 4, 431–44.

Reay, D. (2004b). 'Education and cultural capital: the implications of changing trends in education policies', *Cultural Trends*, 13, 2, 73–86.

Reay, D. (2004c). 'Gendering Bourdieu's concepts of capitals? Emotional capital, women and social class', *The Sociological Review*, 52, S2, 57–74.

Reay, D., David, M. and Ball, S. (2001). 'Making a difference? Institutional habituses and higher education choice', *Sociological Research Online* 5, 4; available online: *htttp://www.socresonline.org.uk/5/4/reay.html*.

Reay, D., David, M. E. and Ball, S. (2005). *Degrees of Choice: Social Class, Race and Gender in Higher Education* (Stoke on Trent, Trentham Books).

Reddy, W. M. (1977). 'The textile trade and the language of the crowd at Rouen, 1752–1871', *Past and Present*, 74, 62–89.

Redman, P. (2005). 'The narrative formation of identity revisited: narrative construction, agency and the unconscious', *Narrative Inquiry*, 15, 1, 25–44.

Rees, A. D. (1950). *Life in a Welsh Countryside* (Cardiff, University of Wales Press).

Reynolds, J. and Taylor, S. (2005). 'Narrating singleness: life stories and deficit identities', *Narrative Inquiry*, 15, 2, 197–215.

Richards, A. J. (1995). *Slate Quarrying in Wales* (Llandysul, Gwasg Carreg Gwalch).

Richards, C. (2005). 'Securing the self: risk and aspiration in the post-16 curriculum', *British Journal of Sociology of Education*, 26, 5, 613–25.

Robbins, D. (1993). 'The practical importance of Bourdieu's analyses of higher education', *Studies in Higher Education*, 18, 2, 151–63.

Robbins, D. (2005). 'The origins, early development and status of Bourdieu's concept of "cultural capital"', *The British Journal of Sociology*, 56, 1, 13–30.

Roberts, B. (2002). *Biographical Research* (Buckingham, Open University Press).

Roberts, K. (1936). *Traed Mewn Cyffion* (Llandysul, Gwasg Gomer).

Rose, N. (1996). 'Governing "advanced" liberal democracies', in A. Barry, T. Osborne and N. Rose (eds), *Foucault and Political Reason: Liberalism, Neo-liberalism, and Rationalities of Government* (Chicago, University of Chicago Press).

Rosen, H. (1972). *Language and Class: A Critical Look at the Theories of Basil Bernstein* (Bristol, Falling Wall Press).

Rosser, C. and Harris, C. (1965). *The Family and Social Change* (London, Routledge and Kegan Paul).

Samuel, R. (1989). *Patriotism: The Making and Unmaking of British National Identity* (London, Routledge).

Sawin, P. E. (2002). 'Performance at the nexus of gender, power, and desire: reconsidering Bauman's *Verbal Art* from the perspective of gendered subjectivity as performance', *Journal of American Folklore*, 115, 455, 28–61.

Schaller, A., Rocha, L. O. and Barshinger, D. (2007). 'Maternal attitudes and parent education: how immigrant mothers support their child's education despite their own low levels of education', *Early Childhood Education Journal*, 34, 5, 351–6.

Schneider, J. (1971). 'Of vigilance and virgins: honor, shame, and access to resources in Mediterranean societies', *Ethnology*, 10, 1, 1–24.

217

Schoon, I. and Parsons, S. (2002). 'Teenage aspirations for future careers and occupational outcomes', *Journal of Vocational Behaviour*, 60, 2, 262–88.

Scourfield, J. and Davies, A. (2005). 'Children's accounts of Wales as racialized and inclusive', *Ethnicities*, 5, 1, 83–107.

Shakespeare, P. (1998). *Aspects of Confused Speech: A Study of Verbal Interaction Between Confused and Normal Speakers* (London, Lawrence Erlbaum).

Skeggs, B. (1997). *Formations of Class and Gender* (London, Sage Publications Inc.).

Skeggs, B. (2004). 'Context and background: Pierre Bourdieu's analysis of class, gender and sexuality', *The Sociological Review*, 52, S2, 19–33.

Smith, D. (1990). *Texts, facts and femininity: Exploring the relations of ruling* (London: Routledge).

Snell, K. D. M. (1999). 'The Sunday-School movement in England and Wales: child labour, denominational control and working-class culture', *Past and Present*, 164, 122–68.

Soloman, B. M. (1985). *In The Company of Educated Women: A History of Women and Higher Education in America* (New Haven, Yale University Press).

Somers, M. R. (1994). 'The narrative constitution of identity: a relational and network approach', *Theory and Society*, 23, 605–49.

Srivastava, A. (2002). 'Good practice in staff development for the retention of students from groups under-represented in higher education', *Widening Participation and Lifelong Learning*, 4, 1, 14–21.

Stanley, L. (1993). 'On auto/biography in sociology', *Sociology*, 27, 1, 41–52.

Sulkunen, P. (1982). 'Society made visible – on the cultural sociology of Pierre Bourdieu', *Acta Sociologica*, 25, 2, 103–15.

Sullivan, A. (2007). 'Cultural capital, cultural knowledge and ability', *Sociological Research Online*, 12, 6, http://www.socresonline.org.uk/12/6/1.html.

Taylor, S. (2001). '"Places I remember": women's talk about residence and other relationships to place', *Auto/Biography*, 9, 33–40.

Taylor, S. (2005). 'Self-narration as rehearsal: a discursive approach to the narrative formation of identity', *Narrative Inquiry*, 15, 45–50.

Taylor, S. and Littleton, K. (2005). 'Narratives of creative journeys: a study of the identity work of novices in artistic and creative fields', paper presented at *Narrative, Memory and Knowledge* Conference, University of Huddersfield, UK.

Taylor, S. and Littleton, K. (2006). 'Biographies in talk: a narrative-discursive research approach', *Qualitative Sociology Review*, 2, 1, 22–38.

Tett, L. (2000). "'I'm working class and proud of it" – gendered experiences of non-traditional participants in higher education', *Gender and Education*, 12, 2, 183–94.

Thomas, L. (2002). 'Student retention in higher education: the role of institutional habitus', *Journal of Education Policy*, 17, 4, 423–42.

Thomas, W. I. and Thomas, D. S. (1928). *The Child in America: Behaviour Problems and Programs* (New York, Knopf).

Tomos, A. (1994). 'A Welsh lady', in J. A. Aaron, S. Betts, T. Rees and M. Vincentelli (eds), *Our Sister's Land: The Changing Identities of Women in Wales* (Cardiff, University of Wales Press).

Van Langenhove, L. and Harré, R. (1993). 'Positioning and autobiography: telling your life', in N. Coupland and J. F. Nussbaum (eds), *Discourse and Life Span Identity* (London, Sage).

Veblen, T. (2001). *The Theory of the Leisure Class* (1899 New York, Random House).

Verter, B. (2003). 'Spiritual Capital: Theorizing Religion with Bourdieu Against Bourdieu', *Sociological Theory*, 21, 2, 150–74.

Wacquant, L. (2004). *Body and Soul: Notes of an Apprentice Boxer* (Oxford: Oxford University Press).

Walkerdine, V. and Lucey, H. (1989). *Democracy in the Kitchen: Regulating Mothers and Socialising Daughters* (London, Virago Press).

Warmington, P. (2003). 'You need a qualification for everything these days: the impact of work, welfare and disaffection upon the aspirations of access to higher education students', *British Journal of Sociology of Education*, 24, 1, 95–108.

Watson, M. (1990). *Contemporary Minority Nationalism* (London, Routledge).

Welsby, C. (1995). "'Warning her as to her future behaviour"; the lives of widows of the Senghenydd mining disaster of 1913', *Llafur: Journal of Welsh Labour History*, 6, 4, 93–109.

Westcott, H. L. and Littleton, K. (2004). 'Interviewing children: context, competence and joint meaning making', in S. M. Greene and D. M. Hogan (eds), *Researching Children's Experience: Approaches and Methods* (London, Sage).

White, E. (2007). *The Welsh Bible* (Stroud, Tempus Publishing).

White, E. and Suggett, R. (2002). 'Language, literacy and aspects of identity in early modern Wales' in A. Fox and D. Woolf (eds), *The Spoken Word: Oral Culture in Britain, 1500–1850* (Manchester, Manchester University Press).

Whittaker, C. (1984). *Great Revivals* (Basingstoke, Marshalls).

Widdershoven, G. A. M. (1993). 'The story of life: hermeneutic perspectives on the relationship between narrative and life history', in R.

Josselson and A. Lieblich (eds), *The Narrative Study of Lives* (London, Sage).

Williams, C. H. and Smith, A. D. (1983). 'The national construction of social space', *Progress in Human Geography*, 7, 502–18.

Williams, D. T. (1934). 'Gower: a study in linguistic movements and historical geography', *Archaeologia Cambrensis*, 89, 302–27.

Williams, G. (2002). *Glanmor Williams: A Life* (Cardiff, University of Wales Press).

Williams, J. G. (1985). *The University College of North Wales, Foundations 1884–1927* (Cardiff, University of Wales Press).

Williams, M. (1991). *The Slate Industry* (Oxford, Shire Publications).

Wood, J. (1997). 'Perceptions of the past in Welsh folklore studies', *Folklore*, 108, 93–102.

Index

SUFFERING IN SILENCE

The Saddle-Fit Link to Physical and Psychological Trauma in Horses

JOCHEN SCHLEESE

Certified Master Saddler and Saddle Ergonomist

Translated by Sabine Schleese

J A Allen • London

First published in 2014 by
J. A. Allen
Clerkenwell House
45–47 Clerkenwell Green
London EC1R 0HT

J.A. Allen is an imprint of Robert Hale Ltd
www.allenbooks.co.uk

Published simultaneously in the United States of America by
Trafalgar Square Books, North Pomfret, VT 05053, USA

ISBN: 978-1-908809-22-3

Disclaimer of Liability
The author and publisher shall have neither liability nor responsibility to
any person or entity with respect to any loss or damage caused or alleged
to be caused directly or indirectly by the information contained in this
book. While the book is as accurate as the author can make it, there may
be errors, omissions, and inaccuracies.

J.A. Allen encourages the use of approved safety helmets in all equestrian
sports and activities.

British Library Cataloguing in Publication Data
A CIP record for this book is available from the British Library.

Front cover top three photo insets © Dusty Perin (www.dustyperin.com)
Cover design by RM Didier
10 9 8 7 6 5 4 3 2 1
Printed in China

DEDICATION

This book is dedicated to my horse Pirat. He was my partner in many successful event competitions in Europe. When signs of increasing lameness appeared and his eyes began to lose their shine, it was already too late to do anything so his career came to an all-too-early end. The diagnosis: irreparable cartilage damage at his scapula. Although at the time I was an apprentice saddler, I had no clue that it was the saddle that had caused him all this pain and lameness. I will never forget nor forgive myself for this; it's because of him, I want to help as many horses as possible avoid the same fate. That's why I founded Saddlefit 4 Life®. And that's why I wrote this book.

TABLE OF CONTENTS

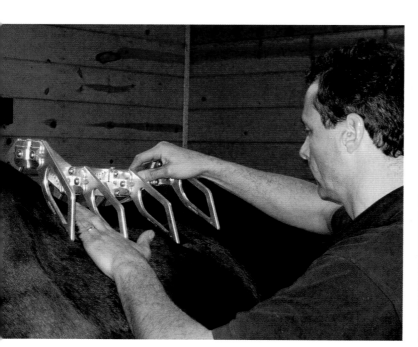

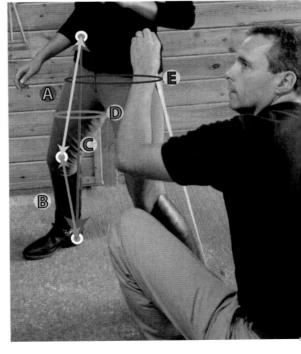

FOREWORD *by Andrea Koslik*

Jochen Schleese's experiences and "aha" moments while working as a saddler are truly unique. It is a great honor that he shares this knowledge with us in his book. The use of his plaster-cast method to take "imprints" of many men and women exemplifies the sometimes circuitous route he used to achieve this level of knowledge. This methodology clearly demonstrated the difference between the male and female pelvis and was integrated into his saddle designs for the benefit of both.

Riding is a very demanding sport and the only one in which the athlete is dependent on the interaction of another being in order to move. As a physiotherapist and a rider myself, I can only state how important it is that finally the difference between male and female anatomy has been taken into consideration to positively impact biomechanics.

The topic of saddle fit is a key consideration when I teach my course in biomechanics of the rider at the German National Riding School in Warendorf. The rider forms the horse and the saddle forms the rider—these two statements are not mutually exclusive.

I often compare the saddle to a shoe, which should be comfortable to wear—except that this "shoe" needs to fit two beings (horse and rider) equally well at the same time. This leaves the saddle-maker with a huge responsibility—one that requires a good basic knowledge in human and equine anatomy. Although many of my students are not consciously aware of the anatomical differences between the male and female pelvis, they are nevertheless adamant that a saddle should work well for either gender (which infers that these differences need to be taken into consideration during design).

Knee rolls are of specific interest to me personally. Through personal observation, which is substantiated by research, opportunities for human activity and movement nowadays continue to dwindle. Children spend much of their time in inactivity: watching TV, playing games on their computers and cell phones. The result is necessary prosthetic compensation to make up for this loss in muscle development; for riders, it is the addition of huge knee rolls on the saddle, which help to keep the rider in a static position while hindering her ability to "go with the motion." A pliable seat for the rider and taking up the rhythm in motion are no longer achievable. Although at first glance it may seem that the rider is sitting properly balanced and straight, it soon becomes apparent that the rider is actually sitting stiffly but thinking that this is the way it should feel. The complementary muscle interactions are not in harmonious states of contraction and relaxation, which means that the rider cannot give the aids properly.

How can she properly relay the message to the horse to achieve even the first three elements of the Training Scale: Rhythm, Suppleness, and Contact? The rider feels cramped, experiences pain and even long-term damage (up to and including slipped discs and torn muscles). This is a possible result regardless of which discipline you ride in and is why the saddle should not only be correct for the rider's gender and anatomy, but also appropriate for the riding discipline.

I can only expect good things to result in the sport of riding when riders, trainers, veterinarians, saddlers, and physiotherapists combine their expertise and experiences for the common good of horse and rider. Only then can the saddler fulfill his role as interface between horse and rider and open the door for discourse. This in a nutshell is the philosophy of Jochen Schleese.

I hope you take away many impressions and revelations and allow this book to alter your point of view as it has mine.

FOREWORD *by Dr. Gerd Heuschmann*

It is a great honor for me to write a foreword for this book.

Jochen Schleese's resumé clearly demonstrates that he is definitely a master in his field, with comprehensive knowledge stemming not only from his training in saddlery but also from his achievements as a rider; he uses these attributes to reach a level of excellence in this multi-faceted industry.

A prerequisite for harmony between horse and rider is the pairing of a healthy, mature horse with a practiced, empathetic, sensitive, and well-trained rider. The saddle is the connection between these two totally disparate living beings: It will either bring them together or distance them—biomechanically speaking. This makes a correctly fitted saddle the key to ensuring commonality in motion, as well as playing a critical role in the successful training of horse and rider. It can help a rider with a good seat find harmony with the horse, but can also restrict and prevent this if it is not fit properly to both.

A well-fitting saddle will quickly allow a good rider on a young horse to attain suppleness. Still, even the best rider will find it impossible to reach harmonious movement on the horse's back when the saddle doesn't fit. There is only one thing that even the best-fitted saddle doesn't guarantee, however: It will never counteract the effect of an unbalanced, tense, rough, and overall poor rider.

As has recently been discussed in numerous publications, riding has become rather far removed from its former idealistic representation. This is seen in dressage especially, which has been brought into a bad light by the actions of a few controversial trainers in the industry. The negative consequences for horse and rider have been, and continue to be, illuminated, discussed, and evaluated. A few saddle manufacturers have reacted to the described issues and made some major design changes in their products.

In my opinion, the main issue is that a rider will have difficulty in finding an independent, pliable, and balanced seat when the horse is held in a position of constant tension, with the rider pushing forward in the seat to go forward while pulling on the bit. The saddle now needs to afford the rider additional support to augment this increased and constant tension on the reins.

As a result, many modern dressage saddles now have extremely deep seats with high cantles, and huge knee rolls. They allow the rider to wedge herself securely and tensely in a deep, inflexible seat behind giant knee rolls, and hang on the reins with tight hands. Many saddle manufacturers are aware of this phenomenon and yet make little or no effort to change it for economic and marketing reasons.

As an experienced rider and certified master saddler, Jochen Schleese has taken an alternate direction with his saddle production, which orients itself toward an unencumbered rider sitting on a relaxed horse. Only a rider who is completely balanced and not forced into position with either his seat or his legs can adhere to the goals of "classical riding." But Jochen's philosophy of saddle fit doesn't stop here: His trees are made to accommodate the specific and individual requirements of both male and female riders. Only a rider with a properly made and fitted saddle can give his horse the proper aids without clamping the thighs, relying on the hands, and sitting unbalanced on the horse's back.

We all want a horse that moves freely and without restriction. The saddle should not cause him pain or hinder his movement. This means that his back muscles need to move freely, which is allowed by a well-fitting saddle, one that may also have to take any asymmetry or unevenness into consideration. These are also parts of the equation considered by Jochen in his work.

I hope that the insights in this book help to reinstate a higher ideal of riding. I wish this important book the highest levels of success.

Gerd Heuschmann

FOREWORD *by Walter A. Zettl*

I have known Jochen as a talented rider and master of his trade since 1986. When I was asked to write a foreword for this book, I agreed with pleasure.

It is easy to recognize how much Jochen Schleese cares about the comfort and well-being of the horse. He uses illustrations and descriptions not only to discuss what a saddle should look like, but also how it should be fit to individual horses. Only then can the animal carry the unaccustomed weight of a rider and the saddle without pain. The horse is not really made to carry any weight on his back—the second most sensitive spot after his mouth. It really only becomes possible to do so after his back has been properly strengthened and trained using specific training and gymnastic exercises.

All of this was taken into consideration by Jochen during his many years of training and studying with his master in Germany, and later as a master saddler himself while establishing his business in his chosen land of Canada. His experience as a successful eventing competitor allowed him to observe and feel the necessity for freedom of movement required under saddle in all three gaits. His own training taught him that only a correct seat will facilitate the right aids to the horse.

What happens when the rider is even slightly out of balance? This is where the saddle comes into the picture: One often sees the rider react by holding his head somewhat to the left or the right. As far as the seat is concerned, this is the first mistake: From this he may collapse at the same hip (left or right) and shift his weight to the other side to compensate. This will, of course, put more pressure on one side of the horse's back. Then the rider pulls more on the opposite rein, the whole other side comes higher, and so forth. The result of such seemingly inconsequential errors in position—ones that may go unnoticed or uncorrected for years—may be a crooked saddle. It will not fit the horse properly any longer and, secondly, continues to place the rider in an incorrect seat. One shouldn't underestimate the frequency or speed with which this crookedness and unevenness can happen. Many rider errors have their origins in poorly fitted saddles—to either horse or rider.

Too many times these issues are simply ignored and that is why I cannot thank Jochen enough for bringing them to our attention in this book, which every rider who loves his horse should own. It discusses what to look for in a saddle and how to ensure it will not cause your horse any pain. Horses did not ask to be ridden, which is why it is so important to Jochen that he protect our four-legged partners from poor saddle fit. He is owed a measure of gratitude from all horses for making their lives bearable and comfortable with properly fitted saddles. I thank him on behalf of riders everywhere, and also his wife Sabine who played just as big a role in the writing of this book.

I wish him every success that he deserves and I am certain that it will be achieved!

ACKNOWLEDGMENTS

This book is meant to be a summary of all I have learned in my 34-plus years of working with horses, riders, and their saddles. I have been driven by simple curiosity and the desire to develop a saddle that is appropriate for the horse's changing conformation. Also included are the epiphanies that came out of conversations with all sorts of equine professionals over the years. Without them, this book never would have happened—you know who you are, and I thank you!

Most of all, however, I want to thank my critics—those who have questioned both my work, my philosophy, and my products—and have engaged in spirited discussions with me and about me. You also know who you are. I thank my parents who gave me the opportunity to begin riding as a child. I am especially grateful for the many hours they spent with me and my youngest brother at horse shows. They made it very clear how much responsibility you take on for another living being when you ride. They taught me to not always take the path of least resistance but to have my own opinion and defend my right to have one. That is the basis upon which I developed Saddlefit 4 Life®.

I owe thanks to the Hans Pracht family, who first offered me the position of Official Saddler for the World Dressage Championships held for the first time in North America in 1986 and thus my introduction to the industry over here. They were the initial reason we first made the leap from Germany to Canada; they allowed me the basis to establish my own company here.

My thanks to everyone who made this book possible—first of all the German publication crew: Isabella Sonntag of Wu Wei, who believed in me from the beginning and gave me the strength and support to begin developing the concept of this book. Nicole Kuenzel, my German ghost writer, who sat with me many hours—and at her computer many more—to put my thoughts on paper in a clear and concise manner. Thanks to graphic designer Christine Orterer and editor Christa-Maria Ossapofsky for their efforts to make the book readable and interesting; Kathrin Woermer of Physically Fit—my model as the saddle ergonomist featured in many of the photos. Frank Reitemeier helped immensely in the original translation of many points from English to German, assisted in formulation of ideas so they made sense, asked the critical questions to take my thought processes even further, and spent many (sleepless!) nights with me going over the original manuscript and editing, re-editing, and deleting!

To Martha Cook of Trafalgar Square Books who has been part of this project almost from day one—thank you for believing in it enough to bring it to the

North American market. To my editor Caroline Robbins for taking the time to fix my mistakes and question my logic. Thank you to Miriam Boutros-Dale and Connie Frantzke who took the time to read the English translation and make sure it was readable. Special thanks to Michelle J. Powell for her proofing, creative design, photoshopping, and editing the illustrations and pictures; to my youngest daughter Danielle who is the talented artist behind some of the drawings used to illustrate points in the text. I thank my oldest daughter Samantha who by showing interest in the progress of the book and her respect for what I do underlines my feeling that I am doing the right thing.

For teaching me about the functional anatomy, biomechanics, and veterinary medical aspects as they relate to saddle design, I thank veterinarians Dr. Gerd Heuschmann, Dr. Joanna Robson, Dr. Carol Vischer, and Osteopath Barbara Welter-Boeller. On the human side of these, especially in articulation of the differences in anatomy between male and female riders, I owe thanks to Dr. James Warson, Andrea Koslik, and Eckart Meyners.

For their limitless knowledge in training horse and rider, and equitation methodology, I thank Jane Savoie and Walter Zettl. Thank you for the illustrative contributions made by Valerie Ponocny, Laura Whitteron, and Christoph Rieser. Also to farrier Barney Cummings for supplying background regarding hooves and horseshoes as they relate to saddle fit.

Thank you to Jaimey and Tina Irwin of Stoney Lake Equestrian and Sue Dunlop of Rainbow's End Farm for allowing us to take innumerable photos of horses on their beautiful properties.

Thank you to Earl and Cathy Rothery, my business partners and our close friends. It is their commitment to our company that allowed me the time I needed for Saddlefit 4 Life® and for this book.

But most of all, I owe thanks to my beautiful partner in life—Sabine. I thank you for your untiring support and for the many hours we spent working on this book, sometimes late at night editing into the wee hours after a day on the road with clients. I thank you for the time you allowed me to realize the dream of actually writing a book; for your patience and understanding and support in taking me one step further in my life's goal to help to protect as many horses and riders as possible from long-term damage arising from poor saddle fit. Thank you for believing in me and in my idea to make a global paradigm shift through the philosophy of Saddlefit 4 Life®, and thank you always for your love. "Wir beide!"

INTRODUCTION

For the Good of the Horse

Dear Reader

From early on I had a dream to become one with the horse—to ride him freely without the use of obvious aids. When I was a young boy living in Argentina, I experienced something I would never forget: My family was stuck on a rural road in a traffic jam when out of nowhere an emu raced by, closely followed by a gaucho (Argentinian cowboy). He was riding without holding the reins and used his hands to swing leather balls attached to a rope (bolo) to hunt the emu. I was fascinated and impressed by how it seemed that horse and rider had become one entity and how beautifully they moved together. That's what I wanted to feel: My ultimate wish was become one with the horse (a centaur, if you will).

When we returned to Germany I was eight years old and I began to bug my parents nonstop to get me a horse. My desire to learn to ride became a driving force; finally they gave in and bought me a series of ponies that I began to compete with. As I began to grow to my present height of 6 feet 4 inches, I had to switch to real horses, but then something strange began to happen. For so many of my peers at the time (and unfortunately something I still observe today) the sheer joy and pleasure in the sport I experienced as a child gave way to the stress of competitive achievement. I began to view my horse as a means to an end; no longer

the childhood friend he used to be, he now needed to perform at his peak for every competition. My ambition, my pride, the pressure: The partnership between my horse and me was changed from what it had been because of these three elements.

The problems with my best horse Pirat, a 17.3 hand Thoroughbred/Hanoverian, began after the 1982 German Eventing Championships. His obvious pain, lameness, and general apathy continued to puzzle us. Examination after examination seemed to yield no answers. In the coming months he would continue to alternate between being sound and showing lameness. I tried using a new veterinarian, experienced various different saddle brands, and used new training methods. I punished him. No obvious cause could be found, but after my qualification for the European Championships in Lastrup 1984, we had to throw in the towel. I simply couldn't figure out what was wrong—nobody could—and so we made the heartbreaking decision to take this highly successful and talented horse into early retirement. He could no longer be used in competition, and was allowed only occasional hacks; the lameness persisted.

Unfortunately for me at that time the diagnostic techniques were not quite what they are today. If I look back at the issues and symptoms Pirat showed

Jochen Schleese and Pirat at the German National Championships in Achselschwang 1982.

I would say with 99 percent certainty that they were caused by his saddle(s)— and this could be substantiated very easily. When I think about what I did, it makes me sad. I am very ashamed for what I unknowingly caused my friend, my pet, my competitive partner—all because I didn't know what I didn't know and didn't know any better!

This very painful revelation for me is one of the reasons for my increas-ing and intensive concentration on all things saddle and saddle fit. I would like to spare you this pain of self-in-duced guilt.

"That's the Way It's Always Been Done!"

It was a series of coincidences that led me to my apprenticeship as a saddler at renowned saddlemaker Passier & Son in Langenhagen in 1978. It was a happy combination of my hobby (riding) and interest—I hoped to use my newly acquired knowledge to find answers to some of the problems my horses were displaying. I began asking questions about the traditional techniques that were being taught. My father (a mathematics and physics teacher) taught me always to question the facts and always ask "why." At this point however, it seemed no one was able to give me the answers as to why a saddle was built "like so" and "not like this" other than "that's the way we've always done it." The answers to some of these questions were only provided to me in later years, fuelled by changes in diagnostic abilities and technology.

A Saddle Made for Women?

After I finished my master's certification a few years later at Passier, I worked at several other companies in both Germany and England. In 1986, I was asked to come to Canada as the Official Saddler for the World Dressage Championships, held for the first time outside of Europe. Out of our original three-year plan to "see how it went," we decided to make Canada our new home. My wife is Canadian so that was somewhat easier to achieve!

Many high-level riders were so pleased with my work that they gave me the impetus to start making my own saddles, rather than just sell other brands. My first custom saddle was made in 1987 for a professional female rider, who was having difficulty and extreme pain in her crotch area because of her saddle, but had no intention of stopping riding.

Her situation led me to speak with my wife's gynecologist (who also happened to be a rider). According to what she told me, many female riders suffer from the same problems: chronic bladder infections, kidney inflammation, and even a proliferation of precancerous cells in the genital region. Many times these women would be cautioned to stop riding altogether. This contributed to the idea of making plaster "butt casts" to show how differently men and women are structured in the pelvic region, a disparity that pointed to an urgent need for an individual saddle seat for both sexes. These three-dimensional objects made obvious differences between men and women extremely clear. Up until then, women were being forced to sit in saddles that for centuries had been built by men, for men. No one had given any consideration to the female anatomy in saddle construction. As a matter of fact, these "male" saddles could actually cause pain and harm to the female anatomy. This needed to change!

A Symbiotic Relationship

After completing this research, I began to design and build my own line of saddles. I soon realized, however, that after fitting these saddles to both horse and rider in accordance with the latest data, it was not enough to have a good horse, a well-fitted saddle, and a competent rider. To achieve optimal training results, it was necessary for all equine professionals around the horse—including trainer, vet, farrier, bodyworkers—to work together in a symbiotic relationship for the good of all concerned. Every one of these professionals is like a spoke in a well-oiled wheel and no less important than the other for the horse to reach his full potential. Only when all the parts are working well together is optimal saddle fit possible.

To further this cooperative effort between all equine professionals, I founded my Saddlefit 4 Life® network (www.saddlefit4life.com), which involves all those who are interested in protecting horse and rider from long-term damage. The philosophy of Saddlefit 4 Life® is being taught at riding schools, universities, veterinary colleges, and various equine associations worldwide.

It was important for me to open a foundation in addition to this network. I, together with Karen Loshbaugh and Joanna Robson, created the HIPPOH Foundation (Horse Industry Professionals Protecting Our Horses), established in California (www.hippohorses.com). HIPPOH's motto is "Horses first, ribbons second," and the goal is to find solutions for problem horses through lectures and presentations by veterinarians (Eastern and Western equine medical experts), saddlers, osteopaths, equine/human physiotherapists, and trainers. This wisdom exchange is

critical and we are finding increasing resonance and willingness to listen and learn in the equestrian industry as a whole. The riding demographic is very interested in education and is becoming critical of unsubstantiated claims. This should be considered a very positive development, even if the questions can occasionally create discomfort. Questions are good; they are key to the well-being of the horse.

I often compare fitting a saddle to finishing a puzzle. Measuring the horse is only one part of it, which becomes a conglomerate of many different influences that are part of the complete picture—leading to a happy horse and happy rider. My happiest moments are when the issues are dealt with and solved; when a cooperative effort by various professionals involved with the horse result in behavioral changes that allow him to again start working freely and comfortably. The first level of this success is usually visible almost immediately to both horse and rider after the initial saddle fitting or refitting.

Well-Trained Saddle Fitters Needed!

I would like to spare you and your horse from what was—and still is—being done to numerous horses (my own included) because of lack of knowledge in saddle fitting. My goal is to help you—whether you are a rider, trainer, veterinarian, saddler, saddle fitter, farrier, physiotherapist or other equine professional—determine whether or not a saddle fits.

I want to give you some relatively easy guidelines on how to choose the best saddle from the plethora of available brands, models, and makes out there. The main questions are simply:

1. Does the saddle fit me and my horse?

2. Is the person (saddle fitter) competent to sell and fit a saddle properly?

I would hope that all riders and trainers begin to question themselves and their associates a little more critically about this. I hope that they know where to go to find the answers they need—from their saddle fitter, their veterinarian, trainer, farrier, or bodyworker—with the ultimate goal of solving problems before long-term damage occurs to either the horse or rider!

We are lucky these days to have the ability to diagnose issues in the horse's back using the newest technology: MRI, fiber-optic cameras, thermography, and computerized saddle pads, to

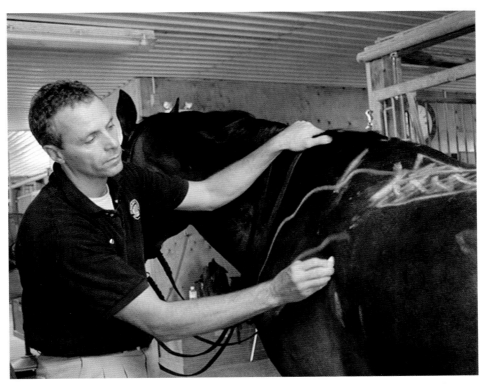

"How, what, why?" The answers to these questions vis-à-vis saddles and saddle fitting has become increasingly important. Here I demonstrate key negative reflex points around the saddle-support area of the horse.

name a few. Knowing what we know, it would therefore seem easy to prevent any physical long-term damage to the horse's back, or psychological issues arising from the pain of poor saddle fit.

With all of these tools at our disposal, there should be no more badly fitting saddles out there. Ignorance should be no excuse, but occasionally things do happen (which I can attest to from my own experiences as a rider and a saddlemaker/fitter). However, when a fitter knows how much damage can be caused to the horse by a saddle, yet still makes the sale because inventory needs to be reduced, in my opinion, is animal abuse and there should be no possible excuse for it!

It gives me great satisfaction to see how many Certified Saddlefit 4 Life® ergonomists are working all over the world to spread the word and my philosophy. Even in Germany, I have found resonance in various high-level riding organizations, where the topic of saddle fitting has since been added to the curriculum; the University of Leipzig has integrated our hypothesis into some of its research. Since 2006, print media all over North America and Europe has included articles on the importance and necessity of good saddle fit (at least for the horse, and more recently, also recognizing the need for it for the rider, as well).

We Want You!

Many riders and trainers intuitively know when something is "off." They turn trustingly to saddlers or fitters for help, however, often these are not necessarily riders themselves, which can mean that they can't, or don't, understand or feel what is really necessary to fit a saddle properly for a specific horse and rider so that long-term damage and issues that can arise in motion are avoided. For me, it is an absolute prerequisite that all saddlers, saddle fitters, and saddle salespersons have a working knowledge in human and equine anatomy, and it is preferably that they are riders. Only then can they actually empathize and feel what the problems could be. Every rider and equine professional should be trained to determine whether or not a saddle fits. The more professionals who have this knowledge, the more pressure will be put on the saddle professionals to consider all sides of the equation for horse and rider in saddle design and fit.

Please don't misunderstand me, I don't want to put my colleagues in this industry on the spot: I want to provide answers and substantiate them with facts and data. My ultimate goal is to reestablish the saddle as a positive interface between horse and rider and, through open discussion, eliminate potential issues.

What I Hope to Achieve with This Book

As a rider, horse owner, master saddler, saddle fit technician, and saddle ergonomist, it is my passion and pride that wants to see every horse and rider work together harmoniously and rhythmically as a result of proper saddle fit. When the saddle melds the two living beings into one, this means more to me than all the money in the world. Each time I see this happening as a result of my involvement it gives me goose bumps. In the truest sense of the word, I want to make a change—this is my happiness and my success, and the best result I could hope for.

I hope this book causes you to re-evaluate, reconsider, and open your mind to new possibilities for the health and well-being of both horse and rider; that you'll find at least one practical takeaway you can apply to your own riding; and that you discover some new insights along with the courage to listen to your horse and your own intuition.

The horse has no choice in the saddle or tack you use—either the "shoe" fits or it doesn't!

Yours in happy riding,

Jochen Schleese

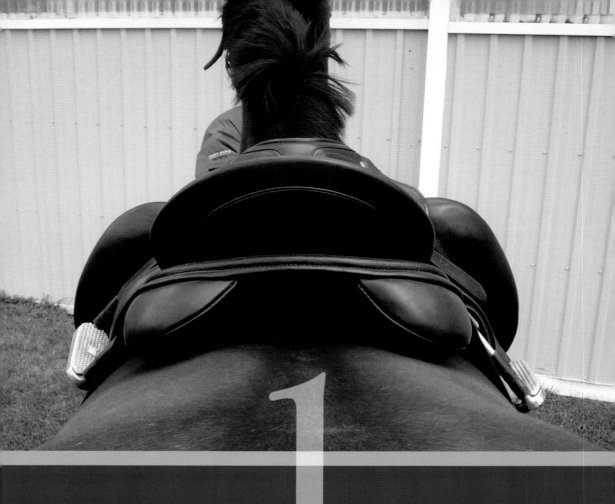

1

IN THE SADDLE

This Is the Way We've Always Done It!—
Past vs. Present

Owning a horse used to be a necessity; it was an important part of earning a living. In agriculture, mining, but also in the military, a man's life could depend on the health and ability of the horse to fulfill its job. A sick or otherwise compromised animal could result in less or even no income. Very few people were financially able to replace a horse, which meant that its loss could lead to economic ruin. And woe to the saddler's reputation if it was proven that the horse's physical condition was due to badly fit tack! Who could afford to lose business like this? This is the reason why proper methods of saddle-making, saddle fitting, and adjusting tack have been handed down from generation to generation.

Nowadays however, horses are used primarily for sport and recreation. The daily closeness that resulted from a working relationship or from military use is no longer the norm, which means much of the closeness and necessary living arrangements between horse and rider has been lost.

Given the amount of literature written by classical riding masters, many excellent trainers and other equine professionals, and the availability of diagnostic tools and research now available, it begs the question why we continue to ignore the impact on the horse of a badly fitted saddles and the importance of proper (classical) training methods. Despite investing huge sums of money, energy, and time in all sorts of issues to do with the horse (shoeing, physiotherapy, pharmaceuticals, for example), many problems continue to persist. These could often be so easily addressed by an adjustment or rebalancing of the saddle, or by changing training or riding methods—just as it was done hundreds of years ago. Too many times, not knowing or not considering the saddle as the cause continues to manifest itself in the symptomatic behavior of the horse or lameness issues, and it is the horse that suffers in the end.

The evolution of modern riding, especially dressage, has been much discussed and criticized inasmuch as it also plays a role in saddle fit and design. A problem with the horse's suspensory ligaments is often seen as a result of poor riding. The basic anatomy and biomechanics of the horse have not changed in thousands of years; many riding masters in the last century preached for the necessity of classical riding to sustain the health of the horse, but newspapers, magazines, and videos are still full of sensational and terrible photos of horses—pictures caused by ignorant and cruel riding methods.

Due to economic and other considerations, many of the riding disciplines— for example, dressage, jumping, and especially racing—often contribute to the unfortunate early demise of many young horses. Forcing them to perform in as short a time as possible for maximum revenue is very detrimental to their well-being and long-term health.

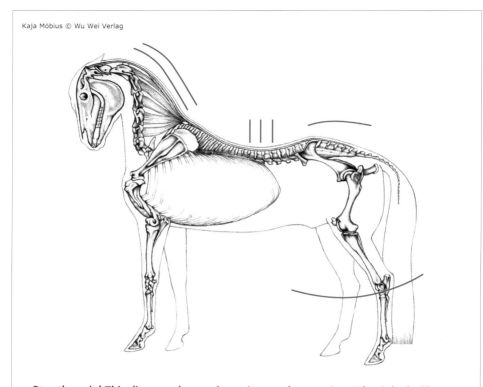

Kaja Möbius © Wu Wei Verlag

Stop the pain! This diagram shows a horse in complete tension: What it looks like when the horse is forced into an artificial position by the rider pulling on the reins. This rider action causes an incorrect arch at the third and fourth cervical vertebrae, and the neck gets tight and the back drops, splaying the hind legs. This forced positioning results in the forehand becoming weighted (the back end is unable to carry weight properly) and it can lead to irreversible, long-term damage.

Instead of being rewarded for keeping a horse motivated and healthy into old age, money and sensationalism talk. The rules and regulations of the various governing bodies (up to and including the FEI) are ignored, even though these organizations should be guiding horse people in accordance with the classical principles of riding and taking the physiology and anatomy of the horse into consideration. As a result, manifestations such as hyperflexion and the "show trot" appear in shows, and are often rewarded with a standing ovation from the uneducated audience.

Most of this audience simply does not know how much physiological and psychological damage is imparted to the horse from these positions and movements. Top riders, who receive high marks from judges who should know better and get applause from an audience that just doesn't know, are obviously also in the dark (or just don't care, which I hope is not the case!) about the long-term damage they are inflicting on the horse they love, and that it is often irreparable.

Taking the saddle alone, what actually happens when the horse is shown in hyperflexion or with a spectacular show trot? His back can't come up, which forces the saddle to sit too far and low in the back, putting the rider behind the center of gravity of the horse. This will cause extra pressure on the last thoracic vertebra, which results in a chain reaction of issues: a) The flocking of the saddle will be compressed under the cantle area because most of the rider's weight is in the back of the saddle; b) pressure increases in the lumbar area, which increases the tension of the spinal ligament system attached to the sacrum; c) this makes it nearly impossible for the horse to step under in suppleness from back to front, which can cause health issues, rider problems, and behavioral mishaps.

A rider needs to experience a paradigm shift: To be considered a true horseman, she needs not only to educate herself with the latest findings, but also learn to intuitively understand her horse's language. Only then will she experience the true harmony that comes from working with a contented horse. The only way to ensure a healthy and happy equine partner is to combine education with an open mind for the latest scientific discoveries, while maintaining classical and time-tested values for training methods. So, having said that, let`s begin!

A HISTORY OF SADDLE MAKING
From Custom to Mass Production

Many of the "latest" innovations in saddle design can actually be traced back in history. Unfortunately, much of this "common knowledge" has been lost over the years. Saddlery is not a new science; saddles have been around and in use for many centuries, and correct saddle fitting has been key. Especially in the cavalry, it was crucial (actually a matter of life and death) for a soldier to have a rideable, healthy horse available for use over long distances.

It used to be one of the jobs of the cavalry officer to teach his men how to make the necessary adjustments to their saddle to bring it back into balance after changes in their horse's musculature or nutrition altered his conformation. Horses used in the mines, in farming, or for transportation purposes also needed properly fitting tack in order to remain capable of working over many years.

In those days, many saddlers actually lived with their horses. And working with them on a daily basis, they became so intimate that they intuitively came to know what was best for their horses. This knowledge was passed on through the generations, mostly from father to son. Most saddles were made on an individual, custom basis, beginning with the horse: The tree was made after the horse's conformation was analyzed and measured, leather was cut accordingly, and the saddle was flocked as needed to accommodate a specific horse's back.

Joseph Sullivan Saddlery, Fort Benton, Montana, around 1900.

THE INDUSTRIAL REVOLUTION

A Rift in the History of Saddle Making

Much of the knowledge about saddlery was lost during the Industrial Revolution and after the two World Wars. But why? The Industrial Revolution is commonly considered to have begun in the eighteenth century in England, then continued onto the European continent through the 1800s, and over to the United States and Japan. It caused massive change to occur through the advancement of

technological innovation within the infrastructure of cities, agricultural areas, and the working world as a whole. With the increasing replacement of both human and animal labor through machinery, many people drifted toward the growing urban landscape to search for alternative work. Horses lost many of their jobs: in transportation, farming, and even the military. This, in turn, resulted in less work for saddlers who also had to look for other careers.

Then in the twentieth century the advent of recognizing the horse for recreational and athletic purposes opened the equestrian industry, led to the rebirth of the trade of saddlery on a whole new level. Women began to ride astride in male saddles, preferring these over the traditional female side saddle. Several saddle manufacturers jumped on the bandwagon, and began mass producing generically fitting saddles for the mainstream recreational market that had developed. Obviously, the profit margins in mass production promised to be higher than in custom and individual manufacture. Demand created the process, and the business was driven by business people rather than knowledgeable saddlers.

Although the horse was still used for cavalry and pulling cannons and the like during World War I (see the popular movie *War Horse*), it became pretty much obsolete for the future military with the increase in the development of modern tanks, jeeps, and artillery. This was another nail in the coffin for the saddlery trade.

(Aside: It is interesting to note, however, that initially, the sport of three-day eventing had its origins in the military. Its first competitors were almost exclusively cavalry officers and the sport is called "military" to this day in the vernacular in Germany.)

CHRISTOPH RIESER

Seven Thousand Years of Development and Optimization of the Relationship Between Man, Horse, and Saddle

In Germany, Rieser, a saddler, master goldsmith, and inventor, has a museum of artifacts dedicated to the history of saddle making. Clients come to him from all over the globe for his custom-made Western saddles.

"Back in the Stone Age, our ancestors knew the horse as prey—it was hunted and eaten, not used for riding. The oldest known sculpture of man with horses is about 30,000 years old and comes from the area of Heidenheim in Germany (just a bit north of Munich in Bavaria). It was not until about 5000 BC that the domestication and use of horses began. The first confirmation that horses were used to transport wagons comes from about 3000–2000 BC. Presumably, they were used as pack animals even earlier than this.

"The question of how man was able to domesticate the horse, and when he actually began to ride it is still unanswered, but it almost certainly was bareback. It would have prophesized the use of a blanket or fur to make riding bareback more comfortable at some point, however. To keep this "pillow" from sliding it would have been useful to fasten it with a strap or rope. It was the increasing need and hope for a more comfortable seat that was the impetus to add increasing layers to this pillow and fashion a more formal cushion to sit on."

The Scythians: The Evolution of the Cushion into a Saddle

"The determining factor in the development of the saddle can be attributed to riding nomads called Scythians who were at the height of their population between 800 and 300 BC. Their territory encompassed the land between the Black Sea, the Caucasus Mountains, Kazakhstan, and Mongolia up to Northern China. They actually divided the seat cushion into two equal halves, which clearly afforded the horse more comfort in

This oldest-known manmade horse sculpture was found in Heidenheim, Germany. It has been estimated to be about 35,000 years old. It is about 2 inches (5 cm) long and made of mammoth ivory.

freeing up the spinal vertebrae. The oldest surviving examples of saddles or saddle fragments using wooden supports can be attributed to this time frame.

"Another key role in the use of saddles for horses can be attributed geographically to the European tundra, which is found between 40° and 50° latitude—from the Danube to Northern China—which is where a proliferation of these riding nomads took place in the 1,000 years before Christ. This corridor connected all of the large territories of the Roman Empire: The riding nomads had contacts in China, Persia, and with Greeks on the north shore of the Black Sea. Attila and his Huns rode all the way into central Europe through this area."

Commonality in Culture: The Saddle Tree

"All riding cultures in the world are connected by the historically documented commonality that the basis for saddle trees arose from the transportable travois (a simple vehicle used by Plains Indians to transport goods behind the horse). The supporting construction—the saddle tree—was born, and it is the saddle tree that to this day determines the functionality of the saddle.

"The saddle tree is the key for the protection of the horse's back. It needs to function for the rider, the horse's back, and for the discipline it is meant for. As a result, there are numerous types and designs of saddle trees, just as there were in the past."

Most of the developments in saddle design can find their origin in the military—usually with "life-or-death" connotations behind them.

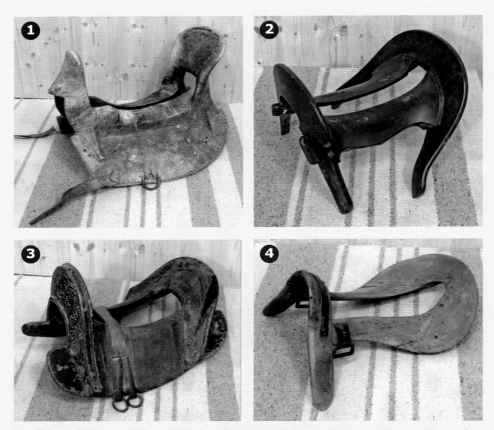

Saddle trees from all over: 1) North African (Arabian) saddle tree; 2) Samurai (Japanese) saddle tree; 3) Chinese saddle tree; 4) English saddle tree.

"The evolution of the saddle tree occurred pretty concurrently and similarly in various cultures and eras in accordance with one principle of design: On the right and left side of the horse's spinal column are two saddle-support areas of varying size, which are connected at the front and back using any number of structures. The photos above from different countries illustrate how different the construction of the saddle tree can be."

The McClellan Saddle: A Milestone

"The McClellan saddle epitomizes how much time and effort went into the design of military saddles: The goal being to produce properly fitting saddles that would keep horses healthy for the longest time.

"The American General George B. McClellan was part of a military commission sent to Europe from April 1855–1856 to undertake a comprehensive analysis of the latest developments by the cavalry in the outfitting of horse and rider, specifically the saddle.

"During his travels, McClellan studied and documented the design, construction, and innovative features of saddles from Hungary, England, France, Prussia, Spain, and Russia. He witnessed many military conflicts, including the battles of the Crimean War.

"He travelled back home laden down with approximately 100 books and numerous sketches on saddles and tack used by the European cavalry. Based on his observations and analyses in Europe, he developed a specific design for the U.S. Army, which was almost certainly the ultimate in saddle-tree innovation at the time."

"The "Model M1859" Saddle: Four Years from Prototype to Market Launch
"The McClellan saddle prototype was approved by the U.S. War Department in 1859 and put into production. From his travels to Europe in 1855 until production in 1859,

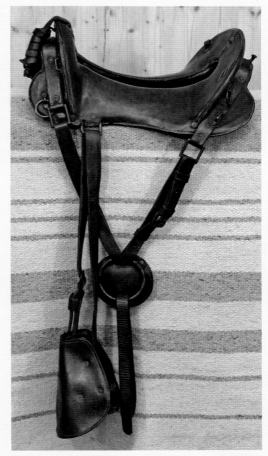

The McClellan saddle is, to this day, the template for many saddles developed for endurance riders.

four years had passed. This impressively indicates how much time, resources, and energy were put into the development of only one saddle-tree model. The first version of the M1859 was actually used during the American Civil War. Even though, over the years, several things changed in its design and detail, it was always recognizable as the McClellan and built for the last time in 1928. It was still in use during the second World War, and has since been used as the basis for the design and development of many endurance saddles.

"Thus it came to be that a saddle that was originally conceptualized for military use has been given a new lease on life and is nowadays more responsible for fun and happiness instead of fear and horror. Times have changed, but the health and comfort of horse and rider still need to be the focus of saddle fit."

THE SADDLERY TRADE TODAY
Cookie-Cutter?

The process that began early in the twentieth century has today become the norm. Developments have led the saddlery trade to become more of an assembly-line process type of industry. By the time a saddle has been completed, it has been touched by the hands of many skilled leather craftsmen. However, it's possible that none of these people has ever built an entire saddle from start to finish, knows anything about traditional saddlery, or has ever even ridden a horse! Building a saddle in its entirety is no longer even part of the apprenticeship curriculum to become a journeyman saddler. Many of the saddle manufacturers that train apprentices will teach them how to make certain parts of the saddle, but never require them to actually put a whole one together. In Germany, for example, the three-year apprenticeship to become a saddler encompasses an internship in a production shop, along with the equivalent of either one day per week at trade school, or trade school in a block of several weeks at a time. Immediately after graduating as a journeyman saddler, the road to becoming a master can begin.

Twenty-five years ago in Europe, the journeyman was required to gain experience in many different saddlery companies before applying to become a master. A master's certification was necessary to then go into business independently. But even the term "master saddler" is somewhat misleading because there are apprenticeships to become a saddler in three

A modern-day saddlery workshop.

There are still many saddlers who prefer to work by hand to manufacture custom goods.

different areas: making luggage, bags and purses; in the automobile industry for car interiors and seats; and in the equestrian industry. Even a master saddler who has been trained in the equestrian industry may have only marginal experience in actually building saddles if he has specialized in making harnesses and strap goods. In other words, even if you have a "master saddler" working with you, it makes sense to do the due diligence and inquire a bit further about his qualifications and experience. (Note: This is not necessarily the case in North America, as the industry is not regulated to this extent and the formal training plans do not exist as in Europe.)

General globalization has also played a role in the saddle-manufacturing industry. Just as in the automobile industry, an increasing level of outsourcing to Third World countries is becoming more common for purely economic reasons. It has become astronomically expensive to have one person make a saddle from start to finish, including patterning, cutting, glueing and sewing, and few people actually have this skill in this day and age. It is for this reason (assembly-line production and outsourcing) that saddles can be sold for relatively high margins with prices that the market will bear. It is not uncommon, for example, to have a saddle with a tree made in China, saddle flaps made in India, and assembly done elsewhere (usually in the country of "manufacture" in order to maintain the "Made in..." label). It would be foolish, however, to view this development in a negative light. Manufacturing components, or even entire saddles, in this manner for economic reasons is absolutely fine as long as the design continues to incorporate the anatomical requirements of both horse and rider.

This is where the dilemma of this type of manufacturing process rears its ugly head in comparison to the more custom type of manufacturing of the last century. It is the loss of the ability to consider the individual requirements of both equine and human anatomy and physiology during this mass production. Horse and rider needs are stuck within a template of "average" design for both.

According to this philosophy, the "average" rider is male, and the "average"

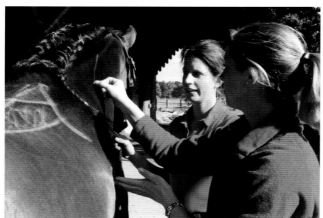

A competent onsite evaluation of horse and rider, and subsequent analysis of these measurements, should be part and parcel of the saddle-consultation process.

horse is a squarely built Warmblood type, with a well-formed, unproblematic saddle-support area.

This standardized requirement for a saddle built for the "average" horse and "average" rider starts with the manufacturer, to the wholesaler, the tack shop, the saddle fitter or saddle salesperson, all the way down to the end consumer (the rider). Experience has shown that there are really only very few well-trained saddle salespeople and fitters who understand the complexities involved for a proper saddle-fit evaluation. Unfortunately, the reality is that many saddlers and saddle fitters today are not what they were 100 years ago—true horse people who grew up with horses and acquired basic equine knowledge, as well as being riders themselves.

How can people who have never ridden understand the needs and wishes of their clients; how can they "feel"

what is required? How can they not only talk the talk, but walk the walk?

There are a minimum of 36 points of consideration when fitting a saddle to a horse. There are approximately 80 points of consideration for a saddler when making a custom saddle, before he even begins production. Beyond the simple measurements taken for horse and rider, there are decisions to be made concerning tree type and shape, leather to be used for certain areas such as panel configuration, and flaps for both the basic construction and the processing during manufacture.

These truly necessary considerations often take a back seat in the real world. Many times the client's wishes hinder making a saddle that is truly what they need. Sometimes, vanity plays a role and the saddler needs to work around this. For example, a rider may insist that she wants a 17-inch saddle when her own body shape would dictate that she would be better off with an 18-inch seat. Other riders want the same saddle that "so-and-so" is using or endorsing, or the same one their friend likes, or what their trainer wants them to use. Still others have a specific budget constraint, or simply dictate a certain design or level of quality, though these last two factors are not necessarily in the best interest of horse and rider since they are frequently related to the latest fad in color, billet length, and style, or other outward appearances.

Truly necessary criteria, such as the saddle actually being made to fit the horse's back and conformation, play a somewhat lesser role for this client: When the rider is more or less comfortable in a saddle used by an Olympic champion or by that gorgeous up-and-coming young trainer, the saddle choice is made without real consideration of whether or not it will actually fit the horse. And, I'm always astonished how much pain and discomfort some female riders will put up with because they are convinced, or have been persuaded, that they have the right saddle.

Saddle manufacturers want to be able to offer many models and many types of saddles to a potentially large market. They want to have "something for everyone," an affordable saddle for the masses without compromising quality and the appearance of exclusivity. This explains the huge range in price points: The manufacturer is under some economic pressure when producing a huge number of saddles for a mass market because these saddles need to be saleable. This becomes a catch-22, because these saddles need to be sold: The end consumer expects an acceptable amount of choice in the tack shop, and this inventory needs to be sold because it is no doubt non-returnable to the manufacturer or wholesaler, which means no refunds! But, in all of this, who thinks for the horse?

The Client's Needs

No rider consciously would want to hurt her horse (one would hope). Much of the long-term damage that results from a poorly fit saddle comes from simply not knowing any better or not having a proper consultation during the sales process rather than from overt negligence. The difficulty here is that: a) The saddle needs to be affordable while, b) optimally fitting both horse and rider on an ongoing basis.

The saddle-fit requirements as indicated by a particular horse are often ignored; maybe the rider has set herself a strict budget that cannot be exceeded, or the seller or saddle fitter has a different (economically driven) agenda and he has a target to achieve. Unfortunately, this is what often happens without the horse and rider's needs being taken into consideration. Obviously, every new horse owner needs to remember that there will be a whole load of expense beyond the initial purchase price of the animal—including buying tack that fits.

THE SAVINGS PARADOX

You would be financially better off if you invested in an adjustable saddle from the get-go. Only then will you actually save money over the years to come.

Buying a saddle that is less expensive but not adjustable may seem like a good idea at the time, but it will not prove the better choice in the long run. Although it may fit your horse for the next year or so, it is not going to accommodate the changing conformation of your horse as he matures and muscles up. What is important to keep in mind is that with consistent and proper training, he will change, and you will need to buy more saddles to accommodate larger muscles and a smaller saddle-support area if you expect peak comfort and performance. (As the horse grows and matures during training, the increasing musculature at the shoulder and withers area will naturally tend to push the saddle farther back, which makes the overall saddle-support area shorter. If the saddle is not changed to accommodate this, the horse's comfort and ability to move and perform properly will be negatively impacted.)

You should view your saddle as a long-term investment for you and your horse's health and comfort. Otherwise, the result could not only be irreparable injuries or damage to you both, but additional cost as you require treatment from a veterinarian, physiotherapist, or chiropractor. This statement may seem somewhat extreme; however, the fact is that many health issues that arise (for both horse and rider) from a bad saddle are often (incorrectly) attributed to many other things. They are then treated symptomatically, rather than at the cause. There is truly the need for more education at all levels within the equine profession to recognize this; the health and well-being of you and your horse should be a number one priority, and you should not be prepared to compromise when it comes to this.

A good quality adjustable saddle (in tree width and tree angle as well as panel flocking) is a smart investment because when it is taken care of properly and maintained and adjusted regularly, it will work for the horse over his whole life. The adjustments should be evaluated and done regularly to keep pace with changes in the horse's conformation as he reacts to training, nutrition, and the maturation process.

Would you buy an expensive car and never change the oil or buy new tires? Even though a car does not change shape or grow, it still needs to be maintained to keep up its performance. Unfortunately, we often hear, "I bought a custom saddle; I expect it to fit forever!" In addition, the term "custom" is also an arguable one. "Custom" does not always mean custom and certainly doesn't always mean adjustable; it may be custom at one point in time only. Doesn't it make more sense to "invest" in a truly adjustable saddle rather than constantly having to go through "saddle-buying hell" to find a new saddle because the old one has become too tight at the withers or too narrow in the gullet—even if at one point it may have been "custom"? Remember, your horse will miss yet another lesson or show because of physical or behavioral issues caused by a saddle that no longer fits.

ECONOMICS VS. EDUCATION

So the question arises, why is there such an extensive offering of saddles, many of which simply do not afford this necessary level of adjustability? There are lots of reasons and excuses offered.

Many of the traditional and newly rediscovered realizations about the cause and effect of saddles, anatomy, and riding were not documented in literature until recently. Saddle fitting is still not part of the curriculum in many of the mainstream educational programs within the equestrian industry—whether for body workers or veterinarians; nor is it yet included in the training to become a professional rider or trainer. It is an unfortunate, though realistic, fact that saddle issues are the cause of many behavioral and training problems, as well as being responsible for a lot of lameness, which is more often than not addressed pharmaceutically rather than physically.

To better accommodate the physiological and anatomical requirements of horse and rider, the saddle industry needs to undergo a shift in willingness to produce a product that takes these into consideration, for example, by incorporating a fully adjustable gullet plate (see p. 151) into the saddle tree.

There are already a number of companies that have embodied into their designs wider gullet channels, adjustable gullet plates, and larger panels for better weight distribution over the saddle support area. However, there are still way too many saddles on the market that are simply not adjustable and do not take the horse's requirements into consideration.

It is not only the lack of knowledge and a certain inherent resistance to change that hinders innovation and

I am demonstrating saddle tree angle and tree width at a 2011 veterinary conference in São Paulo, Brazil.

new designs being introduced to the market. It is a long and expensive process to bring a new product to the consumer; to change an entire mindset to produce completely different saddles using new technologies and state-of-the-art information is even more difficult to achieve.

One of the main obstructions in this process is the simple fact that both manufacturer and retailer likely have a huge inventory of saddles remaining—made and bought without the benefit of this new knowledge—and these still need to be sold! What happens to these thousands and thousands of saddles not made in accordance with these criteria? What about the client who just bought one of these new saddles?

This is an unfortunate situation that is simply ignored by many companies, even if they know that there are alternatives out there that would definitely be better for the horse and rider. This is where the conflict arises between *knowing* what is right and *doing* what is right.

Of course, restocking a saddle inventory that is made using the anatomically correct criteria is an extremely expensive proposition—not only for the above reason. Even the manufacturer could not immediately revamp the entire production process to accommodate these criteria. Developing new saddle models requires planning and beta-testing of prototypes. New molds will need to be made, new patterns designed, and possibly new tools and machinery required. And none of these guarantee instant success or resonance in the marketplace. Even a structured and focused marketing campaign will not result in immediate sales.

Market testing and acceptance by the end consumer are crucial, as are the actual results and changes seen when a saddle is used. The new designs need to be seen as being more effective than what is currently available, and this can take years, given that some of the damage attributed to a poor fitting saddle can take a long time to manifest. The attitude may well be, "If it ain't broke, why fix it?" which leads to some resistance as well. Financial considerations for both manufacturer and retailer also take time to resolve when rolling over the inventory.

Riders will become more and more frustrated and angry as issues arise and saddles don't fit time and time again. The end consumer will become more educated and able to draw her own conclusions, based on findings on the Internet, at conferences, symposia, and seminars, and will be able to ask the relevant questions and raise the arguments for or against saddle designs. The pressure to design a mainstream offering of physiologically and anatomically correct saddles will come from this person. If we ignore this, horses will continue to suffer long-term damage. The more critical the end consumer becomes, the faster saddle manufacturers, wholesalers, and retailers will bow to her wishes.

THE ROLE OF THE SADDLE WITHIN THE CIRCLE OF INFLUENCE

A saddle needs to distribute the weight of the rider correctly over the horse's back so that the rider's center of gravity becomes one with the horse's center of gravity.

The horse will change in conformation over the course of his life due to many influences, least of which are his age and training. To illustrate some of these influences, consider a circle surrounding the horse divided into equal pieces (minimum of eight). One of these pieces represents the rider; other components include the trainer, the veterinarian, body workers (physiotherapists, chiropractors, acupuncturists), nutrition and

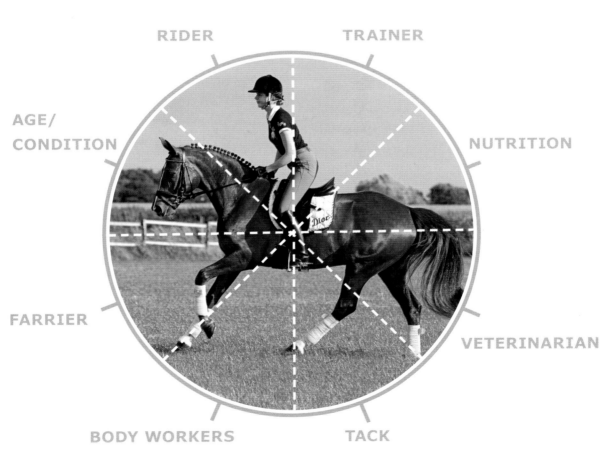

RIDER   TRAINER

AGE/ CONDITION   NUTRITION

FARRIER   VETERINARIAN

BODY WORKERS   TACK

supplements for the horse, the farrier, the horse's age and condition, and last but not least, tack including bits, bridles, saddles, and pads.

I call this the "Circle of Influence" around the horse, in which the saddle and the work of the saddle fitter are never considered in isolation. All the items of influence are interdependent. If, for example, training methods or nutrition are changed or supplemented, the horse's conformation will alter. It follows logically that the saddle will no longer fit, and the reason is not because the saddle fitter did a bad job.

Saddle fitting is nothing more than attempting to prevent long-term damage to the horse by avoiding pressure on his reflex points, and to distribute the rider's weight optimally on the horse's back. Keeping the horse sound and the rider healthy should be the ultimate goal for each one of the "pieces" of the circle that need to work together cooperatively to achieve this. Every change affected by any one of the pieces—whether deemed positive or negative—will have a consequence on the others, which may have the simple end result that the saddle will no longer be balanced. (Let's recall Newton's Third Law here: Every action brings with it an equal and positive reaction!)

For the most part it is not the saddle that changes, it is the horse's three-dimensional back shape that alters the saddle-support area. But without exaggeration, it is the saddle (as interface between horse and rider) that has the potential to inflict the most anatomical and physiological damage—especially to the horse when it no longer fits.

It requires training and empathy for the horse to be able to discover the reason for symptoms like tight muscles, kissing spines, or lameness.

THE HEALTH OF THE HORSE INFLUENCES THE FIT OF THE SADDLE WHEN VIEWED HOLISTICALLY

By Joanna Robson, DVM

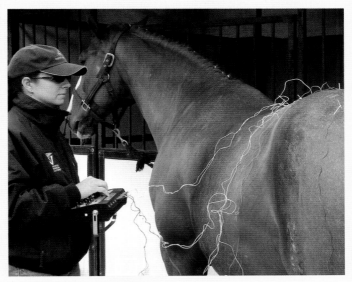

Dr. Robson doing electronic acupuncture.

Dr. Joanna Robson has a holistic veterinary practice in California, combining Eastern and Western medical practices to offer chiropractic, acupuncture, herbal medicine, infrared thermography, and saddle-fit evaluations and analyses.

"If a horse is in physical pain from a disease process such as arthritis, muscle soreness, or tendon-ligament inflammation, the horse's entire physical carriage may be altered, especially through its back, due to primary or compensatory changes. Traditional veterinary medicine employs means such as pharmaceuticals—steroidal (Depo-Medrol®) or non-steroidal anti-inflammatories ('bute,' Banamine®); muscle relaxants (Robaxin®); injections of HA (Legend®) or PSGAG (Adequan®); or intra-articular injections to combat pain associated with arthritis or muscle soreness, and promote soundness and correct carriage. Surgical procedures such as arthroscopy, neurectomy (nerve cutting), and tendon-ligament modification are also employed in an effort to reduce pain and prolong usefulness. Some of these procedures may save the performance of the animal, while others are merely a Band-Aid.

"Holistic veterinary medicine also employs modalities such as acupuncture, veterinary spinal manipulative therapy, laser therapy, mesotherapy, herbal medicine, and homeopathy to restore overall balance to the patient, promote proper nervous-system functioning, employ endogenous endorphins as painkillers, and provide a non-invasive or less-invasive means of ongoing performance maintenance. However, the success of veterinary medicine—traditional or holistic—in maintaining pain-free performance is limited by the tack that is placed on the horse and the means by which it is ridden or trained.

"The body-condition score of a patient will certainly affect the shape of its topline and overall roundness, thus affecting the saddle fit and the horse's ability to sustain exercise and develop muscle. A round horse with fat deposits beneath its skin is not the same as a horse that is round from correct carriage and muscle development in its back.

"Overfeeding of performance and pleasure animals, along with over-supplementation, can lead to behavioral and physical problems that affect performance and training, which may be blamed on other factors such as saddle fit or riding. Underfeeding, and not regulating proper levels of minerals such as selenium, can also affect the horse's conditioning, haircoat, and topline, thus preventing the desired 'bloom' that comes with correct tack and training. Nutrition is only one factor, though a very important one, in the multi-faceted approach to equine wellness."

Dr. Robson performing a chiropractic adjustment.

THE INFLUENCE OF FARRIERY ON SADDLE FIT
By Barney Cummings

Barney Cummings is a certified farrier for the Canadian Equestrian Team and a member of the Ontario and American Farriers Associations.

"The front limbs, unlike the hind legs of the horse, are not joined to the body by skeletal structures. The front legs are supported in a sling of muscles called the *serratus muscles*. When the weight of the saddle and rider are added to the back of the horse, over the thoracic vertebrae, the scapular bones come together slightly as the serratus muscles support that weight. Although proper saddle fit allows for the free movement of the scapula, the bones rotate according to the lower-limb conformation of the individual.

"When the horse's conformation is not correct, the reciprocal muscle movement of the front legs will cause a deviation in hoof-flight pattern and affect the musculature of the back. There will be overdevelopment of one side when it has to work harder to compensate for those faults in the opposite limb or hoof.

"The horse that is *valgus* (toed-in hoof), has an *outward* rotation of the shoulder. The *varus* (toed-out hoof), has an *inward* rotation of the shoulder. The implications to the three-dimensional shape of the horses' back should now be obvious.

"If valgus or varus is caused by injury or poor husbandry, the farrier can trim and shoe to help deliver a truer flight path and footfall for the horse. For example, if a horse has a sheared heel (one heel is longer than the other) from injury or uneven weight bearing, the shorter side carries more weight. When that shear is lateral, or on the outside heel, the horse will need to stand with his weight more under the center of its body mass. The scapula has now been pulled out. The hoof trimming and placement of the shoe can aid in returning weight bearing to its intended position at the base of a straight bony column.

"Saddle fit and farriery are definitely complimentary disciplines of art and science."

2

BALANCE AND RIDER POSITION

We all want a horse that is supple, moves well with propulsive gaits, and responds easily to our aids with respect to timing, transitions, and direction. The goal is to have optimum forward motion with complete suppleness, including the necessary healthy contraction and relaxation of the muscles to accompany each gait transition.

The rider needs to be in harmony with the horse's movement via her own positive muscle responses. This harmony will be particularly evident during the diagonal phases of motion, without unnecessary tension in the seat, legs, or hands. Horse and rider should move rhythmically and in harmony without visible exertion from either side.

We want the horse to move freely without obvious aids from the rider, who should be sitting comfortably in the center of balance and be one with the horse's motion. The ideal rider shows a positive tension (not to be confused with bracing yourself), while not being too relaxed or too loose in the seat.

The seat of the rider—regardless of discipline or style—is the basis of good

The rider's shoulder, hip, and heel should be aligned.

riding. It can take many years of training and practice to achieve this balanced seat. Riding can only be learned by riding, and every good rider knows

The rider's center of balance equals the center of gravity (p. 33). The vestibular system in the inner ear is responsible for maintaining a person's balance. When a rider is standing, or sitting in balance on a saddle, her feet should be directly in line beneath her. This is the reason, in dressage in particular, that it is so critical to maintain the "shoulder-hip-heel" perpendicular "plumb" line body position, because only then, will you feel totally balanced. When the body is not in balance or doesn't feel like it is balanced, the vestibular system causes a reaction, which always leads to movement and a shift in the seat until you feel "straight."

that learning to ride never stops. The saddle is an important interface between horse and rider, and will not achieve the miracle of proper riding by itself—but when it suddenly fits properly, it can feel like one! A poor fitting saddle can hinder the development of a balanced seat for a long time, whereas a well-fitting saddle will support the rider in achieving this balance with ease and suppleness. The rider can use the saddle to help her ride instead of fighting the saddle to maintain position.

THE BALANCE POINT

How and Where Should the Rider Sit?

The rider needs to be in balance in order not to throw the horse off his own center of gravity. Proper balance is an elemental truth—not only in riding, but in life itself.

When you watch a newborn foal, it will attempt to stand within a few minutes of its birth. It tries to stand straight on all four legs, and balances itself more front to back than side to side. The natural balance point* of a static horse is on the forehand pretty much from birth on. Nature has determined that it will be able to move slowly forward while grazing with its head down and most of its weight on the front end. In later life, the rider influences this natural sense of balance quite a bit, as we try to keep the horse "off the forehand."

Humans need to find their sense of balance (center of gravity) on two legs, and this happens around one year of age. In order to ride in harmony and in balance, the rider's legs will be slightly bent at the knee. Her goal is to achieve a straight line from shoulder to hip and through the heel. This is referred to as a "plumb line." When riding, the rider will be almost in a "standing seat" with her legs, back, and pelvis in a plumb line as well, whereas a person who is standing upright, balances herself with her foot position, and when seated, this balancing job is done with the seat bones. The four natural curves of the spinal column and the slightly bent knee position allow the rider to maintain a light and balanced seat in harmony with the movement of the horse, acting as shock absorbers to the horse's motion.

This balance in the saddle can only be achieved if the rider's pelvis is basically in the same position vis-à-vis the rest of her body as it is when she is walking. It is the "feathering"/shock absorption of the feet, knees, and hips, as well as in the spine and through the pelvis, that allows the rider to maintain balance on

---

* The center of gravity or center of balance of the horse is at his sternum. This center of gravity starts farther forward on a green horse's body and moves backward on the horse's body as it is trained.

the moving horse. The diagonal movement of the horse used in all his gaits feels quite natural to the rider, who in the upright position similar to when she walks, will move her arms and legs in this same diagonal way.

The diagonal motion of the horse stimulates the same senses a human uses to walk, which is why horseback riding is often used in physical therapy for paraplegic injuries—with positive results. The rider should sit as comfortably and naturally as possible while carrying her back straight as there is no real back support. She should not clamp on with her knees, thighs, or calves; it is a balancing act and critical for the supple movement of the horse.

One function of the saddle is to position the rider's spinal column and seat bones in such a way to allow the four natural curves of the spine to act as

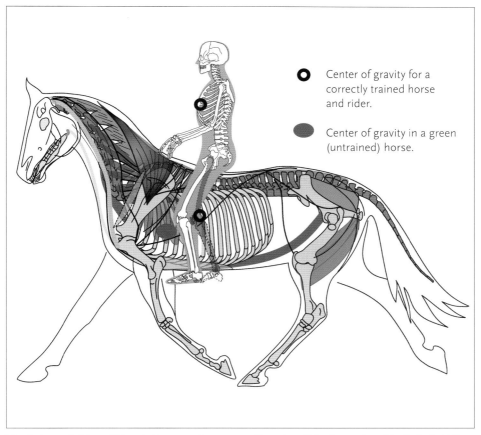

Center of gravity for a correctly trained horse and rider.

Center of gravity in a green (untrained) horse.

The balanced rider will be sitting over the center of gravity of the horse (see black circle.) The red circle shows the position of the center of gravity in an untrained horse and this moves farther back to the black circle after correct training.

A balanced seat and a saddle that fits well are prerequisites to attaining harmony between horse and rider.

shock absorbers and move with the motion of the horse—not work against it. This will allow the natural harmony of horse and rider to enhance the overall movement by compounding the dynamic energy of both.

The horse's balance is certainly impacted—positively or negatively—by the rider, which makes it very important that the saddle fits correctly. If the saddle does not fit the rider properly in the first place, and is causing pain

or discomfort, it will affect the horse and impact the ability of the pair to move in harmony. Saddle fit is the first step to the rider aligning her center of gravity with that of the horse and keeping it there during motion. This "sweet spot" is that certain place the rider sits on the horse's back where they balance each other out; this is where the least movement occurs in the horse's spinal column during motion—even while bucking—which is most obvious when you watch cowboys at the rodeo who are always sitting pretty close to the withers.

It seems that most English saddles lie pretty far forward on the horse's back as well (in the front one-third of the horse) even though logic would dictate that putting the saddle farther back would enhance the horse's ability to stay off the forehand by not interfering with the horse's shoulder movements. It causes a huge problem in an incorrectly designed saddle when the balance point of the saddle is not in alignment with the center of gravity of the horse and rider. Often the rider can't find the proper position for the saddle on the horse's back to sit over the horse's center of gravity, while still ensuring that the saddle is placed behind the horse's scapulae.

One further point to be considered is, of course, the natural balance point of the rider. The horse will only be able to move in harmony with the rider if the rider is sitting balanced and over her center of gravity. Prerequisites to

A CROOKED PELVIS IS NOT A GOOD THING IN HORSE OR RIDER

From Soforthilfe bei Rueckenschmerzen *(Instant Relief from Backache)—Zabert & Sandmann Verlag, Munich) by Lilo Cross.*

Physiological straightness is crucial to the health of every rider. Over time, because of accidents, or one-sided pressure loads (like carrying a bag always on the same side) your balance gets out of whack and away from the "plumb line" position. Many people are "crooked" without realizing it, which can result in a myriad of issues that are not necessarily attributed to their crookedness.

A crooked pelvis can lead to a chain reaction of problems: knee alignment, hip articulation, backaches, slipped discs, migraines, jaw pain, and even vision impairment are all possible results. Treating these individual issues symptomatically rarely brings relief; it is important that the cause—that is, the crooked pelvis—is treated and "fixed."

A well-fitting saddle could help if the rider is sitting crookedly on the horse because of her crooked pelvis. "Dents" in the saddle's seat as well as computerized

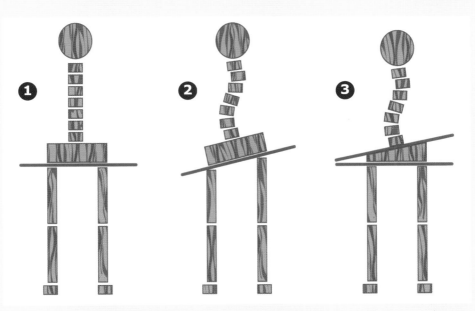

1) **Symmetry displayed by straight pelvis, equally long legs and a healthy static position.**

2) **The legs of this person are uneven causing a misaligned spinal position and crookedness above the pelvic region.**

3) **The legs are equally long but the pelvis is crooked, resulting in a functional difference in leg length and even more overall misalignment in body position with crookedness in the spine.**

pads for pressure underneath the saddle will show exactly if and how much crook-edness is displayed by the rider.

Nowadays, spine and joint issues are among the most common reasons for people to see a doctor or physiotherapist. These result in most cases of disability in the workforce. Often times, the origin of these problems comes from functional differ-ences in leg length, which arise from crookedness in the pelvis that causes body-stressing positional accommodation in order to remain in balance.

Actual practice has shown, however, that it is not that one leg is actually shorter than the other, it is simply a manifestation of a crooked pelvis that makes it appear that way. The body needs to compensate physically somehow for the crookedness of the pelvis, which usually affects its balance and position. This compensation, however, can then result in the manifestation of other symptoms, such as those mentioned previously (backaches, migraines, slipped discs). If we assume that a crooked pelvis usually appears as the result of trauma, then we need to search for its origin in some sort of physical accident, for example, a fall.

The body will try to compensate for this crookedness for a while before the spine, joint or other issues begin to appear—as a rule it takes from five to eight years be-fore they become visibly apparent and require treatment. Treatment of one or other of these symptoms may cause temporary relief, but there will be no healing. And these issues will recur in time when the cause, that is, the crooked pelvis, is not dealt with. Only when this is fixed, can any healing begin.

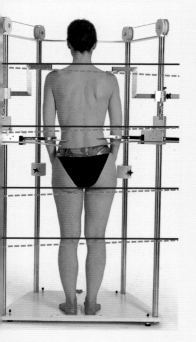

The Cross Method

The Cross method was developed to train the pelvis back into its straight position with simple exercises. In order to achieve complete correction of the position, it is important to take exact diagnostic measurements. Even something as seem-ingly small as being out of alignment by 2 millimeters (one inch equals 25.4 mm) will have serious consequences. This misalignment can't be detected by simple eyeballing, nor can ordinary stretch and muscle-strength tests give a definitive answer. Using the "Acromiopelvimeter" has proven success-ful, because it can determine exactly the extent of the crook-edness of the pelvis before, during, and after treatment.

The Acromiopelvimeter was developed specifically to augment the Cross Method. It is a tool that allows an exact determination of the extent of crookedness of the pelvis without using X-rays or other invasive imaging. Years of research and comparison with X-rays have confirmed that this diagnostic tool, which was developed with the assistance and input of Lilo Cross, will result in a reliable and exact readout of information.

achieving this are not only good riding, but also a correct, well-fitting saddle that allows the rider to find her balance point. This means that the deepest point of the saddle, which is where the rider's seat bones are, should be positioned over the horse's center of gravity; the rider's spine will move as it should, using its four natural curves to absorb the movement. We call this deepest point of the saddle, which allows the rider to find her center of gravity in alignment with that of the horse, the "balance point" or "sweet spot."

It is important to note, however, that this balance point (or whatever you choose to name it) will be different for men and women, given their different anatomy and pelvic structure. If you look at the horizontal axes of balance of pelvises, you will see that a man's pelvis balances exactly in its center whereas a woman's balances in the front one-third of the pelvis. This needs to be taken into consideration when designing a saddle, otherwise even the most talented rider will have difficulty in finding her own center of balance.

Horses were not designed to be ridden and it is their instinct to counteract the effects of a rider. The rider's sense of balance can interfere with the horse's sense of balance. Riding only works when we understand how to bring both of these balance points into one: It's a big challenge to combine the movement of a four-legged animal that moves and balances itself mainly on a horizontal axis with that of a two-

Balance of both horse and rider is influenced by saddle fit.

legged creature that moves and balances itself vertically. This is where the saddle is a crucial piece of the puzzle as it can influence this movement equally in both parts. A common balance point can only be achieved when the saddle is an interface that will perpetuate a harmonic melting of these two axes of movement.

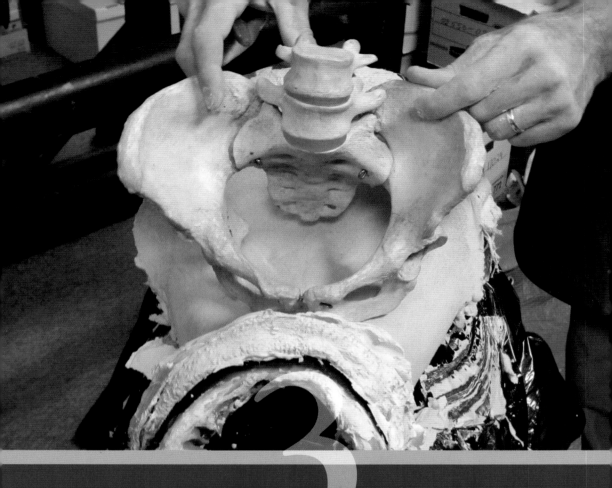

3

WOMEN RIDING IN SADDLES MADE BY MEN, FOR MEN

Many years ago, around 1989, a female rider on the Canadian dressage team approached me. She said, "I have bought a lot of saddles over the years. I'm riding in an 18-inch saddle right now but I feel like I'm sitting behind the motion. If I look at my pictures, it looks like I'm sitting in a 'chair seat.' When I try to fix my position, I'm in constant pain—to the point of being rubbed bloody! Can you help me?"

As a matter of fact, her gynecologist had actually told her to stop riding if she couldn't find a saddle that would alleviate this friction, pain, and physical irritation. She was told that this constant friction and rubbing could actually lead to chronic issues and damage.

I began doing some research and concentrated on finding a solution because I was hearing this type of thing more and more from my clients.

My findings pretty much underlined the fact that over the past 3,000-plus years, men had been making saddles mainly for men (exception was the side saddle for women) because the majority of riders had *been* men: It was men who fought, hunted, and worked with their horses. The idea of women riding was deemed for a long time to be inappropriate and unseemly, and even the development of the side saddle didn't really help to make it a mainstream and acceptable activity.

Of course, with the cultural changes in the last century, and the evolution of the horse as a recreational and athletic partner rather than a working animal, this situation of men versus women riders has reversed. In the last decades, the rapidly increasing numbers of women who ride have actually overtaken the number of male riders. The cliché about "little girls with their horses" is a reality. The statistic of 80 percent female versus 20 percent male riders is probably true for most of the civilized world. Paradoxically, however, this reality was never really accounted for in the realm of saddle design and manufacture.

We began our actual research by making plaster "butt casts" of many men and women, some to actually build custom saddles from, but others just out of simple curiosity. It soon became very obvious that women absolutely

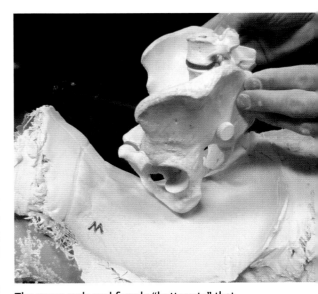

The many male and female "butt casts" that I have made clearly indicate the obvious anatomical differences in pelvic structure between the two sexes.

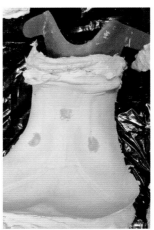

Although these two riders are very similar in body shape on the outside, their "butt casts" clearly show the differences in their pelvic points of reference. The male (right) has two points of contact on the saddle at the seat bones, which are closer together than those of the female (left). In addition, the female pelvis has a third point of contact at the front (her pubic symphysis).

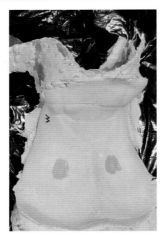

needed a different seat in their saddles than men based on their pelvic skeletal features. This indicated how important it was that this anatomical disparity be taken into consideration during the manufacture of the saddle tree and the forming of the saddle seat.

I then had many conversations with various medical experts and physiotherapists. The consequences of the differences between men and women became even more crucial in my saddle design; now I had to find a way to incorporate them properly into the saddles themselves.

We developed a saddle specifically made for women to allow them to sit properly and comfortably without causing any pain or potential long-term issues. A major change for me was moving from the ubiquitous use of the laminated, beech-wood spring tree to a polyurethane flex tree (see photos). The English spring tree was well known for being pretty comfortable and, well, "springy" and forgiving (middle photo); however, some of the design features, including the forward-facing tree points and non-adjustable gullet plates, makes it less desirable as far as I'm concerned (see p. 151 for more on tree points and gullet plates).

Some of the new plastic trees are pretty stiff and inflexible, even when they have other advantages such as weight reduction. This means, that even if the seat foam (the padding under the area where the rider sits) is very comfortable for the rider, the

A polyurethane saddle tree (AdapTree®) with a patented crotch-comfort system.

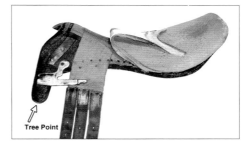

An English spring tree made of laminated beech-wood layers, with seat webbing, and showing forward-facing tree points. The tree points are the bottommost edge of the pommel area and need to accommodate both the size, shape, and angle of the shoulder.

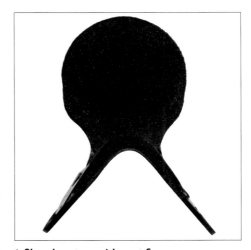

A fiberglass tree with seat foam.

This saddle that was made for a man gives the female rider no other choice but to sit in a chair-seat position.

saddle itself may not accommodate the horse's movement, thus destroying some of the harmony that we are aiming for between horse and rider.

My first design change was based on the fact that I wanted to give the female rider some cushioning in the "ouch zone" (which was the birth of the "crotch comfort" or "cc" cutout). So we developed a very forgiving, flexible, polyurethane tree and patented the cc (see top photo p. 41). It is essentially a padded cut out in the area of the pubic symphysis, which takes the pressure off the contact point here for women. It also works for men, too, for obvious reasons, and takes some of the pressure off their genital area. Even the

bicycle industry became interested in this design and is incorporating it into some of their models.

"I don't care if I'm not comfortable in the saddle, the main thing is that it fits the horse." I'm sure many saddle salespeople and fitters have heard this statement from their customers. Many riders (and fitters) seem to ignore the necessity of the saddle also being comfortable for the rider. The truth is that it is much easier to make a saddle that fits the horse than it is to make it also fit the rider. There are many more points to consider when designing or making a saddle that fits a rider properly to allow him or her to sit in balance on the horse and concentrate on riding rather than fighting the saddle to maintain position. So, let's lose that mindset right now!

We have probably 1,000 more nerve endings in our sensitive crotch region than we do in our fingertips. If these are stimulated even minimally by friction or pressure, we may experience pleasure briefly, but pain for a long time—which will cause us to tense up immediately (even if subconsciously).

The horse will feel this tension in our seat and react to it with a loss of suppleness that will become more and more obvious the longer you ride.

For the most part, women who ride in a saddle made for men experience this discomfort, which is passed on to the horse. (And, to those women who decry this as "bunk," saying they have ridden for all their lives and never had any problems anywhere, they are likely sitting on their inner thighs, or back on their "glutes," and almost certainly can expect knee and hip problems later on.)

You can't argue with anatomy and the fact is that even a horse with a saddle that fits him perfectly will never be protected from long-term damage if the saddle is not fitted to the rider according to her anatomical build. The rider will be out of balance, fall into a chair-seat position, and press the padding down in the back of the saddle into the horse's loins.

Position and balance of the rider are the bases of all riding disciplines, but are especially important in dressage, which requires the most intense and direct aids and a consistently balanced rider in correct position over the course of the horse's training. The placing and balancing of the rider's seat bones are especially key to proper position and balance.

In dressage, for women in particular, it often becomes challenging to achieve the "shoulder-hip-heel" plumb line position because of their pelvic structure and hip-joint articulation. To avoid the pain of sitting on their pubic symphysis, they will collapse at the hip, which shoots the leg forward. It takes some effort to counteract this and place the leg correctly.

"A saddle just for women? I thought this was a joke. I was an emancipated woman—or so I thought—and as such, I should be able to ride in any saddle. That was my mindset until I actually felt the difference between a saddle made for men and one made for women. Without exaggeration, this was truly an eye-opening experience. I rode so naturally without making any effort to have my legs hang straight down where they were supposed to be, and I felt the movement as one with my horse.

"Since then, as a trainer I often think that a saddle that is correctly fitted to my students would definitely help some of their position issues."

—Nicole Künzel, Classical Riding Trainer, Hanover, Germany

"Having spent years doing exercises that supposedly loosen the hips in an attempt to sit deeper in the saddle and prevent my toes from turning out while riding, I have now found that when I sit in a saddle designed for the female rider, I am immediately sitting deep in the saddle with my toes pointing forward— without even warming up. I now wonder what unnecessary damage I've done to myself from the years of putting torque on my joints with those exercises that I learned as a child from an instructional riding book. I wonder how many other people, especially women, have unnecessarily hurt their body believing they struggle with 'tight hips.'"

—Laura Whitteron, Certified Saddle Ergonomist, England

MEN VS. WOMEN

After realizing these anatomical differences and proving them to myself by using the "butt casting" method, I came to understand that they would play a role in rider position, with ramifications for riding as a whole.

The visual charts on the next couple of pages clearly show where these differences lie.

It was a point of discussion around the turn of the nineteenth century, at a time when side saddles were acceptable, about whether or not women could—or should—be allowed to ride astride using a saddle built for men. The arguments pro and con included concerns about physiological health as well as aesthetic and social acceptability points of view. In her 1998 book called *Frauen zu Pferde* (Women on Horses), Gaby Hermsdorf summarizes some of these arguments very succinctly. She includes a quote from an article in a German magazine, *St. Georg*, article from the 1920s that stated, "In my opinion a woman will only be able to ride properly in a male saddle as the exception, not the rule. This is proven if you look at her thighs. A man's muscles are strong and tight around his bones, and his thighs are more hollow on the inside [referring to the hamstring]. A woman's muscles are looser and her thighs are more round. If a woman insists on riding on a saddle like a man, she may only be able to do so if she begins doing it as a young child and develops her muscles accordingly so that she sits properly."

Further to this, Graf von Wrangel in his book *Das Buch vom Pferde* (The Book of Horses) written in 1890 and revised in 1927 wrote, "...because of the difference in anatomy between men and women, women will never achieve a quiet positioning of the lower leg... ."

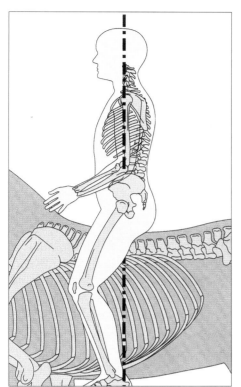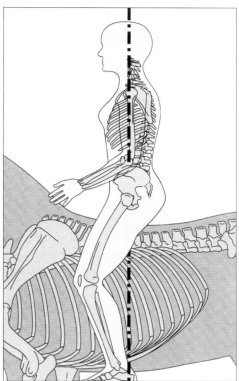

A male (left) and female (right) rider sitting in the shoulder-hip-heel, plumb line alignment on the horse's back. The gluteus maximus muscle of the male has much more contact with the horse, whereas the woman's pelvis is tipped more forward, which lifts her gluteus maximus higher away from the horse's back. This positioning of her butt cheeks is further exacerbated by the stronger curvature in her lower back and her shorter tailbone. In a men's saddle she won't get the support she needs on her pelvis from behind to be able to stay in balance.

And furthermore, from *Reit ABC* (ABCs of Riding) by Richard Schoenbeck: "This doesn't mean that a nicely grown and well-positioned woman doesn't make a pleasing appearance on a male saddle, but everything speaks to the use of a side saddle because female anatomy is simply not conducive to riding astride. If she begins riding like this when young, her body may grow to accommodate the proper position, but a grown woman's body will find it difficult to adjust. Her body shape will make it difficult to maintain balance and proper contact and position on the horse's back...."

Even if the emancipated females of those days turn in their graves to hear this, the facts do substantiate that some of these comments made by men back in the day were not entirely farfetched!

THE DIFFERENCES IN DETAIL

The following charts illustrate the various anatomical differences in the skeletal structures of male and female. In the pages that follow, each of these will be discussed in more detail.

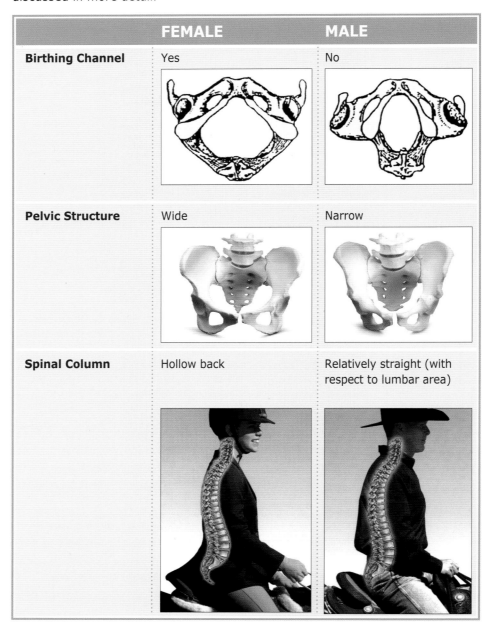

	FEMALE	MALE
Birthing Channel	Yes	No
Pelvic Structure	Wide	Narrow
Spinal Column	Hollow back	Relatively straight (with respect to lumbar area)

	FEMALE	MALE
Balance Point* of Pelvis	Farther forward Shorter pubic symphysis 	Middle of pelvis (on seat bones) Higher pubic symphysis
Pubic Symphysis	Fairly flat and low—will hit the pommel area 	Relatively higher than female pubic symphysis with steeper angles Will sit far away from pommel area
Hip Joints	Articulation is angled to the side Shorter tail bone 	Articulation straight, allowing the leg to hang straight Longer tail bone

*The balance point of the rider or center of gravity is farther forward for women and more in the center for men. Women balance as if on a tripod using their seat bones and pubic symphysis; men can balance on their seat bones only. The axis of balance can be drawn in an imaginary horizontal line on the pelvis between the two hip joints.

	FEMALE	MALE
Upper Leg	Femur is bigger on top and gets narrower down the knee	Femur remains pretty much same thickness from top to bottom
	Articulation at joint has wider angle, which makes it difficult for the leg to hang straight	Articulation angle relatively smaller, allowing leg to hang straight
Quadriceps and Hamstrings	Muscle looks rounder when viewed from front—not much "space" visible between legs	Quadriceps and hamstrings more defined on front and back of leg (less on sides), which leaves more room between the legs at the top
Seat Bones	Farther apart to accommodate birth canal	Closer together

ACCOMMODATING PELVIC ANATOMY

By James Warson, MD

Dr. Warson is the author of The Rider's Pain Free Back *(Trafalgar Square Books, 2007).*

"In riding, it is the rider's pelvis that forms the intimate attachment to the horse. With the pelvis as the anatomical foundation of riding, all other body parts become attachments designed to act in concert to stabilize the pelvis. With each motion, there is an equal and opposite motion (Newton's Third Law of Motion) and the horse's cadence and impulsion become transmitted to the rider through the rider's pelvis for analysis and reaction. Thus the saddle becomes a source of information as well as support.

"A saddle must be designed to effectively transmit touch, position, and even pain in a prompt and intelligible manner through the rider's pelvis to her nervous system. Once this information is processed by that nervous system, impulses must return to the muscles immediately for effective adaptation. These muscles must then act through a saddle that is correctly designed in order to function properly.

"The male pelvis is aligned longitudinally from front to back. This has produced the longitudinal appearance especially noticeable in English saddles. They are the 'descendants' of saddles that were designed to carry soldiers, people in politics, and supervisors of estates, all traditionally male roles. Look at the underside of these saddles and the similarity to the male human buttocks is obvious. When men wanted more comfort than bareback riding afforded, saddles evolved but were based on rider anatomy.

"Mechanization has changed the horse's role for the better. Instead of the horrifying work in the past, including slaughter in battle, the horse now participates in recreational activities and sports, with women riders being in the majority.

"A woman's pelvis is broader than a man's; consequently her hips are located more posteriorly. We see a situation where a woman on a man's saddle becomes something like a teeter-totter, and contact is decreased from medial to lateral in the saddle. The saddle ceases to be able to become the foundation and source of communication that is needed for ultimate riding. While some women may have what is called an 'android,' or male-like pelvis, it is never truly like a man's. I have seen great women riders who learned to adapt well to traditional men's saddles, but they would have been even better in a saddle designed to accommodate their pelvic anatomy."

Pelvic Position

When sitting straight with an erect spinal column, there are considerable differences in the position of the male and female pelvis. Seated persons will carry their weight on both seat bones when they are sitting correctly and comfortably. A man's pubic symphysis, angled significantly more steeply than a woman's, is farther from the chair's surface, whereas the woman's will possibly touch the chair's surface, or at the very least, be a lot closer to it. Conversely, her tailbone is farther away because it is shorter than a man's.

In order to achieve the same erect position, the male and female pelvis will need to be positioned differently given the variations in both the spinal column and the pelvic structure. The balance point (horizontal axis) in the pelvis is found much farther forward in a woman and her tailbone is much shorter (given the need for room in the birth canal).

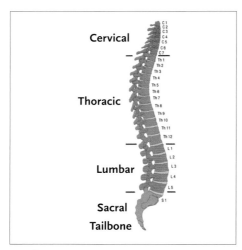

The four curves of the human vertebrae.

Therefore, lacking this natural support at the back of the pelvis, she will often find herself falling back in a saddle if it is not correctly fitted.

In order for a woman to bring her spinal column into a fully erect position, she will have to tilt her pelvis more forward than a man, which a) displaces her balance point or center of gravity, and b) causes her to sit on her pubic bone (see p. 32 for more on balance points and center of gravity). This will happen as a natural result of the flatter angulation of the pubic symphysis as well as the pelvic tilt to sit straight in the saddle. All of her crotch area rubs on the front of the saddle working against the balance point of the saddle as she will be carrying much of her weight here rather than on her seat bones.

In this position, the female rider often has little support under her tailbone and from her gluteus muscles. So in order to escape this "pain," in her crotch area from rubbing her pubic symphysis on the pommel area, she will collapse at her hip to find support under her butt, and position her balance point farther back in the saddle. This results in a further hollowing of her back, changing the natural shock-absorption ability of her spinal column in the lumbar area.

A chair seat is often the result of this "leaning back" to find support under the gluteal muscles, which are usually positioned higher than those of a man to begin with. Her legs will shoot forward as in a pendulum, and this,

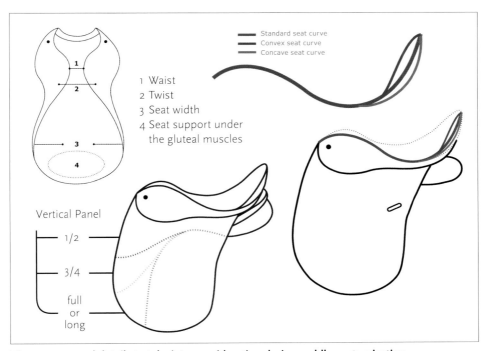

1 Waist
2 Twist
3 Seat width
4 Seat support under the gluteal muscles

Standard seat curve
Convex seat curve
Concave seat curve

Vertical Panel

1/2

3/4

full
or
long

There are several details to take into consideration during saddle customization.

of course, impacts her ability to give the horse the proper aids through her thighs because they are out of alignment. Further, this "bent" position and altered balance to the rear makes it difficult to properly develop and use the abdominals in riding. Without sufficient strength in the core muscles, the rider will find it difficult to sit in a balanced position, give the correct aids, and use her body's natural shock-absorbing capabilities in the spine, hip joints, and knees. Women who continually ride in this position because of a badly fitted saddle will suffer from back pain and possibly slipped discs—particularly in the lower back. Particularly damaging is the slumping position often expe-

rienced by a woman, which increases the curve in her lumbar vertebrae even more, that is, when compared to the straightness of a man's.

The pelvis is wider in women, as is the gluteus muscle. The point of articulation of the hip joint is farther forward on her pelvis, and the hip socket (*acetabulum*) is angled more strongly. When the pelvis is not supported, it is even more difficult for her to keep her legs hanging straight down. The male's hips are articulated more at the side of the pelvis and with a smaller angle, which allows his legs to hang straight down without great effort.

The width of the saddle's seat and the height and angle of the cantle will either support or hinder the rider position. Standard saddles made for men are usually wider in the twist but pretty narrow in the waist (where the saddle seams are), a construction that is uncomfortable for a woman. Her hips will be "wrenched out" over the twist and her seat bones can "hit" the seams on the seat.

Saddles built for women, on the other hand, should be (as a rule) narrower in the twist and wider in the seat (waist). To ride in balance, the deepest point in the saddle should generally be farther forward for women and more centered for men. There were saddle manufacturers in the past that took some of the anatomical differences between men and women into consideration in their saddle designs; however, few to date have really paid systematic attention to the ramifications all of these differences have on a saddle's fit. Too many women are still riding in saddles built for men, which causes all sorts of positional challenges.

The Femur and Its Articulation in the Hip Joint

The female femur tends to become narrower in its overall shape (almost conical) as it nears the knee, and it is attached at the hip with a fairly big angle to the pelvis. The male femur is pretty much the same shape and thickness top to bottom, and its angle of articulation is smaller. Even a man will experience hip or crotch pain when he has a saddle that is not right for him.

The "seat" or position of a rider is not only influenced by the saddle's seat size and construction, but also by the size and shape of the upper leg or thigh area. It is easier for a man to bring his upper inner thigh closer to the horse through the saddle flap because the angle of his hip articulation as well as his quadriceps and hamstring muscles allow him to hang his leg straight.

The femur of the woman will tend to angulate outward from the hip joint, but the better the support of the back end of the saddle seat, the better her chances of maintaining a straight, seated position. Extended stirrup bars will also help her to keep a proper leg position.

The Muscles of the Upper Leg

When viewed from the front the woman has visibly rounder thighs than a man. Regardless how thick or skinny the thighs actually are, there will be less space between the upper inner thigh—to the point of almost being knock-kneed. In a saddle that doesn't fit (or is made for a man) she may experience pain and pressure at both the hips and the knees. Her legs may shoot forward, her upper body falls back—and there she goes into a chair seat!

The male has a much more oval-shaped upper leg, with most of the quadriceps at the front and the hamstrings pretty much all in the back. This leaves much more space between the upper inner thighs from the beginning.

ISSUES IMPACTING RIDER HEALTH CAUSED BY POOR SADDLE FIT OR GENDER-INAPPROPRIATE SADDLES

From Backache to Slipped Discs

A woman should not even be allowed to ride in a saddle that has not taken her unique anatomical requirements into consideration. When there is insufficient support, especially in the lumbar area, backache will result—no question. Many professional female riders have experienced backache, which can go from simple aching after riding all the way to slipped discs and other permanent issues. Part of the problem with a slipped disc could arise from the four natural curves of your spinal column in the cervical, thoracic, lumbar, and sacral regions (see p. 50).

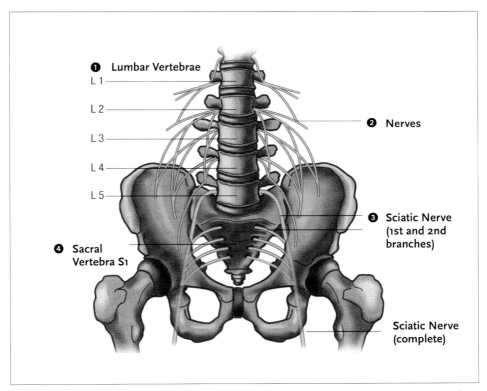

The lumbar vertebrae (1) withstand more pressure from above than the vertebrae in any other region of the spinal column. Nerves branch out from both sides of the spinal column (2), which provide the body with its "energy" to move. Particularly sensitive are the transitional areas between L4 and L5, as well as between L5 and the sacrum (4), which is where the sciatic nerve (3) originates.

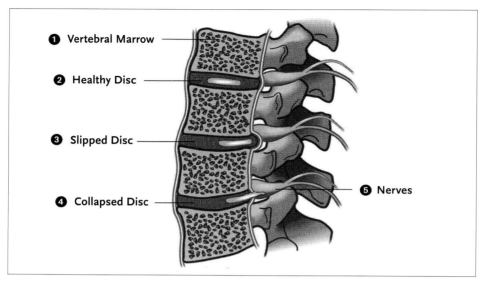

1. Vertebral Marrow
2. Healthy Disc
3. Slipped Disc
4. Collapsed Disc
5. Nerves

A healthy disc is extremely flexible. When it is injured, it can become deformed (protruding or slipped) or collapse (prolapsed disc).

Discs act as shock absorbers between the vertebrae. If the vertebrae are stressed in some way because of incorrect positioning in a badly fit saddle, disc problems can result.

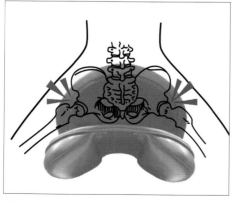

Hip pain can result when the twist of the saddle is too wide for the rider.

Bladder and Kidney Infections

Recurring bladder infections and chronic kidney problems have been thought to be the result of using "gender-inappropriate" saddles (especially where women are concerned). Dr. James Warson, MD, has researched this topic exhaustively for both men and women. In his book, *The Rider's Pain Free Back,* he describes his eye-opening findings, part of which I have taken the liberty of paraphrasing for inclusion in this book. He mentions the fact that kidney and bladder infections can occur in women if the pubic symphysis constantly rubs against the pommel. The skin around the ureter swells, which can cause difficulty in emptying the bladder completely during urination.

As a result, a small amount of urine is constantly retained in the bladder, the bladder becomes irritated and swollen leading to chronic difficulties. Men generally don't have these issues because of the muscles around the testicles, which can literally pull them back into the body cavity (subconsciously—in order to avoid trauma). Underdeveloped *bulbocavernosus* and *dartos* muscles can cause issues with boys before puberty, causing them to experience pain in this area due to malfunctioning of these muscles (see p. 58). This may well lead to boys no longer wanting to ride!

Impotence

If the pressure from the saddle is too great on the sensitive area between the testicles and the anus (the perineum) it can actually hinder blood flow through the artery that leads into the penis. This could eventually cause erectile issues all the way to complete impotence if the blood flow stops totally.

Recognizing this issue, cavalry soldiers began to use the McClellan saddle during the Civil War. It had the cutout in the crotch area that prevented pressure in this sensitive region, thereby reducing the risk of impotence after long periods of time spent in the saddle. This is another one of those "missing or lost" nuggets of information that should be reintegrated into saddle design!

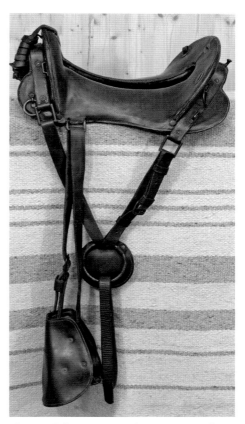

The McClellan saddle with its cutout in the seat was designed to relieve pressure on this sensitive area of the male anatomy.

Illustration of a male pelvis in an AdapTree® which integrates the patented crotch-comfort system.

THE SOLUTION

Gender Correct Saddles for Men and Women

Comfort in the saddle should not be a matter of compromise. Both male and female riders should not be "positioned" in a seat that inhibits the proper giving of aids, as well as causing pain while restricting movement. Rather, a saddle should work like a well-fitting and well-worn shoe: not really noticeable yet protective and supportive.

Women especially need anatomically correct saddles appropriate for their gender. They find it more difficult to move in harmony with the horse's motion because of their anatomy (a shorter tailbone, seat bones that are farther apart, and the angle of articulation of the femur at the hip joint). When they don't have the proper support to maintain their position in a saddle, it costs them muscle strength and energy to even sit straight.

The Characteristics of a Saddle Made for Women

As you can see in the photo on p. 57, a saddle made for a woman has several distinguishing characteristics:

The rear of the seat needs to be much wider to accommodate her wider pelvis and support her larger and higher *gluteus maximus* muscle (photo on p. 57, point 1).

The skirt needs to be attached lower on the seat leather, with extremely flat seat seaming to avoid pressure and pain to the inner upper thigh and the proximal end of the gluteal muscles (2).

The twist is usually much narrower than for a man to allow the upper leg to hang straight and counteract the natural leg turnout that occurs because of the female rounder-shaped thigh, and the angle of articulation of the femur at the hip joint (3).

To avoid hitting the pubic symphsyis at the pommel area, the waist's seaming is usually wider apart and the pommel itself is at a much flatter angle (4). This also helps proper positioning of the seat bones, which are farther apart than a man's. Only when the saddle is made to accommodate these comfortably will the woman be able to sit on her balance point (the "tripod" between the seat bones and pubic symphysis) without undue pressure during the pelvic tilt.

Particular attention needs to be paid to the seat foam of the saddle (foam is put between the tree and the leather covering), which has to support the woman's higher-up gluteal muscles and shorter tailbone at the cantle area (5).

In order to achieve this necessary support area (6), many women resort to riding in saddles that are a size too small, which is not the best solution. This will impact the ability of a woman to properly move with the motion of the horse while forcing the pubic symphysis

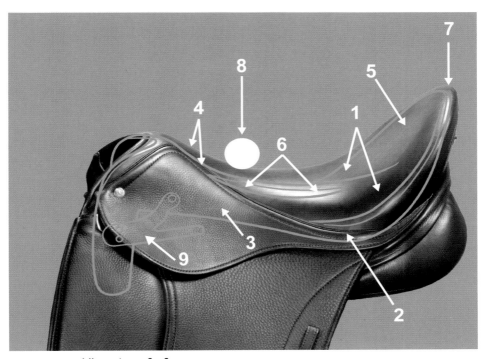

A women's saddle: points of reference.

even more into the pommel area thus taking her out of the balance point of the saddle. Conversely, saddles made for men should have their support area a bit lower down from the cantle, but this is rarely taken into consideration since with their longer tailbone men generally find better natural stability in most saddles.

This area needs special treatment—with air pockets, foam, cutouts and the like—in order to avoid any pressure on the sensitive crotch area (for men, too). Many modern plastic or fiberglass trees are particularly unforgiving and just as inflexible in this region as they are under the larger, more forgiving, glu-

teal area. The resulting pressure that can occur in the crotch area is not only uncomfortable but can lead to chronic health issues. To avoid this happening, I prefer a cutout that is padded with a soft, yet supportive insert material.

A high and steeply angled cantle can provide even more support for the pelvic position of the female rider (7).

The position of the female pelvis requires a saddle that has its deepest point farther forward than one made for men and one that is is considered a "forward-balance" saddle (8).

Most men's upper and lower legs are fairly equal in length. However, most women have a longer upper leg (hip joint to knee is longer than knee to anklebone). At the very least, this indicates the need to position the stirrup bars farther back in order to allow a woman's legs to hang straight, because the natural tendency would be, again, for her leg to shoot forward to achieve its own center of gravity, acting as a pendulum. In many cases, extended, or even extra-extended stirrup bars are required to assist with proper leg position (9). This helps the female avoid having to "clamp" her thighs in order to maintain position and stay out of the "chair" seat. If a man were to ride in a saddle with this stirrup-bar placement, he would feel as though his legs were being pulled back.

A saddler's job is to bring horse and rider as close as possible, which means that the vertical spinal column of the human should be next to the horizontal vertebrae of the horse—while keeping the position of the rider supple and natural—to achieve a flowing harmony in movement between the two. The rider should be as close to the withers as possible without inhibiting the horse's shoulder movement, of course.

WHAT ABOUT CHILDREN?

Children generally demonstrate the ramifications of having ridden in gender-inappropriate and badly fitted saddles when they get older. Many children ride on saddles that are uncomfortable simply because they don't know any better and they just want to ride. They don't care.

Parents would never let their children wear shoes that don't fit. Issues arising from podiatric problems, including leg length and position (for example, bow-legged, knock-kneed), scoliosis, back pain, and pelvic misalignment are usually very difficult to correct in adulthood. That is why, particularly as the child is growing, it is very important that the shoes fit.

But, it is also very important that the saddle fits, especially when the child rides regularly. Incorrect "accommodating" riding positions (because the saddle hurts!) can cause developmental structural issues or chronic health problems that may not appear until long after puberty.

Even the question, "Why don't more boys ride?" may be due to saddle-fitting issues. Let's hear what Dr. James Warson says about this:

"A young man's testicles lie between his pelvis and the saddle. There are three muscular components in the testicles: the *M. dartos tunikum* in the wall of the scrotum, the *vas deferens*, and the *cremaster* (the muscle responsible for 'tightening of the balls' or pulling the testicles back up into the body cavity). The cremaster does not function fully in the boy before puberty so he will ex-

Practice makes perfect, especially when you start young! But please—use a saddle that has been fitted to both horse and rider.

perience his testicles being 'squished' when riding because they cannot be retracted or 'shrunk.' This becomes even more prevalent during trot or canter, which may explain why young boys prefer to do their riding at a walk or in a posting trot. This is, of course, embarrassing to talk about with both the riding instructor and even more so with your mother, so this is probably why boys would rather pursue sports other than riding!"

The development of more supportive breeches and the use of the AdapTree® or a similarly constructed saddle tree could go a long way to make riding more fun for boys. Combined training programs that incorporate team sports such as soccer with access to horses would be one way to awaken the interest as an alternative sport—especially in North America. Riding is not a mainstream sport here like it is in Europe, at least not for most boys.

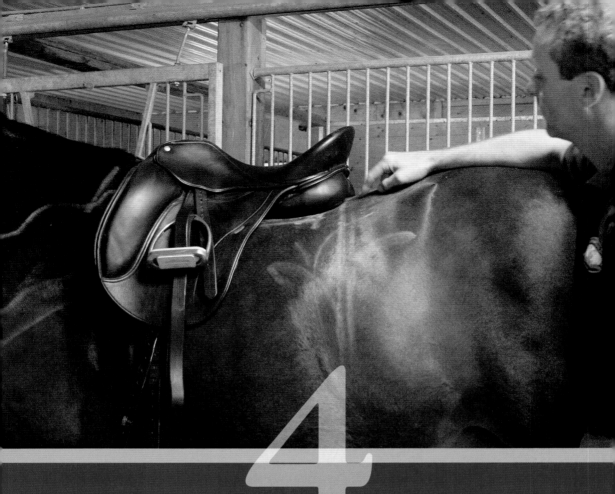

4

EXACTLY WHERE IS THE
SADDLE-SUPPORT AREA?

It still seems somewhat of a mystery to most people in the equine world where the saddle-support area on the horse is exactly. Even riders in the various disciplines cannot come to a generally acceptable consensus and since many veterinarians, farriers, and other equine body workers are not riders themselves, they are not 100 percent certain, nor are they familiar with the actual construction of a saddle as it pertains to the saddle-support area. Many tack shops sell saddles much like a shoe shop sells shoes: They bring out one model after another from their inventory into the store, or even into the barn, and ask how it feels. When the rider feels relatively comfortable and the saddle seems to fit the horse standing in the cross-ties, it's a sale— and this is often a wrong decision. So let's investigate a little more closely this mysterious saddle support area, which it's vital to understand.

In my experience, the tendency to preferentially breed ever more "quadratic" (squarely built) horses will prove a challenge to the saddler and the saddle fitter. The saddle-support area on the horse is getting smaller and smaller, whereas the reality of larger physiques of both men and women in the civilized world indicates the need for a bigger and longer saddle in order to ride comfortably. (Okay, let's stop beating around the bush; riders are getting heavier and backsides are getting larger!)

In any case, frequently, the saddle has to unite these two aspects: a larger seat size for the human component with a shorter panel and weight-bearing surface for the horse's saddle-support area. Over the past years, many saddle companies have made the necessary changes to accommodate the requirements of the larger rider's rear end though without necessarily paying attention to the requirements of the horse's back. Larger and longer saddles are not the answer to maintaining horse health—whether for sport or recreation. There needs to be a different way.

THE HORSE'S BACK

Building Bridges

The horse's skeletal structure can be compared to a suspension bridge. The supporting posts are the front and hind legs and the suspension cables are the ligaments of the neck and back. This suspension bridge (the horse) will support the weight of the rider when the horse brings his hind legs "underneath" him and closer to his forelegs. This allows the back to come up to form an "arch" between his legs (the supporting posts). As riders we want to

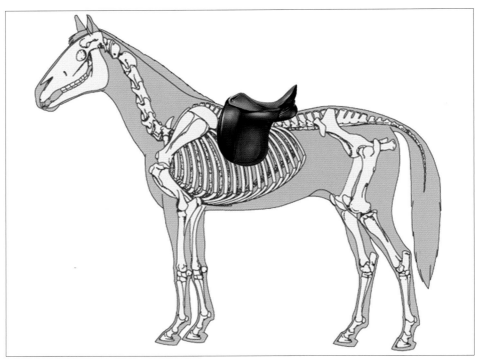

The shoulder blades on a trained and mature horse (as opposed to a younger animal) are higher and rotated more toward the rear, which means that the front of the saddle-support area has moved somewhat more back in order to allow the shoulder enough room to move freely. This actually reduces the saddle-support area. As is shown in the picture, this saddle is minimally too long for this horse's back, as the panel ends just past the last floating rib.

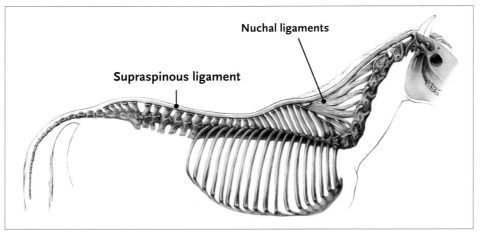

The nuchal and supraspinous ligaments are the "cables" in the suspension bridge of the horse's back.

These are the vertebrae in a relaxed and standing horse. It is clear that the spinal processes face backward at the withers area, then are straight, then face toward the front—with relatively little space between their tips.

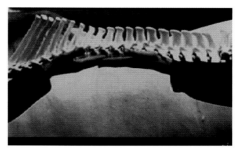

This photo is showing the vertebrae after the horse's back has "come up," which significantly increases the space between the tips of the individual vertebrae.

maintain back health to allow the horse to bring his back up and his hind legs under him in order to be able to carry our weight.

Since horses have no collarbone it means that they are missing this connective anchor between ligaments and tendons that we have to connect the upper arm to the rib cage. Instead, it is a muscle connection that performs this function in the horse: The *Musculus serratus ventralis thoracis* connects to the *Musculi pectorales superficiales*, which is made up of *M. Pectoralis transversus* and *M. pectoralis descendens* to ensure the attachment of the forelegs to the rump (see drawings on pp. 68 and 69). That is why this muscle connection is sometimes described as a "false joint." These muscles are constantly adapting and changing due to training, maturation, nutrition, stabling, shoeing, illness, or simply through the unnatural act of carrying a rider's weight.

When I ride and train my horse to achieve more elevation, the muscles grow and increase the visual distance between the forelegs when viewed from the front. The angle between the upper forelegs increases upward and outward, which means that the distance between the shoulder blades also grows as they move upward and rotate back. The rib cage in front is raised, the withers look higher, and behind the shoulder, the wither angle gets steeper.

In this area of the wither angle the muscles *M. rhomboideus* (rhomboid); *M. Spinalis cervicis* (cervical spinalis muscle); and *M. trapezius* will also get thicker and stronger—just as the biceps or trapezius gets bigger when a human works out. As you move farther back on the horse's back, you encounter the *M. latissimus dorsi*, and the longest back muscle the *M. longissimus dorsi*. On a horse that has been trained properly, the muscle definition will be clearly visible, just as the abdominal muscles (or six-pack) of a well-trained bodybuilder

HORSES ARE NOT THE SAME
Various Breeds Showing Different Back Lengths and Conformation

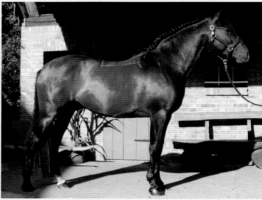

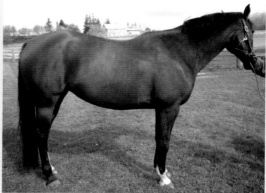

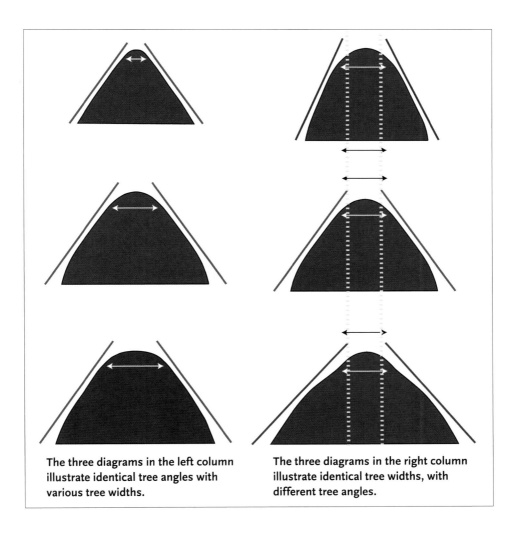

The three diagrams in the left column illustrate identical tree angles with various tree widths.

The three diagrams in the right column illustrate identical tree widths, with different tree angles.

are clearly differentiated from his pectoral muscles, which run from the chest to the upper arms.

The Muscles in the Back

The *M. Longissimus dorsi* simply means "longest back muscle" and is often simply called this. It plays a crucial role for the rider—it needs to stay loose and supple so that the horse can carry the rider with a maximum freedom of movement without causing any damage to his back. Good training ensures that this muscle stays supple and elastic while strengthening the individual muscle fibers without increasing the girth of the muscle itself. (This is true for humans as well as horses.) To allow this to happen and keep it supple as a key player in movement, the support

THE HORSE IS NOT A BEAST OF BURDEN

Nature did not make the horse a natural beast of burden. There are only two instances in nature that the horse is confronted with an additional weight on his back: First, when a stallion mounts a mare and bites her in the withers to immobilize her during mating, and second, when a predator jumps on his back before delivering the kill bite. Both of these situations lead to an instinctual reaction that is completely different from what is expected when we, as riders, put weight on a horse's back. During mating, the stallion needs the mare to stop moving forward, needs her back dropped and her pelvis rotated upward and outward in preparation to be bred. The mare is not able to move forward in collection and suppleness. Obviously, she wouldn't want to move at all in this situation; the point is that she can't really move at all, let alone when under a saddle that has this same effect.

And, when the horse experiences the fear of near death from a predator on his back, he will react by trying to buck it off, then run away—reactions that we don't want when we're sitting on his back!

The domestication of horses over the years has come to allow them to trust us—after the proper relationship building of trust and the correct training—to ride them without significant danger to either party. However, there are situations where the instinctive behavior of the horse will prevail—and one of these is when faced with a badly fitted saddle. If the saddle pinches at the withers (tree width is too narrow and/or the tree angle is too wide, for example) this can seem like the vise grip of the stallion's bite. A saddle that has a gullet channel that is too narrow or too long on the lumbar region, can release the instinct to flee: It can feel to the horse as if a predator is on his back.

posts (the forelegs and the hind legs) need to be close together.

The *M. Longissimus dorsi* inserts at the base of the last four cervical vertebrae and ends at the horse's pelvis. If the horse is restricted from bringing his legs under him (through incorrect riding or an ill-fitting saddle) it feels as though the bridge (his dorsal ligament system) has lost the support from the posts. The asphalt on the bridge would heave and crack, but before the horse would "allow" his spinal column to be damaged, he would react and contract his longissimus muscle to avoid this at all costs. This, in return, would result in a shortening of the forelegs while the back legs splay out—and the horse "falls apart," goes "upside down," or builds the wrong muscles (also known as training and riding "backward").

During movement, first one side and then the other (alternating) of the longissimus contracts and relaxes. One side is more contracted, depending on which lead the horse is cantering. Only when the horse jumps, rears, or bucks is the longissimus contracted evenly on both sides.

The longissimus is about 8 to 10 inches (20 to 25 cm) thick. The trapezius and the spinales muscles (the ones that originate at the spinal processes) are comparatively thinner, being only about one inch (2 to 3) cm thick.

The shoulder blade lies over the longissimus and the *M. spinalis dorsi*, and the shoulder cartilage is very close to where the trapezius insertion occurs.

The spinales muscles (in this case *M. spinalis dorsi*) are located under the trapezius and the shoulder blade. They are situated internally beside the lon-gissimus and are covered in the withers area by the rhomboids. The *M. Splenius cervicis* balances the neck of the horse and lifts it from the base of its insertion area at the base of the neck. The part of the *M. spinales* muscles that lie under the trapezius and the rhomboids and is directly attached to the vertebrae has the function of stabilizing the spinal processes in the withers area. This muscle area is especially prone to significant development—especially with jumpers—because it is continually contracted to accommodate the shock of landing.

The trapezius, the rhomboids, and the spinales muscles all converge in the withers area. One could liken the withers area to a distributor cap since

Sue Harris © Wu Wei Verlag

When the horse has been properly trained and elevates in front, as in this picture, the saddle can be brought out of balance. It is therefore important to fit the saddle, not only in the cross-ties, but also dynamically—that is, when the horse is moving.

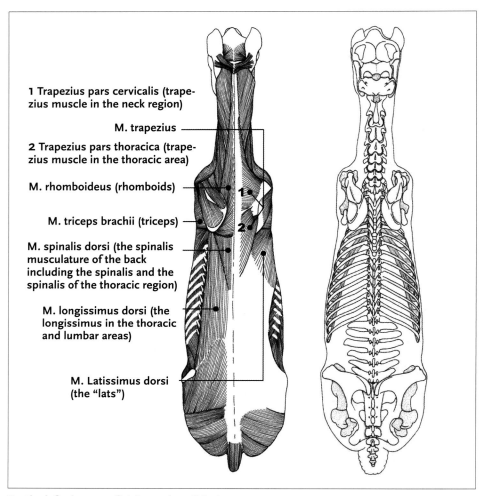

1 Trapezius pars cervicalis (trapezius muscle in the neck region)

M. trapezius

2 Trapezius pars thoracica (trapezius muscle in the thoracic area)

M. rhomboideus (rhomboids)

M. triceps brachii (triceps)

M. spinalis dorsi (the spinalis musculature of the back including the spinalis and the spinalis of the thoracic region)

M. longissimus dorsi (the longissimus in the thoracic and lumbar areas)

M. Latissimus dorsi (the "lats")

On the left, the superficial muscles of the horse.

it contains not only these different muscle groups but also nerve endings, as well as the convergence of both the nuchal- and dorsal-ligament systems. If the saddle puts pressure on this area because it is too tight in the tree, the horse will suffer significant pain. It will respond with a "flight response," contracting his muscles in preparation for running away (or at least trying to!) Riders call this "tensing up," and can feel how heavy the horse is in the reins.

The bones of the vertebrae are relatively well protected through the surrounding musculature in this area; however, in the thoracic area the vertebrae are particularly sensitive to a saddle that pinches and inhibits movement.

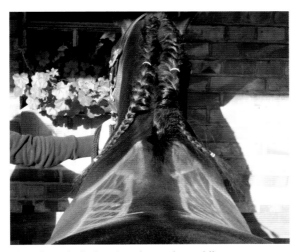

The white chalk drawing shows the saddle-support area and where the saddle should lie; the red triangle on the withers area shows the highly sensitive area where the saddle should *not* be placed.

This saddle demonstrates good distribution of the rider's weight on the saddle-support area and a wide-enough gullet channel.

WARNING

The horse's back has many tendons and ligaments, especially the nuchal- and dorsal-ligament system. Tendons connect the muscles to the bones, and the ligaments connect the bones to each other. That is why the saddle should never put pressure on either the tendons or the ligaments, or cause friction there, because this can lead to significant irritation and long-term damage. Try tapping the top of your hand on the finger tendons for about five minutes a day; after a couple of days the tendons of the back of your hand will be inflamed and you'll be unable to move properly. Once a tendon or ligament has been damaged, it can take much longer than a muscle injury to heal because tendons and ligaments have less blood circulation.

The spinal and transverse processes are nicely surrounded by the longissimus muscle. In the distal end (situated away from the point of attachment) of the vertebrae there are openings for the spinal nerves, which make it critical to ensure the channel width (gullet) of the saddle (the area under the saddle between the two panels) is wide enough: There cannot be any pressure on these vertebrae and there must be enough room for movement. Sometimes the gullet is sufficiently wide at the pommel end, but gets narrower toward the cantle. And it is exactly at the back of the saddle where the vertebrae need to be able to move because of their anatomy and where they should not be impinged due to a narrow gullet channel.

THE GIRTH AND THE RIB CAGE

ry this experiment: Take an hour-glass and try to tie a string around either the top or the bottom half. You will find that the string always migrates to the narrowest part of the glass—that is, the middle, connective piece. Your horse's girth will do the same: It will migrate automatically to the narrowest part of the horse's thoracic area; we call this the girth area. A saddle that has been girthed up anywhere behind this point will slide forward during riding, taking the saddle and the rider with it and leaving the correct saddle-support area on the horse (if it was correctly positioned there during mounting). This natural tendency to find the "area of least resistance" always causes the sad-dle to move forward onto the shoulder.

In dressage nowadays short girths with long billets are the rule. A huge ad-vantage here is that the girth's buckles don't bother the rider at his thighs and usually allow the saddle to be fastened more securely. However, the girth buckles can now be located at a very sensitive area of the horse's rib cage.

The longer girth used with jumping and eventing saddles is usually buck-led on the sweat flap, which means that there is a relatively thick second leather layer protecting the horse's

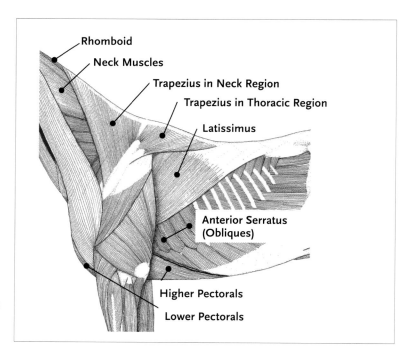

Side view of the superficial muscles of the horse.

Rhomboid
Neck Muscles
Trapezius in Neck Region
Trapezius in Thoracic Region
Latissimus
Anterior Serratus (Obliques)
Higher Pectorals
Lower Pectorals

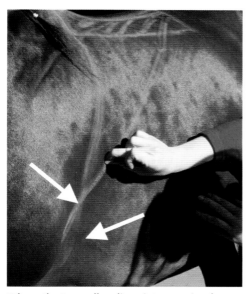

Where the two yellow lines intercept is where the triceps and the latissimus muscles cross. Where these two lines cross and behind the red X is the best spot for the girth buckle to be (the right back region of the "X" as per the arrows shown on the diagram).

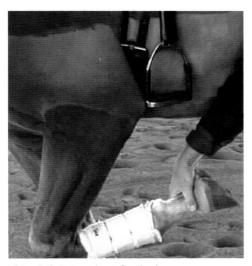

This girth is too short for the horse; you can see that the girth buckle will irritate him at the leg and elbow during movement. This is easily tested when standing like this.

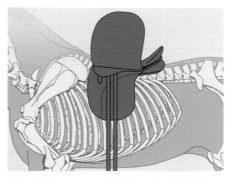

This saddle is positioned behind the shoulder blade but a) is too long for the horse—you can see the panel extends past the insertion of the last floating rib—and b) the billets are set too far back on this particular saddle.

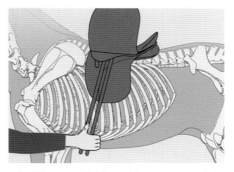

Often billets get pulled forward in an attempt to girth in the correct position.

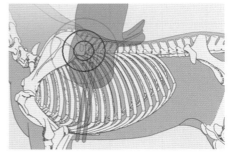

The girth will naturally seek the narrowest spot (point of least resistance) for its positioning. The result will be that the billets pull the saddle forward onto the horse's shoulder blade, potentially damaging its cartilage. The red circle illustrates the point of potential damage at the cartilaginous insertion of the shoulder blade because pulling the billets forward has now positioned the tree points directly onto the horse's shoulder.

flank from the buckle. A short girth is buckled directly on the side of the horse, so that the buckle, which may be protected minimally with one thin layer of leather, may cause pressure here as well. The area where the girth is positioned and buckled is an area where several muscle groups converge and have their sensitive points, which means that we should avoid irritating them if possible.

The girth should be buckled to the billets as close to the widest part of the horse's side as possible (i.e. as high up as possible) so that the buckles are "pulled away" from the rib cage and won't put unnecessary pressure on his side and the insertion points of the *M. Pectoralis profundus*.

In the past, either foregirths and point billets (billets that are inserted directly at the tree point) helped to prevent the saddle from slipping forward, or the saddle was girthed on really tightly to keep it in the correct position. Today we know, however, that it is partially due to the billets, position on the saddle that causes the sliding forward, and their position can be checked simply when the saddle is lying on the horse's back and seeing where the billets hang before girthing up. When they are hanging too far back, chances are that the girth will pull them forward and the saddle will ride up on the shoulder (as described earlier).

A "TRAIN CRASH"

Problems from the Scapula to the Sacroiliac

The horse's shoulder "joint" (also known as a "false joint" or "soft joint") is different from a human's. Unlike human shoulders, which are attached by a collarbone, it is supported by muscles and tendons without any skeletal attachment. This makes the horse's shoulders much more flexible than a human's and increases the range of motion. If a person moves her arm forward and upward, the shoulder moves forward and upward. If a horse moves his foreleg forward and upward, the shoulder moves upward and back-

ward; this means that it has to have room to rotate under the saddle panel. Because of its more flexible support and attachment system, the horse's shoulder is capable of carrying heavier loads and is able to compensate for rougher handling.

The sacroiliac or SI joint is very sensitive to jarring, as it is mainly ligaments (not muscles) that attach the pelvis to the backbone. An apt analogy is the comparison of the SI joint to an old, dry tree branch (brittle, not flexible) versus the shoulder joint, which is

PROBLEMS IN THE MUSCULATURE AND SKELETAL STRUCTURE, WHICH CHANGE THE SPINAL COLUMN AND AFFECT SADDLE FIT

By Barbara Welter-Boeller, Physiotherapist and Osteopath

"Osteopathic treatments can greatly reduce pain through the use of hot and cold compresses, lasers, MRI, or electroshock therapy. Supported by ionizing massages and other manual applications, these counteract any inhibited freedom of motion in the muscles, joints, and connective tissue. Horse management, tack, the way the horse is being used and his training methodology will all be tested, and changed if necessary, in order to support any of the treatment indicated.

"An osteopathic diagnosis usually shows one of two main reasons for reduced mobility: First, a uniform lesion in an area of the spine whereby one or both neighboring vertebrae will show this restriction. This symptom is generally the result of trauma, getting cast or slipping, but it can be from bucking or another reason; treatment is relatively simple by reducing pain and restoring mobility through osteopathic treatment assisted by physiotherapy.

"However, second and more common—and more difficult—is the so-called 'conglomerate' lesion in the vertebrae. In this case, there are usually at least two or more affected areas of the spine, which means that generally they will have occurred because of some compensatory behavior. The cause for this can be muscle injury, muscle cramping, injury to the legs (including suspensory ligaments and muscle damage), saddles that don't fit, incorrect training, and a crooked rider. The individual vertebrae may still feel flexible and move as they should during a diagnosis, however, if the 'avoidance' behavior has been going on for some time, there will be obvious restrictions in mobility. An attempt to find the actual cause should always be made. This optimizes the possibility of success for osteopathic treatments, training therapies, changing tack and the saddle, and different riding techniques that are tried out to counteract the symptoms. Only treating the vertebrae (as a symptom) may result in short-term relief and improvement. This will not, however, address the cause because the horse will continue his compensatory behavior if the issue of the unbalanced saddle or a poor rider are not fixed.

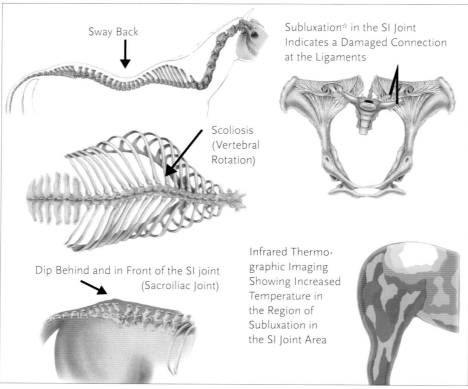

Sway Back

Subluxation* in the SI Joint Indicates a Damaged Connection at the Ligaments

Scoliosis (Vertebral Rotation)

Dip Behind and in Front of the SI joint (Sacroiliac Joint)

Infrared Thermographic Imaging Showing Increased Temperature in the Region of Subluxation in the SI Joint Area

Above are some examples of how the horse's vertebrae can become twisted or subluxated in various areas of the back. There are many causes for this, and most of the indications are not visible to the naked eye. Many veterinarians rely on the use of thermographic imaging to determine where there are changes in circulation and increased temperature.

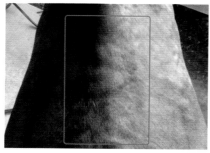

Here is a clearly visible subluxation in the lumbar vertebrae.

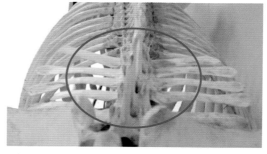

It is easy to determine where the ribs end and where the lumbar vertebrae begin. The saddle should never lie on the lumbar vertebrae with their long transverse processes (which are, in essence, "floating ribs").

*Subluxation: The word implies the presence of an incomplete or partial dislocation (Latin: *luxatio*) of a joint or organ. A medical subluxation is a significant structural displacement and, therefore, visible on static imaging studies. It can lead to inhibition and interference of nerve transmission.

like a young branch (moveable, more forgiving and flexible).

The SI joint is often the hub of all sorts of issues, most of which don't show up until it's too late, for example, a problem with a saddle shifting and twisting to one side: It doesn't fit the horse at the withers area because of uneven shoulder muscling. This will result in a contraction of the horse's longissimus muscle in order to compensate. This contraction then inhibits the freedom of movement of the SI joint and, it follows, that of the pelvis as a whole.

The SI joint is a fairly strong connection between the vertebral column and the pelvis, and acts pretty much like a shock absorber. When the longissimus is in constant contraction, the tendons, ligaments, and the entire SI joint is impacted. One obvious visual result of this is the development of a "dip" just in front of the SI joint. When this issue is not alleviated, vertebral subluxations and twisted vertebrae—especially in the lumbar area—will be the result.

Possible reasons behind this situation can include a rider's hand that is too strong; a rider who is constantly tense and tight in the saddle; or, most often, simply a badly fitting saddle. The end result can be compared to a "train-crash syndrome" where the movement at the front of the train is blocked somehow (the forelegs of the horse), causing the remaining wagons in the train (the vertebrae) to jump out of the tracks.

THE SCAPULAE

The shoulders of the horse can easily change their position because there are no supporting collarbones, as there are for the human. They move the same in every gait—up, back, down, forward. This means that the shoulder blade is constantly moving toward the saddle's position. The more extension in the forward-and-upward movement of the legs, the bigger the forward-and-backward movement in the shoulder. When the saddle is positioned directly behind the horse's shoulder as the horse is standing still, there needs to be enough room for the shoulder to move through and under the tree points (i.e. the gullet plate needs to accommodate this movement along its entire length all the way to the end at the tree points) during motion (see photos on p. 78).

The shoulder blade has a cartilaginous "cap" at the top end. This cap is about 3 to 4 inches (8 to 10 cm) in height and extremely elastic.

This cartilage is easily damaged when the tree points are too tight or constantly hitting it, and when compromised, the muscle fibers surrounding the shoulder blade will also be

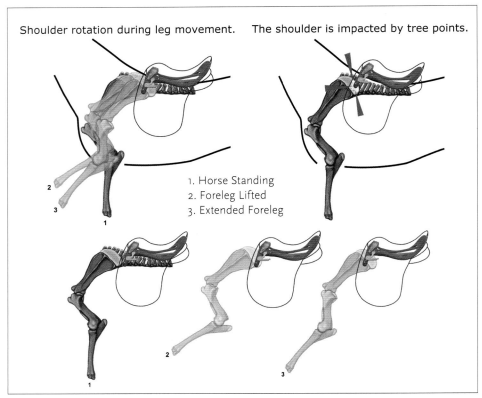

Shoulder rotation during leg movement. The shoulder is impacted by tree points.

1. Horse Standing
2. Foreleg Lifted
3. Extended Foreleg

Shoulder-blade rotation and movement during different foreleg motion. It is obvious that a saddle with an incorrectly adjusted tree angle, incorrect tree width, or when its tree points are angled forward, as in this illustration, can cause potentially serious issues at the shoulder.

impacted, which can lead to extreme pain for the horse to the point of lameness. (This was most likely the issue with my own horse, as I outlined in the introduction!)

To avoid this, the saddle needs to be fitted properly with an adjustable saddle tree so that the tree's width and angle accommodate the horse and allow his shoulder to "slip through" (like a sliding door). The triceps, which are connected to the shoulder and the upper foreleg, are one of the many muscles that are responsible for movement in the shoulder blade and should not be constrained.

This is why it is crucial to girth the first billet parallel to the edge of the triceps muscle, and not on top of the triceps muscle. This might require crossing the billets to accommodate the direction of muscle fibers to allow them proper freedom of movement—while keeping the saddle in position.

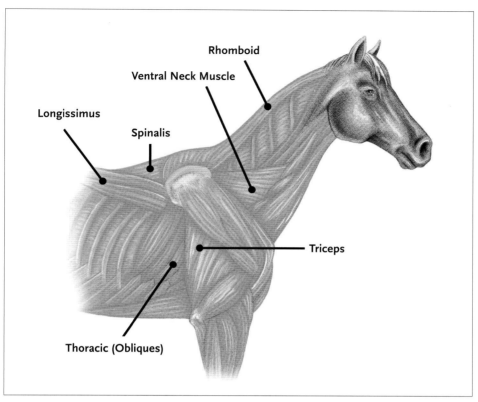

Rhomboid

Ventral Neck Muscle

Longissimus

Spinalis

Triceps

Thoracic (Obliques)

Below the superficial musculature, the longissimus and the shoulder muscles are easy to recognize. The shoulder blade with its attached cartilage cap lies between the spinalis, the rhomboid, the longissimus, and the superficial trapezius. It is critical that cartilage is not damaged because one of its jobs is to help protect the muscles surrounding it when the shoulder moves.

MOVEMENT OF THE SHOULDER BLADE

To actually feel for yourself the range of motion of your horse's shoulder blade, try this experiment. Have someone lead you while you ride bareback. Lay your hands beside the withers, left and right. Once you feel safe and balanced, close your eyes. You will feel the movement of the muscles here even at the walk. You will feel the contractions as well as the movement of the shoulder cartilage rotating up and back.

Now move your hands about 3 to 4 inches lower down—still behind the shoulder blades. During movement, the shoulder blades should glide smoothly through your hands (as long as the horse's longissimus muscle is not in a state of contraction).

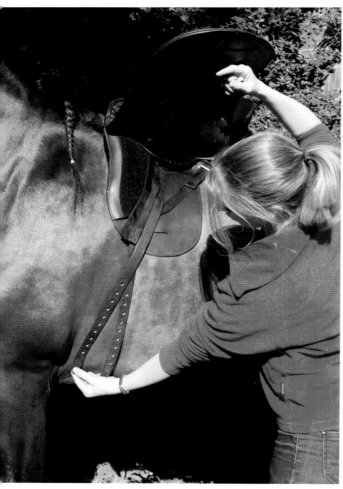

The horse on the left has well-developed triceps (and other shoulder muscles), which is why the saddle ergonomist needs to cross the billets to accommodate the direction of the muscle fibers. The point of intersection of the two billets is where the latissimus crosses under the triceps.

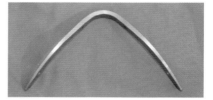

A symmetrical gullet plate (the steel arch under the pommel) may cause problems because it does not accommodate the natural unevenness of horses.

This gullet plate has been opened wider on the left to ensure there's enough room for the bigger left shoulder of this horse.

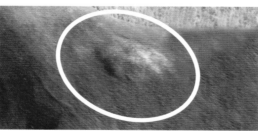

Most often, you will find white hairs on the left side of the horse's withers, which indicate a gullet plate that was too tight and incorrectly fitted, and tree points that were also too tight, incorrectly angled, or forward-facing. (Tree points are illustrated on p. 88 where it shows the difference between those that are forward-facing, a little more vertically placed but still impacting the shoulder cartilage, and rear-facing, which are the only type that don't hurt the shoulder.)

THE NATURAL ASYMMETRY OF THE HORSE

There are many theories concerning the natural unevenness or asymmetry of horse musculature. Some scientists think that there is a genetic predisposition, as in humans, to being left- or right-handed. Even the governing body of riding in Germany, the FN, recognizes in its rule books that most horses are born with a "natural asymmetry" and furthermore: "similarly to the left or right-handedness in humans, this predisposition is cerebral, or determined at birth. It is further supported by the fact that the forelegs are smaller than the hind legs" (*Richtlinien fuer Reiten und Fahren* [Guidelines for Riding and Driving], FN 2005). Others feel that this natural asymmetry could be caused by the way the equine embryo grows in its mother's womb.

In my opinion, however, this natural asymmetry is not really natural at all; rather it is the result of domestication and the conditions under which we keep our equine friends. In the wild, the horse moves all day, more or less slowly, in search of food, and while grazing for most of its waking hours it can cover over 20 miles of ground each day.

Most horses can be observed with their left front leg forward during grazing.

This does not work for domestic horses, even when they are allowed ample paddock or pasture time. Horses have less and less freedom to "run around." They often stand in their stalls 23/7, get fed in one spot, which means they don't have to graze for their food, and don't have to shift their body weight around naturally during the course of their day. Even minimally being let out to pasture or put in a paddock imitates their ability to move in the wild.

That's why I think that "natural asymmetry" develops during the growth phases of the horse. My personal observations are that most of the horses turned out in a flat pasture area generally have their left foreleg forward, which means that most of the weight will be on the right forehand.

This position could be due to the fact that the appendix and most of the gastrointestinal organs are situated on the right. During digestion, these organs are active, which means they will be engorged with blood. This causes pressure on the rib cage on the right side, which the horse compensates for by bending left. This puts extra weight on the right foreleg, while the left is splayed to the front. When there is enough roughage available, a horse will graze for about 17 hours a day with his head lowered and his weight on the right leg. This can lead to a change in conformation of the right humerus because of the constant weight.

"When a horse is born, it must adapt its muscle structure to match its native surroundings, whether natural or man-made. I have seen the physical changes

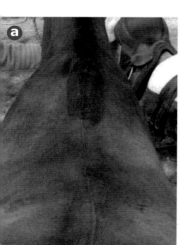  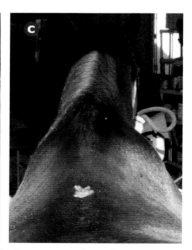

From the measurements that we have accumulated over the last 30 years from about 150,000 different horses, we have determined that about 70 percent are more strongly muscled on the left (a); about 10 percent are evenly muscled (b); and about 20 percent are larger on the right side (c).

a horse goes through once it has been captured from the free environment of pasture and then confined to a small enclosure." (Anthony Gonzales, *PBM: A Diary of Lameness,* p. 61, REF Publishing, Manassas, Virginia, 1986).

In my 34-plus years of working as a master saddler and saddle ergonomist, my technicians and I have measured and documented the results of over 150,000 horses on pretty much every continent (except Antarctica!). Most of these horses were housed in stables or living on pretty flat pastureland—and most of them had a definite increase on the left side over and behind the left shoulder, with a shoulder blade that was obviously higher and farther back on the left.

Some of the horses we looked at were kept outside in more hilly topography. They spent night and day living on this terrain. Because of their constant back-and-forth movement during grazing, they would constantly shift their weight to the "downhill" leg (just like skiers put more weight on this ski to stabilize their balance). Because of the continuing change in directional grazing, they would more evenly balance on both the right and left leg, alternating the one carrying the weight. Most of these horses actually showed a more evenly structured musculature on both sides—the 10 percent of "ambidextrous" horses. However, the development of this more even skeletal structure is really only an influence during the first two years of

the horse's life—thereafter, it really has little impact.

What I can conclude with certainty based on my observations, is that a good 70 percent of those horses that were measured over the years have a more strongly developed shoulder and shoulder muscles, with a farther forward right shoulder. This is what we call the "natural asymmetry" of the horse.

Our general methodology in working with horses would also seem to underline the affinity we have with the left side of the horse. We lead on the left, we saddle from the left, and we mount from the left. Many horses demonstrate "uneasiness" when approached from the right; even when groomed on the right. Perhaps it is because they instinctively want to protect their right side, which houses the digestive organs. This seeming anomaly can also be seen when observing horses fighting; the horse will turn its left shoulder toward the aggressor.

When riding, it is often easier to ride to the left and canter on the left lead. Also, most horse races go to the left (counterclockwise) perhaps because the horse's natural asymmetry is almost always stronger to the left.

It is a very important point to train and ride the horse straight. Even in the German Training Scale it clearly comments and describes the methods that define the rider and provides procedures on how to train and ride their horses to become straight.

It is possible for the rider to counteract the "natural asymmetry" of the horse by training in such a way that the serratus and the pectorales muscles develop evenly on both sides. However, neither trainer, nor veterinarian, nor blacksmith, nor saddle(r) will have any influence on the skeletal structure (even though the growth plates do not entirely close until around six and one-half years).

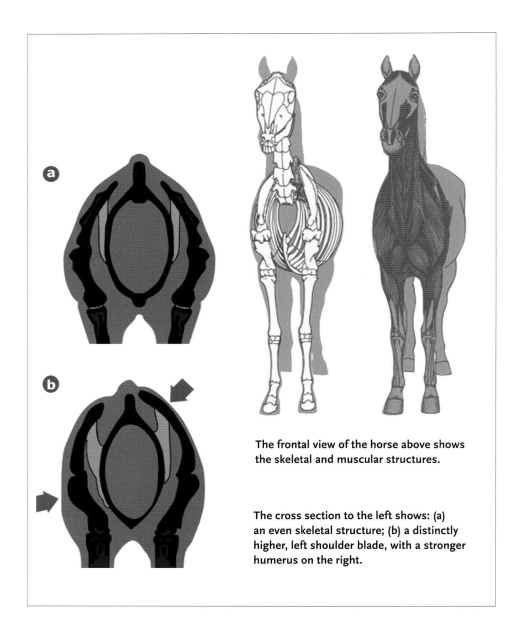

The frontal view of the horse above shows the skeletal and muscular structures.

The cross section to the left shows: (a) an even skeletal structure; (b) a distinctly higher, left shoulder blade, with a stronger humerus on the right.

HOW TO FIX RIDER AND HORSE CROOKEDNESS
By Jane Savoie

Jane Savoie was a member of the 1984 US Olympic Bronze Medal Dressage Team, a former coach of the Canadian Olympic Eventing Team, and the author of several bestselling books from Trafalgar Square Books.

"No matter what kind of riding you do, you want to ride your horse forward and straight. These two ingredients are the cornerstones of correct riding and training in any discipline.

"I'd like to address straightness here because it is an ongoing challenge. That's because both you and your horse are inherently crooked. This crookedness affects how your saddle sits on your horse and vice versa."

Horse Crookedness
"We refer to asymmetry in horses as the stiff and hollow side. To illustrate, cup your left hand in front of your face to form the letter 'C.' The inside (right side) of your hand is your horse's hollow side, and his right hind leg is his weaker hind leg.

"This hollow right side might feel easier to bend, but often you end up with too much bend in the neck and an 'empty' right rein because the right hind leg is not stepping through and 'filling' the right rein.

"The outside (left side) of your hand, in this case, is the stiff side. It feels harder to bend.

"My solution to making your horse straighter so he can develop his strength evenly is to school him by very quietly doing the opposite of what his crooked body wants to do.

"In the above example, when you're tracking to the right with the hollow side on the inside, ride your horse without any bend. You can even keep his body straight and ask him to flex at the poll to the outside (counter-flexion). Ride him as straight as a bus around circles and corners.

"When tracking to the left with his stiff side on the inside, ride him with 'extra bend.' For example, bend him as if he's on the arc of a 10-meter circle even when you're on a larger circle or just going down the long side."

Rider Crookedness
"As your horse's physical therapist, you must sit straight and balanced—both horizontally and vertically—in order to give aids effectively and help your horse become straighter.

"When adjusting your position, always start with your seat. Often, you'll find that other position issues like one leg drifting too far back, or one hand being held too high, get sorted out once you correct your seat."

"Check the following three points:

1. Are you sitting in the middle of your horse?

2. Is your pelvis in a neutral position?

3. Do you have a plumb line running from your ear through your shoulder, through your hip to your heel?

"If not, here are some useful exercises to get you balanced and straight:

1. If you tend to sit off to the right, think about sliding your hips over to the left so you pretend you're placing your right seat bone on the midline of the saddle. You can also pretend you're going to dismount. Put your weight in your left stirrup and move your hips to the left. (Reverse the above if you tend to sit to the left.)

2. To get your pelvis in neutral, imagine that it is a large bucket filled with water. When your pelvis is in neutral, the water stays in the bucket. If you round your lower back, the water spills out of the back of the bucket. You end up sitting in a chair seat putting too much weight in the back of the saddle. If you arch your lower back, the water spills out the front of the bucket. Your back is stiff and your hips are too closed making it hard for you to use them effectively and 'go with' the motion of the horse.

3. If you don't have the classical straight line of ear/shoulder/hip/heel, you won't be in good balance with your horse.

"To help align yourself correctly, ride in a 'standing position' where you stand straight up over the pommel. Do this in the halt as well as the three gaits. The only way you'll be able to stay in a standing position without falling forward or back is when your legs are underneath you properly. The 'natural asymmetry' becomes a central concern when you begin riding because it will make it more difficult to achieve a balanced movement within the requirements of classical dressage."

HOW THE HORSE'S ASYMMETRY AFFECTS SADDLE FIT

The horse's asymmetry has huge ramifications in the consideration of what saddle to buy, and how to fit it properly, because the saddle-support area begins immediately behind the shoulder blade. The natural unevenness is not only seen in the muscles and skeletal structure at the forehand, but it affects all the horse's joints and most of the rest of his anatomy.

The saddle needs to accommodate and be fitted to the unevenness in the horse's frontal anatomy, especially the size and position of the shoulder blades. Muscles can be developed and changed, but bones, as a rule, cannot. It is very difficult to determine whether or not there are anomalies in bone structure in the humerus. Even with today's advanced technology, the veterinarian will not be able to X-ray this area, because an X-ray plate cannot be put between the front two humerus bones. Various other invasive visual diagnostic tools are not (yet) widely available in their applications for horses because of the size of the machines required for this technology. So, we really don't know whether a horse's innate asymmetry is due to bone structure or muscle formation, and that's why we cannot foresee how effective training methods are to alleviate this occurrence.

Particularly the shape and position of the gullet plate—the stiffest and most stable part of the saddle—needs to accommodate the unevenness in the horse's anatomy during saddle fitting. Its necessary function cannot be substituted or eliminated by reflocking, shimming, or the use of other special orthotics in the panel area. Because of the pretty common occurrence of the unevenness at the horse's shoulders, it is usually necessary to fit the gullet plate asymmetrically in order to achieve this necessary support equally well on both sides. Fitting the gullet plate asymmetrically with an AdapTree®, will not result in twisting or making a crooked saddle—this concept is something that many saddlers or fitters simply do not understand. Many use inexpensive saddle trees (where these adjustments are simply not possible) and some have also given poor advice to riders who have had their saddle fitted by us previously in such a way so that the gullet plate is visually crooked (which they don't understand). (What I am saying here is that we have had other "so-called" saddle fitters work on our saddles, open them up and say to the client, "Look how crooked your gullet plate is," because it was correctly adjusted by us to accommodate asymmetry, and denigrate it because they don't understand the reasoning behind it.)

As a matter of fact, if this crucial piece of saddle fitting is ignored, and a saddle with a symmetrical gullet plate is put on a horse with an asymmetrically muscled shoulder, it will inevitably fall to one side as it is pushed there by the more heavily muscled shoulder (usually the left twisting the saddle to the right). You will see many instances of pictures of riders from behind sitting on a saddle that seems to have slipped to the right.

For example, let's say a horse with a bigger left shoulder is fitted with a saddle where the gullet-plate shape has oriented itself to his smaller right shoulder.

This means, in effect, that the gullet plate is really too small for the left side. As a result, during movement, the bigger left shoulder will displace the saddle over to the smaller right—it's simple physics! Farther down the horse's back then, the saddle will actually put pressure on the left side of the spinal column because it no longer lies in proper position in the saddle-support area, which keeps the spinal vertebrae clear of the panel. The saddle, which is being displaced along its horizontal axis, will cause the rider to shift to the right as well. The rider, who uses her vertical axis to balance in the seat, will counteract this fall to the right by shifting her weight more to the left. The rider will find little support from the saddle under her left butt cheek, and may collapse farther at the left hip. This shift in weight will further add pressure to the saddle on this side, shifting it even farther to the right. (Sound familiar?)

Of course, this crooked rider will now have difficulty giving the horse the proper aids, especially the subtle muscle contractions and shifts in weight, which normally cannot be seen. Increased difficulty in a right canter lead is often indicative of a saddle that has shifted to the right somewhat. The shoulder, which rotates 3 to 4 inches during movement (against and under the saddle tree), will also influence the action of the forelegs versus the hind legs.

On the stronger left side, behind which the saddle is now more strongly anchored, the horse will feel the first resistance to movement. The continuous pressure of the saddle on the left side of the vertebral column increases stress to the SI joint, which can cause a crooked pelvis and result in difficulty in the right hind leg—all the way to complete lameness. Inhibition of freedom of movement in the hind leg, of course, becomes evident in the rhythm of the gaits, and causes problems in the knee and stifle as well. "Straightening" the horse is a key impetus to preventing this type of issue from appearing.

However, this does not mean that saddles should be manufactured using crooked trees or uneven flocking. It is the necessity for an adjustable gullet plate—in width and angle—that is the point, and it is here that the unevenness of the horse's anatomy (mainly in the skeletal structure) can be addressed as necessary because the horse will change or even become more symmetrical.

The blacksmith does not usually form the hoof to fit the iron; he fits the iron to the hoof (except for orthopaedic purposes). Along the same vein, a gullet plate should be formed to fit the horse, not be available in only one permanently fixed position.

A saddle will always show a tendency to slide forward anyway, given that the rib cage gets wider toward the back, and, as I have said before, it's another law of nature that items will generally choose the path of least resistance to find their resting position. That is why the girth will also seek the narrowest spot on the chest and pull the saddle along with it. Only a saddle that has been properly fitted to accommodate the horse's individual shoulder

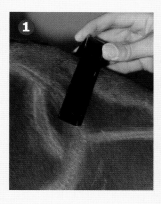
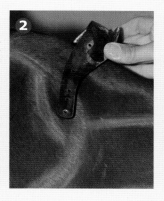
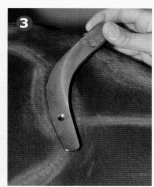

To protect the cartilage cap at the tip of the shoulder blade, it is crucial to fit the gullet plate properly behind both shoulders (especially the larger one). To explain: the gullet plate is attached to the saddle tree under the pommel area and inserts left and right underneath the tree points (which are essentially the two ends of the pommel).

All the gullet plates shown here are placed too far forward. Photos 1 and 2 show gullet plates with forward-facing gullet points, both of which impact the shoulder cartilage even when a saddle sits behind the shoulder blades. Photo 3 shows a gullet plate with rear-facing tree points that would accommodate the shape of the shoulder and protect the cartilage if it was positioned correctly behind the shoulder blades (as on p. 88 bottom left photo). The point here is that regardless of the shape and design of the gullet plate, the tree points (including the gullet plate) must be fitted to both shoulders. In all three of these photos, the gullet plates are not fitted to the left shoulder—even though they fit on the right.

One of the most common reasons for a horse indicating a subluxation in the spine or the SI joint occurs because the gullet plate has not been fitted to accommodate his larger shoulder, which, in this horse is the left. This twists the saddle to the right, puts excess pressure on the back of the left panel, also on the left side of the spine, which the horse tries to avoid by deviating to the right through his right shoulder.

The diagram on the right shows a subluxation due to pressure at the SI joint as a result of a saddle shift like this. It shows that the left lumbar area (including the SI joint) bends to the left, while the horse deviates through the right shoulder (it only looks bigger on the right side because the right shoulder has been thrown out because of the poorly fitting tree, which has not taken the larger left shoulder into consideration). A common problem is that many people try to accommodate this situation either with crooked stuffing or saddle pads and/or shims that just make the situation worse. The only solution is to be able to adjust both sides of the tree—individually, without twisting the tree itself.

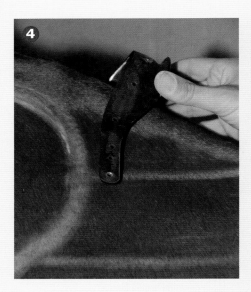

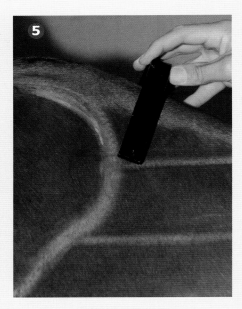

The gullet plate gives the saddle enough stability to sit balanced on the horse's back without slipping to the left or right. The gullet plate supports the tree at the front and gives the saddle the rigidity to keep the saddle off the withers at the pommel without pinching the sides. It needs to be long enough and shaped anatomically correctly to avoid impacting the nerves here (especially Cranial Nerve 11—also called the "spinal accessory nerve," which is a crucial reflex point and described in more detail on p. 117).

Photos 4 and 5 show gullet plates that are not shaped correctly and are not long enough to avoid pinching the withers. Their inherent design flaw will make them uncomfortable regardless what breed, age, or type of horse they are used on. It is clearly recognizable using the chalk outlines that although the tree points shown in Photo 4 stay off the cartilaginous plate at the tip of the shoulder blade, they will still dig into the trapezius muscle.

In Photo 5, the short, forward-facing tree points of this gullet plate will not only dig into the trapezius insertion, but also hit the shoulder cartilage, possibly damaging both areas.

Photo 6 shows a gullet plate with desirable rear-facing tree points that are long enough to support the tree's position in the saddle-support area, stay away from the trapezius, and keep the pressure off to allow maximum freedom of movement at the shoulder.

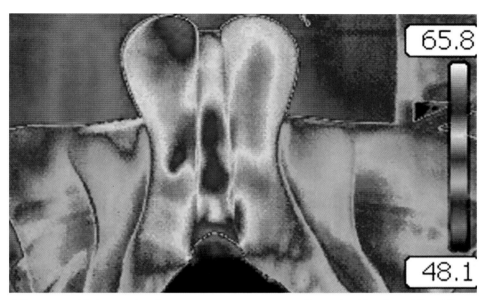

A thermographic image showing uneven pressure areas on the underside of a saddle: at the back left, on the underside in the gullet area, and at the withers. Ideally, you never want to see increased indications of pressure at the pommel or in the gullet. We look for even contact all the way down the panels of the saddle, with no "hotspots."

structure will stay in its proper position behind the shoulders, in balance over the center of gravity, and not shifting to the left or right.

When the gullet plate has been adjusted to accommodate the natural unevenness of a horse's shoulder, the saddle should lie straight on the horse so the rider can sit properly and in balance and there will be no unnecessary pressure on the horse's vertebrae or at the shoulder.

So what happens to your saddle when you need it for a horse that has the opposite shoulder bigger? This is where the advantage, or actually the necessity, for an AdapTree® with an adjustable gullet plate really comes in to play, because the fitter should be able to make any necessary changes as required for any horses over the life of the saddle. The job of the rider is to ride the horse "straight"; the job of the fitter is to make sure that the saddle (i.e. the tree and the gullet plate) is continually fitted correctly to the changing conformational requirements of the horse. This allows optimal interaction between the vertical axis and weight distribution of the rider with the horizontal axis of the horse's back. The saddle needs to be balanced in all directions: front to back, and top to bottom. Only then will both rider and horse vertebrae be able to work as nature intended, protecting their bodies from long-term damage while moving in harmony.

5

TRAINING THE HORSE
TO BE RIDDEN

WHERE SHOULD THE RIDER SIT?

The rider should be sitting over the center of gravity of the horse, which is approximated by drawing a line from the base of the withers down to the sternum. This is the horse's point of balance, that is, where a scale would balance equally on both sides, if you will. However, you should not confuse the center of gravity with the balance point; their actual whereabouts is a point of contention between trainers. According to common belief, the balance point of the horse actually moves on the horse depending on the gait: During the canter or when jumping, it's farther forward; in dressage with greater collection, it is farther back. If you want to get really technical about it, the balance point actually changes with each footfall of the horse. There is argument about where the mysterious center of gravity actually is, as well.

What is actually meant by the term "balance point" is nothing more than the actual point of balance at which the rider and horse become "one," because it is only at this point that a scale would balance—with the horse being able to achieve complete suppleness and harmony with the rider. The rider is neither inhibiting the horse's movement by sitting too far forward, nor "pushing" the horse forward from behind by sitting too far back. The rider's sternum aligns with the end of the horse's sternum.

The farther back the rider sits on the horse, the less ability he has to actually carry his weight. Let's think again

This skeleton is sitting somewhat too far back (behind the horse's center of gravity and off the saddle-support area), which makes it difficult for the horse to round his back. It should sit a bit closer to the front, bringing its balance point closer to the center of gravity of the horse (see diagram on p. 99). A rider should sit approximately at the base of the withers so that his entire body sits in front of the horse's 14th rib—the last rib to connect to the sternum—that in this diagram is located just under the skeleton's hip socket.

about the suspension-bridge analogy (p. 61): It is strongest at its supporting pillars (the legs), which makes it logical that most of the rider's weight should be situated closer to the front since we have already determined that the rider should not be positioned past the last rib and should sit close to the balance point of the horse (at the front end of his sternum). This position will enable the harmonious rhythm of both the horse and rider's vertebrae because there is the least amount of movement in the horse's back itself where horse and rider are in balance. A rodeo cowboy also sits fairly close to the withers area, because it's there that he finds the most secure seat.

It is a myth that the horse can become more "collected" the farther back the rider sits. Proper collection gives the horse better capacity to carry weight in the hindquarters and more ability to bend in the haunches, but this effect will not be helped by placing the saddle too far back (outside of the saddle-support area) nor by leaning the upper body back in an effort to sit heavier and deeper into the back of the saddle.

As I've said, the rider should be sitting in front of the 14th rib (the last rib attached to the sternum) before the first "floating rib," which is actually the 18th lumbar vertebra—and not past the saddle-support area—whenever possible. Some saddles place the rider extremely far back; one in particular that is totally misaligned in this fashion is named after an insect. It purposely seats the rider farther back behind the saddle-support area and behind the center of gravity; this position is necessary because of its huge cutback pommel. Essentially, the supporting panels have the weight-bearing surface of a 13- to 14-inch size saddle, which is an absolutely insufficient size to properly distribute the weight of a normal rider (let alone a plus-sized one).

3—5—8

Conventional equestrian wisdom states that three years is the optimum age for a horse to be started under saddle—to get accustomed to the saddle and the weight of the rider—but a horse really should not begin serious training until he is at least five years old. Until then, activity should be limited to "playtime" riding and training. Around age eight, a well-trained horse's muscles and conformation should be ready to allow him to start training in earnest.

Even if we determine the appropriate discipline of choice for a young horse fairly early on in his life, the necessary physical maturity for difficult dressage tests or for high jumps is not really there. Nor are these intense training methods advisable before he is eight.

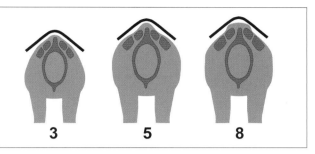

Training during this time will affect the muscular conformation and, as a result, the three-dimensional back shape and its saddle-support area will change.

HOW TO KNOW IF THE HORSE HAS ENOUGH TRAINING TO CARRY A RIDER WITHOUT DAMAGING HIS BACK

These are key points of recognition (see also art on p. 67):

- **The horse's shoulder blade has come up and back, and become very defined and wider.**
- **He has a well-muscled neck, stronger on top (from the poll to the withers) and less muscled from the jawbone to where the neck transitions into the chest area.**
- **He has a well-developed trapezius, defined behind the shoulder blade, with visible and defined longissimus and latissimus muscles.**

To protect the horse from long-term damage and to maintain his ability to carry a rider's weight, not only muscles, but tendons and ligaments, need to be strengthened over a longer period of time and training. Training needs to occur continuously, since lapses reverse any muscle development, which, in turn, increase the possibility of injury to the associated—and now less protected—tendons and ligament systems during riding.

IS A CUSTOM SADDLE NECESSARY FOR A YOUNG HORSE?

Absolutely. This is probably critical; however, this is where many riders fall into thinking that "good enough is close enough" because the horse's conformation can change pretty drastically in the first three to five years of being ridden, and they tell themselves, "I'll have to buy another saddle again soon anyway."

This is probably the worst decision

A saddle should be (and should be able to be) constantly adjusted to accommodate the ever-changing musculature. The photo at right shows muscle atrophy in the loin area, paradoxically caused by an incorrectly fitted gullet plate, which seated the rider too far back thus creating too much pressure in the area.

WHY EVEN A CUSTOM SADDLE NEEDS TO BE ADJUSTED

Unfortunately, it is a fact that a horse's muscles will not develop properly when he is ridden in a bad saddle, and they can even atrophy. When the gullet channel is too narrow; when the tree points face forward and poke into the horse's shoulders; when the saddle is too long; or when the tree width and tree angle are incorrect, correct development of the horse will suffer.

Continued on p. 95

Continued from p. 94

The rider may sit more or less comfortably and quietly on this saddle (which doesn't fit the horse), partly because the horse simply cannot or will not properly swing his back or move freely. The paradox here is that ideally you want the horse to be able to "swing"; however, many cannot "ride" with this much movement. Therefore, they like the fact that the (badly fitting) saddle inhibits this. It becomes somewhat of a catch-22: The saddle doesn't really fit the horse, which inhibits the correct development of the muscles, which means that the good news (if you can call it that?) is that the saddle fitter will need to come out less often to adjust this saddle (if, indeed, it can be adjusted in the gullet plate in the first place) because the horse's musculature has not changed.

So the saddle can stay as it is, but at what cost to the horse? Some people brag about their saddle "that fits all their horses," but these basically simply hang on the spine like a clothespin and sit on the shoulders and "fit" is truly questionable.

The truth is that even a well-fitted saddle (customized, custom, or off the rack—it doesn't matter) will continually have to be adjusted to the horse, because such a saddle will allow the horse the ability to move freely and develop his muscles and conformation accordingly. Isn't that what we want? The positive results of our training should show a visible change in muscle conformation, which is what the well-fitting saddle will support. Some people may not believe in the necessity for constant adaptation of fit as the horse matures, but then behavioral issues and symptomatic lameness are pretty much guaranteed. The sale of a difficult horse is often the only way out for the owner. How sad, when the solution could be such an easy fix!

Customized does not equal "custom," which seems to be quite the catch-all phrase nowadays. A true custom saddle is made using all the rider's conformational requirements and all the horse's specific needs, starting with a butt cast of the rider to truly make a tree that is individually correct. Most companies, at best, only customize an off-the-rack saddle (which comes in your basic narrow, medium, wide tree widths and 16 to 19 half-inch incremental seat sizes) to "more or less" fit a particular rider or a specific horse. Custom Saddlery was truly brilliant in its choice of a company name because all of their products are "custom" saddles whether or not they are actually custom-made! (And in truth, most of them are not—not even customized!)

So custom should mean that a saddle has truly been made from the inside out—from the tree outward—to fit one specific rider and one specific horse. Customized means that a saddle has been adapted to work for one or more riders; for one or more horses.

A young horse on the longe line or under saddle should have the freedom of motion downward and forward, even when his center of gravity is still pretty far forward. A well-balanced saddle plays an important role in helping the horse learn from the start how to balance himself.

a rider can make, because the horse will pretty much associate saddle pain or discomfort with being ridden. This means that the rider's ability to ride correctly, which creates correct muscular development, will probably be hindered. Knowing the impact it will have on the development of their children's feet, who would buy their children shoes that are the wrong size? Long-term damage is difficult to treat orthopedically; it's just as difficult for your horse!

A custom saddle is therefore not only recommended for a young horse, it is easy to justify if you get a saddle that can be adjusted (not just reflocked) in the gullet plate (thus adjusting tree width and tree angle) to accommodate the horse's growth as he is trained and as he matures.

You will need to ascertain the type of tree on a saddle because it affects the adjustability. Is it a plastic, fiberglass, wooden spring tree, or an AdapTree®? Is the gullet plate adjustable? How is the panel made—integrated, independent, shoulder relief, panel relief? And how is it filled—with felt, foam, wool/synthetic mix, or air?

Admittedly, a saddle that is truly adjustable over the life of the horse is probably quite a bit more expensive to buy, however, if you do the math and consider: a) buying an entirely new saddle every one to two years as your horse changes; or b) paying for annual adjustments, you will see that buying this adjustable saddle becomes the smart, and even frugal, decision. You are making an investment into the health of your horse; ensuring that the saddle continues to fit will furthermore potentially save you even more money on vet bills and pharmaceuticals that you would likely have to use to address lameness or other issues that come from ill-fitting saddlery.

A horse will continue to change over the course of its entire life. We need to be cognizant of the fact that our training actually goes against what nature intended: We try to move the horse's natural center of gravity farther back; we try to work against his natural asymmetry in order to allow him to carry a rider over long periods of time.

When a horse has been correctly trained, the weight on his forehand is shifted to his hindquarters, his rib cage lifts, his stamina is increased, and circulation and oxygen exchange improved—that is, the ability to breathe and improve the oxygen/carbon dioxide reaction, providing more oxygen to the blood. An ill-fitting saddle, on the other hand, will always impact your ability to achieve this, while possibly further causing both horse and rider injury in the long term (not to mention pain).

It is important to have your saddle fit evaluated at regular intervals, especially when your horse is in training, or immediately after you start training again after time off. Muscle definition and strength will alter pretty quickly—measurement has demonstrated that significant change can be achieved after only four weeks of intensive training. However, this change can also go the other way: Atrophy happens even faster and the horse returns to his natural conformation relatively quickly when training stops.

Correct riding, as determined by the guidelines of classical dressage, is the basis for horse-friendly methodology and training success—from the breaking in of a young horse to the Grand Prix levels of both dressage and jumping. A poor fitting saddle, however, can impact all efforts of proper training methods just a easily as poor riding itself.

> **Muscle atrophy or reduction in muscle mass will happen about four times quicker than muscle growth. Muscle memory will help in the rebuilding of atrophied muscles if they had already been properly trained in the first place. It will take significantly longer to build up entirely untrained muscles, or muscles that were not correctly trained in the first place.**

EACH RIDING DISCIPLINE REQUIRES ITS OWN SADDLE

Every rider should be familiar with her horse and be able to control it to such a degree that risks to herself, her animal, and her surroundings are minimized. Part of this risk control is not only well-fitting, well-maintained saddle, but also quality and condition of the girth, the leathers, and the irons.

A saddle's center of balance* or deepest point varies for each saddle type. The center of balance is determined not only by discipline and saddle model, but also by the gender of the rider. The saddle needs to facilitate balance between the center of gravity of the horse and the center of gravity of the ride*— whether male or female. For example, in the photographs on p. 100 you can see how the deepest point changes as you look at a dressage saddle versus a jumping or cross-country saddle.

After making the correct choice of saddle to suit the riding discipline and rider gender, the saddle should be regularly adjusted in order to ensure that the ever-changing three-dimensional shape of the horse's back is taken into consideration.

The term "three-dimensional back shape" means that you take into consideration not only the topline of the horse and its cross-section (as in the diagrams on p. 93, except that this is the cross-section only at the withers area to show the growth between ages three, five, and eight) at any given point, but also the change in the conformation as you move from front to back along its length. The horse will be naturally wider at the shoulder area, and narrower toward its rump. Its back may be higher from front to back,

---

* This topic is truly somewhat confusing, but in this instance the term "balance point" and "center of gravity" will be used interchangeably. The center of balance of a horse is the position on the horse's back that correlates closely to the center of gravity of the horse itself. The term may also refer to the horse's center of gravity.

For the best performance by the horse, as well as for better balance of the rider, the rider must be positioned over the center of balance of the horse. The location of the horse's center of balance depends on a combination of speed and degree of collection. For a standing or quietly walking horse, it is slightly behind the heart girth and below the withers. If a horse is moving at a trot or canter, the center of balance shifts slightly forward, and it moves even more forward when the horse is galloping or jumping. If a horse is highly collected, the center of balance will be farther back, regardless of gait, than when the horse is in an extended frame. For movements such as a rein back or the levade, the center of balance of horse and rider may be farther back than at a standstill due to the horse's shift of weight and balance to the hindquarters.

Accordingly, a saddle designed for a specific discipline will attempt to place a rider naturally at the most suitable position for the anticipated activity of the horse. (Bradley, Melvin, and Wayne Loch. "Selecting a Saddle." Department of Animal Sciences, University of Missouri–Columbia, accessed online December 11, 2007).

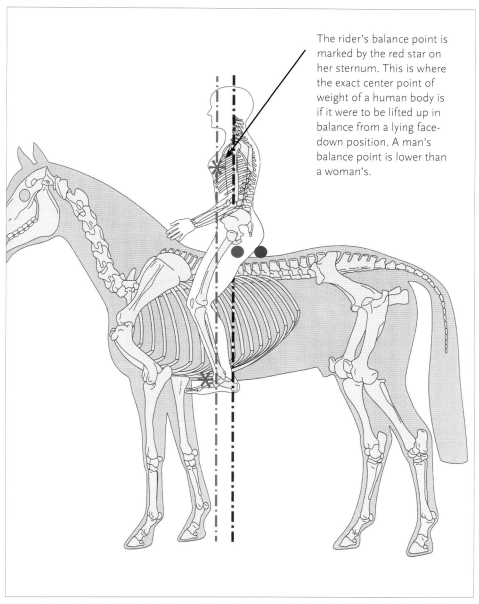

The rider's balance point is marked by the red star on her sternum. This is where the exact center point of weight of a human body is if it were to be lifted up in balance from a lying face-down position. A man's balance point is lower than a woman's.

This is a female rider sitting in balance. Note the perpendicular plumb line aligning with her shoulder, hip, and heels (black dotted line). The center of balance of the saddle is forward (green dot). The deepest point of the horse's back is at the blue dot. It is used to illustrate that the deepest point of the horse's back does not always align with the deepest point of the saddle. The rider is sitting well with her balance point properly positioned over the horse's center of gravity (red star at horse's sternum), as indicated by the red dotted line.

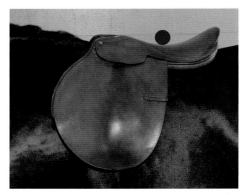

In this general purpose/hunter-pleasure saddle, the center of balance is in the middle.

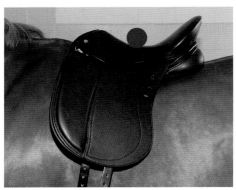

This dressage saddle is made especially for a woman, and the center of balance is more forward.

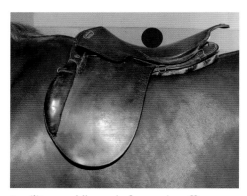

A military saddle made for cavalry officers showing the center of balance in the middle of the saddle.

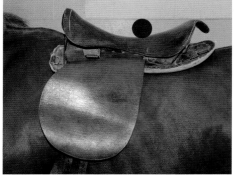

This military saddle made for the cavalry militia had the center of balance farther back, but this could be adjusted by the soldier himself.

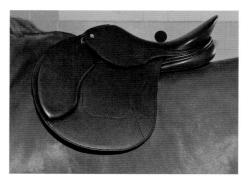

A jumping saddle with the center of balance toward the rear.

A modern, cross-country saddle with the center of balance farther back.

The dot on each saddle seat indicates where the center of balance is for each of the different models. The center of balance is actually the deepest point of the saddle, that is, where the ball comes to rest naturally when the saddle is placed straight on the horse's back. It will change depending on saddle construction or rider preference.

or from back to front, depending on breed, condition, and age.

When the rider's sternum is directly horizontal over the horse's sternum the two will be in balance, as their centers of gravity are aligned. The rider's ability to achieve this depends on two variables: the type of saddle and the gender of the rider. In the sports where the rider does not sit deeply in the saddle and rides with legs more angled in the hips and the knees (show jumping, eventing, steeplechasing, hunting) she is removing much of her weight from the horse's back. In those sports, when the rider actually sits down in the saddle, most of the weight will be carried on her gluteal muscles rather than her seat bones. She will bring her center of gravity over the horse's center of gravity by angling her upper body sharply forward as she goes into a two-point position.

The jumping saddle will always have its deepest point farther back regardless whether the rider is male or female, because this accommodates the ability of the rider to balance in a normal seated position in a jumping saddle. If we tried to bring this point farther forward in a jumping saddle to make it center-balanced or even forward-balanced, the rider would have difficulty finding her own balance and not be able to ride with shortened leathers.

It is different with a dressage saddle, however. It must allow the rider to sit constantly balanced with her center of gravity aligned with that of the horse, in order to achieve the vertical plumb line of ear-shoulder-hip-heel. The dressage rider's leg is only slightly bent at the knee and she carries her weight on the seat bones.

The dressage position requires a saddle that is either center- or forward-balanced with its deepest point either in the middle or closer to the pommel (front) of the saddle. The rider's position will also as a rule require a different saddle for men and women: As discussed previously, the female's different pelvic shape requires her to sit with more of a forward pelvic tilt to achieve the same plumb line position as the male; to assist in achieving this, her saddle will have a more forward balance in the seat. (The optimum position will only be achieved, however, if all the other conformational differences between men and women are taken into consideration during manufacture—this one thing alone, "ain't gonna do it"!)

Obviously, Western riding is quite different from English riding; its origins include the necessity for quick reactions, quick turns, and fast movement. The rider needs to be able to sit in balance while usually only using one hand for the reins. Working with a lasso means the rider needs a secure seat, but one that will allow her to move as needed. A Western working horse such as a Quarter Horse needs to reach top speed very quickly to catch a cow or separate it from a herd. The use of the lasso will only work when the saddle supports him in front and back so he can maintain balance without losing speed.

In order to reach this sprinting ability, most Quarter Horses are built with very strong muscles in the hind end, and Western saddles are built for this breed with their center of balance far back. A saddle constructed in this way that is perfectly balanced for a Quarter Horse should never be used for a breed like a Friesian, for example, since the center of gravity (and too much pressure) will be too far in the back (and likely outside of the horse's saddle-support area).

Although Western saddles have been and can be used on other breeds, they always present a fitting challenge. The saddle industry has somewhat accommodated the wish to use the design for other horses by making "Western trail saddles" or "endurance saddles." These models incorporate the benefits of the Western saddles (such as the comfortable seat) while considering some of the other necessities in design as dictated by other breeds (with more or less success).

The rider needs to align her center of gravity or balance point with that of the horse in order to balance herself —depending on the discipline and situation this balance point will change—and is aided by the choice of saddle. In dressage this point of balance for horse and rider will be pretty centered; when show jumping and on cross-country in eventing, it will be farther forward, but it depends on speed and the height of the jump as well as the saddle and position of the rider.

The goal should always be for the rider to try to achieve whatever the momentary balance point is for the horse. The horse's center of gravity or balance point, will constantly change during movement, but is also influenced by correct riding. The balance of the saddle cannot be forward- and rear-balanced at the same time: It is either forward-, center-, or rear-balanced, and will always stay the same; it depends on the model of the saddle, the riding discipline, and especially in dressage, it also depends on the gender of the rider.

6

A SHORT HISTORY
OF HORSES

OUR RIDING HORSES TODAY

Shifting the Weight from Front to Back

The eohippus was the horse's ancestor, from which evolved the horse breeds we know today. The eohippus is thought to have lived about 50 million years ago, and reached a height of about 16 to 20 inches (30 to 35 cm) at the withers. Eohippus was much higher in the back end so that, like modern horses today, most of his body weight was concentrated on the forehand. As tundra dwellers, for the most part these animals were likely to have spent most of their waking hours grazing in order to get enough nutrition from the bare ground. As a result, they will have had their heads down and moved with a slow walk during their search for food.

Although size and conformation have changed over the millennia, the basic anatomical features have remained. The ideal situation for horses today is still grazing for most of the day with their heads down and most of their weight supported on the forehand. A horse that grazes on pasture has about 60 percent of his weight in front. As he becomes more collected during the course of training under saddle, his center of gravity will move farther back, and the percentage of his weight supported on the forehand is reduced to about 45 percent of total body weight.

This gradual shift of weight distribution and the horse's center of gravity occurs because we, as riders, have an (unnatural) influence on his muscular development, which reacts to the intensity of the training—sometimes more, sometimes less, for whatever reason—in phases. Conceivably, this training period will be affected over a period of several years, but in addition, the horse's conformation will transform naturally on its own due to nutrition, health, and other external factors. In other words, this means that both the muscle development and the conformation of the horse as a whole will undergo many and constant changes, muscles will "atrophy and grow," so fitting a saddle to the horse will in reality only fit for a given short while. It will work for a horse for a specific time, based on his three-dimensional shape at that time. This means, conversely, that there is no way that a saddle fitted during one phase of the horse's training will ever fit him for the rest of his life. However, a good quality saddle should be adjustable to accommodate these conformational changes.

Why is it so important to minimize the weight on the forehand? During the evolution of the horse, its size and conformation have changed considerably because of the specific breeding experiments of man. In nature, a horse only has to carry its own weight and has nothing more to do than graze all day (for the most part—though there may

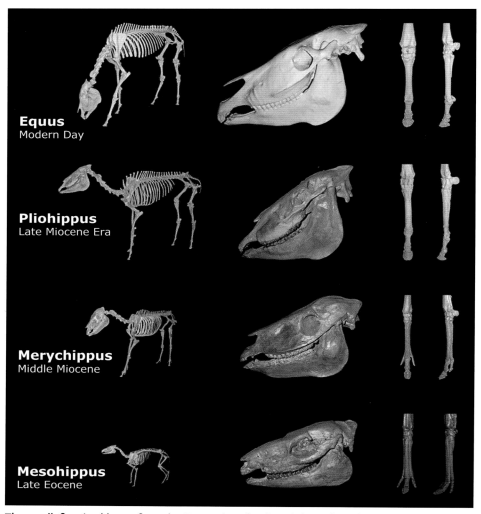

Equus
Modern Day

Pliohippus
Late Miocene Era

Merychippus
Middle Miocene

Mesohippus
Late Eocene

The small, fox-sized horse from the Eocene has developed through evolution and natural selection into the present-day horse, with all its breed variations and size differences (but with basic anatomical similarities).

be some occasional mating activity and escaping predators). This means the horse will naturally be on the forehand.

This weight on the forehand is counteracted by contraction of the nuchal ligament along the back, which tends to pull the spinal processes forward, which in turn, then causes further tension in the dorsal ligament system that allows the horse (without further exertion or muscular action) to stand fully balanced and carry the weight of his rib cage and inner organs (see drawing on p. 107).

If she doesn't follow the guidelines of classical riding (the basis for anatomically and biomechanically correct dressage training), the rider can cause the horse discomfort and pain during training by forcing him to raise his head through the use of the bridle and the reins. Pretty much since horses were recruited for human use, equine professionals (hippologists) have researched how to get the weight off the horse's forehand during collection, while allowing the horse to engage his back ("bring the back up") through the use of proper training and riding methods—and correct saddle fitting. It becomes clear when we consider the horse's development from eohippus to equus that humans have had considerable influence on the selection process, which certainly has impacted the evolutionary changes.

Thus, the horse became a useful partner for man, and partly through human influences developed into a large, strong, and very fast animal as appropriate for the various activities it was destined to perform. The ultimate

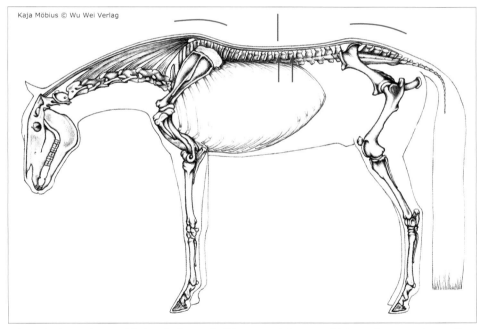

Kaja Möbius © Wu Wei Verlag

When the horse lowers his head, the nuchal ligament tightens, which, at the same time, affects the dorsal ligament system that serves to elevate the horse's back. An elevated back while grazing would allow the horse to easily bring the hindquarters more underneath his body, which results in less weight on the forehand: Tension in the dorsal ligament system allows the horse to graze comfortably. If we understand and honor this predetermined natural law, then the horse can support a rider's weight over a long period of time, but only when we understand and keep engagement of the horse's back viable.

In nature, the horse will spend most of the day (usually around 17 hours) in this position, grazing in a relaxed, and constantly slow-moving state.

A young horse will have a relatively long saddle-support area because his shoulders have not muscled up yet. When they do they move upward and back thus shortening the saddle-support area as the horse ages.

goal in breed differentiation was based on the selected use: as a cart animal to pull wares, for work in the mines and agricultural purposes, as a mode of transportation, or for use in the military.

Nowadays, the number of different breeds—and the use—of horses have changed enormously. For the most part, they are used for recreational and sporting activity, with very few still used for any type of work.

I see many horses during the course of my work that have a saddle-support area that continues to shrink, although they have pretty much finished growing. The reason for this is mainly due to angulation changes in their shoulder blades (see photo on p. 109) usually a result of changes in muscle development or muscular conformation. The horse's torso between his two front legs essentially lifts up as his pectoral muscles continue to develop, and the angle of the scapula gets flatter.

In other words, the cartilaginous cap at the tip of the shoulder blade actually moves upward and back. This, of course, affects the anterior boundary of the saddle-support area, whereas the posterior boundary (at the 18th lumbar vertebra, see photos regarding the saddle-support area, p. 139) stays the same—effectively shortening the saddle-support area. If the horse loses muscle mass in the torso area between the forelegs because of a change in training (or time off), the reverse happens: The angle of the scapula decreases again, which means that the saddle-support area effectively grows again in size.

A correctly trained horse has a higher head carriage than he does when he is grazing. Proper use of a bridle and reins, which result in a stronger back and neck, will show a steeper angulation in his upper arm (humerus), which allows the shoulder blade to move upward and

In a mature horse, the saddle-support area is visibly smaller, particularly because of the muscle development in the forehand and the resulting position of the scapula (shoulder blade). This must be taken into consideration during saddle fitting, and it is one of the key reasons why a saddle that fits the horse at three years will certainly not fit him as he ages and grows.

backward. This also serves to decrease the saddle-support area: We are talking about relatively small amounts here, one inch or less (1 to 2 cm) but still significant, nonetheless! The saddle must not, under any circumstances, push against or lie on the shoulder blade if you want to ensure proper freedom of movement for the shoulder and be positioned far enough back to stay off the forehand. So it becomes important to consider the saddle-support area and to know: a) where it is, and b) how big it is. Only when the saddle panel and tree points do not negatively impact either the shoulder blade or the lumbar vertebrae can you prevent long-term harm and expect maximum extension in the forehand during movement—with proper accompanying movement in the hind end.

This presents a challenge to both the saddle maker and the saddle fitter. The saddle must not lie farther back on the horse's back than the 18th lumbar vertebrae (p. 138), and needs to stay off the shoulder too so that freedom of movement is not compromised in any

of the gaits. This means that those of us in the industry need to be open to incorporating design changes based on the latest research and data available. Although there are, of course, still some breeds and individual horses within any of the breeds that can be ridden with the older style of saddle made for longer saddle-support areas, many of the currently popular breeds require the smaller panels. These include many of the "Baroque-style" horses.

This presents another dilemma because so many riders require larger seats, yet the panels need to be smaller for the horses: Innovations in saddle design that need to be taken into consideration in order to do justice to both sides of the equation. It becomes an undeniable prerequisite for not only the rider, but also the saddlemaker and the saddle fitter, to ensure that with training and proper equipment the horse will be able to carry the rider's weight properly without incurring any long-term damage. The horse's back remains a very sensitive area, despite the goals of targeted selection and breeding.

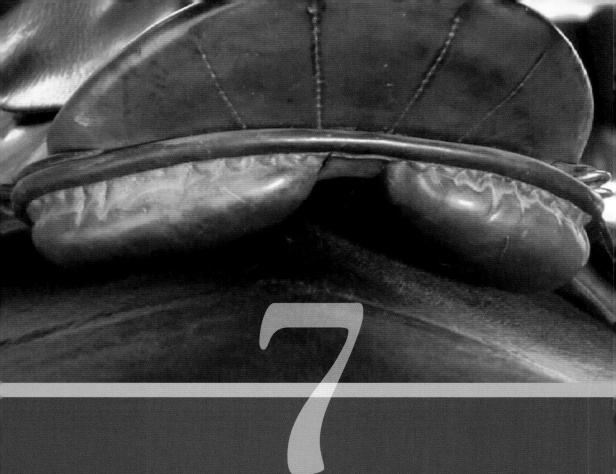

7

WHEN THE SHOE DOESN'T FIT

A horse's sense of touch is many times more sensitive than that of a human. Consider how his skin reacts to even the tiniest fly: He flicks a muscle to remove it. He will feel the slightest pressure, which is why horses can react to even the most subtle of weight changes when the rider gives an aid. As riders, we learn that one of the most important aids is the seat and balance of weight. When, however, the horse seemingly ignores an aid, it could be the result of poor training (he doesn't really know what's expected of him) or because a bad fitting saddle has been constantly putting pressure on one of his reflex points (I'll discuss in more detail later on—see p. 116) so he has basically become "deadened" to the touch.

At this point begins the "battle" between man and horse: constant use of spurs, smacking with the crop, or continuous "flapping" of the rider's legs in an effort to urge the horse forward. A horse does not consciously act out in bad behavior or consciously resist the use of aids; by nature, he is not usually lazy or recalcitrant. More than likely, he is irritated, resigned, afraid, or in pain because of the constant pressure of the saddle on his reflex points and/or poor training by the rider.

A SAD BUT ALL-TOO-COMMON STORY FROM MY EXPERIENCE

I want to tell you about a horse I met recently, a personal encounter that unfortunately is not uncommon. I was called out by the owner of a horse who indicated to me that she was having difficulties with the horse under saddle. I was asked to perform one of my 80-point diagnostic evaluations and determine the possible cause for some of the issues she was experiencing. (Saddlefit 4 Life® has developed a copyrighted, comprehensive, evaluation form that goes into a total of 80 distinct measurements and criteria for determining saddle fit, currently being used by equine and saddle ergonomists worldwide.)

When I came to the barn, neither owner nor trainer were available. I was shocked as the groom brought out this beautiful, but somehow incredibly sad-looking horse. I have rarely encountered such an absolute picture of dejection: Someone or something had totally sucked the life out of him. With some probing, I learned that the owner rode her horse maybe twice a month and that it was the trainer who rode him for the most part—with his own saddle that he used for pretty much every horse he trained. This saddle was clearly too narrow in the gullet channel, with the

Continued on p. 112

Continued from p. 111

result that it constantly pressed on the spinal vertebral processes and was causing nerve damage.

In addition, the saddle was much too long for this horse's saddle-support area, and laid on his back about 1½ inches behind the 18th lumbar vertebra. As I watched the groom ride the horse in order to do a proper dynamic fit, the saddle began sliding forward on the shoulder even during the walk. This, at best, affected the horse's freedom of movement, and at worst, could cause chipping at the cartilaginous cap. The horse stood with his hind legs splayed and was out of body alignment, which indicated the amount of pain this animal was in—even when standing still.

What really made me angry and even sadder was the fact that this horse was being sold because he was "difficult to handle" for the owner and just "too much horse." Too much horse? The animal was simply reacting in a way that would lessen or avoid the pain. In many years of experience as both a rider and a saddle maker and fitter, I have discovered that for the most part, a horse will always try to indicate to us that something is amiss before "bad behavior" becomes the norm.

Horses cannot speak so we need to learn to "read" their signals. Unfortunately, many times a rider is too inexperienced and trainer too arrogant to listen. They ignore signals, manipulate, and punish. Defensive actions are usually the horse's last option and final attempt to escape his fate. This type of behavior, however, is often taken for simple stubbornness or contrariness, and is punished with spurs, whips, and increasingly strong half-halts, which impact the sensitive mouth. The horse really has no chance and resigns himself to the situation.

If only horses could react with tears or by voicing their discomfort, they might get more empathy from their riders. These difficulties in cross-species communication (often simply because we humans don't really want to understand!) often result in a horse being sold without considering that the cause could actually have nothing to do with his character.

In this sad, but unfortunately not rare situation, a number of factors came together: an absolutely inappropriate saddle that wasn't fitted to this horse nor made for this horse; poor training methodology; and insufficient empathy and knowledge on the part of both the trainer and the owner. If nothing else, however, this story served to strengthen my focus in life and showed me that I am on the right path. Education and cooperation between owners, trainers, veterinarians, farriers, and other equine professionals are critical if something is to change and ultimately result in correctly fitting saddles (the interface between all of these influencers).

THE HORSE'S SKIN IS A GOOD INDICATOR OF PAIN

By Carol Vischer, DVM, MS

Dr. Vischer is a Diplomate of the American College of Veterinary Medicine, certified in acupuncture and spinal manipulation.

"It has been my experience that through careful palpation, the veterinarian can gain valuable information about the health of the skin in the thoracolumbar region. The skin is the first line of defense against painful pressure and the skin is subject to changes that can be assessed in the evaluation of pain. It is known that the fascia of the thoracic area (the region where the saddle is placed) is extremely sensitive to pressure and pain due to a richly innervated, connective-tissue web associated with the spinal cord. This is in contrast to the fascia overlying the lumbar region, which is generally more pliable and less sensitive to pain and to excessive pressure than the thoracic fascia.

"It is not always easy to assess the health of the skin of the thoracolumbar region. Healthy skin should be soft, contain adequate moisture and be freely movable from the underlying *cutaneous trunci* muscle and be able to respond to stimuli. One can be readily fooled by horses that tend to respond less to stimuli and be convinced that those horses are not sore. However, most of those horses' fascia is less responsive because the horses are undermuscled and underweight, old, and/or suffering from chronic disease and degenerative conditions, such as kissing spine or impingement of the dorsal spinous processes. In other words, the skin has become numb due to chronic pain.

"Horses that suffer from chronic poor saddle fit usually have skin changes that lead to chronic skin dryness and nerve tissue atrophy with the resulting lack of response. It is unfortunate that these changes are the inevitable consequences of poor saddle fit because they make the detection of pain so much more difficult. As many horses suffer from poor saddle fit, most people are close-minded about the possibility of pain since the detection is not straightforward. It is my hope that through education more horse owners become more cognizant of the damage that inevitably occurs from chronic pressure."

There are, unfortunately, still far too many horses that have literally become crippled because of the use of incorrect or poor fitting saddles. This happens despite that fact that innovations in technology are allowing us to determine, without exception, exactly where and how the saddle should fit. We are able to calculate specifically where issues arise and can act to remove these to achieve the ultimate goal of protection and comfort of the horse's back. Unfortunately, a bad fitting saddle will

> **"Whoever works with horses takes on the responsibility for this living being that has been put into his/her care."**
>
> —The first guideline in the chapter on ethics as established in the Handbook of the German FN

often result in a number of negative chain reactions that, at some point, go beyond the capability of even the best trainer, the best veterinarian, or

THE USE OF THERMOGRAPHY IN THE DIAGNOSIS OF BACK ISSUES

By Dr. Joanna Robson, DVM

Dr. Robson is a practicing veterinarian in California and a partner of Saddlefit 4 Life®. She is the author of the book and DVD Recognizing the Horse in Pain and What You Can Do About It.

"Thermography is a useful tool to assess contact, placement, balance, and pressure points of saddle fit. A proper environment and patient preparation (clean and dry) are necessary. Rider balance may influence the patterning, but steps such as longeing without a rider and videography may be used as additional evidence in an advanced fitting protocol. Friction and pressure create heat. The thermal camera detects infrared waves and creates an image that may be seen by the human eye. These images may then be tuned and manipulated with a digital radiograph to further enhance the diagnostic assessment.

"A saddle that causes pressure points and friction will create an associated pattern in the horse's back and on the underside of the panels and flaps of the saddle. Bridging, narrow, or pinching trees; uneven or lumpy flocking; problems caused by rearward balance or placement too far forward; panel damage from unpadded saddle racks, and much more, can be detected with the correct use of the camera and proper interpretation. Evaluation of symmetry from side to side and front to back lends clues to fitting problems."

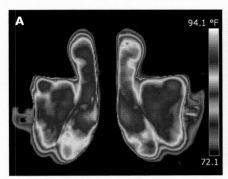

The underside of a close-contact jumping saddle after riding showing that the saddle pinches the horse over the left shoulder and wither and also has uneven panel contact (more on the left, uneven on the right).

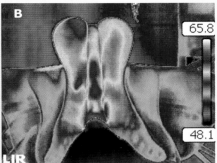

This pattern shows uneven contact on the panels of a dressage saddle. There is not enough freedom at the withers, and the saddle is too close to the horse's back at the pommel and in the center of the gullet channel. There is more heat on the left side, probably indicating that the horse has a stronger left shoulder that is pushing the saddle over to the right. At the rear, the panels impinge upon the horse's vertebrae.

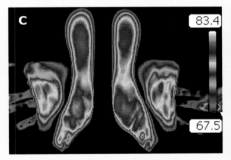

The underside of a dressage saddle that "bridges" (it only contacts the back at the front and back of the panels), results in greater pressure both at the front and the back of the saddle—with less in the middle. This bridging is often seen when the gullet plate is not adjustable, causing greater heat and possibly more damage than a slightly "rocking" saddle. A rocking saddle is one that may have a little more stuffing in the center, causing less contact at both the pommel and cantle areas.

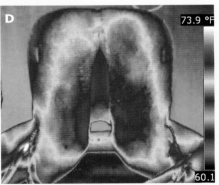

A saddle showing uneven contact through the left horizontal panel, and that the left rear panel is not in contact with the patient's back (lack of heat signature). A saddle blanket that is too thick could cause this patterning, which is common in Western saddles.

the best body worker, to fix. You as the rider are ultimately responsible for your horse's well-being and this includes ensuring that his saddle fits. When this one critical aspect is ignored, your horse can experience long-term, irreparable damage—and suffer for it.

Behavioral problems, tongue hanging out, lameness, stubbornness, irregular gaits and transitions, resistance, tripping—all the way to having to put the horse out to pasture because he sim-

ply cannot be ridden any longer—are just some of the issues that can result from bad fitting saddles. In its ethical guidelines the German FN states that, "No one should cause an animal unnecessary pain or harm." This means, essentially, that any saddle that causes a horse pain or discomfort (even unconsciously and without prejudice) is basically going against these governing guidelines that riders have established for themselves.

THE REFLEX POINTS

Along with "trainable" or conditioned reflexes, both horse and human have many parasympathetic, non-consciously controllable reflex points, where the muscles react to a stimulus of specific nerves. These reflexes work to regulate breathing and heartbeat, among other things, and also come into play during fight-or-flight responses. A stimulus to a nerve end is sent to the brain where it is processed and sends an order to the muscles to produce a specific reflex. It's like two common human reflexes: The doctor hitting your knee at a certain point (the patella ligament below the knee cap), which causes you to kick out; or you hitting your elbow "funny bone." But if these reflex points are stimulated continuously, however, it leads to a gradual deadening of the response so that the natural reflex action is impeded.

A saddle that sits on one of the

horse's specific reflex points can cause many problems. As with humans, the equine spinal column has nerve ends, which protrude between each of its vertebrae. Some of these are actual reflex points, and depending on the length of the horse's saddle-support area, there are between four and six of these along each side of the backbone.

You can test for yourself where these are on your horse's back: Take a piece of chalk and draw a light line from back to front beside the length of the spinal column, starting at the 18th lumbar vertebra and ending at a wither. Using even light pressure you will be able to observe a very subtle muscular reaction and "flicking of the skin"; using greater pressure to approximate the feel of a saddle under a light rider causes the horse to drop his back. If this horse were to do this the whole time a saddle is actually on his back,

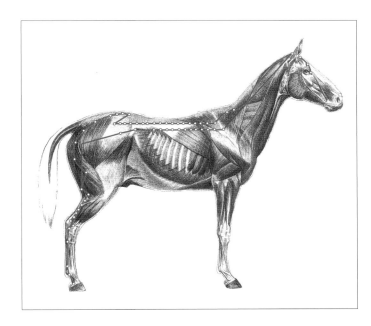

Eastern medicine follows the theory that life energy flows along meridians; humans and equines each have 12 meridians, which can be influenced through acupuncture. When the saddle puts pressure on the meridians (the red lines in the horse's body to the left), the flow of energy is interrupted, which results in various symptomatic issues appearing.

the formation of the condition known as "kissing spine" can result.

If the saddle puts pressure on these reflex points along the spine because, for example, a gullet channel is too narrow, or because the saddle twists during movement because of natural asymmetry (as discussed previously, p. 79), the horse will reflexively lower his back to escape the pressure and/ or pain. The goal of having the horse engage his back and raise it when he is being ridden is unachievable. Forward impulse and momentum is lost. Defensive behavior; not going on the bit; and a rider out of balance are just some of the other ramifications. This results in a frustrating experience for both horse and rider. The horse would like to respond to the aids the rider gives him, but the pressure on his reflex points

inhibits his ability to do so. Think about your knee reflex again: Even if the doctor tells you to try and refrain from kicking him when he taps your patella, you will do it anyway, and there is nothing you can consciously do about it.

So it makes sense that a saddle that consistently puts pressure on the horse's reflex points will be frustrating and, eventually, even damaging to the horse. A rider gives the horse the signal to move forward. However, if the tree angle is too wide, or the tree width is too narrow and the saddle tree is putting too much pressure on Cranial Nerve 11 (more on this on p. 118), the horse cannot really comply. The reason for this is that the saddle is impinging the reflex point, which hinders his ability to move. His instinctive reaction is to drop his back, lock the shoulders, and rotate the pelvis. Despite his best intention, the horse cannot move forward. He experiences the inner battle of wanting to obey his rider ("Let's go forward") and his instinct ("Stay still!"). This is a losing proposition for the horse, and possibly the cause of physical and psychological pain, too, as the rider thinks that this immobility is simply stubbornness and starts using spurs and a whip. (Consider trying to drive your car briskly away with your handbrake still on: tires will squeal; you can only move haltingly; and smoke is generated from burning of the brake pads. That's what your horse goes through, and what it feels like.)

MAIN REFLEX POINTS IN THE SADDLE-SUPPORT AREA

Cranial Nerve 11 (CN11): The Spinal Accessory Nerve

Over 50 million years of equine evolution have seen the stallion biting his opponents in the withers area to determine dominance and literally bring rivals "to their knees." Stallions also bite mares in the exact same area in preparation for mating to stop them from moving forward and to be able to mount them safely. Predators attack horses (and other animals) in this same region of the neck to hinder them in their flight response and bring them down.

This reflex point is known as Cranial Nerve 11 (CN11).* As such, pinching gullet plates, longeing girths, vaulting girths, driving harnesses, and foregirths achieve the same result as the stallion's bite and will act upon the muscles in the horse's withers region like a vise grip. Nature has determined three survival mechanism reflexes for CN11: First, when a mare or a rival are bitten here or when the saddle's gullet plate pinches the side of the withers, this nerve signals to the brain to block movement in the upper arm and shoulder blade. A second signal ensures that the longissimus muscle contracts, thus dropping the horse's back (and that the vertebrae fall into each other as in kissing spine). Third, the pelvis rotates forward as a result of further contraction of the longissimus, opening the area in preparation for mating.

---

*This nerve supplies the sternocleidomastoid and trapezius muscles, which have the following functions:
- Rotation of head away from the side of the contracting sternocleidomastoid muscle.
- Tilting of the head toward the contracting sternocleidomastoid muscle.
- Flexion of the neck by both sternocleidomastoid muscles.
- Elevation of the shoulder by the trapezius.
- Drawing the head back so the face is upward by the trapezius muscles.

With weakness or paralysis these functions are decreased or absent, with possible associated muscle atrophy.

All three of these reactions result in instinctive immobility, and in nature, they are critical for survival: They allow the stallion to mount the mare without being kicked and ensure that a rival is immobilized during a fight for dominance.

The paradox is that we as riders want to achieve exactly the opposite! We like a horse with a loose, supple, and engaged back, and the ability to "step under" his body with his hind end. Only in this way can we be sure we are not riding on the forehand, taking pressure off all the ligaments, tendons, muscles, and bones of the horse to keep him healthy for a full lifetime of enjoyment and riding in harmony.

This goal can only be achieved when there is no pressure on Cranial Nerve 11 from a gullet plate that doesn't fit.

Bucking Reflex Point

This reflex point is located over the fascia behind the 18th lumbar vertebra. The horse's first reaction is to try and get rid of pressure from a saddle that is too long and pressing on the fascia in this area over the transverse processes (see photo on p. 74, bottom right). Further indications of a saddle that is too long are a horse that paces during the walk (both front and hind legs on one side move together rather than diagonally with the opposite side), one that drags the hind legs during the trot, or one that shows a four-beat canter.

Reflex Points to Watch for when Girthing

When using a short girth, watch to be sure that its buckles do not press on the "edge" of the horse's pectoral muscle. And, with a long girth, attention must be paid to the same issue, but avoiding the edge of the latissimus (see photo on p. 71, top left). The edge of a muscle can withstand much less pressure than the flat width of the muscle itself; think about the flat edge of your hand versus the palm as an analogy. Buckles can cause concentrated pressure points in these areas, which cause the muscle fibers of the triceps to contract in an instinctive self-protective measure when trying to avoid this pressure, resulting in potential rub marks. In this situation, a rider will have difficulty finding a good extension in the trot and will experience poor transitions between the gaits: The pectoral muscles need a full range of contraction and relaxation for a "huge" and natural extension; only with complete freedom can the biomechanics work as they should.

Subscapular and Thoracodorsal Nerves

If either the gullet or the billets exert pressure on the subscapular and thoracodorsal nerves, the natural reflex from both or either of these nerves also cause the triceps to contract, inhibiting movement in the front. The horse moves like a "sewing machine" (on the spot, more or less); tripping or stumbling can also result.

IRREPARABLE DAMAGE

The pictures on these next two pages demonstrate clearly some of the long-term, irreversible damage that can result from a badly fitting saddle. Cartilage chipping, nerve pinching, subluxated vertebrae, tongue problems—to mention only a few—can result in further behavioral and even psychological damage to the horse, which will make it almost impossible for horse and rider to find harmony. So please: Listen to what your horse is trying to tell you! If you train him fairly and kindly, he will accept you as the "alpha horse," and once this happens, he can't help but try to please you; it has been in his nature

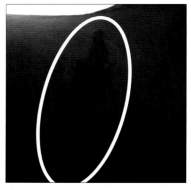

These sweat marks come from damaged sweat glands caused by inappropriate girthing and an incorrect billet system.

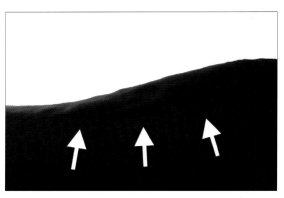

Vertebral and spinal ligament damage caused by too much pressure on the spinal processes.

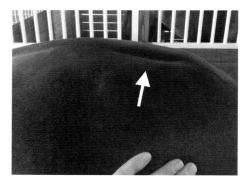

A saddle that was too long, and incorrect training, too, results in abnormal development of the loin muscle area.

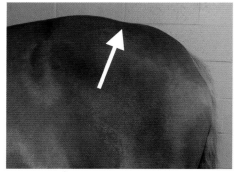

The muscular development at the loins here was due to a gullet channel that was too narrow. You don't want this "dip" at the croup but rather a nice, evenly rounded rump.

for 50 million years. It is the horse's instinct to do what you want him to do as long as you follow the natural and classical training methods. Be aware of the possibility of saddle-fit issues when behavior changes or problems crop up over a longer period (a couple of days), and do your due diligence to avoid the results shown in these photos.

The *M. Subscapularis* refers to the muscle under the shoulder blade, with its accompanying subscapularis nerve. The *thoracodorsal* comes from the Latin *thorax* (chest area) and *dorsum* (back), and describes the area where the thoracodorsal nerve is found—between the chest and the back.

White marks have been caused by either a saddle pad that was too thick or one that was made from "manmade" materials that cannot "breathe."

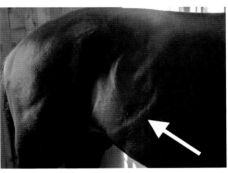

Constant muscular contraction results in an incorrect definition at the flank. This can be caused by a saddle sitting on the withers or one that presses down on the spinal column.

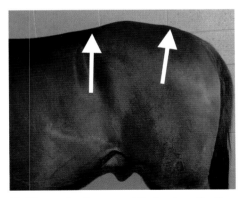

Visible results from a saddle too long for the horse and that exerted too much pressure at and behind the 18th lumbar vertebra.

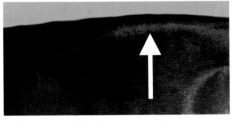

Subluxation of the lumbar vertebrae as a result of pressure at CN11, causing the horse to instinctively block his movement, yet still responding to the rider's impulse to move forward. The subluxation can be likened to the result of trying to drive a car while the hand brake is on; it will move forward (reluctantly) with resulting damage that may show up later.

WHAT IS MUSCLE ATROPHY?

First, when a muscle has been trained for more than it would have been used naturally, and then is not used or trained anymore, the muscle will atrophy back to its shape as determined by nature. The other kind of muscle atrophy we speak of appears when an unbalanced saddle puts too much pressure on a particular muscle, and the horse tries to remove, or avoid, this pressure: He goes into "defensive mode," contracting the area and possibly the surrounding muscles, as well as altering his gaits. In particular, under the point of pressure where circulation is impacted thus reducing nutrients and oxygen to the area, the muscle will develop "back" or it will atrophy. This can only be stopped and reversed when the culprit is removed, or adjusted, to fit properly. A properly fitted saddle and correct training will usually allow the muscle area to regenerate.

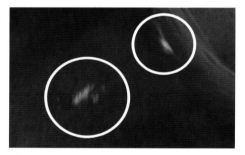

The natural asymmetry of this horse's stronger left shoulder was not taken into consideration during saddle fitting, resulting in white hairs from pressure at the gullet plate, especially at the withers and tree points.

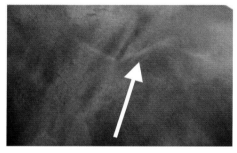

An incorrectly fitted gullet plate putting constant pressure on the side of the withers can result in the formation of a stress line, as well as a constant contraction of the trapezius.

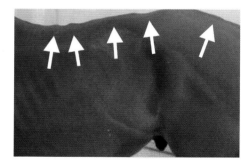

This visibly subluxated back all along its length is the result of poor riding over many years, compounded by an ill-fitting saddle.

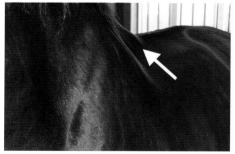

The trapezius muscle can be inflamed like this bulge under the saddle when the tree angle is too wide or too narrow.

WHAT IS MUSCLE DEFINITION?

Muscle definition refers to the generally positive development and growth of a muscle or muscle groups. It can also be negative, however, depending on whether the horse develops his muscular conformation as expected during proper training methods, or whether the muscles are defined incorrectly because of defensive contraction to counteract incorrect riding or a poor fitting saddle. The negative muscle definition is often considered to be "hypertonic," which means that the contraction phase of these muscles is unnaturally long and in a state of abnormally high tension. This results in tight, cramped, and painful muscle development.

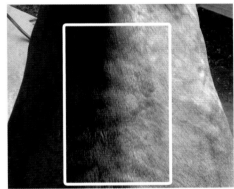

Damage to the dorsal ligament system is often the result of using treeless saddles or from a gullet channel that is too narrow. The rider's weight is not equally or optimally distributed over the weight-bearing surface of the horse's saddle-support area and sits mainly on the spine.

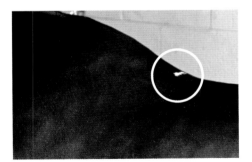

Saddle pads and horse blankets should be anatomically correct and show a withers relief area at the front to avoid pressure spots, which manifest in the appearance of white hairs.

Blisters can result from an incorrect tree width or angle; a horse falling down with the saddle still on; or a sliding saddle pad (among other possible causes, including poor riding).

8

SADDLE-FITTING
EXPERTISE

Horse owners, trainers, veterinarians, body workers, farriers, and you as the rider: Everyone can learn how to diagnose whether or not a saddle fits properly. You don't need to be a saddler or a saddle fitter to do this. If you read this chapter in its entirety and follow along on your own horse, you will able, at the very least, to discern for yourself whether or not the professional you work with is truly an expert at his or her job or someone who is self-taught—that is, someone who may have some idea how to flock but really has very little knowledge about horse anatomy or physiology. In time you yourself will develop the intuition and the "eye" for what a well-fit saddle should look like and what the minimal fit criteria are for both you and your horse.

A trained saddler, whether or not he is at the journeyman or master level, is not always necessarily a good saddle fitter, and to be a good saddle fitter, you don't necessarily have to be trained as a saddler. Veterinarians, trainers, physiotherapists—anyone with a basic knowledge of biomechanics and human and equine anatomy—is capable of learning how to assess and fit a saddle statically and dynamically on-site if the saddle is adjustable.

JOB DESCRIPTIONS FOR SADDLE SPECIALISTS

Saddler: In North America, unfortunately, the saddler trade is still largely unregulated. Together with the Ministry of Skills Development in Ontario, I worked to set up a registered apprenticeship for saddle makers in 1990, making us one of the few authorized training facilities in Canada with a certificate of apprenticeship—especially for English saddlery. There are many skilled craftsmen in North America who have learned the trade from the old "masters"; however, there is no governing body that officially certifies saddle makers. Anyone can call themselves a saddler; people have also recently elevated themselves to "master" status without even having to justify this with the accompanying education or experience. And nobody really cares—least of all, the end consumer.

In the UK, the apprenticeship is more formal, with five years being the norm to achieve journeyman status. The Society of Master Saddlers then deems who can call themselves a master based on years in the trade.

Saddle Salesperson: Saddle salespeople can be from all walks of life, without necessarily having had any training that has anything at all to do with horses

Continued on p. 95

Continued from p. 94

or saddle manufacture or fitting. There is no real focused training available to become a saddle salesperson; much of it is done on the job without any qualifications or certification. Most of this training is done through tack shops, where the owner or the employees sell the saddles. They may have a background in marketing, or know a lot about competitor's saddles and the various makes and models out there, and they may actually be riders themselves. But, there will usually be little or no training about biomechanics or anatomy for either horse or rider. Many tack shops are now beginning to affiliate themselves with a professional saddle fitter to help them sell and fit.

Saddle Fitter: Saddle fitters have been working for many years in one form or another in both North America and in the UK. Training to become a professional saddle fitter has been effected through the Society of Master Saddlers in England as well as through a short-track version in the US. There have also been independent "saddle fitting schools" cropping up here and there, especially in the US, but also as part of the training associated with the selling of various brands of saddles. Many saddle fitters are trained exclusively to sell one specific brand only.

Saddle fitters are able to assess fit and are able to adjust saddles—but are limited somewhat by the materials at hand. Since, as mentioned, there is no real regulation of this trade (especially in North America), many saddle fitters learn what they know by osmosis, or by trial and error, and there are no set standards to give clients a level of security knowing that their fitter is trained properly. Many will do simple repairs on saddles, without having been trained in any way in the saddlery trade.

Saddle Ergonomist: Training to become first an equine ergonomist and then a saddle ergonomist is presently only offered through Saddlefit 4 Life®. Saddle ergonomists are trained to assess the fit of a saddle for both horse and rider, both statically and dynamically, according to the conformational requirements of both parties. They are taught functional equine and human anatomy and how to adjust a saddle properly and completely on-site. The methodology behind Saddlefit 4 Life® training and the expectations for the rider are clearly outlined online (www.saddlefit4life.com). Saddle ergonomists work closely together with all other equine professionals to ensure the ultimate comfort and protection of the horse, which is the common goal for all.

HOW DO I RECOGNIZE A GOOD SADDLE FITTER?

We have noted that just because someone is a trained saddler, does not mean that they necessarily have had any training in saddle fitting. The term "saddle fitter" is pretty much ubiquitous worldwide, without any commonality in qualifications or certification. Basically any person working in a tack shop (a salesperson, a leatherworker, the owner, a manufacturer's rep) can consider themselves a saddle consultant. It becomes necessary for the rider to do the due diligence to determine how much knowledge and experience is really there, which is the purpose of this chapter.

The saddle ergonomist is a copyrighted term introduced through Saddlefit 4 Life®. Everybody with the designation of "saddle ergonomist" has gone through the rigorous training program as set out through Saddlefit 4 Life®, and currently they are establishing themselves on every continent except Africa and Antarctica. Generally, saddle ergonomists always work cooperatively with other equine professionals to ensure a qualified consultation for the rider, and, at the very least, will be open to building these kinds of relationships for the good of the horse. The saddle ergonomist has a good working knowledge of biomechanics, equine and human anatomy, and how these relate to riding and saddle fitting.

He or she is able to adjust the gullet plate of a saddle, re-flock the panels, and do basic repairs and stitching on-site. The advantage is that in this on-site evaluation, the saddle ergonomist can diagnose the issues and discuss the solutions with the rider, and then do what needs to be done to make things work right then and there. (In those instances where a saddle needs a complete and comprehensive overhaul, this will obviously need to be done in the shop as often this job goes beyond what can be done on-site.)

Your saddle consultant/fitter/ergonomist should be a competent and

The saddle ergonomist understands both horse and rider anatomy and biomechanics, and applies this knowledge to other saddle-fitting specifics in order to get the best result for the client with the good of the horse in mind.

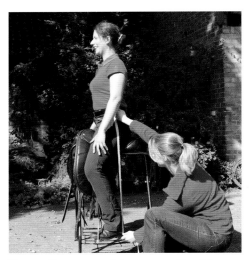

The equine ergonomist measures the rider, checks the saddle flap's length and angle, the stirrup bar position, the length of the stirrup leathers...

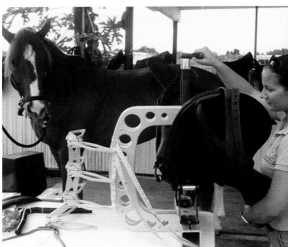

...and changes the tree angle and/or tree width to ensure the saddle fits the horse properly at the withers...

capable expert who has a working knowledge about how the anatomical and physiological requirements of horse and rider relate to one another. It is important to know which muscles and other areas of the horse's body are affected by proper saddle fit, and what is needed to make a saddle fit properly to accommodate these areas.

The fitter also needs to know that the saddle should not cause undue pressure in either the lumbar region, the shoulder area, or on the horse's spine. The fitter will know that the saddle should only be on the saddle-support area, which is mainly on the rib cage and where the longissimus lies. He will also know that the distance between the forelegs will change (hopefully broaden!), which affects the position of the shoulders, that is, if the horse

is being trained according to classical guidelines and is building his muscular conformation correctly. Preferably, the fitter will have some riding background; or at least be aware that the horse's center of gravity slowly moves back as the horse is trained, which takes some of the weight off the forehand, displacing it to the rear. (Critical to assist in accomplishing this, of course, is the ability to continually adjust the saddle as necessary at regular intervals.)

As a saddle consultant or saddle sales rep, he should always have your horse's best interests at heart and make sure that you purchase a saddle that is completely adjustable in order to be able to continually fit it to your horse's ever-changing, three-dimensional back shape. The tree needs to be adjustable in both width and angle

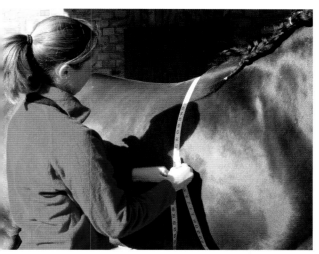

...measures the circumference of the horse to find the best girth option and the optimal area for the girth buckle...

...and makes the necessary adjustments in the flocking to ensure complete and optimal fit on the horse's back.

at the gullet plate, the width of the gullet channel (including panel flocking); the billet system needs to be adaptable as well. The one key prerequisite for a good saddle fitter/ergonomist is that he needs to not only know and understand proper saddle fit, but he must also have the technical ability to adjust the saddle appropriately. To do so, he must be a rider and have extensive knowledge and empathy about and for the horse. That means that optimally he will be able to sit on the horse, if necessary, to be able to feel what the rider is talking about. When he understands terms like "resists, " "falls to the right," and "is not coming through during the changes," then the reason behind a particular issue—and a possible solution—will be easier to find.

It is pretty widely accepted that a saddle needs to fit the horse; as we've discussed it is no less important that the saddle fit the rider (especially critical when the rider is a woman). So this becomes part two of the equation for the saddle fitter: to ensure that the saddle also fits the rider, allows her to sit properly, comfortably, and balanced, and to be able to give the right aids to the horse. Only then will the result be a harmonious coupling. As I've said earlier, it doesn't matter if the horse has the best fitting saddle in the world, when the rider is not comfortable the horse is going to feel it, so neither horse nor rider will perform to the best of their abilities.

In order to assist in ensuring the rider attains the correct and balanced position, the fitter should have a working knowledge of human anatomy and

The saddle fitter should also check saddle length to avoid pressure in the lumbar region...

...check three-dimensional back shape using the Arc Device™...

biomechanics; understand the differences (beyond the obvious) between male and female, in particular the muscles, skeletal structure, tendons, ligaments, and where and how to find the rider's balance point.

The fitter should understand what the correct positioning looks like and why it is so critical to attain.

Of course, a bit of manual dexterity must exist in order to be able to make any necessary adjustments to the saddle on-site. He should be able to at least re-flock, change the billets, narrow or widen the gullet channel, while understanding that even though this might all work while the horse is in the cross-ties when standing still, things may yet again change during motion. This is why it is crucial to watch the horse move during an evaluation: on

the longe line and under saddle (before and after).

A saddle fitter/consultant/ergonomist should be able to assist the rider in the choice of the correct saddle (without manipulating you or having a hidden agenda) because this will affect the ongoing relationship, which should ideally develop between the two. It is inevitable that they will spend quite a bit of time together, which means that there should be enough time for both horse and rider, keeping in mind the subtleties of ongoing customer service that will be required.

It is good when the fitter has competitive information at hand about what's new and on the market vis-a-vis new saddle models and technology, and to be able to discuss the pros and cons and advantages of each. It is also inter-

...check the panel flocking for unevenness and change the billet system...

...and adjust the tree width and/or tree angle one more time, if necessary.

esting to know the various panel stuffing used by manufacturers, and under what philosophy they consider saddle fit in their processes. To be able to offer completely unbiased opinions and information, fitters should not necessarily be affiliated with any one saddle brand or company, but even if they are, it should not impact the ability to give unbiased and educated advice.

A good fitter/ergonomist will always be open to working with other equine professionals, including veterinarians, farriers, trainers, osteopaths, or acupuncturists, to name a few. He should be able to determine if issues have arisen from problems in other areas beyond saddle fit, and be able to refer the rider to the appropriate professional. For example, if there are issues that come from the riding style or poor training methods rather than saddle fit, then he needs to have the courage to mention it diplomatically. He should also have a list of good potential trainers at hand who can work with the rider to address this.

Anyone working with horses should be aware of the fact that we never finish learning. A person who is open to ongoing education, innovations in technology and information, eager to read the latest in available literature and research, and consciously thinks about all the ongoing potential influences on the three-dimensional back shape of the horse, will always have the advantage over anyone who simply thinks, "That is the way we've always done it, and if it ain't broke, don't fix it!"

9

SADDLE FITTING—
IT'S NOT ROCKET SCIENCE
(OR IS IT?)

What Happens in a Saddle-Fit Evaluation?

As a saddle fitter I need to determine exactly where the saddle needs to sit on the horse's back without impeding the rider or possibly damaging the horse. There are several criteria that are generic to any horse and any saddle fitting, and one of these is simply the process of an evaluation. It sounds simple but if you don't follow the logical steps in their correct order, then the possibility of missing something critically important increases.

So for this reason, you begin the saddle-fit evaluation the same way you would begin an evaluation of the horse: You start on the left and observe the horse, first without and then with the saddle, from front to back, and then top to bottom. You repeat this observation exercise on the other side. It is crucial to first observe the horse without a saddle from both sides. This will allow you to determine how defined the horse's musculature is, the shape of the withers, his general condition, and whether there are variations in muscle development that could give some insight into either training methods or saddle fit. This so-called "static" evaluation includes the saddle balance, saddle length, freedom at the withers, tree width, and tree angle. At this point, you should, of course, take a look at the saddle's condition as well, including checking stitching, cleanliness, and billets.

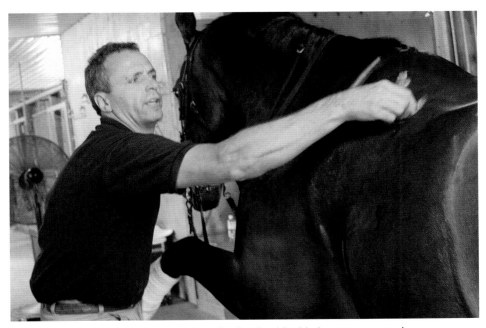

Extending the foreleg demonstrates how far the shoulder blade rotates upward and backward during movement and allows you to delineate its position changes with chalk.

Once you have made this general overview and evaluation, it's time to go into more detail in each of these areas:

1. The saddle should not be on the shoulder cartilage and should have enough room at the top and at the side of the withers muscles (2 to 3 fingers all around, not just at the top).
2. It should not be lying anywhere on the spinal processes nor on the dorsal ligament system (this means the gullet channel needs to be 3 to 4 fingers wide for the entire length of the saddle).
3. The saddle should not go any farther than the 18th lumbar vertebra (where the last floating rib is) and lie on the loins.
4. The saddle panel itself should not be too wide. You can feel where the edges of the longissimus muscle transitions into the internal intercostals (ribs), which is where the panel should end so as not to impede the horse's ability to expand his rib cage properly during breathing and movement.

When you have checked these points statically, have the rider mount and go through all of the gaits—checking to see if what you have determined while the horse was in the cross-ties still works during motion and is reflected in the horse's behavior and in the rider's position. In this dynamic evaluation I watch the rider in the walk, trot, and canter in both directions. (If possible, the saddle should be used without a pad for this exercise.) Specifically, check to see if the saddle moves during each of these gaits. Watch the horse's eyes, ears, tail, and his ability to move freely and, especially, how the muscles move and twitch in front of and behind the saddle. How does the rider feel? Sometimes it is useful to have the trainer or someone else watch with you—someone who is familiar with both horse and rider and can give you enlightening commentary.

WHY IS MY SADDLE TWISTED?

There are basically three components to why a saddle can be twisted on the horse's back: The horse is asymmetrical, the rider is sitting crookedly, or the saddle tree or panels are crooked. To find out exactly which of these components is responsible, a saddle fitter will need to know a number of variables with respect to the horse's conformation, the rider's style of riding, as well as a bit of saddlery background (which, we would hope, is part of the fitter's basic training).

A proper evaluation includes determining shoulder size, position, and angle; and the size and shape of the withers (essentially a cross-section at the spinalis, trapezius, longissimus and

This ergonomist is determining the horse's shoulder angle using the withers gauge from Sprenger.

HorseShape uses a laser device to determine the three-dimensional back shape.

The Topographer® from EquiScan.

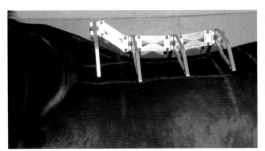

The Arc Device™ from Saddlefit 4 Life®.

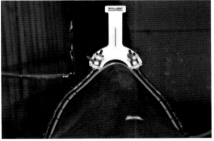

This tool measures the shape of the shoulder musculature.

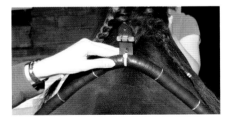

This is the LWT (leather withers tracer) by Schleese, which determines the withers and shoulder-muscle shapes.

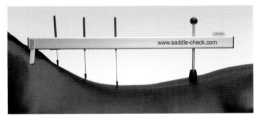

The BVFR (translated to mean the Association of Saddlers and Harness Makers in Germany) uses this standardized device to determine the horse's topline.

latissimus muscles behind the shoulder). To determine this three-dimensional shape of the back, there are a number of commercial devices available (see p. 135) that adequately show any natural asymmetry and the actual position and size of the saddle-support area. (Many of them are "sexy" yet perhaps somewhat cumbersome for actual use in the barn on a regular basis. The results are usually not available immediately, since data has to be input into a computer for analysis.) The use of the relatively simplistic flexible withers gauge augments a simple visual assessment of both horse and rider—statically and dynamically—which shows how the saddle actually fits.

Once the fitter has collected all available information and evaluated the

All measurements are documented on the evaluation form. This horse is making sure that the fitter is not making any mistakes!

data, and the cause of saddle twisting has been determined, only then can he begin to address a solution whether it is to do with the rider, the horse, or the saddle. Documentation of these measurements, diagrams, and suggestions for possible solutions should always be in writing for future reference, and a copy given to the client. This makes it easier to compare results down the road as well: Many times a rider cannot believe the change in her horse's conformation as a result of a properly fitted saddle—sometimes in a relatively short period of time!

Experience has taught me that usually the rider is balanced and the saddle is straight. Any twisting is usually due to the natural asymmetry of the horse, and only when this is taken into consideration during saddle fit will the horse actually have a chance to develop his shoulder muscles as well as all accompanying parallel and diagonal musculature evenly. It's an easy fix: The gullet plate needs to be adjusted to accommodate the bigger shoulder so that it has room on both sides to "slide through" the gullet plate during motion—allowing harmonious movement.

However, we have come across fitters who seemingly do not understand this concept, and want to make an example of a properly fit saddle using one that was already adjusted to accommodate the asymmetry at the shoulder. They want to make the point of demonstrating why the saddle is crooked without realizing why they were adjusted in this

> ### LEARNING FROM ONE ANOTHER
> **Saddlers, saddle fitters, sales people, and ergonomists should all be capable of determining exactly where the saddle-support area on a specific horse is. This allows all of you together—you as the rider, your vet, your trainer, and your fitter—to discuss the optimal placement of your saddle. Thus you can avoid saddle pressures on any of the reflex points I've discussed, and the undesirable horse behavior that accompanies them.**

manner. In essence, all they are demonstrating is their own ignorance. This is just sad, simply wrong and again underlines the need to understand basic equine anatomy when learning to fit a saddle.

THE SADDLE-SUPPORT AREA

You do not need to be an expert to check whether or not your saddle is lying in the correct position on your horse's back. The following photos show you how to check for this by using a simple tool—some chalk! You should check whether the saddle is where it should be before, during, and after riding.

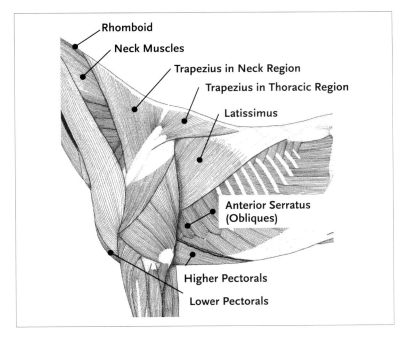

Rhomboid
Neck Muscles
Trapezius in Neck Region
Trapezius in Thoracic Region
Latissimus
Anterior Serratus (Obliques)
Higher Pectorals
Lower Pectorals

Another look at the superficial muscles affected by saddle fit.

Take your chalk and mark a straight line top to bottom at the widest point of the shoulder.

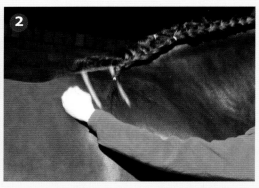

Mark a second line where the shoulder blade ends, parallel to your first line.

Extend the foreleg and make a third line where the shoulder blade now ends (having rotated upward and backward during the leg extension).

Feel where the last floating rib ends (the 18th lumbar vertebra), or you can also see where the two hair directions converge at the hind flank and go up from there, and mark a fourth line.

Behind this fourth line go back another 4 inches (10 cm) and draw a fifth line parallel to the fourth. This is the region where the bucking reflex lies. When the saddle is too long and ends in this area, your horse could buck; go into a four-beat canter; have difficulty with flying changes (an extra "skip" step); pace rather than move diagonally in the gaits; or be unable to achieve collection.

Now return to the area between the third and fourth lines and carefully feel for the spinal vertebrae. Mark a horizontal line between the third and fourth vertical lines to note where the transverse processes of the spine end.

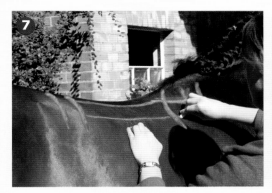

From this horizontal line feel downward where the longissimus ends and inserts into the intercostals (rib muscles). There will be a more or less distinct indentation here. Draw a parallel horizontal line here as well from the second to the fourth vertical lines. There will be about 4 inches of space between these two lines.

Go down 4 inches from the top of second line and draw a diagonal line to connect the second and third lines back to the base of the withers then back to the top of the second line. This triangle is the area where absolutely no contact should be made. The trapezius, the rhomboid, and the spinalis all insert under this region (see illustration on p. 137), as well as the nuchal and dorsal ligament system with all of the accompanying nerve ends. This is the most sensitive area of the withers and, as I've mentioned, where the stallion bites a mare to immobilize her during mating.

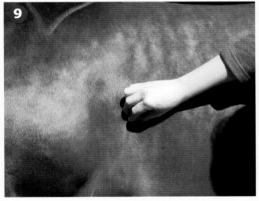

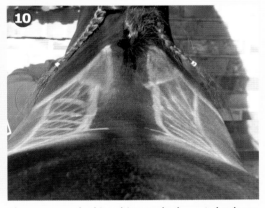

For your own visible information draw red chalk "X"s everywhere where the saddle and the girth should not lie—that is, between the first and second vertical chalk lines, and between the fourth and fifth vertical chalk lines; in the sensitive area of the withers; and above the first horizontal line on the horse's back/spine. The girth buckles should avoid the area of the edge of the pectorals and the latissimus at the elbow, and at the side of the horse.

The areas marked in white on the horse's back are the saddle-support areas, which are essentially the position of the longissimus muscles.

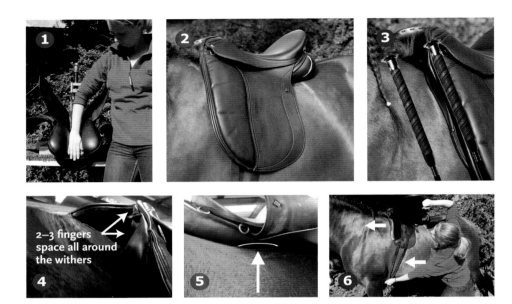

2–3 fingers space all around the withers

Based on the chalk marks from pp. 138 and 139 you can check static fit and determine whether (see photos above):

1. Your saddle has a large enough and evenly spaced (3 to 4 fingers width) gullet channel all the way from front to back. (Some horses will need a hand-width space here—4 inches or more!)

2. Your saddle goes farther beyond the fourth vertical line and is therefore lying on the sensitive reflex point in the loin area that can cause bucking and other behavioral issues, as well as soft-tissue damage.

3. The gullet plate is parallel to the shoulder blade and wide enough for the shoulder muscle. The angle is easily visible when you place a pencil (or other straight object like your crop) against the first vertical line, and a second straight object along the front piping of the saddle panel to determine that these are parallel (what you need). If this is the case, then the shoulder should easily "slide under" (like a sliding door) the points of the tree during movement.

4. There is enough room at the withers, not only at the top but all around the pommel area: 2 to 3 fingers or 1 to 2 inches above where the panel's padding starts. If the withers and the accompanying transverse spinal processes are not free to move here, your horse will have particular difficulty during circles, bending, and when turning corners.

5. The horizontal panel is lying flat on the horse's back. You can test this by running your flat hand underneath and checking the panel's position by lifting the sweat flap to look. You don't want to see light through the middle, which

would indicate bridging, or light at either or both ends, which can cause the saddle to rock.

6. The billets are hanging correctly. Their position is crucial for maintaining the saddle in its correct place in the saddle-support area, and not sliding up or back during riding.

If the saddle is positioned correctly behind the second vertical chalk line, you can expect that the saddle tree with its rigid gullet plate will also stay behind the shoulder during movement. This does not mean that certain parts of the saddle (the flap in a jumping saddle, for example) cannot lie in front of this line because a flap is flexible and does not exert constant pressure—allowing the shoulder to come back and under the flap during movement.

You can check the position of the tree points by seeing where the D-rings are; they are usually attached in front of the gullet plate. When the D-ring is located at the pommel on the same line as the second vertical chalk line, then the gullet plate is in correct position behind the second vertical line. When the saddle is behind this second vertical line, the girth needs to stay in its proper position as well, in order to avoid the saddle sliding forward. Remember that the girth will always migrate to the point of least resistance: the narrowest point behind the elbow, which is the correct position for the girth to be in. This means that the billets need to be correctly attached to hang straight down toward this area.

To be sure it is correct, girth up loosely and check that it is in the proper position, that is, you don't need to pull the billets forward (as shown in photo 6 on p. 140).

Dynamic Fit

Put the saddle on the horse's back without a pad and girth it up correctly. Work with your horse and ride him for about 15 minutes—at least two circles in each direction walk, trot, canter—then do a 20-meter figure-eight at sitting and rising trot in both directions.

Remove the saddle by lifting it up and off the horse's back, being careful not to disturb the hair. The dust pattern that the saddle leaves (without a pad interfering) should not be visible in front of the second vertical line, nor behind the fourth line (behind the 18th lumbar vertebra). When you look over the top of the horse's back from behind, the dust pattern should be even on both sides.

To check whether or not the spinal processes have enough room, the gullet channel must be wide enough from front to back. I often see gullet channels that are wide at the front but narrow toward the back. (This makes no sense, but seems to be a design flaw in some saddle brands.) The saddle should not have twisted either to the left or the right, which would be indicated by the horse's hair or the dust pattern. This too can be easily seen if you stand on a stool and look over the horse's topline from behind.

10

SADDLE FITTING 101

The Basics in Detail

SADDLE LENGTH

The saddle-support area ends at the 18th vertebra. There are some saddles available that are longer than this area would indicate, but they do not put pressure on the horse's back beyond this point. For example, some Western saddles (although they may look too long) "float" in this region and carry no actual weight, nor do they place consistent pressure on the horse's back there. Every saddle should adhere to the principles of weight distribution, regardless of discipline.

FINDING THE LAST RIB

There are a couple of methods to determine where this is. In the flank you can see where the two directions of hair growth converge (the area that I call the "rain line"): When a horse sweats, this is where the sweat runs off. If you follow this line up to the spine, you will approximately hit this 18th vertebra, and you can feel where the last rib is. If you follow this rib up to the spine with a slight curvature to the front, you will also find where the 18th rib inserts into the spine (where the fourth vertical line should be and where the saddle-support area ends).

After the saddle fitter has used chalk to determine the saddle-support area, it is easy to see whether the saddle fits lengthwise (top right), or is too long for the horse's back (bottom right).

THE SADDLE-SUPPORT AREA

The horizontal panel of the saddle, which runs under the length of the entire tree from front to back, is what supports the saddle on the horse's back and distributes the rider's weight.

The center of gravity of the rider should be found approximately at the base of the withers. The goal is to have the first third of the saddle carry about 30 percent of the rider's weight, the middle third of the saddle to carry 40 percent, and the back third of the saddle again only 30 percent. It is the middle third of the saddle that places the rider correctly behind the withers over the horse's center of gravity. This is where there is the least movement in the horse's back itself, especially when compared to the front (due to the musculature contractions in the withers and movement in the shoulder area), and to the back (due to the motion in the spinal column). In order to achieve this proper weight distribution of the rider, most saddle trees have a slight curve in their naked form. This is what allows the saddler to put more flocking in at

the front and the back to accommodate the greater inherent movement of the horse's back there. This also ensures that the flocking is soft and comfortable for the horse, while providing the "close contact" area in the middle of the saddle where the rider wants to get as near to the horse as possible.

If you observe the horse in motion with a time-lapse camera, you can see that first the back arches up, the hind leg comes under, the horse lifts the front of his rib cage, and his center of balance moves back to release pressure off the forehand. The forelegs can then easily extend out and the shoulders rotate upward and backward under the saddle—in effect, pushing the saddle up in the center (and, for that split second where this happens, decreasing the load from the front and back thirds of the saddle and concentrating it onto the middle).

At the same time, the horse will engage and raise his back and the shoulder blade needs to be able to "glide" through a properly fitted gullet plate

The saddle-support area is effectively in the middle of the longissimus muscle...

...and to ensure that it remains unencumbered during riding, the saddle should not bridge.

TOO MUCH OR TOO LITTLE MOVEMENT?

Most riders would prefer a saddle that doesn't move, doesn't rock. However, to maintain the ability for loose, harmonious, and supple movement of the horse's back and to ensure the rider's body is in positive tension, the saddle should actually be able to "rock" (very slightly) front to back. If it rocks too much, it will continually smack the rider (not the horse) in the butt. If the saddle doesn't move at all in this area, but actually has contact all the way to the cantle, or it bridges, it will cause constant pressure on the horse's back at this point and can actually lead to muscle atrophy in this area. Too often we see saddles that don't move at all on the back, thus putting too much pressure on the floating ribs and on the sensitive part of the horse`s back outside the saddle-support area (behind the 18th lumbar vertebra).

A rider may have a hard time getting used to the change in feel when a saddle like this has been adjusted—from not moving and digging into the horse's loins to one that allows this slight "rocking." The horse will be able to demonstrate a greater dynamism in movement than in a saddle that previously didn't move and kept the rider sitting more still. The increase in "swing" and suppleness during movement will, at first, be felt as too much bounce and takes some getting accustomed to. This difference in feel can sometimes cause lactic acid to build up in the rider's abdominals or back muscles because she will be feeling the positive tension (muscle contractions) that she will need to ride with in order to be able to sit this new level of movement correctly. Often, the horse will also demonstrate "symptomatic lameness" due to lactic acid buildup in the muscles from this increased ability to move; both rider and horse will be using muscles that were heretofore repressed!

This will certainly go away in a few days. Think of the movement in the back when it comes up to meet the saddle: There is no room to do this when the saddle is sitting flush while the horse is standing still. Good riders welcome this movement ability in the horse's back; insecure, beginner, unfit, or unbalanced riders have difficulty with it and, consequently, choose a saddle that sits quietly (does not move) and digs into the horse's loin—obviously to the horse's detriment.

and tree points. (To clarify: The tree points can be part of the gullet plate, but the tree points are part of the tree structure itself and need to fit on their own. The gullet plate needs to ensure enough freedom all around the withers, and the tree points need to allow room for the shoulder blade to move. Sometimes the gullet plate is long enough that the ends are attached to the tree points of the saddle tree.)

It is, of course, important that the

saddle panel lies flat and evenly along the length of the horse's back, that is, not hollow (not touching the back) in the middle (bridging, in other words). To test this, run a flat hand under the panel from front to back. Start at the stirrup bars using one hand below (palm side up and hand flat) and one hand above on the saddle to exert a light pressure.

It is not necessarily a problem if the saddle rocks slightly at the back end during this exercise (i.e. is not showing consistent contact on the horse's back at the cantle area). However, when it rocks a lot it can affect the seat and position of the rider, and the horse will experience too much pressure, especially from the middle third of the saddle. This is akin to the feel of a "treeless" saddle (essentially bareback pads). A saddle can also rock too much at the pommel end, which is usually an indication that the saddle will be completely out of balance under the rider's weight,

fall forward and come up in the back end. When this is the case, it is advisable to check whether this is due to uneven flocking, or whether the saddle is simply too wide at the gullet plate for the horse's conformation.

If the saddle panel has depressions in it (especially under the weight-bearing areas), this indicates the need for a re-stuffing because the flocking has shifted during riding. Otherwise, there is no guarantee of even rider weight distribution, and the area around the depression(s) will exert even more pressure on the horse's back—possibly causing him pain, but certainly discomfort. You should be able to feel these areas when testing the saddle panel for evenness as just explained, even if they are not immediately obvious to the eye.

How the saddle is stored may also cause indentations on the saddle panel. The commonly used red metal saddle racks mounted to the wall are huge perpetrators of this by putting huge

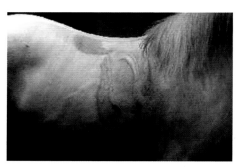

Sweat marks occur in areas where there is friction and air circulation.

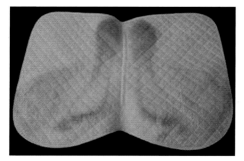

Similar to a collar on a white shirt, most of the dirt occurs where there is the most access to air circulation and friction. Here we see an excellent (from a correctly fit saddle) dust pattern on a saddle pad.

dents into the vertical and horizontal panels. The best way to store an English saddle is to have the saddle sit on a round, 2-inch polyvinylchloride (type of plastic) pipe with nothing whatsoever touching the panels.

Sweat Patterns

Horses sweat just like humans in order to regulate their body temperature. The horse's back actually has only a few sweat glands, most of them are found along his sides, at the neck or flank—areas that have a broad and open surface to allow the natural influence of air and wind to cool the body with the help of sweat. This is why the large saddle flaps (the bottom flap when there are two, the monoflap when there is one) are called sweat flaps.

The horse will be able to sweat under the saddle when friction and air circulation are present. In other words, no sweat will form in the areas that are in constant contact (without movement) with the horse's back. Most of the friction occurs at the front (pommel area) and back (cantle area) of the saddle, since presumably the center of the saddle (where there is the least amount of movement on the back) has constant pressure.

In the front, the horse's shoulder rotates upward and backward anywhere between 4 to 6 inches during movement. The latter third of the saddle should rock slightly in accompaniment to the horse's motion. In the center of the saddle where the billets work to keep the saddle still and in position, and where the gullet plate and stirrup bars assist in keeping the saddle off the horse's spinal processes, there must be no movement or twisting.

Since there is no real amount of friction (at least, there shouldn't be!) under the stirrup bars or at the gullet plate at the withers, this is the area where the horse will sweat least—and last. Of course, this also depends on the season, coat length, where and how the horse is stabled, his breed, overall health and condition, and how he is ridden. Large kidney-shaped (6 to 8 inches long) dry spots are acceptable under the stirrup bar, but dry spots found on the saddle-support area that have a circumference of around an inch could indicate points of concentrated pressure.

VERTICAL PANELS

The vertical panels are found at the front of the saddle as a natural extension coming from the horizontal panels into the sweat flap, and are designed to protect the horse from undue pressure from the tree itself (its gullet plate, its screws, its nails). This part of the panel also serves to stabilize the saddle along its sides on the horse's back, but the panels should

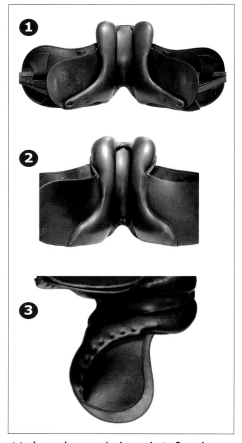

1) Independent vertical panels (referred to as "French" style) with ¾ panels and shoulder relief cutouts.

2) Integrated vertical panels with ½ panels.

3) Integrated vertical panels showing full-length panels.

not interfere with the movement of the horse. The vertical panels can take several forms and vary in length: long, three-quarter, or short panels, which the saddler will designate as "full," "¾," or "½" panels (see diagram on p. 51). Their size will depend mainly on

horse, rider, or some combination of the needs of both. For dressage saddles, for example, full-size vertical panels are good for Thoroughbred-type horses (with narrow rib cages), and for inexperienced riders. The full-length vertical panels will impact the freedom of the trapezius somewhat, which is probably good for the rider who is just beginning to learn dressage. It can be compared to training wheels on a bicycle—support for the beginner. The rider has this supportive feel at the thigh, which can increase the feeling of a secure seat.

Jumping or eventing saddles often have longer vertical panels that do not impede the rider's leg or the horse's triceps muscle because they are situated farther forward on the saddle (lying slightly beyond the shoulder and the triceps). The sweat flap on these saddles is shorter than a sweat flap on the dressage models.

Shoulder Relief Cutouts

More experienced riders who are aiming for a balanced seat (without needing to depend on the additional security of "hanging" onto their reins for balance)—regardless of whether they event, jump, or do dressage—often prefer the ¾ panel, which is cut back a bit at the shoulder ("shoulder relief panel") and therefore provides complete freedom of movement in this area. The seat of the rider is not as "wedged in" as she might feel with a normal full-length vertical panel, but there is still a bit of support. This is especially advantageous for younger horses and the slimmer horse breeds as the vertical panel with the cutout doesn't interfere with their freedom of movement at the shoulder.

The shortened vertical panel system (½ panel) is one of the oldest methods used for panels, and can be seen in military, ceremonial, and dressage saddles. The ½ panel ensures complete freedom for the rider's leg, but one disadvantage is that the ½ panel cannot include a shoulder-relief cutout because this could possibly lead to a concentrated pressure point right at the base of the vertical panel. It is difficult to stabilize the saddle with a ½ panel on slimmer breeds, and the inexperienced rider can miss the additional support at the thigh.

Panels can also differ in the method of attachment to the seat leather and sweat flaps. We differentiate between integrated and independent (French style) panel systems. The integrated panel is stitched to the sweat flap all the way around and is actually considered part of the sweat flap itself. The independent panel is only attached to the saddle at the front and back with no attachment of the panel under the saddle tree to the sweat flap. The advantage here is that because it is truly independent of the rest of the saddle, it can be easily fitted to the horse's three-dimensional back shape and flocked exactly as required before attachment, and also, of course, after it has been attached and needs to be refitted.

PANEL WEDGE OR NOT?

We differentiate between round panels and panel wedges, which refer to the shape of the panel under the cantle. The traditional form is a round panel, which basically requires one complete piece of leather to make. The panel wedge is actually a separate wedge-shaped piece of leather that is inserted at the back end of the panel so that the panel itself can lie completely flat on the horse's back all the way to the cantle. The huge advantage of a panel wedge is that it serves to distribute the rider's weight more evenly because of the increased surface area of the panel itself. The back end of the panel can then be flocked in accordance with the horse's breed and conformation. Ideally, a good saddle manufacturer should be able to accommodate every rider, large or small, using any size and type of panel as needed: A so-called "relief wedge" will work for a short-backed horse needing to accommodate a larger rider (18-inch seat for rider with a 17½-inch panel, for example).

The size and shape of the panel wedge will determine not only the size of the panel on the horse's saddle-support area, but it can actually shorten or widen the weight-bearing surface under the rider.

The distance between the underside of the pommel and the top of the withers should be 2 to 3 fingers in height.

This same distance (2 to 3 fingers) should also be evident along the sides of the withers bone above where the panel starts.

WITHERS FREEDOM

Enough space at the withers area is of huge importance to the comfort of the horse under saddle. As such, pretty much everyone who has anything to do with fitting the saddle (including the rider who uses the saddle) must ensure that there is 2 to 3 fingers clearance here. Unfortunately, just having 2 to 3 fingers clearance between pommel and withers is really only half the equation: What is usually ignored is that you also need this same clearance at the sides of the withers!

This freedom at the sides of the withers under the pommel, which is so necessary, is often neglected by saddle fitters. This negligence has resulted in irreparable damage to the shoulder cartilage, or at the very least, caused white hairs to develop on the sides of the withers.

If you observe the movement of a horse from behind, you will notice a slight pendular motion of the abdomen from left to right. This motion is accompanied by the natural movement of the transverse spinal processes. When training a horse in lateral movements or riding around a corner—during which a horse should bend supply to the right or left—the horizontal axis of the saddle does not actually bend with the horse. However, to ensure that this saddle resistance does not hinder or harm the horse during these movements, it is very important that the space available to move at the side of the withers muscle is as great as the space above it (2 to 3 fingers high).

The saddle ergonomist measures 4 inches down from the start of the vertical panel at the pommel and marks this spot as "L."

Measuring between the two starting points of the panels (4 inches above L) left and right will give you the "T" measurement.

THE GULLET PLATE

The gullet plate and the accompanying spring steel pieces (that strengthen the saddle tree along its length) work together to support the saddle behind the shoulder. The saddle tree should never break, slip, or injure the withers or the spine. The gullet plate gives the saddle tree enough stability to allow the rider to sit balanced and work in harmony with the horse. It needs to be rigid enough to take the pressure off the withers at the top and sides (keeping the saddle from sitting on the withers with the rider on top, and in effect, "building a bridge" over the withers). To ensure this happens, both width and angle of the gullet plate is critical: Correct fit helps to allow the shoulder blade enough room to slide through the tree points during movement.

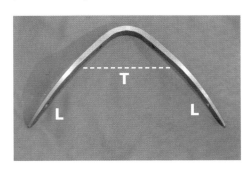

Gullet Angle and Gullet Width

As shown in the photos on p. 150 and this page, the gullet plate is measured to determine both width and angle: L, which is determined at the base of the gullet plate (4 inches down from the start of the vertical panel on both sides); and T, which is 4 inches above L at the start of the vertical panel on both sides.

The shorter the distance between the two T and the two L markers, the narrower the gullet angle; the longer the distance is, the wider the angle. There are no standards for "narrow, medium, wide" in the industry; these are fairly arbitrary descriptions. Most saddles you will find on the market today are adjustable in their angles at the tree points, but not their gullet-plate width. The chart on p. 152 discusses some of the causes and effects of changing T and L in the gullet plate. As an analogy, place your hands together as though you are praying—palm to palm. Move your hands apart parallel and upright—this is gullet width. The angle of your hands doesn't change whether you spread your hands 10 inches apart or one inch apart.

Now put just the tips of your fingers together as in an upside-down V to make an angle. You can change this angle by keeping your finger tips together but spreading your hands apart, all the way to 180 degrees! You can change the angle, but the width (at the top of the gullet or where your finger tips are) doesn't change.

The chart shows that changes made to the tree width at T do not necessarily mean an automatic change in tree angle. However, the effect as shown in the chart is not always the result of

ACTION	HOW TO DO IT	WIDTH OF GULLET PLATE AT T	WIDTH OF GULLET PLATE AT L (NEAR THE TREE POINTS)	EFFECT
Widen the Tree	The sides of the gullet will be evenly spread.	Gets wider	Gets wider	Angle gets wider
Narrow the Tree	The sides of the gullet will be evenly closed.	Gets narrower	Gets narrower	Angle gets steeper
Making the Angle Steeper	Pressure on T at the inner gullet will narrow the angle.	Stays the same	Gets narrower	Tree width stays the same
Making the Angle Wider	Pressure on T at the outer gullet flattens the angle (makes it wider).	Stays the same	Gets wider	Tree width stays the same

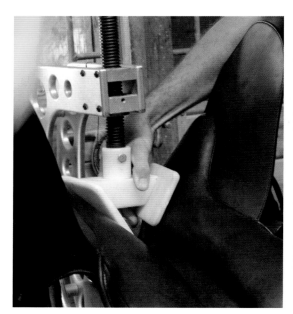

The Saddlesizer™ tree machine can adjust both tree angle and tree width.

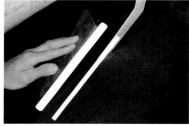

You can determine the shoulder's angle by using the Sprenger gauge.

Here, this tree's width is being adjusted asymmetrically.

changing the angle, because horses with wide withers muscles and/or wide shoulder muscles do not necessarily have flat shoulder blades. Therefore, it is not always enough that the gullet plate's angle can be changed; its width should always also be adjustable, too. The ability to do this is particularly lacking in the "self-adjustable" saddles that come with tools to work on them. (In particular, the self-changeable gullet plates as seen in the Bates saddle don't address this requirement; changing them will actually change the angle of the tree points, but does not change the actual width of the gullet at T.)

It is important to consider the points of the tree to be sure they lie flush to the horse's muscles, thereby avoiding adding extra pressure at the sides of the withers. The angle of the gullet plate needs to be the same as the angle of the shoulder blades, as previously discussed. What is important here is that the shoulders may have different angles because of the asymmetry of the horse, which means that the gullet plate needs to be asymmetrically adjustable—which most aren't. Only this adjustment on each side will allow the rotating shoulder blade the freedom for unencumbered backward and upward movement through the vertical tree panel point during motion on each side.

Tree width (the width of the gullet plate) is always considered in regard to its relationship to the width of horse's the shoulders: The farther apart they are, the wider the tree needs to be.

Show jumpers and eventers, in particular, will appreciate our accommodating their shoulder width because both shoulders rotate upward and backward at the same time over a jump (as opposed to flatwork, where one shoulder at a time needs the room.)

Several companies have developed measuring tools to determine shoulder and wither angles (see photos p. 152). The fitted saddle needs to lie within the saddle-support area of the horse's back and the gullet plate needs to accommodate the shoulders' angles, which can differ from left to right. The shoulder-angle measurement is the angle between the vertical axis of the horse and the distance to the shoulder blade, as well as measuring the distance between the two shoulder blades. You can really only determine how much freedom at the shoulder is actually required by knowing this angle.

You can take this shoulder-angle measurement to a tack shop to determine whether or not the front panel seam of the vertical panel is parallel to the shoulder before you even take out a specific saddle to try. Just as the blacksmith can customize each horseshoe for each foot and each horse, the saddle should be fitted on-site to ensure—especially at the gullet plate—it fits the horse. If the gullet plate is too tight on one side (because of the natural asymmetry of the horse's musculature or bone structure) and the angle doesn't line up with that of the shoulder blade, it will follow that the saddle will slip to one side of the back during movement. Rotation of the shoulder blade and the bigger muscles on the one side will push the saddle out of position when the gullet plate is not fitted to accommodate this asymmetry. One of the results of this situation, which we must do our very best to avoid, is the irreparable damage that can occur to the shoulder cartilage when the horse's shoulder measurements are not taken into account.

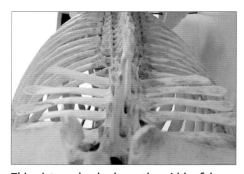

This picture clearly shows the width of the spinal vertebrae and the transverse processes. Notice the height difference between last rib and the lumbar spinal transverse processes. This is why a saddle should never lie on the spinal processes!

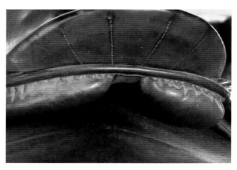

This saddle has slipped to the right and is lying on the vertebrae (sitting on the spine) on the left hind. The saddle has twisted and the gullet channel is obviously too narrow for this horse, as well.

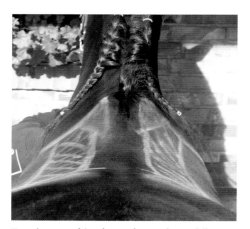

To reiterate, this photo shows the saddle-support area as shown by the white chalk on the horse's back, with the sensitive area at the withers in red (that is, the saddle should never sit here).

This saddle fits well, has a wide enough gullet channel for the horse's spine and sits straight on the horse's back in front of the lumbar spinal processes.

THE GULLET CHANNEL

The gullet channel needs to be wide enough through the entire length of the saddle to accommodate the spinal processes, ligaments, and nerve endings from front to back. The width of the gullet channel will, of course, impact the size of the panel itself, which means that the wider the gullet channel, the smaller the panel—and the less weight-bearing surface available to the rider. This means that gullet-channel width cannot be an arbitrary decision: The saddler has to ensure that there is still enough weight-bearing surface on the panels to avoid the tree itself slipping into the gullet channel. The tree is supported by the panels on the horse's back—if these panels get too far apart when the gullet gets too wide, there may not be enough leather surrounding the tree making it possible it can hit the horse's back in its "naked" form.

The optimum width of the gullet channel lies somewhere between 2½ to 4 inches (6 to 10 cm); it will seldom be wider than this and should never be narrower. A somewhat-too-wide gullet channel is still better than one that is too narrow. Although there are those who contend that a gullet channel wider than 3½ inches (about 8 cm) can cause breathing difficulties for the horse, there is no real proof that substantiates this claim. Every single traditional military and Western saddle that has been built—and is still being built—using a 4-inch gullet channel would have to cause breathing problems, and this is not the case, because otherwise, none of these horses would perform the way they need(ed) to. Therefore, I cannot support this opinion.

Many riders think that using extra thick saddle pads will help the horse's back when they notice pressure points or sensitivity on the horse's spine. This is a case where meaning well does not necessarily end well. A saddle with a gullet channel that is too tight will only get tighter when you add extra padding (regardless of what the padding is made of). It's like trying to fix a pair of shoes that doesn't fit because they are too tight and causing blisters with another pair of socks. It doesn't work! Who would do that?

A gullet channel that is wide enough for the horse's spine will not impinge the movement nor cause long-term damage. The saddle should not sit on either the vertebral processes, the dorsal ligament system (runs along the horse's back), or on the nerve ends that originate all along the spine. Only when the gullet channel is wide enough for the horse will he be able to move properly and freely in all gaits, lateral movements, and over jumps without uncomfortable pressure originating from the saddle.

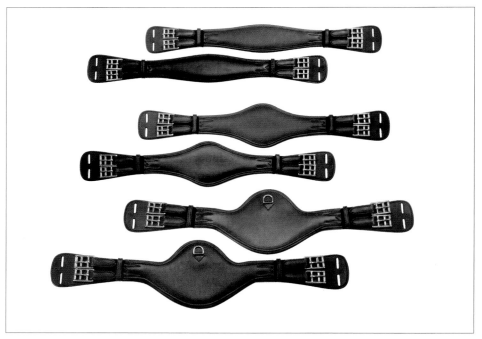

The more a girth is able to distribute weight over a larger surface area, the more comfortable the horse will be. These are all "BSE" (both sides elastic) diamond girths, with 4-, 6-, and 8-inch sternum shields.

THE GIRTH

In my experience, whether or not a saddle can fit properly and lie balanced on the horse's back has a lot to do with the saddle pad and the girth because about 20 percent of slipping or instability issues arise from these two accessories.

There are many different types, lengths, and versions of girths available today. They have different forms and functions and are paired with the saddle billets in their necessary length. The main considerations should be form and elasticity of the girth while remembering that it is the girth's job to keep the saddle in place within the saddle-support area. It has the potential to put immense pressure on the horse's musculature, which means that it should displace this pressure as evenly as possibly along its length. Ideally, it should have a bit of a wider surface area along the sternum of the horse, which is the strongest point of contact. A girth like this is called a "diamond girth" because of its shape and it is anatomically accommodating by narrowing at the ends that sit under the elbow area. Many horses have an issue with the girth pinching at the elbow because it tends to sit pretty close to this area (finding the narrowest spot) and because, of course, the saddle is sitting closely behind the shoulder.

The girth should be narrowest at the spot where it sits under the elbow and widen to between 4 to 8 inches at the sternum (6 inches is a good happy medium and works for most horses to help displace the optimum amount of pressure along its length). Some dressage girths are 8 inches wide (20 cm) wide in this area.

More often, however, you will see girths being used that are neither wide enough nor long enough, with too much elastic at the buckles. The result is that they actually "cut" into the pectoralis muscle. This type is referred to as a "knife girth."

A wider girth is always advantageous. It ensures distribution of pressure and weight over the biggest surface area possible, without impinging on the reflex points or causing rub marks. It should be narrower at the ends to accommodate freedom of movement without interference behind the elbows. Opinions vary as to the effectiveness of elastic; however, it is an unarguable fact that a bit of give equally on both sides at the buckles is more comfortable for the horse and allows him to breathe better.

The horse's rib cage gets wider from front to back, which is why tension on the buckles from left to right and front to back vary. Too much elastic at the buckles can cause the rider to inadvertently girth up too tightly: elastic continues to be able to be stretched longer when pulling the girth tightly and this

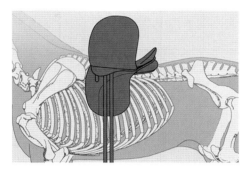

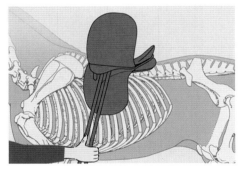

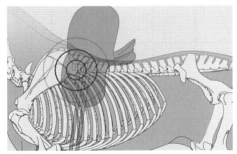

When the billets are not positioned correctly on the saddle, the saddle will automatically slide forward during girthing (the billets and girth seek the narrowest spot behind the elbow), which can cause damage to the horse's shoulder from the gullet plate of the saddle tree.

The red "X" marks the spot where the triceps and the latissimus intercept.

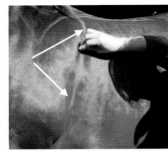

This line shows the outer edge of the triceps muscle (where it ends).

This is the outer edge or lengthwise "border" of the latissimus muscle.

These billets do not fall correctly (hang straight down), which means that during movement, the saddle will definitely slide forward.

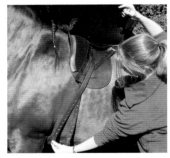

The billets are crossed in order to ensure that they will follow the direction of the muscle fibers in the triceps and the latissimus muscles.

This is the point where the triceps and the latissimus muscles actually cross each other (intersect).

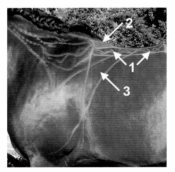

Chalk drawings on the horse's back illustrate where the various muscle groups are actually located in their entirety, including the saddle-support area (longissimus), the sensitive area at the withers (trapezius) and the triceps and latissimus muscles.

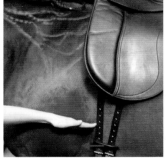

This girth is too short for this horse because the buckles are sitting at the edge of the pectoralis muscle. The hand shows where the buckles should ideally be sitting.

Here the buckles are located correctly; they do not interfere with the pectoralis (shown by the hand).

impedes the horse's ability to breathe deeply, resulting in the horse tiring more quickly.

Ideally, a long girth should have no more than 2 inches (5 cm) of elastic at the buckles, and a short girth no more than one inch (2½ cm) based on elastic used with stretch ability as per standard industry guidelines. If the bottom hole of the billets is about one inch (2 cm) from the sweat flap, after tightening the girth (with long billets/short girth) there should be maximum 2 to 3 open holes left at the top of the billet. This will ensure elbow freedom

If the girth is too short, the buckles will pinch (you can test this by lifting your horse's leg up once you have girthed up) and the horse will not be able to fully extend during movement.

and no pressure on the edge of the pectoralis muscle.

THE BILLET SYSTEMS

There are long and short billet systems, each with their own advantages and disadvantages. Long billets have the major advantage of ensuring that the girth buckles are not positioned under the sweat flap, which can annoy the rider (at least), or cause pressure points on the rider's inner leg (worse). Short billets on the other hand, usually provide a more stable saddle position after girthing. But whatever billet system is preferred—or being used on the saddle according to discipline—it is absolutely key to ensure that pressure from the girth buckles never lies on the edge of the muscle, but rather on its mass (flatness)—for example, the pectoralis or the latissimus (see photos on p. 158). The buckles should also never cause pressure points for either horse or rider, or interfere with riding and moving freely, without pain. Remember that the saddle-support area will change in response to shoulder movement during motion and this, of course, also influences the billets positioning.

The billets and the girth should always hang straight down from the horse's back and fall at the correct girthing position at the elbow and the sternum. (This "straightness" may change slightly once the girth has been tightened; however, you should begin in the correct position!) The horse's breed, condition, weight fluctuations, size of the rib cage—all these influence the position of the girth and billets and they change over time. When the billets hang in such a way that when tightened they can "flow" with the direction of the muscle fibers, you avoid pressure points, and it is easier for the horse to be able to carry a heavy load without "stressing" (stretching) the girth. Accommodating the muscle fibers can be assisted with the use of cross-billets, V-billets, or donut billet systems.

The rule is that the girth will always seek the point of least resistance at the narrowest point of the horse's chest, and when this fact is ignored as decisions are being made about the billets and choosing the right girth, the saddle will always slip forward over the shoulder during motion. As already discussed, this causes physical and behavioral issues, as well as long-term damage.

SADDLE PADS

I could write a whole book on this subject alone. There are so many different pads available—each of which probably has a myriad of uses (beyond simply being an interface between your saddle and the horse's back). Saddle pads can be heat-deflecting, sweat-absorbing, pressure-distributing, saddle-balancing, rider-cushioning, you name it. They generate a huge amount of revenue within the equine industry, and when it comes to overall unit sales, are probably among the top sellers for any tack shop.

One of the reasons for their growing popularity—aside from certain fads, bright colors, and other optical designs—is simply that there are so many bad-fitting saddles. Saddle pads are still widely seen as the band-aid solution for poor fit—to the point that sometimes even brand new saddles are sold with accompanying "shimmable" pads to ensure that the saddle will fit the horse properly. Truth is, fixing fit problems with saddle pads and shims should always be an interim solution, and only when their use doesn't impact the gullet angle and width, or impact the gullet channel freedom for the spine. The original use of the saddle pad was as a thin interface between saddle and horse to keep the sweat off the leather; a well-fit saddle should not need a pad of any kind! A saddle pad should merely be considered as "underwear" for your saddle.

The saddle pad should be shaped to accommodate the natural topline of the horse, including room for the withers at the front (wither-relief pad).

WHAT TO WATCH FOR WHEN CHOOSING A SADDLE PAD

- The pad should have a seam along the center, that is, a topline that follows that of the horse, including the withers (with a withers-relief shape at the front).

- The girth loop should not be too far back otherwise the billets will shift the pad forward. It should be over the girth position on both sides so that the billets and girth align properly through it.

- The pad should be made of natural rather than man-made fibers. Where the outside and the inside layers of the pad are made of two different materials, be sure that the inner side that lies on the horse's skin is made of a natural fiber (cotton or wool).

- Functional, orthopedic pads, such as gel or memory foam, should be covered by a natural fiber, or failing that, at least with state-of-the-art, heat-and-sweat-absorbing technology.

- Make sure to adjust the pad into the saddle's gullet channel at both the pommel and the cantle ends to avoid pulling and pressure over the withers.

- Never wash your saddle pads with fabric softener. Many horses react with great sensitivity to the chemicals in this and also to some strong detergents; also the chemicals can quickly destroy the fibers in the pad, especially the ones used for sweat and heat absorption.

- Quilted pads should use nylon-based "wool" (a wool/synthetic mix, as nylon dries quickly) not foam, as filling; foam disintegrates quickly during regular washing.

- Wash your pads regularly since dirt causes rub marks and pressure points on your horse's skin.

- It really is often true with pads that you "get what you pay for." The more expensive ones are usually worth it because they will have been made with better quality materials and workmanship.

- Less is more! Using more than one pad (for example, cotton pad, wool/felt pad, and gel pad all together) will cause instability in your saddle position and balance, and also seat you farther away from the horse. If that much padding is necessary, there is likely something really wrong with the fit of the saddle.

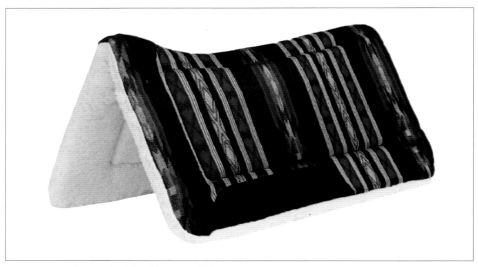

A Western saddle pad with wither-relief shaping.

Using Saddle Pads

The function of a saddle pad is based partly on the style of the saddle it was made for. For reasons of clarity, I will keep the categories to two.

There are two basic types of saddles. The first includes those saddles such as military, pack, and Western saddles, where the saddle tree is in direct contact with the horse's back. For these types of saddles, a saddle pad is absolutely necessary as padding to keep the tree from directly contacting the horse's back. Originally, it was a rolled wool blanket folded and used under a saddle, or a pad made of felt was called into service to keep the horse's back comfortable. Nowadays there are other materials to pad these types of saddles.

The second type has a fairly flat saddle tree with attached panels containing flocking made of wool, felt, rubber, air, or a synthetic wool mix. These saddles really do not need any type of pad to ensure the horse's comfort, that is, if they fit properly! Saddle pads for these saddles are really only supposed to be protection from rub marks arising from dirt or sweat, and also to protect the saddle's leather from the horse's sweat. Of course, pads can be used as a temporary expedient to assist in proper fit, but the important word here is temporary. Even the best saddle pad in the world is not a good substitute for regular saddle-fit adjustments.

It is important to make sure that the saddle pad does not impact the positive designs of the saddle. It shouldn't interfere with the width of the gullet channel (thus pinching the spinal vertebrae and dorsal-ligament system), nor should it "pull" or pinch over the wither. It should lie flat and without folds under the saddle.

Many saddle pads are really thick and cushiony and, therefore, they change the three-dimensional, saddle-support area of the horse: In effect, they negate any saddle-fitting work that has been done. When at a saddle-fit evaluation, it is important to bring along any saddle pads you use while riding so they can be taken into the equation when determining necessary adjustments.

There are, of course, horses that react with great sensitivity to being ridden without their usual saddle pad. However, any horse—if he is not ill or showing skin issues such as blis-

ters, rub marks, or the like, which will increase his sensitivity—can get used to a thin cotton pad that will not impact the fit of a properly adjusted saddle.

I remember watching my first jumping show when I came to Canada and seeing some of the top riders (who shall remain nameless) using the popular jumping saddle of the day. These close-contact models were different than what we used for jumping in Germany: a) Most of them were way too far on the shoulder, which, of course, meant that they were too low in back, and b) without exception, they all had numerous pads, including keyhole foam pads (lollipop pads) underneath them to bring them back up in the cantle area. How is that "close contact"?

11

DOES THE SADDLE
FIT THE RIDER?

THE SADDLE'S SEAT

This area on the saddle is where the rider puts his seat. It consists of a foam "mattress" (base) and covered tree area (usually leather). But even the skirts of the saddle are considered part of the seat. The skirts are the small leather "flaps" that are between the actual seat leather and the (sweat) flaps, and cover the stirrup bars. The balance, size, seaming, and foaming of the saddle's seat are critical for the comfort and position of the rider, and quickly allow her to decide whether a saddle is going to work for her or not.

YOUR PERSONAL SADDLE CHECKLIST

Use these points to help you decide whether or not a particular saddle is going to work for you:

- **Does your leg hang comfortably and loosely straight down?**
- **Is the saddle comfortable for you between your upper inner thighs (this is where the twist is) or do you feel "pulled apart" in this area, that is, with soreness in the hips?**
- **Can you feel your seat bones?**
- **Are the stirrup bars in the correct position to allow you to achieve the shoulder-hip-heel straight line?**
- **Is your knee comfortably placed on the flap or is it angled outward?**
- **Is the flap visible behind your leg when you are in the stirrups?**
- **Can you perform a pelvic tilt (forward and backward movement) without any pain at your pubic symphysis or crotch area?**
- **Do the thigh/knee rolls impede movement at the hips, knees, or ankles? Are they too long, big, or small? Do they support you, or are they in the way?**
- **Can you post comfortably?**
- **Is there enough room in front and behind your pelvis so that during posting you don't hit your pubic bone, and during sitting trot you are not thrown out of the saddle at the cantle area?**
- **Is the saddle flap long enough so your boot top doesn't catch on it?**
- **Is the seat seam uncomfortable and noticeable?**
- **Are you in balance during the walk? Do you have enough support from the saddle to be able to sit properly in position while the horse is walking?**

Once you have answered these questions for yourself and feel comfortable in the saddle, then it is probably a good choice. If you still have questions, your saddle fitter should be able to help you.

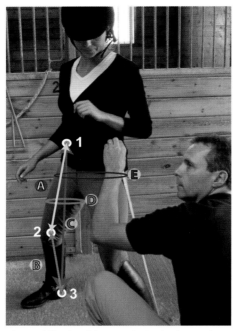

The saddle should not only fit the horse, but just as critically, fit the rider, too. Taking the following measurements is key:

• **Length of the upper (A) and lower (B) leg:** sacroiliac crest (1—just below the waist) to knee bone (2) and knee bone to ankle bone (3). This is to determine the proper stirrup-bar position.
• **The entire leg length (C)** is measured from the edge of the sacroiliac crest (1) to the back of the heel (3) while you sit in the saddle with your feet in the stirrup leathers, as well as on the ground as shown here.
• **Circumference at the hips (E widest part) and circumference at the widest part of the upper thigh (D).** This aids in determining proper seat and flap size.

Besides having to be comfortable for the rider, the saddle's seat has a huge influence on the rider's ability to sit properly and in balance; to be able to give good aids; and to become one with the horse so that the exercises are harmonious.

Across the industry and in the many disciplines, there are various interpretations about the term "seat depth." Some tack shop owners, for example, contend that seat depth simply indicates how tightly the rider is positioned between the saddle's pommel and cantle. Many trainers (and as a result, riders who train with them) think that seat depth is more an indication of how close the rider actually feels to the horse, while maintaining enough freedom to move in both the front and back of the saddle. Whatever the definition (which is really not important) the understanding should be simply that whatever seat depth means, the rider should never be wedged into the saddle so that absolutely no movement is possible.

As a saddler, I understand that the seat depth refers to the deepest physical point of the saddle between pommel and cantle. In other words, the "depth" of the center of gravity of the saddle (and where a round object naturally lies—as shown in the pictures on p. 100—if you want to determine visually where this is on your saddle). You can measure this in inches: Take a straight ruler, lay it straight across the pommel to the cantle and see where there is the greatest space between ruler and saddle seat. The general rule is: the higher the cantle, the deeper the seat.

In other words, seat depth really has nothing to do with how close a rider's contact actually is to the horse. It

POINTS OF REFERENCE ON THE SADDLE

Key criteria when fitting the saddle to the rider:

The front of the saddle (1 in drawing) should not be uncomfortable at either the pubic symphysis or crotch area. This can be easily tested when you try saddles out for size in the shop or on the horse. Test the saddle wearing jeans with lots of seaming in the crotch area. Sit on the saddle and lean far forward and far back. You should be able to feel your jean seams only when you are out of the natural shoulder-hip-heel, plumb-line position. If you can feel the seams in the full range of this motion exercise, the saddle is not for you. Take a friend along to tell you when you are actually sitting straight.

In the middle of the saddle (2) the rider should feel an absolutely even distribution of pressure between the inner upper thighs and the crotch area. If the saddle doesn't fit here, the knees and the feet will be turned out instead of hanging straight down. Your thighs will also feel "pulled apart" and your hips will hurt. The other extreme in this area could have you feel as though there is very little contact between the upper inner thighs and the saddle—almost as if you were sitting on a tepee.

In the rear of the saddle (3) the rider should feel supported in the seat bones and in the gluteal muscles. If the seat area is too small, the seat bones can feel as if they're sitting on nothing, hanging over the edge. If the seat area is too big, the edge of the tree (at line 3) will press against the rider's thighs, pushing the rider's leg forward. The back of the saddle seat will feel like a flat, hard piece of wood. The rider should never feel the pommel or the cantle while moving through any of the gaits; this would definitely impact any semblance of balance or suppleness while riding.

The area behind the seat area (4) should have enough foam support to accommodate the rider's gluteal muscles (butt cheeks). When there is too much foam here, the rider will be forced into arching her back (even when the saddle itself is in balance) Many riders complain about sore spots or rub marks between their butt cheeks, or too much pressure on the gland at the base of the tailbone. If too little foam, the rider will fall back and collapse at the pelvis—especially when tired or when the horse is in an uphill frame. This is a common issue for women, especially since they have shorter tailbones and pelvises that are angled forward when they sit upright. They are absolutely dependent on better support in this area than men are.

A slipped disc can be caused over a period of time from the same repetitive motion when the rider's pelvis falls back in the saddle (not enough support), and the rider has to continue to force the correct upright position to keep over the horse's center of gravity. In the top left photo, we are looking at a pelvis with two lumbar vertebrae out of alignment.

When determining the actual seat size (length) keep in mind that there is always about 2 inches of room for the saddler to position the saddle nails. That is why a 17-inch saddle is not always 17 inches!

A slipped disc can easily occur when the pelvis is tilted back continuously (in a "chair" seat where the saddle is out of balance). The rider tries to bring her upper body closer to the balance point by pushing her lumbar vertebrae forward. In order to achieve a flexible seat and protect both the rider's and the horse's back, the rider needs to pivot her pelvis forward on the seat bones so that the vertebrae align properly with their discs.

basically only tells you how much differential (space) there is between the pommel and the cantle, and how high the cantle is. Close contact to the horse is determined by the type of tree and its construction, the amount of flocking and shape of the panel, and the number and type of saddle pads used.

The rider's preference for either a soft, medium, or hard seat is pretty personal, and also depends somewhat on the shape, size, and distance between the seat bones as well as the position of the pubic symphysis. Whatever the preference, the seat needs to offer stability and security to the rider without wedging her into the saddle. The

rider should not feel discomfort or pain under the seat bones, nor should she feel like she is swimming in the saddle.

Let's take another quick look at the form and function of the human spine. We account for the movement of the spine in four shock-absorbing natural curves: at the tailbone, lumbar area, shoulder area, and neck. We get additional shock-absorption assistance through the ankles, knees, and hips. If the knee is blocked because of a saddle that doesn't fit (wrong flap, wrong thigh blocks); if the ankle is pulled up to keep the rider steady on the saddle; or if the hips are pulled apart because the saddle is too wide, then any of these issues

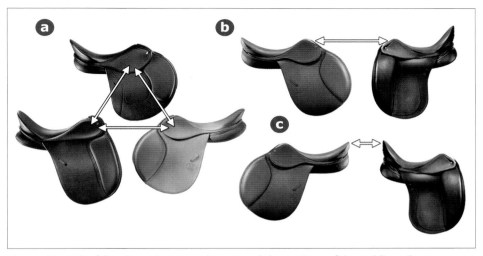

The position (a) of the stirrup bars can change, and the position of the saddle nails can vary depending on model and riding discipline. Pommel height or cutback (b) and cantle height (c) are other variables dependent on model and discipline.

can cause the rider to tense or cramp up from head to toe, leaving the entire problem of maintaining balance in the seat up to the seat bones! Even the softest, most comfortable saddle seat will get hard as rock under the seat bones, causing rider backaches—not to mention what the horse will feel under the saddle. (You think that this is minimal for the horse? Recall how he feels even a fly landing on his skin—think of the princess and the pea!)

The bottom line is: Gender correct, properly fitted saddle seats are necessary to allow the natural shock absorbers of the human skeletal system to work properly. I can see some of you female readers rolling your eyes and saying, "My saddle is 15 years old and probably made for a man, but it fits me just fine!" My response to this is:

"Really? Are you sure? Have you even tried something else?"

You might be surprised. I often find that people sometimes just don't know what they just don't know! The status quo has become so ingrained in their riding life that they accept it for being what it is and can't imagine an alternative. Remember, having a saddle that helps your position does not mean you are a bad rider, it means that you are an informed rider and know what's good for you and your horse.

A soft, supple seat can only be achieved when the rider can move in harmony with the horse—with both in balance. Both her back and abdominal muscles are properly and lightly contracted (not tense or cramped) when the rider is sitting in the correct straight position. This allows the discs between the vertebrae to do their job as shock absorbers and keep the vertebrae in proper alignment vis-à-vis their neighbors. When the saddle supports the rider, her spine will do its job and keep the SI joint healthy.

STIRRUP-BAR POSITION

A balanced and upright position in the saddle is possible when the rider's shoulder, hip, and heel line up vertically—in a plumb line. This position can usually only be achieved when riding without stirrups or when the stirrup bar is attached at the correct position (as described in the photo on this page) to the tree for an individual's leg during manufacture. The position of the stirrup leathers and the stirrup irons are absolutely dependent on the position of the stirrup bars, which are essentially metal hooks to hang the leathers on. When the stirrup iron doesn't hang right for an individual rider's leg, she will immediately go into a "cramping" mode as the lower leg is artificially pulled forward—or backward—out of the plumb-line position.

The rear small section of every stirrup bar should be able to open up in the case of a fall; should a rider's foot get stuck in an iron in the process of falling off, the stirrup leather (and iron) can slip out of the stirrup bar so the rider doesn't get dragged by the horse.

Here, once again, the anatomical differences between male and female play a crucial role. Whereas men generally have equal length upper and lower legs, women usually have longer upper legs. This has enormous ramifications regarding proper stirrup bar position and length, since it is the stirrup bar that impacts the stirrup-leather position. Mostly depending on the ratio between the upper—and lower-leg length, the leg itself will be positioned differently on the horse to allow the rider to achieve the plumb-line position. The stirrup bar's placement and length should allow the rider to have her leg hang di-

Stirrup bar "A" is considered "extended" (positioned farther back) by one inch; stirrup bar "B" is considered "extra-extended" by 2 inches. The stirrup bar's position is dependent on the ratio of the length of the upper leg to the length of the lower leg and needs to be placed where necessary during the manufacture of the saddle.

A regular stirrup bar will be even shorter in the front (the length between the rivet by A or B and the first vertical indented line as you move from left to right on the stirrup bar).

rectly beneath her, without feeling that the lower leg is being pulled forward or back and forcing the rider into either a chair seat or a crouched seat.

Men generally have regular length stirrup bars (not "extended" or "extra-extended") attached in a more forward position, while women often have the extended or extra-extended bars attached farther back on the flap. Women using a saddle made for men, with the stirrup bar placement for a man, will find that their legs hang forward ("Get that leg back!" Sound familiar?) because of the natural center of grav-

This dressage saddle has a flap that is slightly forward—beyond the vertical—and an extra long thigh roll that is meant for a rider with a very long upper leg.

ity due to the difference in upper- and lower-leg length.

THE SADDLE FLAP

Since the rider's upper leg is placed directly against the saddle flap, it should at least be long enough to prevent the top edge of the boot (or half chaps, as the case may be) from getting caught under it. The rule of thumb is to have a flap end about a hand-width below the knee.

The function of the saddle flap is to keep the horse's sweat from its flanks away from the rider's leg. The thickness of the flap may vary, but a rider should

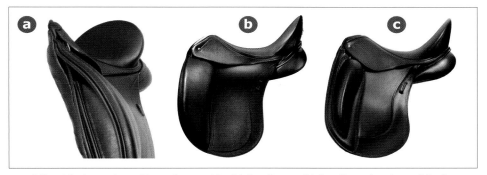

A saddle with the option of interchangeable thigh rolls (a); thigh rolls under the saddle flap on this saddle are made for a rider with shorter, strong upper legs (b); a monoflap with an example of a long thigh roll that can be switched as needed to another shape, size, or type of thigh roll by the rider, depending on her preference and need (c).

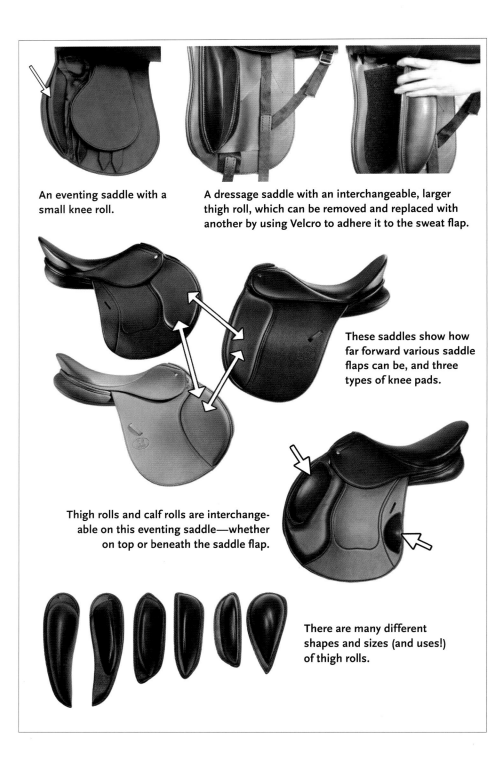

An eventing saddle with a small knee roll.

A dressage saddle with an interchangeable, larger thigh roll, which can be removed and replaced with another by using Velcro to adhere it to the sweat flap.

These saddles show how far forward various saddle flaps can be, and three types of knee pads.

Thigh rolls and calf rolls are interchangeable on this eventing saddle—whether on top or beneath the saddle flap.

There are many different shapes and sizes (and uses!) of thigh rolls.

be able to feel the horse through the flap, which means that the ideal thickness (for a monoflap without an additional sweat flap beneath it) should be about 1/5 inch (4 to 4½ mm). Obviously, the addition of a sweat flap and a buckle guard (it protects the horse from buckle pressure and the saddle flap from buckle rubbing) increases the distance between the horse's flank and the rider's leg. Even with a monoflap,

it is important that the billets do not touch the horse until they reach the bottom edge of the flap.

When the saddle flap is optimal for the rider, her leg should lie pretty much in the center of the flap. There should be about one inch (2 to 3 cm) of the flap visible in front of the knee, and at least ½ inch (1 cm) visible behind the back of the thigh.

THIGH ROLLS

Thigh rolls were not added to saddles until around the time that riding became a recreational pastime. They were totally unheard of in Western or military models. They were mainly developed to help inexperienced riders find a more secure seat, and for use in the more dangerous disciplines (steeplechase, eventing, jumping). The use and necessity for thigh rolls has been a "bone of contention" pretty much since they were "invented." No other design feature on the saddle has been the source for so much dissention. Many trainers and riders think that thigh rolls are absolutely unnecessary; others find small ones all right, whereas others swear by thigh rolls in any shape, size, or form.

The correct and well-placed thigh roll will offer the rider an additional feeling of security, especially when riding

a younger horse. However, if the thigh roll is too big, it can block the rider's leg and prevent the transmission of the proper aids to the horse. When the thigh roll is not right, the rider will end up with a head-bobbing, wedged-in feeling and possible backache. In addition, the thigh roll will hit on the rider's sensitive knee reflex point, causing an "avoidance" movement that will turn the leg out from the upper thigh down all the way to the toes. As a result of this unwanted leg position, the rider will adjust his seat to get more comfortable, and can then fall behind the bal-

> **Thigh rolls that are too large, paradoxically, give the rider a feeling of automatic security, while, in actuality, they negatively impact the rider's balance and position.**

ance point and center of gravity. This will cause a "fidgety" heavy seat in the back one-third of the saddle. The larger thigh rolls, instead of offering additional security to an inexperienced rider or a rider on a younger horse, will actually increase the likelihood of an insecure and uncomfortable seat position.

The knee roll is often confused with a knee pad. The knee pad is the padded area sewn in at the very front of the saddle flap, whereas the knee roll is a smaller, thinner version of the thigh roll attached on top of the saddle flap and acting as a support (see photos on p. 172). Nowadays, there are really no actual knee rolls; they are more of an elongated, slimmer version of the thigh roll that can be situated to run parallel to the front of the knee along the patella. While a thigh roll is meant to give added support to the rider, it should never act to wedge him in.

When the rider's knee is blocked with a thigh roll that is too large or poorly placed on the flap, his ability to achieve a soft, supple, and harmonious melding of horse and rider is negatively impacted. The knee is not able to absorb the natural motion that originates in the hips when the thigh roll blocks it. (To feel it yourself: Jump off two steps and don't absorb the landing in your knees. You will experience a jolt all the way to your backbone. When you bend at the knees to absorb the landing, you land softly without experiencing any jolting.)

It is the same when riding: When a knee is blocked it cannot direct the motion all the way down to the heel of the foot and thereby absorb the "jolt" as one of the natural shock

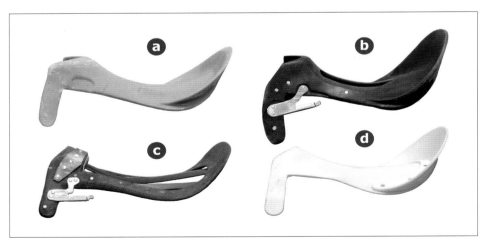

Various types of saddle trees and their different tree-points orientation: a) "Flex" tree with straight tree points; b) AdapTree® (flexible polyurethane) with rear-facing tree points; c) laminated wooden English-style spring tree showing an English riveted gullet plate and forward-facing tree points; d) a plastic tree with straight tree points.

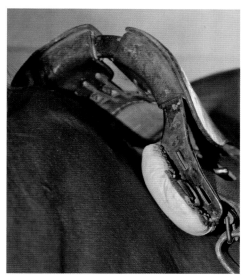

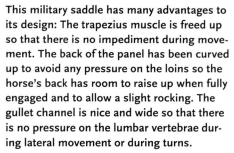

This military saddle has many advantages to its design: The trapezius muscle is freed up so that there is no impediment during movement. The back of the panel has been curved up to avoid any pressure on the loins so the horse's back has room to raise up when fully engaged and to allow a slight rocking. The gullet channel is nice and wide so that there is no pressure on the lumbar vertebrae during lateral movement or during turns.

absorbers; instead, the entire force of motion remains in the knee. This affects the entire area upward through the thighs and into the hips, which, in turn, will not be able to perform their shock-absorbing function during motion so the force will hit your lower back and hurt your lumbar vertebrae.

Just as important as the length and width of the thigh rolls is their correct angle and position. The upper thigh should have at least one inch (2½ cm) room before hitting the thigh roll in

Military types of saddles ensure that the spinal column is free and bridged with the use of two support panels that lie to the left and right of the vertebrae and are connected only at the front and back ends. The saddle's seat is built into the area between the pommel and the cantle at the distal ends of the panel.

Conversely, in English-style saddles, the tree is an uninterrupted, slightly curved structure that acts as both the connection for the panels as well as the base for the saddle seat. The spinal column is protected by a divided panel that lies along either side (and that needs a wide enough gullet channel between the two sides of the panel to avoid touching the vertebrae). This type of saddle lends itself to the use of more subtle, defined aids, as it will generally be of less weight than other saddle types.

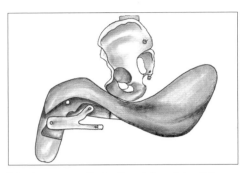

It's clear to see that a female's pelvis sitting in an ordinary saddle based on the traditional design made for men will not have the necessary support she needs at the back of her pelvis and under the tailbone. Additionally, her pubic symphysis hits the pommel area.

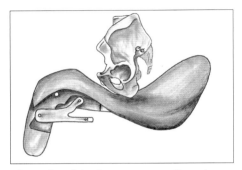

The male pelvis sits more naturally and balanced in the same saddle, with support under his seat bones, no impact to his pubic bone, and enough support.

order to ensure that all the other parts that are impacted during movement (hips, knees, heels) have enough room to do their job. The thigh rolls should never hit the rider's knee, because it can react reflexively, changing your leg position.

TREE VS. NO TREE

Treeless saddles present an ongoing controversy that will seemingly not go away. They have their proponents and opponents, but the "pro-tree" facts do speak for themselves. You can argue till you're blue in the face, but this doesn't change the realities of the effects a treeless saddle can have on the horse's back over time. A treeless saddle may work for a short period of time as an interim solution to a poorly fitting saddle with a tree, but in the long run, it is not going to do your horse any favors.

The job of a saddle tree to is to optimally place the rider's weight correctly over the saddle-support area of the horse's back. A treeless saddle (or bareback pad) will not have this support structure that allows proper weight distribution of the rider on the horse's back. Most of the rider's weight in these "saddles" (and I do use the term loosely, because, for the most part—even if they resemble saddles at first glance—they are still more closely related to bareback pads) will be under the seat bones or cause individual pressure points on the horse's back. The saddle tree, by contrast, distributes the weight evenly over the longissimus (if, of course, the saddle has been fit correctly). In the middle of the saddle-support area the horse's transverse spinal processes are completely straight—a treeless saddle means that 100 percent of the rider's weight is concentrated right here.

I always recommend a (well-fitting) treed saddle over a treeless one. We know that pressure points can impede circulation and cause muscle atrophy, along with tendonitis and ligament damage. We want to avoid symptomatic long-term damage and pain, but also incorrect muscle contraction leading to atrophy when the horse reacts parasympathetically to try and avoid pressure.*

The truth is, it is much easier (less time and expense) from a craftsman's point of view as a saddler to build a treeless saddle than to build a treed saddle. The first trees were built out of rawhide, straw, or wood. Beech is still a popular wood used in saddle-tree manufacture—many traditional "English" style saddles are built using these trees made of several layers of laminated beech wood that are heat-glued together (called "wooden spring trees"). It has only been in the last 50 years or so that polyurethane, vinyl, and plastic

In a treeless saddle—as well as a saddle with a tree—made for a man, a woman does not have the necessary support behind her pelvic area to sit correctly in balance and in position. This female pelvis on the horse's back is shown in the approximate position it would be in a treeless saddle. The photo shows that she is lacking the necessary support a treed saddle would give her from behind in order to change her position to the plumb line (shown in green) and that she is tilted backward from the vertical (along the axis shown by the red lines).

trees have come into fashion and they have their advantages and disadvantages, as well as their supporters and naysayers.

*While the sympathetic system is also known as the "fight or flight" response, the parasympathetic is often called "relax and renew." Interestingly, the parasympathetic functions in opposition to the sympathetic nervous system. When the sympathetic system activates in response to some sort of stressor, the parasympathetic reacts, in turn, to bring the body back to a state of equilibrium. The parasympathetic system is consistently active at a low level, but levels of activity increase when it is necessary to bring the body back to a balanced state from a state of elevated sympathetic activity. The primary parasympathetic nerve is the vagus nerve, also known as cranial nerve X.

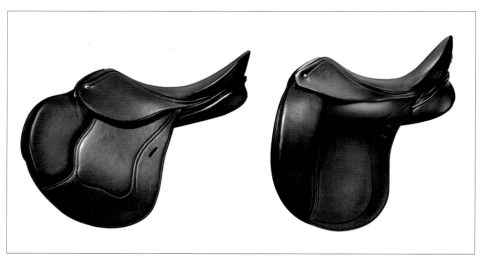

A jumping saddle (left) will generally have a flatter seat to allow the rider more freedom of movement as she changes her position over jumps. A dressage saddle (right) generally has many more options regarding seat size and balance to allow the individual rider a better opportunity to achieve the proper balanced position.

I find that a polyurethane tree (although minimally heavier by about 1½ to 2 pounds) is infinitely more durable, pliable, flexible, and easy to work with than the traditional wooden spring tree still used by many of the English saddle manufacturers. The synthetic tree is also quite a bit more expensive as it is usually made with the use of injection molds, but that's the trade off. Solid wood trees are still being used for the other style saddles, such as Western models.

Laminated spring trees usually last a long time and are pretty flexible ("spring"), and they are cheaper and lighter than solid wood trees. They are strengthened with a gullet plate at the front and with spring steel along their length, but are generally not adjustable in either tree width or tree angle.

As a result, more and more synthetically made trees are appearing on the market. Their advantages should not be underestimated: they are generally lighter than laminated wood trees, less likely to become twisted, and can be cheaper and easier to produce (depending on the actual chemical mix of materials and the types of molds used). There are various permutations of synthetic compounds used to make these trees, but some are absolutely inflexible so they cannot be adjusted in any way. They are made and fit the way they come.

Some of the synthetic trees are adjustable when heated, and some are actually adjustable over and over again with the use of a tree machine and without having to separate the panel from the seat leather. Many of these synthetic trees incorporate some mixture of polyurethane, which allows the saddle to retain its flexibility, not only front to back, but also side to side, to accompany the horse's natural diagonal motion. The stiffness of the saddle can be affected by using various lengths, thicknesses, and strengths of added spring steel along its length underneath. The rider will feel the difference—the longer and thicker the spring steel, the stiffer the saddle will feel and the resulting hardness of the seat impacts the rider's comfort. The hardness from the spring steel is only minimally impacted by the addition of foam in the seat. It is important, however, not to make a flex polyurethane tree too flexible or soft, because it can actually cause pressure—even all the way through the panel flocking—onto the horse's back, especially in cases where the rider is heavier. There has been some development in the "self-adjustable" market recently with saddles that the rider can adjust or replace the gullet plates herself. However, these innovations rarely take tree width into consideration, and these adjustments or replacements usually only deal with changes in tree angle over the withers.

I'll give you one thing: A treeless saddle allows the rider to feel the horse's motion more closely and gets her closer to the horse. It is, however, physiologically difficult—impossible actually—for women to sit properly and correctly and comfortably in a treeless saddle. The necessary support for the gluteus and tailbone is simply missing, and as such, truly harmonious and supple movement can never be achieved. In addition and to repeat: The biggest disadvantage with a treeless saddle is that it is simply unable to properly distribute the rider's weight over the saddle-support area, and it will always cause pressure points under the seat bones. The best advantage of a treeless saddle is in its construction; it has no stiff or immoveable parts that could force the horse into an unnatural muscular reaction, and it never has to be refit to the horse as he changes and matures. But this doesn't make up for its disadvantages: In addition to causing pressure points, it is difficult for the rider to give the proper aids, and it is almost impossible to prevent the horse from experiencing long-term damage to his muscles, nerves, ligaments, and tendons in his back.

A horse with pressure points on his back is unable to bring his back up properly to counteract a rider's weight and move freely when carrying a rider. The inability to do so because of the impact of a treeless saddle impedes the entire functionality of the biomechanics and load-carrying ability of the horse, which not only can, but will, lead to health issues. There are many diagnostic tools available that will illustrate the damage done (MRI, thermography, fiberoptic cameras, X-ray, to name a few).

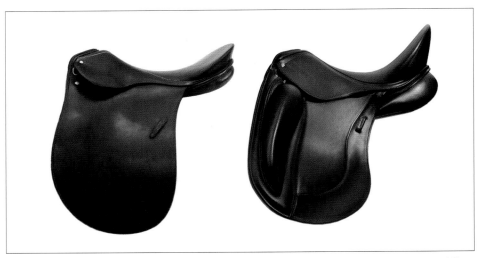

A dressage saddle with a fairly flat seat and minimal leg support (left) and a dressage saddle with an extremely deep seat (high cantle) and a lot of leg support (right). The not very politically correct nickname (especially in Germany) for this type of saddle is a "prosthesis."

A SADDLE OR A "PROSTHESIS*"?

The question of how a saddle should be used to support a rider in finding a balanced and secure seat has been a much discussed question in the horse industry. Some maintain that a "pure" saddle with a flat seat and no thigh/calf/knee rolls is the only true option for an experienced and well-trained rider. Such a rider shouldn't need any of these "bells and whistles" to be able to ride. Others continue to insist that saddles with well-thought-out design features such as leg supports, higher pommels and cantles, and various seat sizes absolutely have their place—especially for more inexperienced or elderly riders. The nickname for such a saddle in Germany is actually "prosthesis." The idea is the rider needs these little extras to be able to achieve a balanced and secure seat, to allow her to ride in harmony.

---

*Webster's defines prosthesis as "an artificial device used to augment an impaired or missing part of the body." It is used here to mean that saddles are sometimes seen as a support for the inexperienced rider when they should be used to improve the ability of an already capable rider, not replace the ability to ride.

The idea of the saddle as an artificial support for the rider has been argued about for many years. When a horse is moving with full suppleness and engagement ("swinging") a beginner rider has a hard time staying put. So why not add a thigh roll for a little more security in the saddle? It can be used for a limited time to give the rider the feeling of more stability until his ability increases. The rider should, however, keep in mind that the goal is to be able to ride securely and in balance without the use of a thigh roll. An experienced and balanced rider will have overcome his initial insecurity and won't be using his legs as a clamp to stay on the saddle. Thigh rolls that are too large or long can even impede his ability to ride properly at this point.

Nowadays, many riders don't start riding until a later age. The demographics of the industry have changed immensely even in the last two decades. Aging female baby boomers are the fastest growing market segment: either starting to ride again or just learning to ride. They want to feel secure in their pastime. Many of them haven't grown up with horses and need these little "training wheels"—especially in the first few years—to feel comfortable. The other side of the coin is the experienced rider who has such a personal biomechanical effect that correctly positioned larger thigh rolls are actually necessary to empower this rider to give the right aids at the right time.

The bottom line is that every rider needs to find what works for him at any given time during the course of learning how to ride, and based on the horse's level, too. Without a doubt, a comfortable and secure seat (while still ensuring freedom to move as necessary) is an absolute prerequisite for good riding.

The more a saddle helps a rider to find a secure and comfortable seat, the more it can also inhibit the ability to ride freely. There is always an individual solution that works by trial and error—you have to go with what feels right for you—but this does not absolve the trainer, the tack shop, or the saddler from their responsibility to learn how to distinguish the fine line between helping or hindering a rider.

FINAL WORDS

Saddlers, tack shop owners, saddle ergonomists, trainers, veterinarians, body workers of all kinds, blacksmiths—all of us are equine professionals in our various areas of expertise and every one of us has a wealth of experience and training to fall back on in our everyday work with horses.

In those instances where our paths collide when working holistically around the horse, we should all be open to thinking "outside the box" to learn from each other. Only when we keep in mind the circle of influence to the horse will all of us be able to really work together for the common good of the horse and rider.

Often the focus on continuing personal development is necessary to put this goal into practice, since there is an unfortunate lack of overlap in the educational paths of all of these professions. A master saddler learns little to nothing about the anatomy of horse and human; nothing about riding techniques, and nothing about the commonalities and interfaces of all of these subjects. Even a veterinarian or a physiotherapist is taught little about saddle construction and design, and how it actually affects horse health and behavior. Trainers and professional riders—those who have the most influence on both the horse and his owner—often lack basic knowledge in other areas that contribute to the well-being of the horse and are not able to provide a comprehensive "overview" to what these issues might be.

Many equine professionals have chosen their career path out of a passion for horses, because they have been involved with horses since childhood, or perhaps because it has been a family business. The bottom line though is probably the fact that they truly love working with horses—in whatever capacity. This prerequisite of having empathy for the horse should be evident in whatever career path is chosen in the equestrian industry. My personal impetus to learn about saddlery from the ground up came out of my involvement in the sport as recreation and then as a competitor, but also because this was how I wanted to make a living: by combining the best of both worlds. The responsibility this career choice brought with it, however, only became clear to me several years later.

I have been working in this industry for the better part of my life now—over 34 years. In that time, I have met many, many people who earn their money by working with horses in some capacity. With some dismay I had to come to the realization, however, that there were a number of my "colleagues" around the horse—and there are people like this in every industry, I guess—who were not always in this business for the good of the horse.

The reasons for this are difficult to pinpoint. Maybe it's because of (false) pride or pressure to succeed and perform either economically or competitively, thereby wanting to maintain the procedural status quo. Egotism and lack of willingness to work cooperatively with other equine professionals around the horse often result in actions that do not have the best interests of the animal in mind. And last but not least, maybe the most important reason is simply the fact that too many times the almighty "buck" rules.

Sometimes, though, it is truly scary how little true knowledge some of these so-called experts have, and how they subscribe—without thinking—to theories that are "traditional" but do not take the latest research, findings, and innovation into consideration. And then there are other companies that develop "the latest designs" for the horse in gullet-plate shapes, panel shapes or whatever—without referring to the actual anatomical realities of the horse. The results are actions that get in the way of doing what is right for the horse. The horse's owner, rider, and saddle purchaser trust the advice of these experts, and expect that their trainer, veterinarian, saddler, and body workers know what is correct and will advise them properly—up to, and including, their choice in saddles.

It is our solemn duty to do everything in our power to spare these horses, these beautiful and noble animals, any pain. But this will only be achieved if we work together cooperatively; we need to stop questioning each other's decisions or competence in front of the client and work with, instead of against, each other.

As renowned German trainer Hans Heinrich Isenbart said: "And—don't forget the horses!" That pretty much sums it up. I personally have learned so much over the years from my dealings with all sorts of fitters, saddlers, veterinarians, osteopaths, farriers, trainers, and human and equine physiotherapists that I am now absolutely certain that only a symbiotic relationship between all of these minds will lead to the perfect saddle fit.

My personal curiosity and interest in achieving the best possible solution for horse and rider—and in this way protecting them both from long-term damage caused by badly fitting saddles—continue to motivate me to reach this goal. I don't really care about selling as many saddles as possible. My goal is to teach the philosophy of Saddlefit 4 Life® to as many people as possible. It is education that will change the industry. I can only hope that curiosity ("What's this all about?" "Is there anything to this?"), and the presumed goal of doing the best job possible with the given variables, will restore the passion in any and all of these various professionals and lead them to investigate what Saddlefit 4 Life® is all about. This is the first step to achieving a cooperative way of working together and not against each other that I am talking about.

Saddlefit 4 Life® is not about selling a particular saddle brand; it is about recognizing that even an inexpensive saddle can be used as long as it adheres to the philosophy, and as long as it is exchanged as often as necessary to make sure, at all times, optimal fit to the animal is ensured. The saddle as the reason behind health and behavioral issues that arise for both horse and rider is more and more the focus in the equine industry. It is, I hope, only a matter of time before riders and owners insist on a cooperative effort between the equine professionals around their horses.

It needs to become more of a habit, beyond constant further education and personal development, that riders, owners, (and trainers, especially), make saddle-fit evaluation as much of a regular event as shoeing and hoof care is. After people buy a saddle, too many check it once in the first year or so, but thereafter very irregularly, if at all, and then only to see if the padding is still okay. I have seen riders who bought saddles 10 or even 15 years ago who have never had their saddle fit evaluated—they "don't believe in it." Poor horse is all I can say....

This is not good enough by any stretch of the imagination. A young horse especially needs his saddle fit checked two to three times a year between the ages of three and six.

These young horses change their conformation drastically in the first couple of years, depending on training methods and intensity of training. Once the horse is seven or older, an annual evaluation should be adequate, unless he has been ill, unsound, or had changes in training or nutrition that could have af-

fected conformation. After age 16, the number of evaluations per year should go up again to two or even three times.

I sometimes hear from colleagues in the saddle-fitting industry that people complain about the necessity and cost of having their saddles evaluated. I don't accept this argument. Horse owners spend literally fortunes on various external therapy: pharmaceuticals, physiotherapy, and supplements (not to mention shoeing every 6 weeks). A properly trained saddle fitter or saddle ergonomist who is able to competently fit a saddle based on the anatomical requirements of both horse and rider, and who is able to talk to a client intelligently about her saddle choice, is at a professional level equal to any body worker or blacksmith. Adequate compensation is not only earned, but also justified. But I think time is on our side because people have become more aware of the differences offered by the variously trained professionals they have available to them, and understand that a saddle fitter needs to be compensated for his time and expertise just like any other equine professional.

To continue with the increased awareness, it becomes necessary to strengthen this with more regulation in the training of saddlers, saddle fitters, and equine or saddle ergonomists in this industry and market the expertise of properly trained professionals more diligently. Clients will then become more and more open to paying for the expertise that is provided regardless of what they actually do with the information they are given at a diagnostic evaluation. They can choose to ignore what they learned and continue on as before; they can make the necessary changes to their saddle or their saddle's fit as recommended, or they can buy a new horse to fit the saddle they already have. Best of all would be if they then went to their local tack shop with their new knowledge and created the demand for saddles that could accommodate the requirements of their changing horse. Only then will manufacturers react—when it hits their bottom line!

A comprehensive evaluation of saddle fit always requires that a specific procedure is followed from start to finish in order to determine all the variables. It requires both a static and dynamic evaluation, with all the results documented for both the client and the fitter to use for future reference. It becomes difficult to fit a saddle unless both the horse and rider have been evaluated in these aspects. I do not support a simple "re-flocking" as a properly offered service.

A good result for both horse and rider (and one that justifies the fee charged for the evaluation itself) is best achieved when the saddle can be adjusted at the facility where the horse lives. This means that the client is not without her saddle for an unreasonable amount of time. Unfortunately, this sometimes happens; it depends on whether certain repairs have to be done that cannot be attended to on-site (this happens, in particular, when dealing

with many of the "not really" adjustable saddles). The rider can constantly "retest" the adjustment dynamically (riding in it) while the fitter is still there to continue working on the saddle.

This complete and proper evaluation procedure requires approximately two hours per horse. The fitter should tell the rider or owner about the work: what needs to be done and at what cost. There should always be several options for the rider to choose from.

I have rarely experienced a rider who does not agree to have necessary adjustments done on his saddle. Most of them, including work done at the gullet plate (widening, narrowing, changing angle—that is, assuming the saddle can be fitted or adjusted at the gullet plate in the first place, which many can't); re-flocking or doing a completely new flocking; re-stitching; or attaching billets can be pretty much done on-site. This allows the rider to immediately test whether the adjustment has been successful for both himself and the horse. The rider can watch the fitter work and ask any questions that come to mind right then and there, and the good thing is that he will not have to give up his saddle for days, weeks, or (sometimes) even months while it is at the shop being repaired. Obviously, however, regardless of what work is actually done to the saddle, the evaluation itself needs to be paid for; it is the know-how that is being offered here and the evaluation itself is a valuable service to educate and inform the rider about the issues.

Saddlefit 4 Life® is proliferating and becoming established all through North and South America, Africa, Europe, and Australia. Income from using Saddlefit 4 Life® protocols for evaluations is becoming a significant factor in the revenue stream for saddle ergonomists and tack shop owners. I am absolutely convinced that riders all over the world can be educated and become convinced of the necessity for ongoing professional saddle-fit evaluations and adjustments. The desirable outcome of improved performance capability for both horse and rider—and the avoidance of potential injury to either—will improve the willingness (and justification) to pay for the expertise of an on-site evaluation by a saddle ergonomist.

Saddlers, saddle fitters, tack shop owners—any equine professional really—need to recognize the value in the ability to perform this on-site evaluation correctly, and get qualifications to do them through Saddlefit 4 Life® or other recognized saddle fitting "schools." As long as saddle fitting "hell" is still in the vernacular and considered to be a more or less necessary evil, it will be difficult to make a decent living from this service. I personally see how incredibly grateful my clients (and their horses!) are after an evaluation and adjustment, and that they do understand how much we as professionals help them with the issues that can arise from this one absolutely critical piece of the "riding puzzle."

There are several other organizations beyond Saddlefit 4 Life® that have made the topic of saddle fit the focus of their existence. Thanks to social media and the availability of the Internet it is much easier to stay informed and avail yourself of education and knowledge. As professionals (in any industry) it forces us as well to stay informed and educate ourselves—to stay ahead of the curve! Ongoing education is the key here, with only one goal: preventing long-term damage to horse and rider that will allow you many years of enjoyment of working together.

The visual accompaniment to this book is available on the Schleese Youtube channel or in the DVD *Beyond the 9 Points of Saddle Fit* available at www.saddlesforwomen.com.

Dear Reader

I wrote this book on the basis of my own 34 (and more) years of experience working in the equestrian industry. I incorporated insights gained from my own apprenticeship and master's training, from associating with numerous other industry professionals and picking their brains, and from doing evaluations (personally and through my company) on approximately 150,000 horses of all breeds, ages, condition, and ability during these years. All opinions and comments come from my own experiences and education, and any omissions or factual and technical errors are mine alone.

I hope you have taken the time to read the book in its entirety; perhaps you have only flipped through it and read those chapters that appealed to you. I thank you for your interest, and I hope that you will look at your saddle and its fit a little more critically in the future, and use the guidelines in this book to evaluate your status quo. Perhaps you will go to your saddle fitter and ask him or her to do a proper evaluation based on what you have read in this book. You will have achieved a level of knowledge that is not inherent in many of the people who are working with saddles in the industry—your fitter, saddler, or tack shop owner may make recommendations that are in direct opposition to what you have learned here. You will also experience scepticism: "It's all smoke and mirrors," or "It is absolutely unnecessary to put so much emphasis on saddle fit." People may try to persuade you that the saddle you just bought is absolutely the best thing for you and your horse. If you use the most basic criteria I outlined in this book and realize that the saddle just really doesn't fit you or your horse correctly, you need to stand behind your knowledge—in front of the tack shop owner or in front of your trainer.

You need to ask your fitter the right questions to reassure yourself that either he is right or find out that he doesn't really have a clue. You need to be steadfast. Insist on the answers you need to make an educated decision. Question the qualifications and training of the people you work with and don't be afraid to ask! I can honestly maintain that I personally have fit and evaluated more horses in my life than most saddle fitters or tack shop owners. I have probably learned and taught more about saddle fit than most people who call themselves experts in this field. You need to decide who you want to put your faith in. *YOU* carry the responsibility for the well-being of your horse. It's really only common sense and simple logic.

I wish you continued success, health, and happiness with your horse; I wish for you a well-fitting saddle that will guarantee you enjoyment with your horse; I wish you access to a well-trained and competent circle of professionals all around your horse to keep you riding for many years to come!

ABOUT THE AUTHOR

Jochen Schleese has been working in the equestrian industry as a master saddler and saddle fitter for over 34 years and studied and built "gender-appropriate saddles" for over 20 of those. He completed both his journeyman's and master's certification at Passier and Sohn in Germany. In 1986 he was asked to come to Canada as the Official Saddler for the World Dressage Championships, held for the first time outside of Europe, and in 2005, 2007, and 2009 he held the same position for the World Cup Finals in Las Vegas, Nevada.

In 1990, Jochen developed a three-year certification program for the trade of saddlery together with the Ontario Ministry of Skills Development. He received a US Patent in 1996 for his innovative adjustable AdapTree® saddle tree, which is specifically made for the female anatomy, and he has been featured twice on Discovery Channel (*How It's Made* and *Harrowsmith Country Life*). Jochen has been the recipient of numerous business and industry awards over the years and is featured as a regular educational contributor to many equestrian magazines in United States and Canada. He teaches his Saddlefit 4 Life® philosophy all over the world in conjunction with the German National Riding School, United States Dressage Federation, Ontario Equestrian Federation, Professional Trainers Verband in Germany, and at veterinary conferences in Brazil. Jochen is truly a leader in the concept of saddle fit: he has changed the way saddles are made, sold, and fitted all over the world, with the good of the horse and the comfort of the rider in mind.

Nicole Künzel assisted in the writing of the original German edition of this book. Nicole is the author of *Eleganz im Damensattel* and *Am Langen Zügel* and runs her own training facility in Hanover, Germany, where she specializes in classical dressage and promoting the ideals of harmony and joy between horse and rider.

The English language edition of this book was translated from German by Sabine Schleese.

RECOMMENDED WEBSITES*

www.evipo.de	Nicole Künzel
www.christine-orterer.de	Christine Orterer
www.facedprofessionalmakeupandartistry.com	Danielle Schleese
www.inspiritusequine.com	Dr. Joanna Robson
www.linkedin.com/pub/dir/James/Warson	Dr. James Warson
www.welter-boeller.de	Barbara Welter-Böller
www.gerdheuschmann.com	Dr. Gerd Heuschmann
www.steinfurt.city-map.de/de/andrea-koslik	Andrea Koslik
www.ahorngreen.de	Angelika Schleese
www.balimo.info	Eckart Meyners
www.janesavoie.com	Jane Savoie
www.nancynicholson.tel	Dr. Nancy Nicholson
www.walterzettl.net	Walter Zettl
www.ergo-saddlefit.com	Valerie Ponocny
www.physicallyfit.de	Kathrin Wörmer
www.ergonomicsaddlefitting.co.uk	Laura Whitteron
www.professionalfarriers.com	Barney Cummings
www.schleese-gmbh.de	Frank Reitemeier
www.saddlefit4life.com	
www.horobin.com.au	Peter Horobin
www.tom-buettner.de	Tom Büttner
www.rieser-sattel.de	Christoph Rieser
www.horseshape.com	Andreas Bauer
www.axelkock.de	Axel Kock Medienbüro für Gestaltung
www.stoneylakeequestrian.ca	Jaimey and Tina Irwin
www.sonnenhofstables.ca	Dieter Busse
www.youtube.com/user/Padmavideo	Kathryn Lauritzen

*Please excuse us for those we may have inadvertently forgotten!

RECOMMENDED READING

In German:

Am Langen Zügel von Saskia Gunzer und Nicole Künzel, WuWei Verlag, 2011

Aufwärmprogramm für Reiter von Eckart Meyners, Franckh-Kosmos Verlag, 2008

Balance in der Bewegung von Susanne von Dietze, FN Verlag, 2003

Balanceakt von Dr. Gerd Heuschmann, WuWei Verlag, 2011

Bausteine Dressur Reiten von Corinna Lehmann, Müller-Rüschlikon Verlag, 2009

Der Reiter formt das Pferd von Udo Bürger und Otto Zietzschmann, FN Verlag, 2007

Die Psyche des Pferdes—sein Wesen, seine Sinne, sein Verhalten von Ulrike Thiel, Franckh-Kosmos Verlag, 2007

Die Schiefen Therapie—Pferde geraderichten mit System von Gabriele Rachen-Schöneich und Klaus Schöneich, Müller Rüschlikon Verlag, 2010

Dressur in Harmonie— von der Basis bis zum Grand Prix von Walter Zettl, FN Verlag der Deutschen Reiterlichen Vereinigung, 2003

Finger in der Wunde von Dr. Gerd Heuschmann, WuWei Verlag, 2006

Gutes für den Pferderücken von Christoph Rieser, Cadmos Verlag, 2008

Illusion Pferdeosteopathie. Von ausgerenkten Wirbeln und anderen Märchen von Tanja Richter, WuWei Verlag, 2010

Reiten mit Verstand und Gefühl von Michael Putz, FN Verlag, 2004

Soforthilfe bei Rückenschmerzen von Lilo Cross, Zabert & Sandmann Verlag, 2007

Xenophon Reitkunst von Dr. Phil. Klaus Widdra, WuWei Verlag, 2007

In English:

40 Fundamentals of English Riding by Hollie H. McNeil, Storey Publishing, 2011

ABC of the Horse—Anatomy, Biomechanics, Conditioning by Pauli Grönberg, Pg-Team Oy, 2007

BioMechanical Riding & Dressage: A Rider's Atlas by Nancy Nicholson, PhD, Zip Publishing, 2005

Care and Rehabilitation of the Equine Foot by Pete Ramey, Hoof Rehabilitation Publishing, 2011

P.B.M. A Diary of Lameness—Proper Balance Movement: A Gift for Your Horse by Tony Gonzales, REF Publishing, 1986

Practical Saddle Fitting by Ken Lyndon-Dykes, J.A.Allen, 2005

Recognizing the Horse in Pain and What You Can Do About It by Dr. Joanna Robson, DVM, Inspiritus Equine Inc., 2009

The Horse's Pain Free Back and Saddle-Fit Book by Joyce Harmann, DVM, Trafalgar Square Books, 2004

The Rider Forms the Horse by Udo Bürger and Otto Zietzschmann, FN Verlag, 2007

The Rider's Pain Free Back by James Warson, MD, Trafalgar Square Books, 2007

Top Massage for Top Balance by Jean-Pierre Hourdebaigt, LMT, Massage Awareness Inc., 2008

Tug of War: Classical vs. "Modern" Dressage by Dr. Gerd Heuschmann, Trafalgar Square Books, 2007

PHOTO & ILLUSTRATION CREDITS

Photos:

Schleese: vi *left and top right,* 5, 8, 18, 19 *top left,* 20 *right,* 38, 39, 40, 60, 64 *bottom right,* 69 *right,* 71 *bottom left,* 102 *middle,* 103 *right,* 123 *top left and bottom right,* 132, 133, 136, 142, 146, 152 *left and top right,* 154 *bottom right,* 162, 166, 171

Steffi Neumann: vi *bottom right,* vii *bottom left,* 20 *left,* 64 *top right,* 69 *left,* 71 *top left,* 78 *left,* 90, 106, 127, 128 *left,* 129, 130 *left,* 131 *left,* 135 *top right and bottom left,* 138, 139, 140 *top row and bottom right,* 143, 144 *left,* 150 *bottom middle and bottom right,* 152 *bottom right,* 154 *bottom left,* 158, 164, 168, 177 with Michelle J. Powell

Michelle J. Powell: vii *right,* 41, 48, 148, 160, 169, 171 *bottom,* 172, 174, 178, 180, 182

Kathryn Lauritzen: xvi, 42, 63, 74 *right,* 94 *bottom,* 110, 140 *bottom left,* 150 *top row,* 154 *top left*

Hugo M. Czerny: 2

Daniel Hagerman: 12

Wikipedia: 13, 106

Christoph Rieser: 14, 15, 16, 17, 55 *right,* 135 *middle right*

Ron Katz, Kamdar: 19 *top right,* 156

Solange Mikail: 23

Kathrin Hester: 25, 102 *left,* 108 *right*

Elisa Bandermann: 26

Joanna Robson: 27, 28, 74 *middle right and bottom left,* 80, 89, 115, 122 *bottom right,* 159

Anke Panzner: 30, 34, 37, 96, 109

Christina Wunderlich: 31

Dr. James Warson: 46 *bottom row*

Laura Whitteron: 47 *middle,* 126, 130 *right,* 131 *right,* 135 *top left*

Barbara Hensch: 59

Hilltop Farm: 64 *top left and middle right*

Iron Springs Farm: 64 *middle right*

Dieter Busse: 78 *right,* 79, 87, 88, 100 with Michelle J. Powell, 108 *left,* 120, 121, 122 *top row,* 123 *top right and bottom left,* 135 *row three,* 140 *bottom middle,* 144 *right,* 151, 154 *top right,* 175

Peter Horobin: 112

Andreas Bauer: 135 *left row two*

Tom Büttner: 135 *bottom right*

Katja Schmiedeskamp: xviii, 90, 189

Illustrations:

Michelle J. Powell: v, viii, 45, 46 *top and middle,* 47 *bottom,* 48 *bottom,* 51, 54 *bottom,* 62 *top,* 65, 68 with Peter C. Goody, 71, 76, 82, 87 with Peter C. Goody, 93, 99, 117 (Gottfried Bammes), 157, 167

Danielle Schleese: vii, 47 *top,* 55, 176

Wu Wei Verlag Archive: 10

Nancy Nicholson: 33, 91

Axel Kock: 35, 50, 53, 54 *top*

Lilo Cross: 36

Schleese: 57

Equistar Publications: 62 *bottom,* 74 *all but lower right,* 77

Sue Harris: 67

Peter C. Goody: 70, 137

Kaja Möbius: 107

INDEX